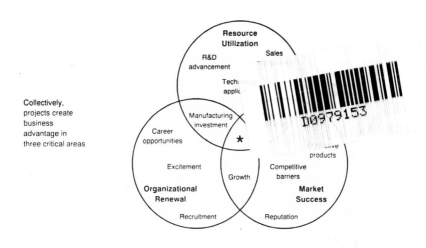

Collectively, projects create business advantage in three critical areas

Resource Utilization

R&D advancement

Sales

Tech application

Manufacturing investment

Career opportunities

Excitement

Growth

Competitive barriers

products

Organizational Renewal

Recruitment

Market Success

Reputation

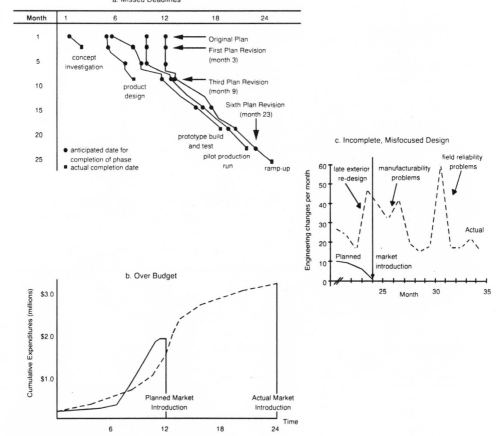

a. Missed Deadlines

Month	1	6	12	18	24

concept investigation

Original Plan

First Plan Revision (month 3)

product design

Third Plan Revision (month 9)

Sixth Plan Revision (month 23)

● anticipated date for completion of phase
■ actual completion date

prototype build and test

pilot production run

ramp-up

c. Incomplete, Misfocused Design

Engineering changes per month

late exterior re-design

manufacturability problems

field reliability problems

Actual

Planned

market introduction

Month

b. Over Budget

Cumulative Expenditures (millions)

$3.0

$2.0

$1.0

Planned Market Introduction

Actual Market Introduction

Time

6 12 18 24

*Revolutionizing
Product
Development*

STEVEN C. WHEELWRIGHT
KIM B. CLARK

Revolutionizing Product Development

Quantum Leaps in Speed, Efficiency, and Quality

THE FREE PRESS
A Division of Macmillan, Inc.
NEW YORK

Maxwell Macmillan Canada
TORONTO

Maxwell Macmillan International
NEW YORK   OXFORD   SINGAPORE   SYDNEY

The Free Press
A Division of Macmillan, Inc.
866 Third Avenue, New York, N.Y. 10022

Maxwell Macmillan Canada, Inc.
1200 Eglinton Avenue East
Suite 200
Don Mills, Ontario M3C 3N1

Macmillan, Inc. is part of the Maxwell Communication
Group of Companies.

printed in the United States of America

printing number
3 4 5 6 7 8 9 10

Library of Congress Cataloging-in-Publication Data

Wheelwright, Steven C.
    Revolutionizing product development: quantum leaps in speed,
efficiency, and quality / Steven C. Wheelwright, Kim B. Clark.
        p.   cm.
    Includes bibliographical references and index.
    ISBN 0-02-905515-6
    1. New products.   2. Product management.   I. Clark, Kim B.
II. Title.
HF5415.153.W44   1992
658.5'75—dc20   91-38170
                                                          CIP

To
Margaret and Sue,
who make it all worthwhile by keeping
us focused on the developments
that really matter

Contents

PREFACE   xi

CHAPTER *1*   *Competing Through
Development Capability*   *1*

The New Industrial Competition: Driving Forces and
Development Realities
Assessing the Promise and Reality: The A14 Stereo Project
The Characteristics of Effective Development
The Fast-Cycle Competitor
The Plan for the Book

CHAPTER *2*   *The Concept of a
Development Strategy*   *28*

A Framework for Development Strategy
Technology Planning and Strategy
Product/Market Planning and Strategy
Development Goals and Objectives
The Aggregate Project Plan
Project Management
Post-Project Learning
Honda: An Example of Development Strategy in Action

CHAPTER 3   Maps and Mapping: Functional
             Strategies in Pre-Project Planning   57

The Concept of Functional Maps
The Mapping Process
Apple Computer: The Need and Opportunity for Maps

CHAPTER 4   The Aggregate Project Plan   86

Aggregate Project Plans: Promise and Reality
Types of Development Projects
Using Project Types: The Benefits
Developing an Aggregate Project Plan

CHAPTER 5   Structuring the Development Funnel   111

Basic Concepts and Their Application
Creating the Development Funnel: Alternative Models
Diagnosing and Correcting Critical Issues in the Development
    Funnel

CHAPTER 6   A Framework for Development   133

Basic Elements of the Framework
The Framework for Development at Medical Electronics Incor-
    porated
Applying the Development Framework: Comparing Four
    Approaches
Creating an Effective Development Process: Common Themes and
    Basic Principles

CHAPTER 7   Cross-Functional Integration   165

The MEI Experience
A Framework for Cross-Functional Integration
Achieving Cross-Functional Integration

CHAPTER 8   Organizing and Leading Project Teams
                                                 188

Project Organization and Leadership
The Heavyweight Team Structure
Building Capability for Multiple Approaches

CHAPTER 9   *Tools and Methods*   218

A Framework: The Design-Build-Test Cycle
Structured Methodologies for Effective Problem Solving
Computer-Based Systems
Appendix to Chapter 9

CHAPTER 10   *Prototype/Test Cycles*   255

The Traditional Approach to Prototyping
Prototyping: A Managerial Perspective
Matching Prototyping and Development Project Requirements

CHAPTER 11   *Learning from Development Projects*
                                                   284

A Framework for Learning
Capturing Insight and Learning to Change the Development
    Process
The Project Audit: A Framework for Learning
Conclusions and Implications

CHAPTER 12   *Building Development Capability*   311

Four Approaches to Building Capability
Building Capability: A Comparison of Alternatives
Creating New Development Capability: General Observations
Changing Behavior and Overcoming Obstacles
Building Capability: Management Leadership

NOTES   339

INDEX   347

Preface

Why do some companies move quickly and efficiently to bring to market outstanding new products, while others expend tremendous resources to develop products that are late and poorly designed? How do designers, engineers, marketers, manufacturers, and senior executives in these companies combine their skills to build competitive advantage around product and process development? What are the critical concepts, ideas, practices, and processes that lie behind truly outstanding performance in the development of new products and processes? And what can managers do to bring about significant improvement in the performance of their development process? These are the kinds of questions we try to answer in this book.

Our interest in product development is rooted in our long-term focus on the performance of manufacturing companies. Throughout the late 1970s and early 1980s our research and case writing took us into hundreds of factories around the world as we sought understanding of the wide differences in productivity, quality, cost, and flexibility we observed among competitors in a wide variety of industries. Time after time that search led us to product design, the engineering organization, and the speed and effectiveness of the development process as explanations for superior performance. Moreover, in industry after industry and company after company we found senior executives convinced of the competitive importance of development but without a solid base of concepts, ideas, and understanding to guide their efforts to manage and improve the development process.

While much has been written about the management of research and research laboratories, little effort has been focused on the engineering process that lies behind new products, the integration of marketing, manufacturing, and engineering, and, in particular, the role of senior management in leading and guiding the effort. Indeed, business schools included all the major business functions in their curricula (e.g., marketing, operations, finance, accounting, and human resources) except engineering and the development of new products and processes. What was needed, therefore, was not only a base of knowledge and understanding born of research, but also teaching materials and courses to make that knowledge accessible to students of all ages and levels in the organization.

We set out to do research, write cases, develop courses, and teach and work with companies in bringing about significant improvement in development performance. This book is the result of our efforts over the last seven years. The ideas presented here have been tested in research and in classroom interactions with hundreds of executives, and put into practice in many companies. In all of our research, teaching, and interactions we have tried to find the general principles that can guide executive action. But we have also sought to ground our principles and perspective in an understanding of the details of practice: the actual day-to-day work of development. Like the components of a great product, a crucial part of the magic in a great development process is in the details of strategy, planning, designing, engineering, testing, and implementing, and these we have tried to capture. But a great process is not complete unless the details fit together into an effective, coherent whole. How firms fit those details together to create an effective pattern of development is thus a crucial focus of *Revolutionizing Product Development*.

Many people have helped us in writing this book. Literally hundreds of managers, engineers, designers, and marketers in many different companies throughout the world have spent time with us sharing their experience, insights, and perspective. Without their cooperation we could have neither conducted the research, written the cases, nor learned firsthand what it means to develop a new product. Although we cannot recognize them here by name, we have thanked them personally and would like to acknowledge their support.

We have been blessed with great colleagues and a stimulating, supportive environment at the Harvard Business School. We are especially grateful to Dean John McArthur for his encouragement, and particularly for the faith he had in us when it was not clear that any of this would actually work. Jay Lorsch headed up the Division of Research and was always there when we needed support. Bob Hayes chaired our Area and took a lot of flak while keeping our administrative burdens relatively light. (We have been in his debt for many years, but he is starting to collect!) Earl Sasser was co-author on the first paper on maps, and was among the very first of our colleagues to recognize the crucial role of product development. Dorothy Leonard-Barton, Marco Iansiti, and Brent Barnett have worked with us on related research; we have benefited from their field work and ideas. Our doctoral students past and present, especially Taka Fujimoto, Rebecca Henderson, Marcie Tyre, Mike Watkins, Clayton Christensen, and Dave Ellison, have been a crucial source of research assistance and stimulating ideas. We especially want to thank Mike Watkins for his help with Chapter 9, and Dave Ellison for his inputs to Chapter 10. Geoff Gill wrote many of the cases that lie behind the material in the book.

We are happy to report that the field of product and process development is a growth area for research and teaching. Many colleagues have contributed ideas, offered encouragement, used our case material, and otherwise helped us in our work. We are especially indebted to members of the "Manufacturing Vision Group," a research consortium of five companies and engineering and business schools in four universities that has focused on product and process development. We have been part of the group since its inception and have benefited greatly from our involvement. We want to thank especially Kent Bowen, Tom Eagar, Jim Solberg, Carolyn Woo, Phil Barkan, Chuck Holloway, George Stephanopoulos, Richard Billington, Al Brune, Bill Hanson, Gordon Forward, Hal Edmondson, Sara Beckman, Max Jurosek, Jack Rittler, Rohn Harmer, John Owen, Robin Farran, and Doug Braithwaite.

Throughout the writing of the book and the preparation of the manuscript we have received tremendous support from numerous people. Bill Handy, Director of Development at the *Wichita Eagle*, and a former Executive student of ours, was kind enough to apply his critical reading, editing, and creative skills to the final manuscript. He supplied us with many improvements and suggestions. We appreciate the time and energy he spent making a significant contribution to this effort. Bob Wallace, our editor at The Free Press, was an enthusiastic supporter from the beginning and kept after us to make it happen. Elisabeth Peter kept the office humming along and helped us with drafts and revisions. Much of the burden of dealing with two authors, complex graphics, and multiple drafts fell on Jean Smith. She managed the manuscript, designed and executed the graphics, and kept us focused. We could not have done it without her.

Finally and most importantly we want to thank our families for their love and support during these many years. For the Wheelwrights, their dad's involvement meant more than preoccupation and nights out of town; it eventually moved them from Palo Alto, California, to Belmont, Massachusetts. Fortunately, Belmont is a great place to live and the story has a happy ending, but we are grateful for the love and support that lay behind that move. For some of the Clark children (Jennifer and Julia) this has been a lifelong (seven-year) project; for Bryce, Erin, Jon, Andrew, and Michael it only seems that way. Finally, our love and thanks to Margaret and Sue, who are happy that we like to write books, but have always kept us focused on the things that really matter.

*Revolutionizing
Product
Development*

CHAPTER 1

Competing Through Development Capability

In a competitive environment that is global, intense, and dynamic, the development of new products and processes increasingly is a focal point of competition. Firms that get to market faster and more efficiently with products that are well matched to the needs and expectations of target customers create significant competitive leverage. Firms that are slow to market with products that match neither customer expectations nor the products of their rivals are destined to see their market position erode and financial performance falter. In a turbulent environment, doing product and process development well has become a requirement for being a player in the competitive game; doing development extraordinarily well has become a competitive advantage.

The New Industrial Competition: Driving Forces and Development Realities

The importance of product and process development is not limited to industries or businesses built around new scientific findings, with sig-

nificant levels of R&D spending, or where new products have traditionally accounted for a major fraction of annual sales. The forces driving
development are far more general. Three are particularly critical:

- *Intense international competition.* In business after business, the number
  of competitors capable of competing at a world-class level has grown at
  the same time that those competitors have become more aggressive.
  As world trade has expanded and international markets have become
  more accessible, the list of one's toughest competitors now includes
  firms that may have grown up in very different environments in North
  America, Europe, and Asia. The effect has been to make competition
  more intense, demanding, and rigorous, creating a less forgiving environment.
- *Fragmented, demanding markets.* Customers have grown more sophisticated and demanding. Previously unheard of levels of performance
  and reliability are today the expected standard. Increasing sophistication means that customers are more sensitive to nuances and differences in a product, and are attracted to products that provide solutions
  to their particular problems and needs. Yet they expect these solutions
  in easy-to-use forms.
- *Diverse and rapidly changing technologies.* The growing breadth and depth
  of technological and scientific knowledge has created new options for
  meeting the needs of an increasingly diverse and demanding market.
  The development of novel technologies and a new understanding of
  existing technologies increases the variety of possible solutions available to engineers and marketers in their search for new products.
  Furthermore, the new solutions are not only diverse, but also poten-
  tially transforming. New technologies in areas such as materials, electronics, and biology have the capacity to change fundamentally the
  character of a business and the nature of competition.

These forces are at work across a wide range of industries. They are
central to competition in young, technically dynamic industries, but also
affect mature industries where life cycles historically were relatively
long, technologies mature, and demands stable. In the world auto industry, for example, the growing intensity of international competition,
exploding product variety, and diversity in technology have created a
turbulent environment.[1] The number of world-scale competitors has
grown from less than five in the early 1960s to more than twenty today.
But perhaps more importantly, those twenty competitors come from
very different environments and possess a level of capability far exceeding the standard prevailing twenty-five years ago. Much the same is true
of customers. Levels of product quality once considered extraordinary

are now a minimum requirement for doing business. As customers have grown more sophisticated and demanding, the variety of products has increased dramatically. In the mid 1960s, for example, the largest selling automobile in the United States was the Chevrolet Impala. The platform on which it was based sold approximately 1.5 million units per year. In 1991, the largest selling automobile in the United States was the Honda Accord, which sold about 400,000 units. Thus, in a market that is today larger than it was in 1965, the volume per model has dropped by a factor of four. Currently over 600 different automobile models are offered for sale on the U.S. market.

Similarly, technological change has had dramatic consequences. In 1970, one basic engine-drive train technology (a V8 engine, longitudinally mounted, water cooled, carbureted, hooked up to a three-speed automatic transmission with rear wheel drive) accounted for close to 80 percent of all automobile production in the United States.[2] Indeed, there were only five engine-drive train technologies in production. By the early 1980s that number had grown to thirty-three. The growing importance of electronics, new materials, and new design concepts in engines, transmissions, suspensions, and body technologies has accelerated the pace and diversity of technological change in the 1980s. Simply keeping up with those technologies is a challenge, but an often straightforward one in comparison with having to integrate them in development efforts.

Similar forces have been at work in other traditional, mature industries. In textiles and apparel, for example, firms such as Benetton and The Limited have used information technology to create a production and distribution network which links retail outlets directly to distribution centers and back into factories and suppliers in the chain of production from fiber to finished product. The thrust of these networks is the ability to respond quickly to changing customer demands at relatively low cost.[3] Fueled in part by availability and in part by growing demands for differentiated products, product variety has expanded significantly. In plant after plant, one finds vast increases in the number of styles produced and a sharp decline in the length of production runs. These are not changes of 10 or 20 percent; in the 1980s, it was common for apparel plants to experience a four- to fivefold increase in the number of styles produced. These increases in garment variety have pushed back into the textile plants as well. For example, the average lot size for dying at Greenwood Mills, a U.S. textile firm, declined in the 1980s from 120,000 to 11,000 yards.

Changes in markets and technologies for automobile and textile firms have accentuated the importance of speed and variety in product development. But changes in competition, customer demand, and technology have also had dramatic effects on newer, less mature industries in which product innovation has always been an important part of competition. In industries such as computer disk drives and medical equipment, already short life cycles have shrunk further and product variety has increased. In addition, competition has placed increased pressure on product reliability and product cost. In disk drives, for example, the market for Winchester-technology hard disks has expanded from a base in high-end systems for mainframe computers to include a spectrum of applications ranging from notebook personal computers to large-scale supercomputers.[4] Even within an application segment, the number of sizes, capacities, access times, and features has increased sharply. In addition to this *explosion of variety*, firms in the hard disk drive industry have had to meet demands for *dramatic increases in reliability* (tenfold in five years) and *decreases in cost* (5 percent to 8 percent quarterly). These have been met in part by incremental improvements in established technologies and in part through the introduction of new design concepts, production technologies, materials, and software.

Much the same has been true in the market for new medical devices. Innovation has always been important in the creation of new medical devices, but by the 1980s success required the ability to follow an innovative product with sustained improvements in performance, application to new segments, improved reliability, and lower cost. In the case of devices for angioplasty (a procedure using a balloon on a small wire to expand clogged arteries), the initial innovation was followed by a variety of developments that offered the physician greater control of a smaller device, making access easier and creating additional applications. In concert with process changes that substantially improved or reduced variability of performance characteristics, changes in the product have opened up new applications and treatment of a more diverse set of clinical problems and patients, worldwide.

The Competitive Imperatives

Rigorous international competition, the explosion of market segments and niches, and accelerating technological change have created a set of competitive imperatives for the development of new products and processes in industries as diverse as medical instruments and automobiles, textiles, and high-end disk drives. Exhibit 1–1 identifies three of these imperatives—speed, efficiency, and quality—and suggests some of their implications. To succeed, firms must be responsive to changing customer demands and the moves of their competitors. This means that they must be fast.[5] The ability to identify opportunities, mount the requisite development effort, and bring to market new products and

Exhibit 1–1

The Development Imperatives

Required Capability	Driving Force	Implications
1. Fast and Responsive	Intense competition; changing customer expectations; accelerating technological change	Shorter development cycles; better targeted products
2. High Development Productivity	Exploding product variety; sophisticated, discerning customers; technical diversity	Leverage from critical resources; increased number of successful development projects per engineer
3. Products with Distinction and Integrity	Demanding customers; crowded markets; intense competition	Creativity combined with total product quality; customers integrated with truly cross-functional development process

processes quickly is critical to effective competition. But firms also must bring new products and processes to market efficiently. Because the number of new products and new process technologies has increased while model lives and life cycles have shrunk, firms must mount more development projects than has traditionally been the case utilizing substantially fewer resources per project. In the U.S. automobile market, for example, the growth of models and market segments over the last twenty-five years has meant that an auto firm must mount close to four times as many development projects simply to maintain its market share position. But smaller volumes per model and shorter design lives mean resource requirements must drop dramatically. Effective competition requires highly efficient engineering, design, and development activities.

Being fast and efficient is essential but not enough. The products and processes that a firm introduces must also meet demands in the market for value, reliability, and distinctive performance. Demanding customers and capable competitors mean that the ante keeps going up—requirements of performance, reliability, ease of use, and total value increase with each product introduction. When competition is intense firms must attract and satisfy customers in a very crowded market. More and more this means offering a product that is distinctive; that not only satisfies, but also surprises and delights a customer. Moreover, attention to the total product experience and thus to total product quality is critical.

The Opportunity and the Challenge

Firms that step up to the challenge and meet these competitive imperatives enjoy a significant advantage in the market place. The development of outstanding products not only opens new markets and attracts new customers, but also leverages existing assets and builds new capability in the organization. Getting a succession of distinctive new disk drives or a string of new medical devices to market quickly and consistently requires the solution of technical problems that builds know-how. Moreover, it stimulates the creation of greater capability in problem solving, prototype construction, and testing that can be applied in future projects. All of these skills and capabilities enhance a firm's ability to compete. But there is more. Successful new products also unleash a virtuous cycle in reputation and enthusiasm within and outside the organization. Inside, successful new products energize the organization; confidence, pride, and morale grow. The best employees remain challenged and enthused. Outside, outstanding new products create broad interest in the firm and its products, enhance the firm's ability to recruit new employees, and facilitate the building of relationships with other organizations. The organization's momentum builds and reinforces itself.

While the potential opportunities to be realized in developing new products and processes are exciting, making them happen is a demanding challenge. New product or process development entails a complex set of activities that cuts across most functions in a business, as suggested by Exhibit 1–2, which lays out the phases of activity in a typical development project—a new product. In the first two phases—concept development and product planning—information about market opportunities, competitive moves, technical possibilities, and production requirements must be combined to lay down the architecture of the new product. This includes its conceptual design, target market, desired level of performance, investment requirements, and financial impact. Before a new product development program is approved, firms also attempt to prove out the concept through small–scale testing, the construction of models, and, often, discussions with potential customers.

Once approved, a new product project moves into detailed engineering. The primary activity in this phase of development is the design and construction of working prototypes and the development of tools and equipment to be used in commerical production. At the heart of detailed product and process engineering is the "design-build-test" cycle. Both products and processes are laid out in concept, captured in a working model (which may exist on a computer or in physical form), and then subjected to tests that simulate product use. If the model fails to deliver the desired performance characteristics, engineers search for design

EXHIBIT 1–2
Typical Phases of Product Development*

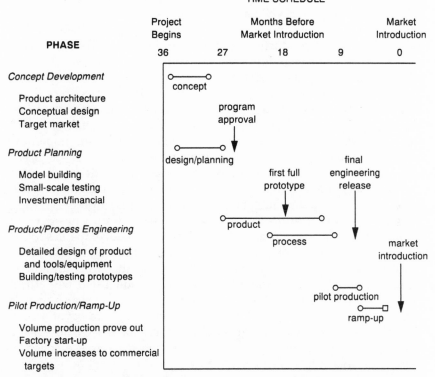

TIME SCHEDULE

	Project Begins		Months Before Market Introduction		Market Introduction
PHASE	36	27	18	9	0

Concept Development

Product architecture
Conceptual design
Target market

Product Planning

Model building
Small-scale testing
Investment/financial

Product/Process Engineering

Detailed design of product
  and tools/equipment
Building/testing prototypes

Pilot Production/Ramp-Up

Volume production prove out
Factory start-up
Volume increases to commercial
  targets

concept

program
approval

design/planning

first full
prototype

final
engineering
release

product

process

market
introduction

pilot production

ramp-up

* This development process assumes a thirty-six-month cycle time and four primary phases. Vertical arrows indicate major events; horizontal lines indicate the duration of the activities.

changes that will close the gap and the design-build-test cycle is repeated. The conclusion of the detailed engineering phase of development is marked by an engineering "release" or "sign off" that signifies that the final design meets requirements.

At this time the firm typically moves development into a pilot manufacturing phase, during which the individual components, built and tested on production equipment, are assembled and tested as a system in the factory. During pilot production many units of the product are produced and the ability of the new or modified manufacturing process to execute at a commerical level is tested. At this stage all commercial tooling and equipment should be in place and all parts suppliers should be geared up and ready for volume production. This is the point in development at which the total system—design, detailed engineering, tools and equipment, parts, assembly sequences, production supervisors, operators, and technicians—comes together.

The final phase of development is ramp-up. The process has been refined and debugged, but has yet to operate at a sustained level of high-yield, volume production. In ramp-up the firm starts commerical production at a relatively low level of volume; as the organization develops confidence in its (and its suppliers') abilities to execute production consistently and marketing's abilities to sell the product, the volume increases. At the conclusion of the ramp-up phase, the production system has achieved its target levels of volume, cost, and quality. In this phase, the firm produces units for commercial sale and, hopefully, brings the volume of production up to its targeted level.

An obstacle to achieving rapid, efficient, high-quality development is the complexity and uncertainty that confronts engineers, marketers, and manufacturers. At a fundamental level the development process creates the future, and that future is often several years away. Consider, for example, the case of a new automobile. The very best companies in the world in 1990 could develop a new car in three to three and a half years. At the outset of a new car development program, therefore, designers, engineers, and marketers must conceive of a product that will attract customers three years into the future. But that product must also survive in the marketplace for at least another four to five years beyond that. Thus the challenge is to design and develop a product whose basic architecture will continue to be effective in the marketplace seven to eight years after it has been conceived.

The problems that uncertainty creates—e.g., different views on the appropriate course of action, new circumstances that change the validity of basic assumptions, and unforeseen problems—are compounded by the complexity of the product and the production process. A product such as a small copier, for example, may have hundreds of parts that must work together with a high degree of precision. Other products, such as the handle of Gillette's Sensor razor, appear to be fairly simple devices but, because of very demanding performance requirements, are complex in design and come out of a manufacturing process involving sophisticated equipment and a large number of operations. Moreover, products may be evaluated across a number of criteria by potential customers. Thus the market itself may be relatively complex with a variety of customers who value different product attributes in different ways. This means that the firm typically draws on a number of people with a variety of specialized skills to achieve desired, yet hard to specify, levels of cost and functionality. To work effectively, these skills and perspectives must be integrated to form an effective whole. It is not enough to have a great idea, superior conceptual design, an excellent prototype facility, or capable tooling engineers; the whole product—its design system, production process, and interaction with customers—must be created, integrated, and made operational in the development process.

But an individual development project is not an island unto itself. It interacts with other development projects and must fit with the operating organization to be effective. Projects may share critical components and use the same support groups (e.g., model shops, testing labs). Additionally, products may require compatability in design and function: models of computers use the same operating system, and different industrial control products conform to the same standards for safety. These interactions create another level of complexity in design and development. Critical links also exist with the operating organization. A new design requires the development of new tools and equipment and uses the skills and capability of operators and technicians in the manufacturing plant. Further, it must be sold by the sales group and serviced by the field organization. Of course, new products often require new skills and capabilities, but, whether relying on new or old, the success of the new product depends in part on how well it fits with the operating units and their chosen capabilities. Thus, effective development means designing and developing many elements that fit and work well as a total system.

Assessing the Promise and Reality: The A14 Stereo Project

The uncertainty and complexity that characterizes the development of new products and processes means that managing any development effort is difficult; managing major development activities effectively is very difficult. Thus, while the promise of a new development project is often bright and exciting, the reality is often quite different. The following story, based on a composite of several situations we have encountered, illustrates typical problems in product development.

In September 1989, Marta Sorensen, product manager for mid-range stereo systems at Northern Electronics Company, a large consumer electronics firm, laid out a plan for a new compact stereo system utilizing advanced technology and providing superior sound quality. Sorenson's marketing group at Northern felt that the company needed to respond quickly to the expected introduction of a new compact system by one of its toughest competitors. The plan Sorenson presented at the beginning of the concept investigation stage called for a development cycle time of one year, with volume production commencing in September 1990. (See Exhibit 1–3 for the initial schedule and subsequent changes.) This would give the factory time to fill distribution and retail channels for the all-important Christmas season in late 1990.

As the exhibit suggests, the schedule began to slip almost immediately. Because of problems in freeing up resources and scheduling meetings, and disagreements about desired product features, the concept investigation stage was not completed until November 1989, six weeks later than originally planned. At that point, no change was made to the schedule for commerical introduction or start of pilot production, but two months were added to the prototype build and test schedule. This additional time was needed as a result of the selection of a new speaker technology that the engineering group had lobbied for during the concept development stage. It was assumed that the time originally allowed for pilot production could somehow be overlapped and/or compressed.

By February 1990 new design problems had emerged. The compact size of the product created unexpected difficulties in fitting the components into a small space while maintaining sound quality. Furthermore, delays with a chip supplier and the speaker technology supplier set back the project schedule several weeks. A revised schedule, established in February 1990, called for completion of the design in April and completion of the prototype-build-test cycle by June. However, no changes were made to the schedule for pilot production or ramp-up. This meant a significant compression of the time between completion of prototype testing to commerical production; process engineering and manufacturing groups were asked to begin preparing the process for production even though the design was still incomplete.

Design engineers worked hard to solve problems with product size, and cost and completed the design in May 1990. By that time, however, new problems had emerged with the prototypes and with the production process. Part of the delay in prototyping reflected late deliveries of parts from suppliers, overambitious testing schedules, and problems in scheduling meetings for milestone reviews. But part of the delay also reflected technical problems with the introduction of surface mount technology in the printed circuit boards for the product. Moreover, process engineering had experienced difficulties with production tooling. There had been a significant number of engineering changes to accommodate changes in exterior appearance as well as performance problems with the product. As a result, the completion of prototype testing was rescheduled for August and pilot production and ramp-up were scheduled to occur in rapid fire succession thereafter.

Even the new schedule proved optimistic. As the fall months wore

EXHIBIT 1–3

Schedule Slippage in the A14 Stereo Project at Northern Electronics*

Anticipated and Actual Phase Completion Dates

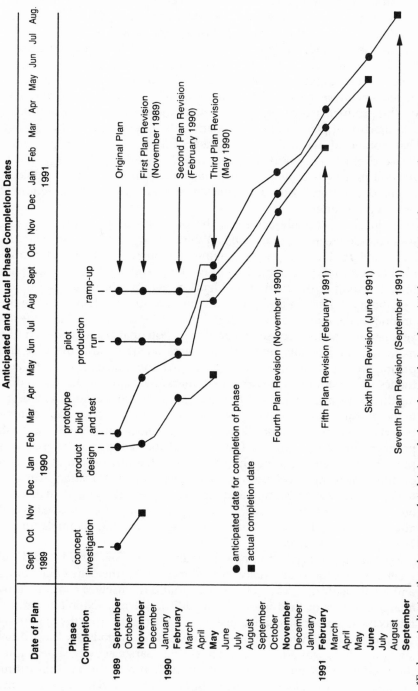

*Each row indicates the phases completed (■) and planned completion dates (●) for remaining phases as of a given date.

on and the project continued to slip, Sorenson and her marketing team realized that they would not meet the critical Christmas season deadline. Much of the latest delay had been caused by interaction between the product design and new automated assembly equipment that the manufacturing organization had installed. In order to meet product cost targets, manufacturing had chosen to move to an automated assembly system that would significantly reduce variable cost on the product. However, while design engineering was aware of the manufacturing plan, there were many subtle details of product design that conflicted with the capabilities of the automated equipment. These conflicts only surfaced late in 1990 as attempts were made to run full prototype units on the automated equipment. These problems required additional product redesign and slowed the completion of prototype testing.

Engineers eventually corrected the problems and prototype testing was completed in February 1991. While compression of the schedule had made product and process engineering operate in parallel, the completion of prototype testing did not mark the end of design changes nor the alleviation of production problems in pilot production.

Although Sorenson and the marketing group were happy to see the product make it through prototype testing, the fact that it was almost a year late had serious consequences for its potential attractiveness in the market. Sound quality and features were adequate and the cost and pricing were in line with expectations, but some of the product's aesthetics were out of synch with recent market developments. Thus, during the spring and summer of 1991 marketing pushed through a redesign of the product's exterior package to make it more attractive and contemporary. This caused some delays as engineering put through a crash program for new tooling and testing, but the redesigned exterior was put into production during the early fall. While the design of the new exterior was being developed, the manufacturing organization struggled to debug the new equipment and achieve consistent levels of quality. By September the plant had solved most of its major process problems and attention was shifted to increasing volume and filling channels for the 1991 Christmas season.

Market acceptance of the new product was satisfactory, but did not meet the projections originally laid out in 1989. Further, the engineering and manufacturing organizations soon found themselves confronted by a large number of field-identified quality problems. Exhibit 1–4 documents the engineering change history of the product from the beginning of pilot production to its post-Christmas sales period. As the exhibit suggests, there was a flurry of engineering change activity shortly after the product went into commerical production and the manufacturing organization struggled to achieve target levels of yield and volume.

EXHIBIT 1–4

Engineering Changes in the A14 Stereo Project, May 1991–July 1992*

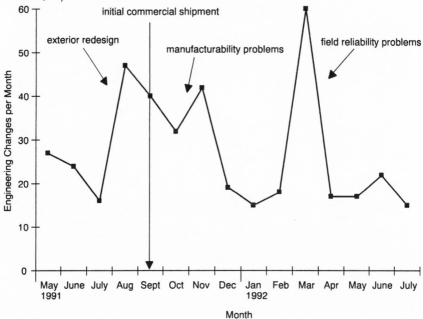

* Arrows indicate major events against which the monthly rate of engineering changes can be referenced. The peak in November 1991 resulted from feedback from early adopters; in March 1992 from feedback from Christmas season customers.

Many of these engineering changes were intended to improve manu-facturability. The significant peak in March 1992 reflected consumer experience with the product following the Christmas season. In February and March of 1992 design engineering launched a crash program to solve several field problems with product reliability.

The Characteristics of Effective Development

The experience of Northern Electronics with the A14 stereo system is not a pathological example. It reflects experience that is all too common in the world of product and process development. The failure of the A14 project to meet its original potential and expectations was not due to a lack of

Exhibit 1–5
Central Themes in Ineffective and Effective Development Projects

PROBLEMATIC PROJECTS		OUTSTANDING PROJECTS
Characteristics	*Consequences*	*Selected Themes*
• Multiple, ambiguous objectives; different functional agendas	• Long planning stage; project becomes vehicle for achieving consensus; late conflicts	• Clear objectives and shared understanding of project's intent throughout organization; early conflict resolution at low levels
• Focus on current customers and confusion about future target customers	• Moving targets; surprises and disappointments in market tests; late redesigns; mismatch between design and market	• Actively anticipating future customers' needs; providing continuity in offerings
• Narrow engineering focus on intrinsic elegance of solutions; little concern with time	• Slipping schedules; schedule compression in final phases	• Maintaining strong focus on time-to-market while solving problems creatively; system view of project concept
• Reliance on engineering changes and manufacturing ramp-up to catch and solve problems; "we'll put a change order on it when we get to manufacturing"	• Poor, unrepresentative prototypes; many late changes; poor manufacturability; scramble in ramp-up; lower than planned yields	• Testing and validating product and process designs before hard tooling or commercial production; "design it right the first time"
• Narrow specialists in functional "chimneys"	• Engineering "ping-pong"; miscommunication and misdirected effort; use of time to substitute for integration	• Broad expertise in critical functions, team responsibility, and integrated problem solving across functions
• Unclear direction; no one in charge; accountability limited	• Lack of a coherent, shared vision of project concept; buck passing; many false starts and dead ends	• Strong leadership and widespread accountability

creative people, management desire, technical skills, or market understanding. The company had excellent marketing information, good relationships with its dealers and customers, recognized competence in engineering and design, and was known for its technical expertise. The A14's problems were rooted far more in the inability of the organization to bring together its insight and understanding and the expertise of its people in a coherent and effective way. In short, the A14 had problems because Northern lacked critical capabilities for integration.

Column 1 of Exhibit 1–5 summarizes typical characteristics of problematic projects like the A14, and column 2 identifies some of their implications. Problems on the A14 were rooted in the nature of the development process and its organization and the absence of a coherent and shared cross-functional plan for competing in the compact stereo market. Different functional groups (e.g., marketing and engineering) had different agendas and there was no organizational process to resolve issues before they surfaced throughout the phases of the A14 development effort. This led to delays and miscommunications throughout.

The development process itself contributed to delay and poor design. The many late engineering changes reflected in part a poorly organized and executed prototyping process. Some prototype parts came from suppliers unfamiliar with the commerical production environment at Northern and were late and poorly built. Delays getting into manufacturing were caused by a narrow focus on product performance in design choices (no design for manufacturability) and barriers to communications between engineering and manufacturing. Management treated the development of new products as the responsibility of the engineering group. Manufacturing was not of primary concern, at least not until problems with the new automated process began to surface. Without strong leadership, problems in the project went undiscovered, surfaced late, and were difficult to resolve.

In contrast to the A14 experience, column 3 in Exhibit 1–5 lays out selected themes in an outstanding development project. Objectives and accountability are clear and widely shared and stem from a concept development and product planning process that brings marketing, engineering, and manufacturing together. Moreover, early-stage development builds on clear strategies in the organization for the product line and major functions. In effect, the outstanding organization starts development projects with concept development on a firm foundation.

Once the concept has been developed and plans for the product have been laid out, execution in outstanding programs has a distinctive character. Guided by strong leadership, engineers with broad skills work in a coherent team with skilled people from marketing and manufacturing. "Integrated" describes day-to-day problem solving across departments and functional groups right down at the working level. Strong, collaborative relationships across departments are rooted in intensive communication, a shared responsibility for product performance, and an appreciation of the value to be added by each group. In this context an excellent engineering design is one that not only achieves outstanding performance but also is manufacturable and comes to market rapidly.

Indeed, time-to-market is such a critical dimension of performance in the outstanding project that all of the processes, systems, and activities in development are geared to fast action. This is particularly true for the critical design-build-test cycles that are at the heart of problem solving in development. Thus, the outstanding project has a prototyping process that creates representative components, subassemblies, and complete units of high quality. These prototypes in turn come out of a design process in which careful and simultaneous attention to the details and behavior of the product as a system catches numerous problems and identifies important opportunities early in the process. In this setup, engineers concentrate on eliminating redesigns caused by mistakes, poor communication, and lack of process understanding, and maximizing product performance and distinctiveness for its target market. "Design it right the first time" is critical because it creates products of high quality and saves valuable time.

Outstanding projects of this kind are not possible without leadership. In contrast to problematic projects where direction is lacking and responsibility diffuse, the excellent project has a project leader who gives conceptual direction and stimulates and nurtures working-level integration. Moreover, that leadership extends to linkages with critical suppliers, customers, and the market. The outstanding project leader fosters internal integration and integrates customer needs into the details of design. Effective product development is not the result of a single individual, but strong leadership makes a difference.

The Fast-Cycle Competitor

The themes that characterize outstanding development projects—clarity of objectives, focus on time to market, integration inside and out, high-quality prototypes, and strong leadership, to name a few—reflect capabilities that lead to rapid, efficient development of attractive products and manufacturing processes. The power of such capabilities lies in the competitive leverage they provide. A firm that develops high-quality products rapidly has several competitive options it may pursue. It may start a new product development project at the same time as the competitors, but introduce the product to the market much sooner. Alternatively, it may delay the beginning of a new development project in order to acquire better information about market developments, customer requirements, or critical technologies, introducing its product at the same time as its competitors but bringing to market a product much better suited to the needs of its customers. Furthermore, if it also has achieved speed and quality in an efficient way, it may use its resources to develop additional focused products that more closely meet the de-

mands of specific customer niches and segments. Whatever the mix of customer targeting, speed to market, and product breadth the firm chooses to pursue, its advantages in fundamental capabilities give it competitive edge.

For a firm like Northern—with slipping development schedules, late design changes, and problems with field failures—competing against a firm capable of rapid but effective product development can be a bewildering, discouraging, and ultimately unprofitable experience. Exhibit 1–6A illustrates just such an episode in Northern's history. Consider first Panel A, which graphs the price, cost, and product generation experience of Northern and its principal competitor, Southern Electronics Company, from 1978 until 1985.

Until 1985, both Northern and Southern followed standard industry cycles in new product development, pricing, and manufacturing costs. With a product development cycle of eighteen to twenty months, both firms introduced new generations of product every two years. Between major generational changes in products there were frequent model upgrades and price declines as the cost of key components and manufacturing fell with increasing volume. Thus, until the mid 1980s, both Southern and Northern had prices and costs that tracked each other closely, and both mirrored industry averages.

Improvement Efforts at Southern Electronics

In the early 1980s, changes in Southern laid the foundation for a significant change in the nature of competition in the industry. Stimulated by the efforts of Greg Jones, the new vice president of engineering, Southern embarked on a concerted effort to reduce its product development lead time. Without compromising quality, Jones and the entire organization began to develop the characteristics sketched out in column 3 of Exhibit 1–5. Stronger leadership, more effective cross-functional integration, greater attention to issues of manufacturability and design, more effective prototyping, and a revamped development process gradually led to a reduction in development lead time from eighteen to twelve months. By 1986 Southern could develop a comparable compact stereo system about six months faster than Northern.

As Panel B of Exhibit 1–6B suggests, Southern began to use its new development capability in early 1986. At that point it broke with industry tradition and introduced its next generation of stereo product about six months sooner than expected. With a more advanced system and superior performance, Southern was able to achieve a premium price in the marketplace. Although Northern followed six months later on a standard cycle, its next generation stereo was unable to command its

Eхнibit 1–6A

Panel A: Standard Competitive Patterns for the Compact Stereo Market*

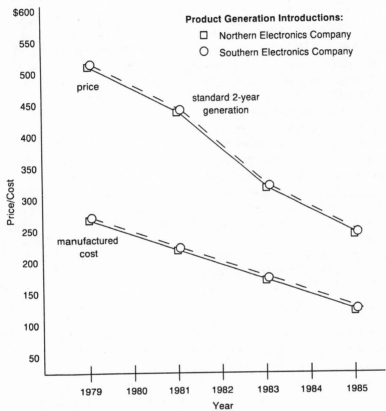

* Prior to 1986, both competitors introduced their new stereo products on the same two-year cycle, adopted similar pricing strategies, and experienced comparable manufacturing costs.

---

traditional market share. As a result, Northern's volume increased more slowly than expected and its cost position began to erode slightly relative to Southern.

Southern Electronics introduced its next generation product eighteen months later in the fall of 1987. Once again the product achieved a premium price in the market. However, Southern did not fully exploit its premium pricing opportunity. Instead, it lowered prices somewhat to increase further its market share. At that point, not only was Northern

EXHIBIT 1–6B

Panel B: Competition on Rapid Development Capabilities in the Compact Stereo Market*

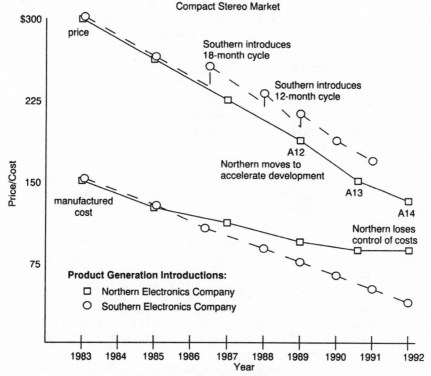

Compact Stereo Market

* Beginning in 1986, Southern moved first to an eighteen-month product introduction cycle and then to a twelve-month cycle; Northern moved to an eighteen-month cycle only in 1990. The consequences were continuing price premiums and cost advantages for Southern.

behind in product features and technology, but Southern's aggressive pricing posture put even more pressure on Northern's sales volume and margins. Although Northern fought back with price discounts, increased advertising, and promotions to dealers, it was unable to stem the erosion of its historical market position. The result was an even greater disparity in the cost positions of Northern and Southern Electronics.

Northern's Competitive Reaction

In late 1988, Northern introduced its next generation stereo system, the A12. Developed under the motto "beat Southern," Northern's executives felt that the A12 would be the product to regain their former competitive position in the market. Much to their surprise, however, the rollout of the A12 in early 1989 was met by Southern's introduction of its next generation stereo system: Southern had moved to a twelve-month product introduction cycle in late 1988. At that point Northern was a full generation of technology behind Southern in its market offerings. Northern's management determined that the only course of action open was to accelerate development of the next generation system, the A13. They thus embarked on a crash development effort to bring the A13 to market in early 1990. At the same time Sorenson and her colleagues began development on the A14, which they targeted for the Christmas 1990 selling season. The A14 was to get them back into the competitive ball game on solid footing—a "close the gap" strategy.

While Northern's strategic intent was to catch up to Southern with accelerated product development, the reality was much different. Northern brought the A13 to market in early 1990, but the development process was so hectic and the ramp-up in manufacturing so strained that the company effectively lost control of its costs. The product came to market but was much more expensive and less effective than the company had planned. Because of its many problems, scarce development resources that were to have been moved to the A14 in early 1990 were focused instead on correcting problems and cleaning up the A13's design. To make matters worse, Southern continued to follow its twelve-month introduction cycle and actually beat Northern to the market with its next generation product. The result for Northern was a further erosion in margins and market position.

Without making fundamental changes in its development process, which management considered neither necessary nor within the charter of Sorenson and those working on the A14, Northern's attempt to push ahead with the A14 for the 1990 Christmas season was a dismal failure. The A14 product had so many problems in the field and was so expensive to manufacture that the product line became a serious financial drain on the company.

The Sources of Advantage

The key to Southern's success in the compact stereo market was its consistent ability to bring excellent products to market before its competitors. This ability was rooted in fundamental changes that Jones and others had made in its development process. These included obtaining broad-based organizational and individual buy-in to key project goals, at the onset, and empowering and encouraging development teams to modify the development process while developing the needed products. In addition it harnessed that capability to a marketing and pricing strategy that was well targeted at Northern's weaknesses. In effect, Southern changed the nature of competition in the industry; Northern was forced to play a game for which it was ill suited—a game Northern never fully comprehended until it was years behind in capability.

Southern Electronics' ability to bring a competitive product to market more rapidly than its chief rivals created significant competitive opportunities. How Southern chose to exploit those opportunities depended on the nature of its competition and its own strategy. But the ability to move quickly in product development created at least three potential sources of advantage:

- *Quality of design.* Because Southern had a twelve-month development cycle, it could begin the development of a new product closer to the market introduction date than its competitors. Whereas Northern had to begin eighteen to twenty months before market introduction, Southern's designers and marketers could gather and refine an additional six months of information before setting out to design a new product. In a turbulent environment, designers face a high degree of uncertainty in the early stages of development about which set of product characteristics will be most attractive to target customers. Additional time to secure feedback on the most recently introduced generation and to learn about market developments and emerging customer preferences may mean the difference between winning and mediocre products. Although the product may use the same basic technologies, additional market information may yield a much better configuration. The product's features and aesthetics may be fresher, more up-to-date, and more closely matched to customer expectations. Thus, Southern could exploit its lead time advantage by waiting to launch its development effort until more and better market information became available. Even though its product would arrive on the market at the same time as its competitors, its product would offer the customer a superior experience.
- *Product performance.* A much faster development cycle gave Southern Electronics the opportunity to launch a new product program well in advance of its competitors. It could use that lead to introduce the next generation of product technology. In this case, the advantage of speed lay not in superior market or customer intelligence, but rather in the ability to exploit technological developments and bring them to market faster than its competitors. The gap in performance this created is depicted in Exhibit 1–7 for a single product generation. As illustrated in the exhibit, a six-month jump on competitors in a market accustomed to eighteen- to twenty-four-month design lives can translate into as much as three times the profit over the market life of the

Exhibit 1–7

The Impact of Market Introduction Timing on Lifetime Profits of a Major New Product*

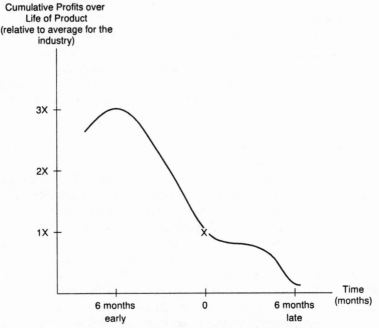

Cumulative Profits over
Life of Product
(relative to average for the
industry)

3X

2X

1X

Time
(months)

6 months | 0 | 6 months
early | | late

Time of Market Introduction Relative to Competitors

* Introducing at the same time as competitors (0 on the horizontal axis) leads to average profits over the life of the product (1x on the vertical axis). Introducing a new product six months ahead of competitors can triple (3x) total profits over the life of the product; introducing six months behind competitors may mean simply breaking even. Note that getting too far ahead of the market (greater than six months) can be less than optimal.

design. Conversely, being late to market with a new product can lead to break-even results and zero profit. This provided Southern with the leverage to control not only their own profits and returns, but also those of their chief competitor, Northern. Putting a sequence of such developments together further widens the competitive gap, as depicted in Exhibit 1–8. The slow-cycle competitor brings new technology to market every two years. The fast-cycle competitor, in contrast, achieves the same performance improvement every twelve months. While the initial advantage of the fast-cycle competitor is relatively small, the ability to move quickly to market eventually creates a significant performance gap. To the extent that customers can discern the difference in performance and to the extent that the gap offers them valuable improvements, a faster time to market creates a superior product.

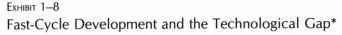

EXHIBIT 1–8

Fast-Cycle Development and the Technological Gap*

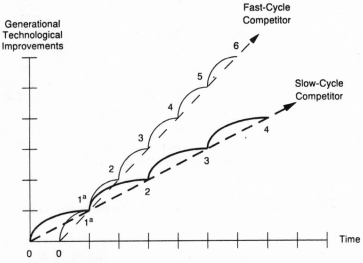

ᵃIndicates product generation.

* This example assumes both competitors incorporate similar amounts of technological change in each generation of product, but the slow competitor lets twice as much time elapse between product generation introductions as the fast competitor. This is what was happening between Northern and Southern Electronics in the compact stereo market (see Exhibit 1–6B, Panel B).

- *Market share and cost.* A better product design and superior product performance gave Southern the opportunity to achieve premium prices in the market. However, a firm may also choose to price its product to create superior value for its customers, thereby translating advantage in design and performance into increases in market share. Where lower costs are driven by growth and increases in volume, increases in market share may translate into improved cost position for the fast-cycle operator. Thus, even if two competitors operate on the same learning curve, the fast-cycle competitor will achieve a cost advantage. However, it may also be the case that the capabilities which underlie fast development cycles create a steeper learning curve. Speed in development is rooted in the ability to solve problems quickly and to integrate insight and understanding from engineering with critical pieces of knowledge in manufacturing. This set of capabilities likewise is critical in achieving cost reductions in established products. Thus, when costs are sensitive to volume and fast-cycle capability enhances a firm's overall learning capacity, the fast-cycle competitor enjoys double leverage in improving its manufacturing costs.

23

How a fast-cycle competitor chooses to exploit the potential advantages in design, product performance, and manufacturing cost will depend on the competitive environment and the firm's strategy. In the case of Southern Electronics, all three dimensions of advantage were important. Initially, Southern used its six-month advantage in lead time to obtain better market information and still introduced its 1986 compact stereo about six months before its competition. In the second generation, however, Southern accelerated its model introduction and began to exploit its development capacity to achieve superior product performance. By 1990, Southern was a generation ahead of its competitors in product technology. It used its superior design and performance to achieve some price premium in the market, but it did not raise prices as much as its performance advantage warranted. The result was a superior value for customers, increases in market share, and steeper slopes on its manufacturing learning curve. Thus, Southern used its advantage in performance and cost both to expand its market share and increase its margins.

But perhaps the most powerful effect of Southern's fast-cycle capability was its ability to change the nature of competition. By improving its development productivity and shortening the time between product generations, Southern forced Northern to play a competitive game that Northern was not prepared to play. Northern would have faced competitive difficulties no matter how it responded to the Southern challenge, but it compounded its problems by failing to change fundamentally its approach to product development. By attempting accelerated development in the context of its traditional systems, Northern created internal confusion, strained its resources, and actually reduced the effectiveness of its development organization. In addition, previously enthusiastic, capable, and hard-working product managers such as Sorenson became frustrated and disappointed. Thus, at the start of the 1990s, Northern Electronics faced the challenge of undertaking a major overhaul of its development process while its margins were eroding, market position was slipping, and morale among some of its best development people was declining. Southern's fast-cycle capability had clearly put Northern and its other major competitors at a significant competitive disadvantage while generating additional enthusiasm and competence among people such as Jones and individual project contributors. Southern was continuing to build momentum as Northern and other competitors continued to lose it.

Achieving competitive advantage through effective development capability is not just a theory. Effective fast-cycle competitors have emerged in a wide range of industries. Firms such as Honda in automobiles, Applied Materials in semiconductor production equipment, ACS in angioplasty, Sony in audio products, Matsushita in VCRs, The

Limited in apparel, Philips in computer monitors, Hill-Rom in hospital beds, and Quantum in disk drives have made the ability to bring outstanding products to market rapidly a central feature of their competitive strategy. Once achieved, and subsequently maintained as the organization grows, an advantage built around fast-cycle capability seems to be strong and enduring. In the first place, the advantage is based on capabilities—human and organizational skills, processes and systems, and know-how—that are difficult to copy. Moreover, effective, rapid development creates superior products and offers customers superior value. It therefore helps to create a market franchise and brand equity. A real product advantage rooted in difficult-to-copy capabilities and a translation of that product advantage into a fundamental market franchise that reinforces its own momentum is a powerful combination. Although product development is difficult, doing it well confers significant advantage. Furthermore, the more challenging the development requirements, the more dramatic the potential impact.

The Plan for the Book

In this book we lay out concepts for the effective organization and management of product and process development. Each chapter frames a particular problem or issue in development, provides a set of ideas for effective management, and illustrates those ideas and their application with several examples. The cases accompanying each chapter in the College version provide an opportunity to apply and develop the concepts and ideas in a practical context.

The first part of the book focuses on the front end of the development process. In Chapters 2 through 5 we discuss the concept of development strategy, the use of maps and mapping to chart an organization's path through the development terrain, the creation of an aggregate project plan to guide a portfolio of development efforts, and the challenge of creating an overall development process that effectively initiates and selects projects and focuses the organization's resources to bring the most attractive projects to market rapidly and efficiently. The thrust of these chapters is laying the foundation for effective development efforts. While the actual development project is a natural locus of attention and effort in organizations, individually effective development projects depend on a strong foundation in strategy, a shared understanding across functional organizations, and an overall process that effectively allocates and concentrates time, energy, attention, and resources on the most attractive opportunities.

Chapters 6 through 10 focus on the management of individual development projects. We first work through an overall framework for evaluating development efforts, including identification of the important phases of development, the measurement of performance, and the critical areas of leverage and choice for managing projects. We then examine the problems of cross-functional integration. A central theme in this part of the book is the power of integrated problem solving. Chapter 8 deals with the problem of organizing development projects. Our emphasis is on the organizational structure, the processes the organization uses to carry out development, and the impact of development leadership. We lay out four contrasting approaches to development project organization and focus particular attention on what we call heavyweight project teams.

The challenge of integration applies not only to large functional organizations like marketing, manufacturing, and engineering, but also at the working level within those organizations and across departments and work groups with different disciplines, tasks, and experiences. Chapter 9 focuses on recent developments in systematic methods and tools for product (and process) development. Concepts such as quality function deployment, design for manufacturability, computer-aided design, and computer-aided engineering represent new design and development methodologies. Much of the thrust of these methodologies is the creation of more effective integration in the development process. In Chapter 10 we examine prototyping, testing, and convergence to a final design. Much of development is a sequence of design-build-test cycles in which prototyping and testing play a central role. Effective management of prototyping is therefore a critical element of effective development capability.

In the final chapters of the book, we shift our attention from the planning and execution of specific projects to the problem of managing the improvement of the development organization and its processes. In Chapter 11 we examine the problem of learning from individual development experiences. This involves not only capturing the insight and understanding that come from current experience, but also capturing that experience in the form of changes in the development process. In addition, learning from experience involves building resources and capabilities to conduct development efforts more effectively in the future. Thus the major focus of Chapter 11 is on mastery of the building blocks for superior development capability and the associated investment in people, skills, tools, and systems.

The book concludes with a chapter on making it happen. We examine alternative improvement paths and focus on the peculiar nature of the development process and consequent issues that managers must examine in pursuing an overall improvement plan. A central theme in this final chapter—and, indeed, throughout the entire book—is the importance of learning by achieving consistency and balance across a wide range of development activities. There are no "three easy steps" to effective development performance. The capabilities that allow an organization to move quickly and efficiently to the market are rooted in people and their skills, organizational structure and procedures, strategies and tactics, tools and methodologies, and managerial processes. This is what makes it so difficult for organizations to improve—and why they acquire such a strong competitive advantage when they do.

CHAPTER 2

The Concept of a Development Strategy

Perhaps no activity in business is more heralded for its promise and approached with more justified optimism than new-product and new-process development. The anticipated benefits almost defy description. This is true whether the business is engaged in an old-line manufacturing-intensive activity such as steel or machine tools, the manufacture of consumer goods such as appliances or personal care products, the production of industrial products such as material transfer systems or heavy equipment, or the creation of technology-intensive products such as pharmaceuticals or electronics.

The potential benefits of effective development efforts are of three types—market position, resource utilization, and organizational renewal and enhancement. In terms of *market position*, ideally a new product can set industry standards—standards that become a barrier to competitors—or open up whole new markets, such as the Sony Walkman or Polaroid camera. Superior products and processes are a means to get a jump on the competitors, build on existing advantages by creating stronger competitive barriers, establish a leadership image that translates into market dominant designs, extend existing product offerings, and increase market share.

Anticipated benefits in *resource utilization* include capitalizing on prior

R&D investments (applying lab discoveries), improving the return on existing assets (such as the sales force, factories, and field service network), applying new technologies for both products and manufacturing processes, and eliminating or overcoming past weaknesses that prevented other products or processes from reaching their full potential. The potential leverage on a variety of resources can be substantial.

Perhaps the most exciting type of development benefit is the prospect of *renewal and transformation of the organization*. The excitement, image, and growth associated with product and process development efforts capture the commitment, innovation, and creativity of the entire organization. This success, in turn, enhances the firm's ability to recruit the best people, improve their integration, and accelerate the pace of change. Furthermore, development projects themselves often are the vehicle by which new approaches and new thinking are adopted and take on institutional reality.

Finally, it is anticipated that all of these benefits will drop to the bottom line, providing rich financial rewards such as improved return on investment, higher margins, expanded sales volume, increased value added, lower costs, and improved productivity. Little wonder that development prospects build excitement and anticipation throughout an organization and its people.

Unfortunately, in most firms the promise is seldom fully realized. Even in many very successful companies, new product development is tinged with significant disappointment and disillusionment, often falling short of both its full potential in general and its specific opportunities on individual projects. In fact, many individuals directly involved in creating new products and processes suffer burnout or a longing to return to the status quo (business as usual), and may even depart from the company.

Problems in New Product and New Process Development

To understand what causes the great disparity between promise and reality, and, more important, to take corrective action, it is useful to explore some ways in which development problems manifest themselves. From experience in a variety of firms and industries, a handful of obvious pitfalls emerge.

The Moving Target. Too often the basic product or process concept misses a shifting technology or market, resulting in a mismatch. This can be caused by locking into a technology before it is sufficiently stable, targeting a market that changes unexpectedly, or making assumptions about the distribution channel that don't hold. In each of these cases, the project gets in trouble because of inadequate consistency of focus throughout its duration and an eventual misalignment with reality. Once the target starts to shift, the problem compounds itself: the project lengthens, and longer projects invariably drift as the target continues to shift. Dramatic examples of such mismatches include the Ford Edsel in the mid 1950s, Texas Instruments' home computer in the late 1970s, and Kodak's disk camera in the 1980s. Even very successful products like the Apple Macintosh can experience a rocky beginning and have to iterate through revisions into an appropriate focus and positioning because of moving targets.

Mismatches Between Functions. While the moving target problem usually reflects a mismatch between an organization and its external environment, mismatches also often occur within an organization. What one part of the organization expects or imagines another part can deliver may prove to be unrealistic or even impossible. For instance, engineering may design a product that its factories cannot produce, at least not consistently, at low cost and with high quality. Similarly, engineering may design features into the product that marketing's established distribution channels and selling approach cannot utilize fully or existing customers do not need. Or manufacturing may assume a certain mix of new products in planning its requirements, while marketing makes different assumptions, confident that manufacturing can alter its mix dramatically on short notice when, in fact, it cannot. Such mismatches may result from a lack of communication among the functions or from a sequential, over-the-wall approach to project management; in either case, development suffers. One of the most startling mismatches we've encountered was at an aerospace firm where manufacturing built an assembly plant using one set of new product specs only to find that it was too small to accommodate the wing span of the aircraft it ultimately had to produce.

Lack of Product Distinctiveness. Often new product development terminates in disappointment because the new product is not as unique or defensible as the organization anticipated. If the organization gets locked into a concept too quickly, it may not bring differing perspectives to the analysis. The market may dry up, or the critical technologies may be sufficiently widespread that imitators appear overnight. Plus Development introduced Hardcard®, a hard disc that fits into a PC expansion slot, after a year and a half of development work. The company thought it had a unique product with at least a nine-month lead on competitors. But by the fifth day of the industry show where Hardcard® was introduced, a competitor was showing a prototype of a competing version. And within three months of Plus's market introduction, the competitor was shipping its new product.[1]

Unexpected Technical Problems. Delays and cost overruns often can be traced to overestimates of the company's technical capabilities or simply to its lack of depth and resources. Projects can suffer delays and stall in midcourse if essential inventions are not completed and drawn into the designers' repertoire before the development project starts. An industrial controls company encountered both problems: it changed a part from metal to plastic only to discover that its manufacturing processes could not hold the required tolerances and that its supplier could not provide raw material of consistent quality.

Problem-Solving Delays. Every new product development activity involves uncertainty, with regard both to specific problems and conflicts that will inevitably arise, and the resources required to resolve them. Too often organizations allocate all of their development resources to known project requirements, leaving little or no cushion for the unexpected. Subsequently, when the inevitable, unanticipated problem occurs and the project experiences delay, managers rob Peter to pay Paul. This siphoning of resources cascades into delays on other projects. Once delays occur, costs increase, pressures mount to cut corners, and further problems erupt. The cycle is familiar. A major project gets into trouble, and managers pull key people off of other projects only to discover that the reassigned people take weeks to get up to speed—thus, the project is almost as late as it would have been without them. In addition, several other projects suffer delays and escalating costs.

Unresolved Policy Issues. A number of very specific choices and decisions must be made during any product or process development project. If major policies have not been articulated clearly and shared, these choices often force a decision on the policy issue for the entire organization. While such forcing is not inherently bad, it inevitably involves more senior levels of management in resolving specific issues. Resolving policy issues during the "heat of the battle" and at senior (more politically oriented) levels of the organization inevitably engenders delay and further complications. One industrial products firm that lacked a clear policy on make-versus-by and vertical integration changed the manufacturing location for a new product four times—from a headquarters plant to offshore Mexico, to offshore Japan, to a local subcontractor—before actual start-up. Each change entailed months of delay and costly design modifications. In effect, the project became the forum for making major strategic decisions.

The reality is that much can and does go wrong during development projects in most firms. When it does, most often it is not because the project team was not smart or was unwilling to work. Nor is it because they do not want to do a good job or that senior management lacked good intentions. The problem is a much more fundamental one—managers fail to plan sufficiently in advance to provide the requisite skills and resources, to define the project and its purposes appropriately, and to integrate the development project with other basic strategies. Rather, managers often seek to respond to problems as their importance becomes apparent; at that point they are unavoidable.

A visit we made to an automotive plant revealed the shortcomings of a focus on "after-the-fact" problem solving rather than problem prevention through effective pre-project planning. In touring the assembly line, we were surprised to find a workstation where the worker's tools consisted of a rubber mallet and a two-by-four. The tour guide explained that the worker was aligning the doors so that each automobile would pass the subsequent leak test. Further questioning revealed that the designers had gone to a new aerodynamic design that eliminated rain gutters and had the doors joining the roof at a point over the driver's (or passenger's) shoulder. This required much tighter tolerances than on previous models—tolerances that this plant could not meet routinely. While several long-term options were available, the short-term fix was a rubber mallet and a two-by-four.

Additional investigation found that the pattern of management's involvement in the development of this particular car and its production start-up followed the pattern shown in Exhibit 2–1. In the early part of the development effort, when management had the ability to make a substantial impact on the eventual outcome, they had been only minimally involved. It was not until pilot production started and the factory discovered it could not make a watertight passenger compartment that management got heavily involved. While the engineers thought the rubber mallet and two-by-four had solved the problem, when the factory began shipping the car in volume, dealers experienced heavy warranty claims for leaks. The problem was that as customers leaned (or hung) on the car door, it again became misaligned. This caused a second flurry of management attention. Subsequently, dealers were trained in the use of rubber mallets and two-by-fours.

This example provides a vivid illustration of why worrying about a development project only when problems become apparent (late in the development cycle) leaves the organization behind the power curve and in a reactive mode. Under such circumstances tremendous amounts of management, technical, and functional expertise do get applied, but largely to avoid competitive disaster rather than to provide competitive advantage. Managers need a much more comprehensive approach—creation and pursuit of an overarching development strategy—in order to apply development resources, including senior management's time, in a manner that is preemptive, proactive, and of maximum value.

Exhibit 2–1

Timing and Impact of Management Attention and Influence*

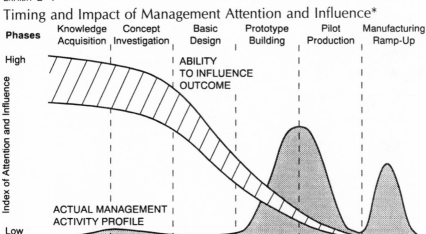

* Management's ability to influence a development project's outcome is high early in development (diagonally shaded area). Yet typically, management's actual activity profile (darkly shaded area) is very limited early on and only becomes significant late in the project, when the effort is in trouble.

SOURCE: R. H. Hayes, S. C. Wheelwright, and K. B. Clark, *Dynamic Manufacturing* (New York: The Free Press, 1988), p. 279. See also F. Gluck and R. Foster. "Managing Technological Change: A Box of Cigars for Brad." *Harvard Business Review* (1975, September–October), p. 141.

A Framework for Development Strategy

In reality, too many firms use an approach to product and process development (depicted in Exhibit 2–2) in which the critical elements of strategy—a plan for technology and a plan for product-market position—are only connected (and then loosely) in individual projects. The major shortcomings of such an approach are (a) a failure to bound and focus the individual project sufficiently to guarantee its rapid, productive execution; (b) a failure to provide sufficient up-front planning to effectively link individual development projects to these two key strategies; and (c) an unreasonable burden on the individual project, so that it must address policy issues, functional mismatches, and other fundamental organizational needs, as well as meet the challenges inherent in any development project. As a result, individual projects fall short of their potential to implement the technology and product market strategies and to capture market position, improve resource utilization, and facilitate organizational renewal.

Exhibit 2–2

Conventional Approach to Development Projects*

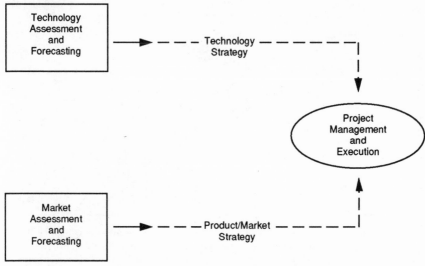

* Traditionally, most firms make only a loose assessment and forecast of technology and market evolution. Futhermore, even the technology and product/market strategies are not explicitly integrated with individual product development projects.

Our research on and experience with firms that have superior development capabilities suggests that a much more comprehensive framework for development strategy, as shown in Exhibit 2–3, provides a far more secure foundation for individual projects. This framework addresses the four main purposes of a development strategy.

- Creating, defining, and selecting a set of development projects that will provide superior products and processes.
- Integrating and coordinating functional tasks, technical tasks, and organizational units involved in development activities over time.
- Managing development efforts so they converge to achieve business purposes as effectively and efficiently as possible.
- Creating and improving the capabilities needed to make development a competitive advantage over the long term.

This expanded framework accomplishes these purposes by adding two pre-project focal points—development goals and an aggregate project plan—where technology strategy and product/market strategy can be discussed and integrated. These explicit pre-project activities

ᴇxʜɪʙɪᴛ 2–3

Development Strategy Framework*

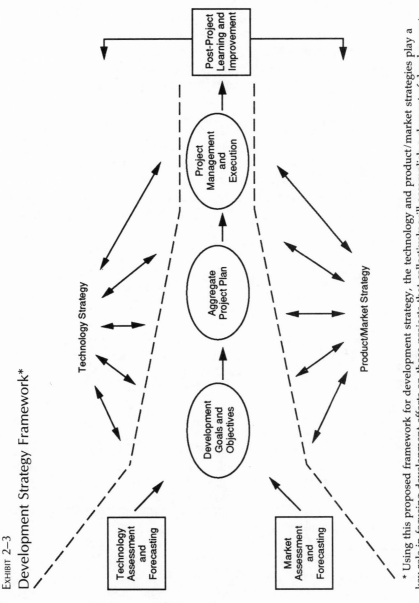

* Using this proposed framework for development strategy, the technology and product/market strategies play a key role in focusing development efforts on those projects that collectively will accomplish a clear set of development goals and objectives. In addition, individual projects are undertaken as part of a stream of projects that not only accomplish strategic goals and objectives, but lead to systematic learning and improvement.

35

provide a way for managers to address policy issues and cross-project concerns, and to set bounds on individual projects. By limiting the scope of individual projects, senior executives make projects more manageable and facilitate refinement and improvement of project management procedures. The framework thus recognizes the need for ongoing learning and provides mechanisms for capturing and applying learning beyond the local efforts of individual team members. The framework provides much more robust phases for pre-project planning and post-project learning that complement and support work on specific projects.

In the remainder of this chapter, we discuss and illustrate each of the elements of the development strategy framework. We place particular emphasis on pre-project steps and their linkages to technology and product/market strategies. Chapters 3, 4, and 5 then deal with concepts, tools, and procedures that have proved extremely effective in operationalizing and implementing these pre-project elements. We will touch only briefly on the project and post-project phases of the framework, since they are the primary focus of Chapters 6 through 10, and Chapters 11 and 12, respectively. We conclude this chapter with an example of development strategy in action.

Technology Planning and Strategy

The objective of technology strategy is to guide the firm in acquiring, developing, and applying technology for competitive advantage.[2] Linking this element of development strategy to the success of a specific development project requires a clear understanding of what technology is, the characteristics of a strong technology strategy, the key issues such a strategy must address, and a plan for achieving it through a set of projects and complementary actions that build the organization's technical skills.

A strategy for technology must confront, in the first instance, what the focus of technical development will be. The question is what technologies are critical to the firm's competitive advantage. In this context, technology must include the "know-how" the firm needs to create, produce, and market its products and deliver them to customers. While some of this knowledge may be based on years of practical experience, some may be rooted in science and scientific research. Such knowledge is "know-why"—a deep understanding of why the products or processes work as they do. While technical knowledge and understanding may therefore have different sources and take different forms, what matters for competition is the firm's technical capability—its ability to use its "know-why" and its "know-how" to achieve very specific results in its products and processes.

As the first step in creating a technology strategy, *focus* defines those capabilities where the firm seeks to achieve a distinctive advantage relative to competitors. For most firms, there are a large number of important areas of technological "know-how" but only a handful where the firm will seek to create truly superior capability. In the steel industry, for example, a firm might seek to build an advantage in the quality and speed of its continuous casting operations. This is a technology based on the sciences of metallurgy, thermodynamics, mechanics, and electronic control; it requires know-how in machine design, computer modeling, materials development, metallurgy, and electrical engineering. There are many other areas of know-how required to be an outstanding competitor in the steel business, but a technology strategy focuses attention on those few areas of distinct advantage. The strategy additionally defines those areas where the firm will seek mastery, if not superiority, and may also define areas where it will rely on generally available, standard technologies.

Establishing focus defines targets for investment in technical capability, but leaves open the question of *source*. This is the second critical aspect of technology strategy. Technological capability may be developed internally through investment in people, equipment, facilities, and methodologies, or through advanced development projects. But technology may also be acquired from outside the firm through sponsored research in universities, joint ventures, licensing, and outright purchase. Inside and outside sources are not mutually exclusive. Indeed, the specific mix of internal and external sources is a crucial dimension of the strategy. Although one source may be dominant, the other usually plays an important role. For example, our steel firm that seeks an edge in continuous casting might engage in significant internal development—building experimental machines, developing prototype control systems—but also may enter into a partnership with equipment suppliers in the development of advanced controls and fund university research on heat transfer modeling. Even where the primary source is external (e.g., licensing coating technologies for special applications), the steel firm needs some internal capability to evaluate the external work and to integrate it into the internal operations. Thus, the key questions the technology strategy must answer about sources are: (1) what roles will external and internal sources play, and (2) how will they be integrated?

Having determined the focus of technical development and the source of capability, the firm must establish the *timing and frequency of implementation*. Part of the timing issue involves developing technical capability, and part involves introducing technology into the market. Our steel firm, for example, may decide to pioneer a new technique for metal forming by conducting advanced development projects, but may choose to delay market introduction until others have paved the way. Though the firm will be a relatively early player in the game, others are the commerical pioneers. Without the advanced development work, the firm's only choice would be to be a follower (possibly a slow follower).

The frequency of implementation and the associated risks will depend in part of the nature of the technology and the markets involved (disk drive technology changes more frequently than automotive engine technology, for example), but in part on strategic choice. At the extremes, a firm may adopt what has been called the "rapid inch-up" strategy— frequent, small changes in technology that cumulatively lead to continuous performance improvement. In the case of the steel company, this would involve introducing many new technologies into the continuous casting process as they are developed. The polar opposite is what might be called the "great leap forward" strategy. In this approach, a firm chooses to make infrequent but large-scale changes in technology that substantially advance the state of the art. In the steel case, this would involve collecting all the individual pieces of new technology and creating a totally new system that is implemented in one large project.

Critical Issues in Technology Strategy

Integrating technology strategy with specific product or process development projects requires managers to articulate the strategy in terms of a plan for development and implementation of capability. Advanced development projects and external acquisitions need to be phased to connect in time with the planned development of products and processes. In developing these plans and linking them to specific development projects, there are two critical issues: separation of technology invention from technology application and integration of product and manufacturing process technology paths.

The *first* issue—separating invention from application—is one of the few development guidelines upon which everyone (practitioners and academics) seems to agree. When invention (for which the timing, prerequisites, resources, and specific outcomes are largely unpredictable) is included in a development project, it invariably causes delay, backtracking, and disappointment. However, when done in advance so that its results are available for application, development of new technology may contribute significantly to project success. The implication is that required inventions should be proven (i.e., feasibility demonstrated) beforehand, off the critical path of commerical development.

The challenge lies in foreseeing when the guideline is likely to be violated and taking the pre-project actions needed to prevent it. A comprehensive process for creating a development strategy can do much to address this issue by forcing clarification of the technology strategy, articulating the relationship of its goals and objectives to those of the development strategy, and defining a set of advanced technology projects (as part of the aggregate project plan) that ensure required inventions precede their application in development.

To highlight the importance of separating the invention of technology from its application, one of Hewlett Packard's major businesses created what they refer to as the "pizza bin" approach. As shown in Exhibit 2–4, their framework for development strategy requires explicit identification of the technologies required in each of the primary business functions *before* proceeding with a development project. It also recognizes the desirability of having several technology options "on the shelf" so that development projects can apply those that are most appropriate.

The *second* critical technology issue—integration of the paths of product and manufacturing process technology evolution—also can be largely preempted through use of the comprehensive development strategy framework. While this issue is not as universal as the separation of invention and application, it is frequently a major pitfall. Basically, the issue arises because most firms develop a rather narrow technology strategy—one that addresses only product technology. In the framework of Exhibit 2–3, technology strategy is defined broadly (as Hewlett Packard did in Exhibit 2–4) and covers manufacturing process and service delivery technologies, as well as product technology.

All too often "development projects" means "product development projects," the assumption being that process technology can be acquired easily if and when the need for it becomes obvious. Unfortunately, such a view results frequently in the full benefits of the product technology never being realized—the manufacturing process simply cannot deliver the quality, cost, or timeliness the product requires. In addition, the potential for competitive advantage from superior process technology, either by doing things others cannot do (at least, not easily) or by protecting proprietary product technology, is never realized.

A comprehensive development strategy can do much to address this issue by providing a long-term focus on product and process technology evolution and an intermediate-term focus on development projects that apply those technologies in an integrated and complementary way. Many of IBM's businesses, for example, have detailed this aspect of development strategy as shown in Exhibit 2–5. There are four subparts in IBM's approach: pursuing long-term inventions in product and process as part of the technology strategy, engaging in medium-term advanced development projects to refine and prepare technology for commerical application (filling the pizza bins), executing numerous near-term product and process development projects to apply technical advances, and matching product and process "windows" (generations) in order to maximize the competitive benefits of product and process improvements.

Exhibit 2–4

Development Strategy at Hewlett Packard Emphasizing the Separation of Technology Invention and Its Application in Development Projects*

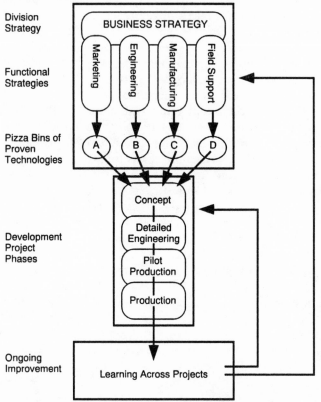

* Hewlett Packard conceives of the business and functional strategies as key drivers in assessing which technological opportunities hold the greatest promise for a business. Advanced development projects around those technologies then prove technical feasibility *prior* to their application in specific development projects. (Note that HP uses a standard four-phase process in development, followed by efforts to consolidate learning across the set of projects.)

Product/Market Planning and Strategy

A product/market strategy for a business addresses four important questions:[3]

- What products will be offered (i.e., the breadth and depth of the product line)?

40

EXHIBIT 2–5

Linking Technology Evolution (Advanced Development) Efforts with Product and Process Development Projects at IBM*

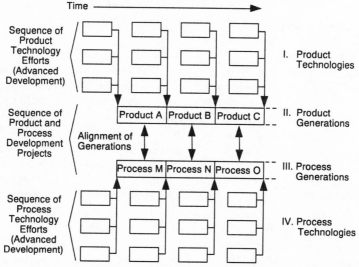

* Each row represents the evolution over time of a set of product technologies (I), the product line (II), the process line (III), or set of process technologies (IV). Advanced development efforts precede and provide inputs to next generation product and process development efforts, which are aligned to ensure that products and processes introduced to the market are complementary.

- Who will be the target customers (i.e., the boundaries of the market segments to be served)?
- How will the products reach those customers (i.e., the distribution channels to be used)?
- Why will customers prefer our products to those of competitors (i.e., the distinctive attributes and value to be provided)?

From the perspective of product and process development, the critical issues in the product/market strategy are the number of platform (or core) products, the number of enhanced (or derivative) products, and the frequency of new product introductions. Development projects are, after all, the primary vehicle by which such changes in the product line are accomplished.

There are a variety of patterns of platform and derivative projects. Some firms choose to have relatively few core product offerings that change only infrequently, but offer a variety of product variations based on the core product. Steinway, with its handful of upright and grand piano models, introduced only one major new model between 1970 and

41

1990. It customizes each piano, however, making it a work of art. Thus Steinway offers no two identical pianos, yet produces only a handful of core models. Other firms choose to have a few core products that change much more frequently, in addition to offering numerous variations. Sony's Walkman (a portable, personal audio system with earphones) illustrates this strategy. By 1990, Sony offered over 180 models of Walkman, with almost half of them introduced in the preceding twelve months. That wide variety, however, was derived through incremental changes to one of three platform products. Each of those platform products in turn was redesigned to provide a "next generation" core product every eighteen to twenty-four months.[4]

In other industries the frequency in performance improvement increments of platform products is set largely by an industry standards group, with firms free to offer as much variety around those platforms as they think appropriate. The alternating current (AC) electric motor industry in the United States, with its seven-year cycle of rerating standards set by the National Electrical Manufacturers Association (NEMA), is an excellent example of this. Reliance Electric chooses to offer extensive variety around current standards, while Emerson Electric's variety is more limited. In relatively young industries, such as medical instruments, every development effort appears to be a platform effort (to broaden the firm's market coverage), with incremental changes targeted primarily at correcting deficiencies in the platform products (as originally introduced).[5]

Critical Issues in Product/Market Strategy

Linking product/market strategy to specific development projects raises two critical issues: (1) the number, timing, and rate of change of platform products, and (2) the number, timing, frequency, and relationship to the product/market strategy of derivative products.

The way a firm deals with the first issue defines the generations of platform products. There are five specific factors involved in the choices the firm makes about platform generations:

1. *Technology evolution.* The rate of technology change impacts how much new knowledge is available, and when it can go into a next-generation platform product.
2. *Competition.* The rate and time at which competitors introduce new generations of platform products affects how long an existing generation can remain in the marketplace and still be viable.
3. *Return on investment.* The investment required to develop the next-generation product (and its associated process), in concert with the contribution margins generated by the new product, determines the

cumulative sales volume required for that product to provide a sufficient return before the next-generation product is introduced.

4. *Customer support*. Providing a continuous flow of products that meets the needs of targeted markets and channels for product "freshness," customization, and performance affects the timing and structure of the generational products offered.

5. *Available resources*. Generally, next-generation platform development efforts require significant resources over an extended period. Available resources—constrained by existing people, productivity, and the R&D expenditures the business can support—usually can execute only a handful of generational projects every couple of years.

What the firm does with platform generations will affect its approach to derivative products. Derivative products range from defeatured, cost-reduced versions of platform products to enhanced and even hybrid versions. While the marketplace often makes only minor distinctions among platform and derivative products in the line, for development planning (and manufacturing) the distinctions are significant because of the differences in resources required to develop and support them. The development strategy, in conjunction with the product/market strategy, needs to bring these differences into sharp focus and address these concerns:

- The timing of derivative products and developments and market introductions *relative* to the timing and life cycle of platform generation developments from which they derive.
- The fraction of sales expected to come from derivative versus platform products.
- The nature of the markets and channels served by the derivative products (e.g., niche or custom segments) in contrast to those served by platform products (e.g., the volume segment or the early adopters).
- The leverage on development resource investments as well as operating investments (e.g., sales force, factories, field service) to be provided by derivative products.
- The role of derivative products in extending the life cycle of platform products and "holding" market position (preempting competitors) until a next generation can be completed and introduced.

These choices and the factors related to them need to be addressed at both the strategic and tactical levels. At the strategic level, choices must be made such that the product/market strategy and the longer-term development and business goals are compatible and do-able. At the tactical level, decision rules and disciplines must be adopted that enable the aggregate project plan and individual projects to implement successfully the product/market and development strategies.

The leverage provided by effective integration of the product/market strategy and the development strategy can be significant. Consider the experiences of two companies, a scientific instruments firm and an electric hospital bed firm. Historically, the scientific instruments firm had developed and introduced a highly featured, generational platform product every four or five years, followed by a cost-reduced derivative product and some minor "fixes" a year or two later. As part of a comprehensive development strategy, they decided to develop and introduce the derivative, low-cost model concurrent with the high-end platform model and to target the derivative product at the high-volume market segment. Through the use of software options, a common manufacturing process, and extensive testing to design in reliability, they were able to introduce two winning products off a single platform, and achieve very aggressive business and development goals while implementing a new product/market strategy.

A leading hospital bed company consolidated a formerly "all things to all people" product line around three platform products while maintaining breadth of line through modularized options. This increased significantly their return on development and manufacturing investments, enabling them to expand into other related product fields. Through additional investments in technology and market research, they began shortening the time between platform generations. This in turn increased the value of their products to customers, making it attractive to hospitals to replace beds more rapidly. The result was increased volumes, market share, and profit margins.

Development Goals and Objectives

A strategy for technology and for products/markets gives the development effort guidance and direction. But to ensure consistency and coherence across these strategies and to link them explicitly to business as well as development objectives, a firm must define its basic development goals and objectives. At the aggregate level, the goals and objectives need to be made explicit and then juxtapositioned to examine their compatibility and complementarity. The purpose of this process is to provide integration both in the aggregate and at the level of the individual project. Typically, these goals range from market share (by customer segment and channel) to revenues and profits, and from dates for platform generation introductions and technology achievements to new product/new process performance objectives. When effectively tied together, these goals provide an organization with confidence that their

EXHIBIT 2–6

Motorola Life Cycle Planning—Relating Business Goals to New Product Development and Market Introductions*

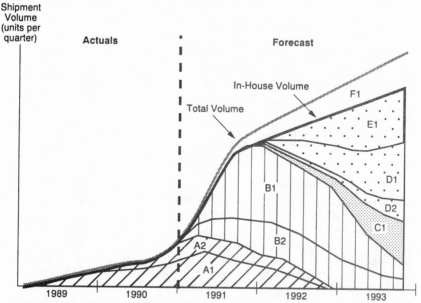

* Starting with development plans for product families (A through F), business unit revenue planning and budgets can be linked to individual development projects (A1, A2, B1, etc.), their market introduction dates, and their product life cycles.

SOURCE: Adapted from C. H. Willyard and C. W. McClees, "Motorola's Technology Road-map Process," *Research Management*, vol. 30, No. 3 (September–October 1987), pp. 13–19.

strategies will generate the business performance desired. They also can serve as a guide for investment decisions and a benchmark for monitoring ongoing progress.

For such goals to be credible, they must be linked directly to the set of development projects the firm intends to undertake. That is, the sum of the parts (the projects) must provide the aggregate performance desired. One way of determining whether this will indeed be the case is to model financially the development projects and their expected results. Exhibit 2–6 illustrates the use of one such model applied at a Motorola business unit. In 1990, this business offered a single platform (A) in two primary forms (A1 and A2). The plan is to introduce a second platform (B) in 1991, again in two forms (B1 and B2), that will replace the current platform (A) by the end of 1992. They also expect to add another primary platform offering (F1) in 1991, but that will be produced by a

EXHIBIT 2–7

Establishing Generational Development Goals that Tie Product Families to Business Strategy Goals at Northern Electronics*

	1990	1992	Mid 1993
Family generation	I	II	III
Number of components	3100	1250	1150
• PC Boards	27	11	8
• ICs	90	32	27
• Semiconductors	400	140	170
Defective units (final assembly)	28%	14%	5%
Service call rate	32%	11%	6%
Services costs/set sold (indexed)	100	50	20
Volume (indexed)	100	125	320
Factory cost (indexed)	100	70	40
• Work content	100	60	34
• Material	100	65	42
• Overhead	100	80	40

* In the late 1980s, Northern Electronics prepared plans for three generations (I, II, and III) of a consumer product, to be introduced in 1990, 1992, and mid-1993, respectively. They then set performance goals for both product and process development that would first close the competitive gap, then achieve parity, and finally provide a competitive advantage by the third generation.

---

supplier. Finally, by early 1992, they plan to introduce three more platforms (C, D, and E). Similar graphs could be developed to show factory utilization, development resource commitments, revenues, profits, or any other measure of interest.

In addition to meeting aggregate business goals, the collective set of projects also must meet technical performance goals. Consider, for example, the competitive interaction between Northern and Southern Electronics discussed in Chapter 1. When Northern found itself slipping behind, they could have looked carefully across the product generations and established goals to regain competitive position. Exhibit 2–7 presents an example of what these goals might have looked like. Such goals would have helped significantly in linking individual projects to the longer-term strategic problems at Northern.

At the operating level, there is also a need for goals that can guide the individual project, yet connect its contribution to longer-term objectives. Typically, firms that measure development focus their attention on either resource productivity (especially of engineering) or design quality (delivery of new features). Only recently have time-to-market and production quality (manufacturability) gained widespread attention as im-

EXHIBIT 2–8

Performance Measures for Development Projects

Performance Dimension	Measures	Impact on Competitiveness
Time-to-Market	• Frequency of new product introductions • Time from initial concept to market introduction • Number started and number completed Actual versus plan • Percent of sales coming from new products	• Responsiveness to customers/ competitors • Quality of design – close to market • Frequency of projects – model life
Productivity	• Engineering hours per project • Cost of materials and tooling per project Actual versus plan	• Number of projects – freshness and breadth of line • Frequency of projects – economics of development
Quality	• Conformance – reliability in use • Design – performance and customer satisfaction • Yield – factory and field	• Reputation – customer loyalty • Relative attractiveness to customers – market share • Profitability – cost of ongoing service

portant measures for individual projects. In most competitive environments, however, managers need multiple measures on all four performance dimensions. Moreover, the primary emphasis must be on improving all of the dimensions simultaneously. As part of the development strategy, it is important to define what measures are to be used and why, and to apply them consistently in evaluating development performance. Exhibit 2–8 presents examples of performance measures and their connection to competition.

Taken together, time, quality, and productivity define the performance of development, and, in combination with other activities—sales, manufacturing, advertising, and customer service—determine the market impact of the project and its profitability. In order to integrate the dimensions of development performance so that general management, the functional areas, and the development team can better monitor, evaluate, and learn from individual projects, Hewlett Packard has defined what they call "the return map." As shown in Exhibit 2–9, this concept presents graphically the relationship of several key measures important to development projects. For example, it captures both money and time, as well as market acceptance. This single diagram conveys the time-to-market for a project, its break-even time (when cumulative product contribution has repaid the development and start-up investments), and the return factor (the ratio of contribution to original investment over a given sales period). Hewlett Packard found that since it shows investment, cost, revenue, and profit over time, a variety of groups

Exhibit 2–9

Hewlett Packard's Development Project Return Map*

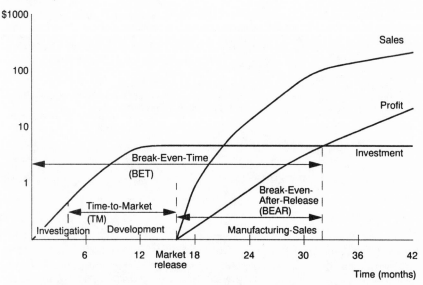

* As a way to make comparisons among projects, Hewlett Packard has developed and refined the set of measures shown here. These are now used as management tools by both the team and senior management on all product development projects.

SOURCE: Reprinted by permission of *Harvard Business Review*. An exhibit from "The Return Map: Tracking Product Teams," by C. H. House and R. L. Price (January–February 1991), pp. 92–101. Copyright © 1991 by the President and Fellows of Harvard College; all rights reserved.

charged with making decisions that impact the development strategy can use the map as a common reference point.

The Aggregate Project Plan

The process of working out development goals and objectives integrates technology and commerical plans from the standpoint of purpose and intent. The aggregate project plan brings a second stage of integration down to the level of specific projects and resources. The purpose of creating such a plan is to ensure that the collective set of projects will accomplish the development goals and objectives *and* build the organizational capabilities needed for ongoing development success. While an

EXHIBIT 2–10

Four Types of Product / Process Development Projects*

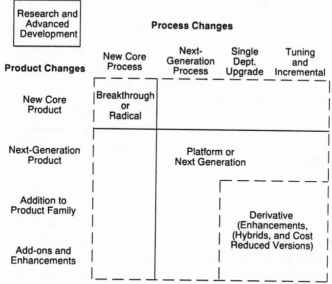

* The amount of product and process change determines the type and magnitude of the development effort required. Research and advanced development involves proving the feasibility of new technology. The other three types of projects involve the application of proven technologies to create commercial products and manufacturing processes that will achieve business objectives.

aggregate project plan is absent in the vast majority of firms we have studied, the concept is relatively simple and straightforward. (Chapter 4 deals with the practical challenges that must be addressed to operationalize the concept fully.)

The first step in developing an aggregate project plan is to ensure that development resources are applied to the appropriate types and mix of projects. For most firms, development projects—both product and process—fall into one of the four types shown in Exhibit 2–10. Briefly, these are defined as follows:

• *Research or advanced development projects.* These aim at inventing new science or capturing new know-how so that required knowledge will be available for application in specific development projects. Often they are conducted by a research or advanced development group that is separate from the main development organization.

• *Breakthrough development projects.* These involve creating the first gen-

49

eration of an entirely new product and process. They are "break-through" in the sense that their core concepts and technologies break new ground for the organization. If successful, they are likely to constitute a whole new product/process family for the organization.

- *Platform or generational development projects.* These are the platform or core development projects mentioned earlier in this chapter. Typically they have a design life of several years and establish the basic architecture for a set of follow-on derivative projects.
- *Derivative development projects.* These tend to be substantially narrower in scope and resource requirements than platform projects. They refine and improve selected performance dimensions to better meet the needs of specific market segments. Often they are referred to as "incremental."

While these four project types may vary in the degree of product and process change they incorporate, a fifth type can be distinguished by who does the work. In *alliance or partnered projects,* the firm "buys" a newly designed product and/or process from another firm. The possibility of subcontracting a development project to a partner needs to be included in the aggregate project plan because it can leverage in-house effort, yet requires some resources for coordination and integration.

By indicating the number and mix of these types of projects the aggregate project plan helps an organization allocate its efforts in proportion to the need for and benefits from projects of each type. In addition, it makes explicit the connection between research projects and development projects. Finally, the mix by type translates the product/market and technology strategies into more specific bounds for development efforts and gives the organization the ability to deliver on intermediate-term operating objectives and goals.

The second step is to develop a capacity plan. In virtually all organizations, the demands or opportunities for development projects far exceed the capacity of available resources to work on them. Furthermore, when organizations overextend their resources, productivity declines, the number of projects "in process" increases, projects take longer to complete, and the rate of project completions declines.

As part of the aggregate project plan, the expected resource requirements for representative projects of each of the five types need to be estimated. These estimates, multiplied by the number of projects of each type, can be compared with the available resources to estimate the capacity utilization levels. Initially when this is done, it is not unusual for project commitments to exceed available development capacity by 50 to 100 percent or more. Over time, as demand and capacity are brought into better balance—usually by reducing significantly the number of projects underway at any given point in time—more refined estimates of project requirements can be developed and used to schedule at a detailed level.

The final step in the aggregate plan is to examine the effect of the proposed projects on fundamental skills and capabilities required for future development projects. This includes planning net additions to development resources, but more importantly, providing a set of projects wherein individual contributors, project leaders, and teams can sharpen their skills over time. This aspect of the plan comprehends the fact that development projects build skills and capability, in addition to creating new products and processes.

Project Management

The aggregate project plan and the goals and objectives set the stage for execution of individual projects, a subject we examine in detail in Chapters 6 through 10. But the firm's approach to project management is also part of its development strategy. Since a primary objective of development strategy is to better focus, bound, and set the stage for individual projects, individual projects must build on prior planning by starting with their own planning phase. In essence, each project needs to create its own project strategy and plan that fits with the development strategy. Thus, at the front end of an individual project, the firm needs a process to connect the project in its details to the broader strategy and direction of the business. An important part of that connection is the establishment of clear, measurable goals that can guide development and ensure the project's contribution to overall development objectives.

With the project firmly linked to the business's overall strategy and objectives, project leaders have a much clearer sense of mission and purpose. That clarity in turn simplifies the project and brings focus to the actual work of development. Getting that work done is a matter of detailed design, engineering problem solving, building and testing of prototypes, marketing planning, process planning and development, and manufacturing ramp-up. But the way the firm approaches that detailed work—how it is broadly structured and organized—is part of its development strategy. There may be several different "models" or "approaches" that the firm may develop to apply to different kinds of projects. Crafting a complete development strategy, therefore, involves deciding what those approaches need to be and how they ought to be developed and used in different circumstances. As Exhibit 2–11 makes clear, the key components of individual project management must be not only integrated among themselves, but also linked effectively with the aggregate project plan and the other elements of the development strategy.

EXHIBIT 2–11

Integrating and Linking Project Management Elements to
Development Strategy

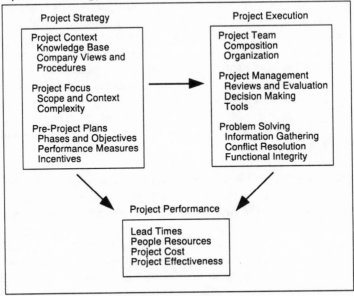

Development Strategy Context

Post-Project Learning

The final element of a development strategy, the focus of Chapters 11
and 12, is post-project learning. Its goal is to ensure that the lessons
available from each project are identified, shared, and applied throughout the organization. In doing so, it closes the loop on continuous improvement by strengthening the foundation for the next iteration of the
development strategy.

Learning from individual development projects has proven to be an
elusive goal for too many organizations. This is due in part to the prevalent view of how such learning occurs. Many firms think of improvement in development as fixing problems. Unfortunately, the "ideas" for
improvement are often little more than short-term reactions to problems
the firm has experienced. Taken together, they may add new procedures, steps, tests, and organizations that only increase the bureaucracy
of the process. The accumulation of fixes then sets the stage for a major
overhaul of the development process in which the firm strips away all
the added steps and procedures. Overall performance, therefore, goes

up and down, but on average changes very little. In contrast, the most successful organizations at learning *and* improving are those that follow a path of continuous improvement in the fundamental capabilities that drive development performance. Each project results in an incremental, but cumulatively significant, improvement in the capabilities of the organization.

Another reason many firms find improvement and learning elusive is that they fail to plan for learning across a sequence of projects. Their goal on each project is to get the product or process into the marketplace (or factory) as rapidly as possible, without significant regard for the means by which they accomplish it. They fail to capture and embed learning in people's behavior, complementary tools, supporting systems, and the organization's structure during each project. Furthermore, even across generations of product and process or even in derivative projects, they fail to plan systematically for the performance and capability improvements they desire.

To make continuous improvement a reality, the post-project phase of the development strategy needs to address the how, who, what, and where of such learning. A particularly effective part of *how* is the project audit, described in detail Chapter 11. Such audits seek to identify the lessons learned and determine how best to apply them. The *who* consists of the entire organization. However, focused steering committees, continual management attention, and a cadre of trained project managers help ensure that the lessons identified in the audits get applied fully. The *what* involves investing—in training, new tools, and new skills. This investment is both in people and procedures, ranging from support groups to the development engineers, and from project planning systems to computer-aided design tools. The *where* is largely in the development projects themselves, targeting some to demonstrate new tools, others to train new people, but all to improve incrementally the organization's collective capabilities.

Honda: An Example of Development Strategy in Action

Honda's competitive performance in the world auto industry over the last decade illustrates the power of a coherent development strategy. Beginning in the 1970s with the Civic, Honda has successfully expanded its product line and established a reputation for innovative products that offer outstanding performance and reliability. Honda's development process has been crucial in establishing that reputation. Continued growth and market success will depend on ongoing improvements in development skills and capabilities.

The challenge that Honda faces in the 1990s is to meet distinctive demands in different regions and market segments, and yet offer a consistent image and product character across models. As Honda moves from its position as a niche player to a full line producer, it must nurture and sustain its reputation for innovative, exciting products while meeting increasingly rigorous competition on cost and quality. Moreover, the global nature of Honda's business and the regional nature of markets means that Honda's product development process must address the need to be both local and global at the same time.

To address the challenges of the 1990s Honda has organized regionally with capability for marketing, manufacturing, design, and engineering established in each of the major regions of the world—Asia (Japan), North America, and Europe. Compared to the challenge of the 1980s, Honda's product line is more complex, its technical requirements more demanding, and its target markets more diverse. Nobuhiko Kawamoto, Honda's CEO, has made it clear that more and more effective up-front planning is crucial to Honda's continued success.

Honda's development strategy has several distinctive elements. Advanced technology has always been a centerpiece of Honda's approach to competition. But at Honda, advanced technology has a particular character. Consider engines, for example. Honda's roots are in motorcycles where highly efficient yet powerful small engines are critical to success. This philosophy has carried over into automobiles. Honda has used Formula 1 racing activities to test and refine engine concepts that deliver very high performance with a minimum of weight and space. Moreover, Honda's engines deliver high performance without add-on devices like turbochargers. In engines, as in other technologies such as four-wheel steering, the hallmarks of Honda's approach are innovation and simplicity.

Looking forward, Honda (and the rest of the world auto industry) faces major technical challenges from the environment (i.e., emissions and recyclability), energy use, safety, and ergonomics. It is likely that meeting these challenges will require the integration of science into the R&D program at Honda. Individual projects will need more focused, deeper technical knowledge and advanced components and systems that have been developed and tested prior to the project's launch. The need for depth and advanced development places an even greater premium on close links between planning for technology and advanced development, and planning for the product line. In our terms, the aggregate project plan, including advanced development as well as commercial products and processes, will be crucial.

Honda's experience with the Today, a micro-mini car sold in Japan, illustrates the power of a close link between advanced development and the product plan.[6] Changes in government regulations in 1988 created new standards for engine and body size for micro-mini cars in Japan. Honda had done advanced work on engine designs for micro-minis that fed directly into the Today redesign. The total development process for the Today took twelve months (compared to a normal development cycle of twenty-four to thirty-six months for such projects), a speed that would not have been possible without the advanced engine development work.

Not all of Honda's development efforts have been unmitigated successes, but the company seems to learn rapidly from each of them. Indeed, the capability for learning seems to be a significant part of Honda's overall success in development. Consider, for example, the project to develop the 1990 Accord, a mid-size family sedan. Honda chose to develop models for the U.S. and Japanese markets from essentially the same platform (body structure, interior, chassis) with different engines, but the two markets proved to be quite different. While a conservative design worked well in the United States, Japanese customers in that segment seemed to be much more interested in innovative concepts and advanced technology. Honda's senior managers have learned that the next generation Accord not only must be more exciting and innovative, but that the two markets probably need different concepts and possibly different platforms. The 1994 Accord project, therefore, is likely to be really two or three projects with distinctive concepts, conducted in a way to achieve coordinated development that leverages common skills and technologies.

One part of the changing development strategy to meet the challenge of multiple platforms yet common identity and character is Honda's approach to project leadership and project teams. For incremental projects, they have defined a type of "small project leader" who, having worked on a preceding development effort for that car model, is given management responsibility for a derivative product or enhancement. A more expanded type of leader is the "regular project leader," who heads a platform effort such as the one resulting in the 1990 Honda Accord. Above this regular project leader is a "large project leader," having responsibility for a group of projects such as the three Accord platforms that will be introduced in 1993–1994. Finally, at the corporate level, there is an executive, or "large, large project leader," who oversees all projects in a broad part of the product line (e.g., one each for small, medium, and large cars).

A final aspect of Honda's project management has been the creation of and continued improvement in the tools and techniques used for carrying out projects. An integral part of this effort has been improving the transfer and introduction of newly designed products into Honda's worldwide manufacturing network. In the future, Honda anticipates that R&D will increasingly focus its attention on platform and technical projects while manufacturing and sales and marketing organizations will handle more of the incremental, derivative, and enhancement projects. One of the reasons for giving the operating organization more development responsibility is to create the same opportunities for renewal and innovation as the R&D organization has. This also would provide a means for implementing a fundamental tenet at Honda: "every organizational unit must break old habits, even good ones."

Honda has used development strategy to build distinctive capabilities and to address the issues raised at the outset of this chapter: avoiding the moving target syndrome, aligning the efforts of individual functions, creating distinctive products while avoiding unexpected technical problems, shaping policies in advance of individual projects, and avoiding unanticipated delays. The success of Honda's efforts is evident in individual projects such as the "Today" as well as in rapid development time for platform projects (three to three-and-a-half years—among the fastest in the worldwide auto industry) and in the completion of factory and supply chain changeovers for new car models in a single weekend, thereby avoiding costly plant shutdowns. Honda has occasionally stumbled in the past, and it faces significant challenges in the future. However, its experience illustrates the power of a development strategy and suggests that continual success will be found by paying close attention to pre-project planning, linking technical strategy to the aggregate project plan, and creating an approach to leadership and organization that matches the need for distinctive, innovative products that create an attractive, coherent image in the marketplace.

CHAPTER 3

Maps and Mapping: Functional Strategies in Pre-Project Planning

Effective managers lay the foundation for a successful development project long before the project begins. When the project starts, the project leader and members of the project team need a clear sense of strategic direction in the business and in its critical functions. A typical business plan—focused on financial and marketing information, prepared by a staff group—is not enough. Nor is it sufficient to take a business plan and add sections on functional plans. What is needed is an understanding of where the business is going, what the functions are going to do to get it there, and how this project fits into that picture. Thus, behind the foundation of a successful development project must be a process that identifies and integrates the strategies and the functions, and links them to the overall direction of the business. To see the importance of a process and a plan that links functional strategies to the details of specific projects, consider the case of a company we will call WHZ Medical Electronics.[1]

The Missing Cable

Peter Culver, project manager for a new portable monitoring unit, couldn't believe what he was reading. With only six months to go before market introduction of a new instrument, the head of electrical design for the project, Werina Milbury, had just discovered that a cable she designed into the product would not be available for commerical production. The cable was produced in one of the company's component plants in upstate New York. The plant manufactured a wide range of electrical components for several of the company's divisions. Werina learned that the plant was scheduled to be shut down and that products in the plant had been farmed out principally to suppliers; the cable she had designed into the new instrument, however, was part of a long list of components scheduled to be discontinued. Werina estimated that redesign to use available cables would require a few additional weeks of design and testing. The net effect was a two-month slip in the introduction schedule.

With the project already running behind schedule, an additional two months of delays was a major problem. To shorten that lead time, Pete put together a crash program that brought the product with its new cable to market with a delay of only one month. The crash effort was such a traumatic experience that Pete and his team spent several days trying to get at the root causes of the missing cable. What they found was sobering.

The decision to close the components plant in upstate New York and transfer many of the products to outside suppliers was made about a year before design of the new instrument started. That decision was part of a long-term strategy in the components group to sharply reduce their in-house manufacturing capacity. Thus, information on the components group's strategy and its implications for electrical components was well-known long before the new portable instrument project was launched.

Pete and his team were also perplexed to find that representatives from the manufacturing division (of which the components group was a part) had participated in the concept development stage of the instrument project as well as subsequent design reviews. Furthermore, the project team had purchased small quantities of the cable from the electrical components plant and had clearly indicated on invoices that the orders were for prototype units of a new instrument. The fact that the cable would no longer be available only came to light when the project team began to arrange for volume purchases of the cable for commerical production.

Pete's conclusion was that information about the cable was readily available in the organization long before design of the new instrument was initiated. In spite of a detailed business planning process, manufacturing feasibility studies, and design reviews to which all functions were invited—and, indeed, in which all functions had participated—that information had never been brought to bear in designing the product.

The experience of WHZ Medical Electronics is not uncommon. Our research and case writing over the last several years have brought us in contact with numerous firms that experienced similar problems. We have seen product designers develop a conservative, classically styled product for a marketing division whose advertising campaign focused on a sporty, youthful image. We have seen a manufacturing organization launch an aggressive low-cost, highly automated production process at the same time that a product development team was creating a complex new family of products requiring significant customization. And we have seen a product development team launch the design of a more sophisticated, highly featured version of an established general-purpose product while customers were demanding less complex and more tailored, customized versions. As in the case of WHZ Medical Electronics, these problems in development reflect a mismatch between the strategies of different functions. But they also reflect a failure to acquire and use readily available information. In effect, WHZ (like many other firms) failed to bring together the right people with the right information in the right forum *before* the project was launched. As a result, the team set off with a poor sense of direction and an incomplete picture of the context and setting into which their results were to be integrated.

The analogy between launching a project and setting out on a journey seems appropriate. Indeed, laying the foundation for effective product and process development is much like making preparations for an expedition into unknown territory. A central part of that preparation is developing plans for the journey, which includes acquiring all of the information available about the terrain ahead as well as likely contingencies that one may encounter. Experience has taught the thoughtful traveler than an essential part of preparation for an extended journey is the acquisition of good maps of the areas in which the journey will occur. In a similar way, we have found the mapping of the competitive terrain in each of a business's functions to be a powerful link between business and functional strategies and the details of specific development projects. Functional maps provide both the process and substance for functional integration, establish a context for a stream of development projects over time, and offer guidance and direction for an individual development project.

Maps and mapping are the focus of this chapter. We first lay out what we mean by a map and provide several examples taken from the wide variety of maps we have found useful in development. We then examine the process of mapping and develop guidelines for effective implementation. The chapter concludes with an application of maps to the story of Apple Computer's development of the Macintosh personal computer.

The Concept of Functional Maps

In every business, and every function in the business, there are driving forces that define the critical dimensions of competition.[2] In the marketing of household appliances, for example, an important driving force may be the changing nature of distribution channels as discount retailers and emerging superstores become the outlet of choice for more and more customers. In the same business, the introduction of electronic controls, plastic materials, and small but powerful electric motors may create product opportunities that open up new segments in the marketplace. At the same time, expansion of variety may be accompanied by a drive for lower cost in a highly competitive market. These forces place significant pressure on the appliance manufacturing process, where traditional approaches to cost reduction (e.g., standardization and automation) may be in conflict with the need for flexibility and expansion of variety.

Mapping has a clear objective: capture the driving forces for the business and the functions, and portray their implications for competition graphically. Defined in these terms, a functional map has the following distinguishing characteristics: it is a visual, graphic display of the driving forces in the market, and the firm's position along critical dimensions of competition over time and relative to its competitors. Each of these elements is critical. The very purpose of a map is to give managers a way to see the evolution of critical dimensions in the market, the technology and the manufacturing processes. Although good maps are based on data and analysis, we have found that pulling together that analysis in a visual format greatly enhances communication and the development of insight.

The requirement that a map show driving forces and critical dimensions of competition *over time* is central to achieving its fundamental purpose: helping managers to see where they are, where they have been, and where they may be going. Laying out developments in marketing, engineering, or manufacturing over time helps to uncover underlying trends and provides a useful context in which to evaluate alternative courses of action. In effect, putting driving forces and critical dimensions of competition in their historical context is an important element of providing strategic direction for product and process development.

With a visual, graphic display of critical dimensions of competition over time, functions in a business have a set of maps that facilitate communication, focus attention on salient issues, and provide historical context. What is missing, however, is a benchmark—a standard of comparison that creates perspective. Thus, the last requirement for an effective map is comparison with competitors. Finding out "where we are" and "where we are going" cannot be done only with internal data. The relevant standards are not past budgets or plans, but what the toughest competitors have accomplished. Furthermore, seeing what competitors have done may yield important insights into differences in competitive performance. We may discover, for example, that while our company has followed a broad line strategy, our strongest competitors have focused their marketing and development resources in a few key product areas where they dominate the business.

Such insight is invaluable in crafting a business strategy and provides an important context for decisions in new product and process development. Maps help to ensure that all functions share a collective vision of where they are going and of how individual projects contribute to their common purpose. Moreover, mapping facilitates effective mobilization of all the organization's resources, capabilities, and skills. Maps provide a tool for guiding the development of functional excellence, and they facilitate the strategic integration of that excellence around a common purpose. Additionally, maps help an organization to target its investments. By displaying underlying forces at work in the marketplace, maps help to clarify choices firms face regarding which markets to serve with which products, which manufacturing facilities to employ, what process technologies to use, and what directions to take in the development of product designs.

The specific maps that a business team chooses to develop will vary depending on the circumstances of the business, but we have found a small number of maps to be particularly useful across a wide range of businesses. These maps are listed in Exhibit 3–1, along with an indication of the specific measures used in the maps and likely sources of information. Their relation to each other, to key strategies, and to operating plans are depicted in Exhibit 3–2. To illustrate what maps such as these look like and to suggest a way in which maps may be used to identify important strategic issues in a business's various functions, we present here a set of maps developed for a company—we will call it the Coolidge Corporation—engaged in the design, development, production, and marketing of vacuum cleaners.[3] We present a small number of maps developed for the three principal functions of the business: marketing, engineering, and manufacturing. In each case, we have tried to

Exhibit 3–1

Examples of Functional Maps

Functional Area/Map Type	Concepts and Specific Measures Used	Sources of Data
Marketing		
Product profile	Product attributes; position relative to competitors	Customer interviews; market research; product testing
Channels of distribution	Sales by channel; market share by channel	Sales organization; trade publications; surveys
Product generation	Timing of new products; life cycle of models; relationship of products to one another	Sales documents
Engineering		
Critical skills	Skill composition of engineering work force	Internal personal research; interviews or comments of engineering managers
Performance tradeoffs	Range of performance combinations possible among dimensions that may conflict (e.g., weight and efficiency)	Test data; product performance specifications
Component technology	Performance of critical components using different technologies	Test data; product ratings
Manufacturing		
Process technology	Degree of automation; fraction of output in different types of processes	Production research; project data
Vertical integration	Role of suppliers; internal operations by component	Purchasing research; internal operating plans
Cost structure	Cost by volume levels; cost by factor of production	Cost accounting research

capture dimensions of competition that are central to the effectiveness of the function and to the business's competitive position. In addition to these functional maps, we also present a set of integrative maps that depict driving forces that cut across functional areas.

Marketing Maps

The mix of product attributes offered to potential customers is critical for the marketing organization. Exhibit 3–3 lays out a map of the customer and product profile for Coolidge's vacuum cleaners between 1980 and 1990. For each of the critical attributes of the product, we have identified a spectrum of performance and positioned Coolidge's offering in the middle price segment in 1980 and 1990. This provides us some perspective on the improvement in Coolidge's product performance over that period of time. In addition, we have indicated the performance position

EXHIBIT 3–2

Relating Functional Strategies and Maps to Other Strategies and Plans*

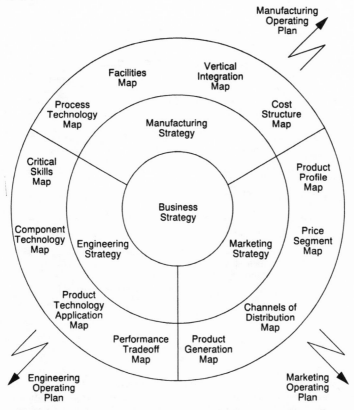

* The individual functional maps—twelve of which are shown in the outer circle—link the departmental plans to the functional and business strategies. Thus they provide an essential bridge between day-to-day activities and long-term directions.

---

of Coolidge's toughest competitor in 1990—the Fillmore Corporation. The diagram makes clear that Coolidge's product moved from being relatively heavy, loud, large, and somewhat difficult to operate to being relatively compact, lightweight, and easy to use. The Coolidge product offers advantages in cleaning performance and dust bag hygiene relative to its competitor, but is moderately behind in most other product attributes.

In addition to product position along the performance spectrum, we have indicated the relative importance that customers place on attributes. In the right-hand column of the diagram we have indicated a

EXHIBIT 3–3

Customer / Product Profile (Middle Price Segment)*

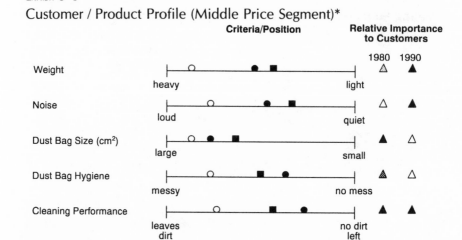

Criteria/Position — Relative Importance to Customers

	1980	1990

O Coolidge, 1980
● Coolidge, 1990
■ Fillmore, 1990

△ △ ◮ ◮ ▲
least —— most

* The right-hand columns illustrate the relative importance of each performance criterion to customers in 1980 and 1990, respectively. The horizontal continuums indicate the progress made by Coolidge between 1980 and 1990, and the position of their primary competitor, Fillmore, in 1990.

clear shift in focus of customer choice from 1980 to 1990. While customers have tended to focus on cleaning performance and dust bag size in 1980, by 1990, the principal issues were weight, noise, and cleaning performance. Overall, the map suggests that Coolidge may have some problems in the middle price segment. Except for cleaning performance, where it has a clear edge, it is at a disadvantage to its primary competitor in weight, noise, size, and ease of use, all areas of increasing customer focus.

Exhibit 3–4 maps changes in distribution channels in the vacuum cleaner business from 1975 to 1990. Vacuum cleaners are sold through multiple channels, and changes in the relative importance and mix of

Exhibit 3–4

Channels of Distribution.*

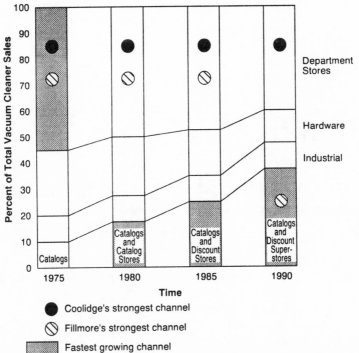

● Coolidge's strongest channel

⊘ Fillmore's strongest channel

▨ Fastest growing channel

* Between 1975 and 1990, two trends in the channels of distribution occurred: the importance of department and hardware stores declined (from 80 percent to about 55 percent), and the importance of catalog and discount stores increased (from ten percent to about thirty-five percent). In the second half of the 1980s, Fillmore responded effectively to these trends; Coolidge did not.

channels may have an important influence on Coolidge's market share. The diagram shows a dramatic change in the channel mix over this period. Catalogues and especially discount superstores have become a critical factor in the business, while the share of sales going through department stores—a traditional area of strength for Coolidge—declined sharply. Looking back over the decade of the 1980s, it is clear that Fillmore moved aggressively into discount operations, while Coolidge continued to focus on its traditional channel. By 1990, Fillmore had developed its strongest position in the fastest growing channel in the market.

The final marketing map that we present for Coolidge is the product generation map. The product generation map in Exhibit 3–5 lays out the

EXHIBIT 3–5

Product Generation Maps*

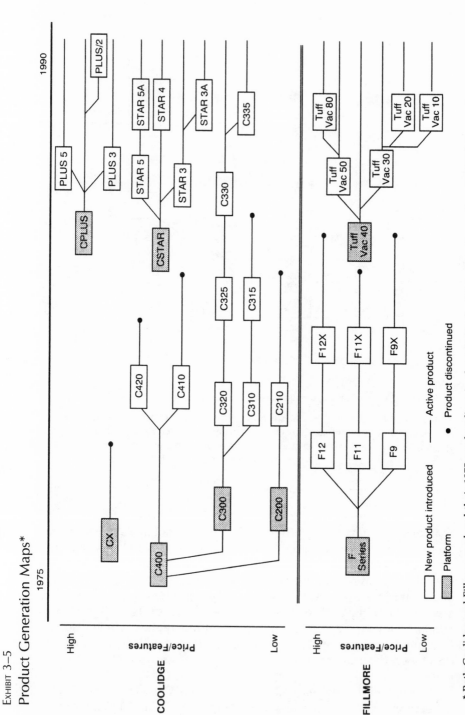

* Both Coolidge and Fillmore replaced their 1975 product lines in about 1985. Coolidge chose to continue its C300 line so that it would have three families of product in the market. In contrast, Fillmore chose in 1985 to offer a single family of products off the Tuff Vac 40 platform.

evolution of the Coolidge product line from 1975 until 1990. The diagram documents not only the major generations of product, but also how product line extensions and enhanced and lower-priced versions emerged from a core product offering. Products are arrayed in the map so that their position in the price/features spectrum is apparent; thus, high-end, high-price, high-feature products are near the top of the diagram while low-end, low-price, low-feature versions are near the bottom. The maps suggest that Coolidge systematically shifted its product line from relatively low-price cleaners to medium-price products and is moving increasingly toward more high-end offerings. In addition, the number of product families and total products offered in the market have both expanded rapidly.

The companion product generation map for Fillmore indicates a somewhat different product development strategy. Fillmore competes in the same market segments as Coolidge, but does so with a much narrower product line. Although it too expanded that line over time, its development has been much more focused. Moreover, it is evident that Fillmore leveraged a single product platform to reach diverse market segments. In contrast, Coolidge tended to launch independent development programs for specific market segments.

Engineering Maps

An important driver for the engineering function is the shifting mix of critical skills required in the design, development, and engineering of products and processes. Exhibit 3–6 depicts that shifting mix for Coolidge. This kind of map is particularly useful when product technologies, for example, are undergoing significant change. From a situation in the mid 1970s in which the engineering organization was composed of individuals with backgrounds in mechanical engineering, electromechanical design, and plastics, Coolidge has seen an increasing role for engineers trained in electronics, ergonomics, acoustics, and software. This shifting mix of skills reflects the growing sophistication of product design and the growing importance of new dimensions of the product, including noise and ease of use (electronic controls and ergonomics).

Exhibit 3–7 depicts a second important driving force in the engineering function: the shift from metal to plastic materials in the product's design, and the increasing significance of expanding the capacity for cleaning relative to the unit's weight. The diagram illustrates that Coolidge was able to expand the volume of its vacuum cleaner between 1975 and 1980 while reducing weight through substitution of plastic for metal. Between 1980 and 1990 weight declined further with only a small reduction in volume through design changes and continued use of plas-

ExHIBIT 3–6
Critical Skills in Engineering*

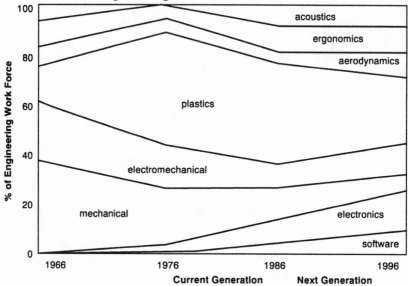

* Over time, the mix of engineering skills at Coolidge changed significantly. The proportion of mechanical engineers declined from its peak in the 1960s as plastics specialists increased and, later, electronics engineers were added. Most recently, software engineers were added, replacing some of the plastics specialists.

---

tic. The data suggest, however, that while Coolidge made significant progress in its volume-to-weight ratio, its competitors moved more aggressively both on design and on the use of plastic parts and by 1990 achieved an advantage over Coolidge. Fillmore, for example, offered a product with slightly less volume but considerably less weight than Coolidge. A second competitor, Harding, specialized in much smaller units.

Design changes also had an important influence on the design of motors over this period. Exhibit 3–8 documents the trajectory of motor development, again in the middle price segment for Coolidge and Fillmore. Both companies increased their cleaning performance during this time period, but adopted very different approaches to achieve it. While Coolidge (as we saw earlier) achieved significant improvement in cleaning through a larger, more powerful motor, Fillmore opted for somewhat less but equivalent cleaning performance with a substantially smaller, but much more efficient, motor. Thus, while Coolidge motors in 1990 were the same design as the 1980 model (only larger), Fillmore had

Exhibit 3–7

Engineering Design—Capacity and Weight* (Middle Price Segment)

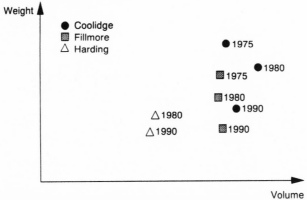

* Over time, both Coolidge and Fillmore reduced the weight of their units but did not alter their capacity (volume). Over the past decade, a third competitor—Harding —established itself with a lighter weight, smaller capacity product.

adopted a radically new motor design that offered much greater efficiency in a more compact package. The redesign of the Fillmore motor was an important element in reducing the overall size of the vacuum cleaner.

Manufacturing Maps

While the manufacturing function often finds itself involved at the tail end of product development, reacting to product designs and marketing initiatives, there are important strategic developments in manufacturing that can have decisive influence on the success of new products. It is important, therefore, that driving forces in manufacturing be evident and taken into account in the early stages of new product development. Exhibit 3–9, for example, documents trends in manufacturing processes for final assembly at Coolidge. The basic process for final assembly at the Homewood plant (the original Coolidge production facility) was a manual operation conducted with a combination of a line flow of raw materials and a stall build setup in which workers assembled significant portions of the product from parts that had previously been kitted together. In 1980, Coolidge had built a new plant (Plant A) that employed asynchronous conveyer lines in subassembly operations with a predominantly manual operation. Finishing was completed in the traditional

Exhibit 3–8

Motor Size and Cleaning Performance*

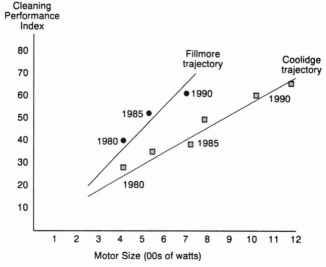

* While both Fillmore and Coolidge have improved the cleaning performance of their products significantly, Fillmore has done so with a much smaller, more efficient motor than Coolidge.

stall build mode. Plant B, built in 1987, added increased automation and material handing with some robotics (particularly in subassembly operations, e.g., motor and compressor assembly and the body of the unit). Plant B employed a limited number of traditional stalls for small-volume products but largely employed a manual, asynchronous assembly line process.

In contrast, Fillmore moved aggressively during the 1980s to automate the assembly process. Its main assembly plant in the mid 1970s was much like the Coolidge facility, but Fillmore engineers adopted a flow line concept in the early 1980s. Fillmore built a second line in its main assembly plant in the mid 1980s that employed robotics along with an assembly line concept. By the late 1980s, assembly at Fillmore was significantly automated with the use of robotics and material handing equipment. The main line likewise migrated from a manual to mixed mode in which people and robots shared assembly in what Fillmore called its flexible assembly system. In this system, Fillmore could assemble several of its models on the same line with minimal changeover time. The automated line was dedicated to the production of two high volume models.

Exhibit 3–9

Final Assembly Process Generations*

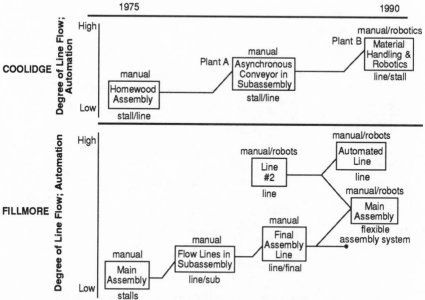

* Fillmore has been more aggressive than Coolidge in upgrading its manufacturing processes. Fillmore started in the late 1970s to redo layouts to provide line flows, then to adopt automation, and most recently, to adopt a flexible assembly system. Although Coolidge has built new facilities, they have stayed with some stall-built operations.

During the 1980s Coolidge made important changes in its level of vertical integration and in the role suppliers played in its production process. Exhibit 3–10 maps out the structure of vertical integration at Coolidge in 1980 and 1990. Whereas in 1980 Coolidge primarily focused on in-house assembly and purchased motors, electronics, plastic parts, and accessories, by 1990 Coolidge had backward integrated into motors and complex plastic parts. The drive for increased vertical integration was dictated largely by increasing pressure on margins and the vice president of manufacturing's decision to try to lower costs by bringing critical activities in-house.

Fillmore adopted a quite different strategy. The map makes clear that Fillmore was in much the same position as Coolidge in 1980, but during the 1980s chose to vertically integrate not only motors but also electronics. Fillmore additionally cultivated a network of suppliers that could provide simple and complex plastic parts and accessories and began to rely on suppliers for subassembly and assembly operations of finished

EXHIBIT 3–10

Patterns of Vertical Integration*

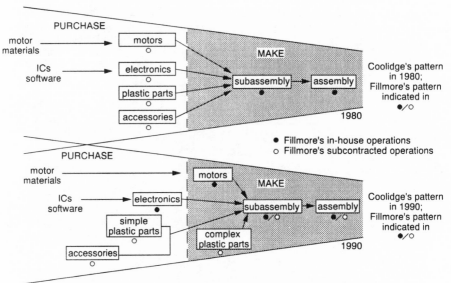

* In 1980, Fillmore and Coolidge had similar levels of vertical integration. By 1990, both firms had brought motor manufacturing in-house. Fillmore also brought electronics in-house but started outsourcing some of its sub- and final assembly requirements. Coolidge, in contrast, chose to either make or buy 100 percent of each production step.

products. Fillmore's strategy was to concentrate on control over motors and electronics while retaining flexibility to move production inside or outside in final assembly.

The final manufacturing map—Exhibit 3–11—lays out the relationship between manufacturing cost per unit and the volume of production per plant. In 1990, Coolidge operated three plants: Homewood, Plant A, and Plant B. The figure shows that Plant B, the high-volume plant, actually had a manufacturing cost per unit slightly above or equivalent to costs at Homewood. The lowest-cost facility was Plant A, the medium-volume plant. The diagram suggests that Coolidge may have suffered diseconomies of scale in Plant B. Fillmore operated a single facility in 1990 which it had broken down into two distinct plants. The main plant operated at a volume level similar to Homewood but had lower costs. Fillmore's automated line—its most efficient facility—was much higher volume but did not suffer the diseconomies of scale apparent in Plant B at Coolidge, and operated with substantially lower costs. There is also evidence in this diagram that Fillmore's costs on its automated line

Exhibit 3–11
Cost and Volume*

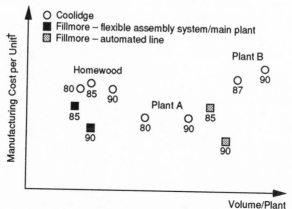

* Fillmore continued to push products toward either a low- or high-volume line and to improve its cost position at both volume levels. Coolidge neither forced products toward preferred volume levels nor pushed to reduce costs for a given volume level.

† Cost has been adjusted for product complexity and inflation.

---

declined substantially since its introduction in 1985. In contrast, costs either rose or stayed roughly the same at Plants A and B and at Homewood.

Integrative Maps

The functional maps suggest important issues confronting Coolidge as it looks to competition in the 1990s. Many of the issues, however, cut across functional areas. In order to illustrate the interaction across areas we have prepared a set of *integrative maps*. An integrative map attempts to identify important dimensions in multiple functions that interact with each other and that together provide important context for strategic decision making. Exhibit 3–12, for example, presents the product/process matrix—a map of the relationship between the manufacturing processes at Coolidge and the evolving structure of the product line.[4]

The map suggests that Coolidge may confront a mismatch between its evolving product structure and the characteristics of the manufacturing process. The diagram shows that evolution out of its home base in Homewood has created three production facilities. Homewood concentrates on low-volume products, while Plant A uses a somewhat automated, less manual operation to produce the mid-range of the product line. Plant B produces high-volume, lower-cost, more standardized

73

Exhibit 3–12
Product / Process Matrix Assembly Plants*

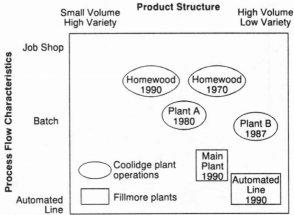

* Coolidge's choice of less automated, more batch type processes, even in their high-volume Plant B, stands in sharp contrast to Fillmore's choice of process flow characteristics.

---

products but does so with a production process that is still predominantly a manual assembly operation. There is some line flow at Plant B, but it is largely a batch process with heavy manual operations. The contrast with Fillmore, also laid out in the map, is quite sharp. In the standardized high-volume lines, Coolidge competes against a facility that is much more automated that the process in Plant B. Moreover, it is evident that Fillmore has focused its product line at the same time it has focused its manufacturing facilities. The result is a quite powerful advantage in terms of cost and ability to meet the requirements of specific market segments. It appears that Coolidge is at a distinct disadvantage.

The second integrative map examines interaction between manufacturing and engineering. The map in Exhibit 3–13 lays out the relationship between manufacturing cost and product complexity measured in terms of the number of parts and features in the product. A number of important developments emerge from this map. First, there is clearly a positive association between the complexity of the product and its manufacturing cost. Second, Coolidge systematically increased its product complexity and therefore experienced increasing cost in its product line. Fillmore, on the other hand, while also increasing the complexity of its products, did not experience the same degree of cost increase. This is likely a reflection of the manufacturing strategy at Fillmore in which the products are produced in a much more focused manufacturing facility

Exhibit 3–13

Manufacturing Performance and Product Complexity*
(Mid-range Family)

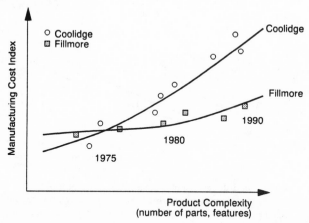

* While both Coolidge and Fillmore have seen the complexity of their products increase dramatically with time, Fillmore has controlled the increase's impact on production costs much more effectively than has Coolidge.

where there is greater process control and where additional complexity can be managed more effectively. The implication of this map is that Coolidge must cope with the market-driven increases in complexity much more efficiently if it is to overcome the apparent disadvantage against Fillmore.

The third integrative map—Exhibit 3–14—looks at the connections between marketing and engineering. It lays out the relationship between price and performance over time from 1975 to 1990, and makes clear that the price performance curve improved substantially. Customers could buy products in 1990 with much higher levels of performance than, but at the same price as, products they bought in 1975. In addition, it is clear that marketing and engineering combined to introduce much higher-priced products with a greater level of performance than were available on the market in 1975. In this sense it is clear that the market's range has increased. The map also underscores the advantage that Fillmore achieved over this period of time. Though in 1975 Coolidge and Fillmore had an equivalent price performance curve, by 1990 Fillmore had a significant advantage. It could offer products of equivalent performance at much lower prices than Coolidge, or products at the same price as Coolidge but with much higher levels of performance. The sources of Fillmore's advantage are evident in the functional maps out-

EXHIBIT 3–14
Price / Performance Map*

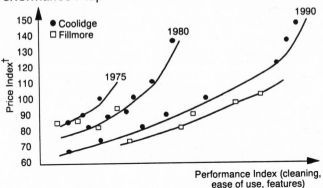

* By 1990, both firms had dramatically increased their top end product performance and the breadth of their performance offerings. However, for all but the lowest performing Coolidge product, Fillmore offered comparable performance at a lower price than Coolidge.

† $100 = average price.

---

lined earlier. Changes in product design, marketing channels, and manufacturing processes gave Fillmore a cost advantage and a performance advantage from the customer's perspective.

The Mapping Process

Maps like those developed for Coolidge underscore the critical driving forces in the business and help to clarify the important strategic decisions and directions confronting an organization. But the true power of maps is not so much in the graphs or the documents themselves, but in the process used to create them. What is important in laying the foundation for effective development projects is the creation of shared understanding among senior executives, among heads of the major functions of the business, and among engineers, marketers, and manufacturing people who make the product happen. While important insight and pieces of knowledge are incorporated into the maps, shared understanding grows out of the process that underlies them. If the maps are not actively used to structure and inform decisions and actions, they have little value. But when developed and used in an effective process, maps may play an important role in creating shared understanding.

An effective mapping process has two parts. In the first, managers define the critical driving forces in the business and the functions, and

Exhibit 3–15

An Effective Mapping Process*

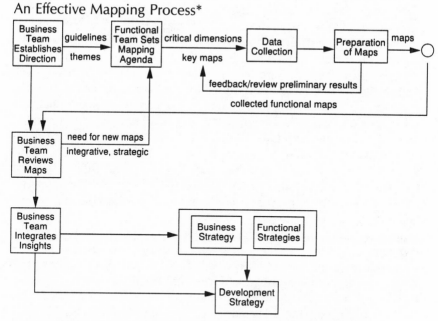

* The process for creating a set of functional maps incorporates two critical concepts. First, the business team plays a central role in establishing the context and direction for mapping and in reviewing and integrating the results. Second, the functions—those who know the specialized areas best—create the maps and work to resolve differences, gain consistency, and build consensus on future choices and detailed plans.

then acquire the data necessary to map those forces over time, against principal competitors. In the second, managers from different functions in the business develop insights from the maps and share those insights with their colleagues on the business team. In that context maps provide a new language. By visually presenting the important dimensions of competition and the business's relative position, maps give managers versed in different disciplines and endowed with different experiences the ability to communicate their ideas more effectively. Where it works well, the mapping process thus creates both a language of communication and channels within which important insights and understanding may be communicated.

Although there are many different variations of the mapping process, the central features of an effective process are laid out in Exhibit 3–15. Mapping is an iterative process carried out by managers in marketing, engineering, and manufacturing working separately, as well as jointly as a business team under the direction of the general manager. After meeting together as a business to plan out the mapping agenda, identify important guidelines (e.g., the number of maps to be developed, timing of map development, etc.), and establish overall business themes, the individual functional teams decide which maps to develop and how to get the work done. Working together as a team and involving knowledgeable individuals within the function, the functional teams identify the driving forces affecting their function and sketch out a set of maps to capture those forces. This involves deciding what dimensions to map, in what combinations, and laying out guidelines for the number of maps and methods of data acquisition. With the mapping agenda laid out, the functional teams proceed to collect data and prepare maps. Once the maps have been developed, the final step within the functional team is to meet, review the maps, discuss their implications, and develop guidelines for functional strategies.

Once the functional teams have developed a set of maps, members from each function meet as a business team to share their respective maps, identify important insights and issues, and develop guidelines for future directions and strategic choices. The business team may then identify further issues that need to be mapped, particularly those that involve cross-functional integration. In addition, the functional teams may meet again to develop strategic maps—maps that look forward and lay out the strategic direction of the business in terms of the critical driving forces captured in functional maps.

Armed with integrative and strategic maps, the business team meets again to integrate the insights, strategic directions, and plans into overall functional strategies and a business strategy. The point is not only to refine and develop the maps themselves, but also to establish guidelines for future development projects. In that sense, functional heads, project managers, and senior executives can use the maps as starting points for developing and implementing operational plans, communicating a sense of direction within their organizations, and providing a context within which plans for specific product and process development projects may be undertaken.

Getting the Most Out of Mapping

If we look at the role maps are expected to play, it is evident that the mapping process must have a certain character. We expect maps to be linked directly to development efforts. In order to be effective they must be translated into operational plans within each function and used to develop criteria for allocating resources to specific projects. One of the things that the mapping process should do is help answer questions about priorities, goals, and research allocation for the set of development projects facing the business over the planning horizon. Maps and mapping, therefore, are not simply an exercise or a tool to be used for staff analysis. Where effective, they are an integral part of the general management of the business. To make that happen, the mapping process needs to develop objectivity and to use both internal and external data sources. Managers need to evaluate performance relative to their principal competitors, not just their own internal objectives. Key people involved in the functions and the business team must be involved and committed to the maps that emerge out of the process. Mapping will not work as a staff activity, or when it is delegated to lower-level subordinates possessing little insight into the problems confronting senior managers. Additionally, if maps go into such detail that senior managers see them as tactical rather than strategic, they will lose their power and fail to play their role. Maps need to be developed in the context of face-to-face meetings involving all the major functions of the business working together as peers on the business team. In this way key issues may be raised and resolved rather than set aside or buried in a blizzard of data and detail. Finally, it is important that maps be communicated throughout the organization in order to serve as a framework and guide for development activities.

While mapping is not a panacea, it is a process that can assist in laying a foundation for effective product development. Much remains to be learned about how to use maps and make mapping effective, but our research and case writing to date suggest a number of pitfalls to avoid:

- Delegating maps and mapping to junior staffers
- Viewing mapping as "filling out forms"
- Using only internal information
- Sticking to conventional wisdom
- Ignoring historical trends
- Using only historical trends
- Getting bogged down in details
- Treating maps as an end unto themselves
- Not sharing information early
- Allowing one function to dominate
- Failing to use maps to guide and direct decision making

Apple Computer: The Need and Opportunity for Maps

Creating coherent functional strategies is essential to the success of new products and processes. Getting straight the driving forces in the business and function, the position of competitors, and the choices confronting the business is essential to picking the right projects, establishing support capabilities, and achieving effective projects. Maps can play a critical role in clarifying choices and facilitating communication. The saga of Apple Computer illustrates the potential power of maps and the mapping process. We first examine developments at Apple in the early 1980s and then review that history through a set of maps.[5]

Creating the Macintosh at Apple

In the early 1980s, Apple was riding the crest of its success with the Apple II personal computer. The product line was manufactured in both Singapore and a recently constructed facility in Dallas, Texas, while many peripheral components, such as disk drives and keyboards, were manufactured by Apple in southern California. Product development, marketing, and corporate headquarters were located near San Francisco.

In 1982, Apple's CEO, Steve Jobs, initiated the development of a new product family, the Lisa-Macintosh personal computers. The Lisa-Macintosh development effort was established as a small, dedicated team reporting directly to Jobs. Its challenge was to make major leaps in both product (hardware and software) and manufacturing process development. An extremely ambitious project, development of the Lisa-Macintosh was assigned to very capable people and had Job's personal backing and day-to-day involvement.

The Lisa, priced at $8,000 to $10,000 per unit, was initially regarded as the core of the product family. It would be the family flagship, demonstrating the power of its new technology and serving as the base from which to launch a derivative, but much higher unit-volume product: the Macintosh. Thus, the Lisa was to be developed first and was expected to provide a significant share of the family's combined profits, although not the bulk of its sales volume. The Macintosh was eventually to have its own production facility, but the low-volume Lisa was to be produced in the Dallas factory (which would also continue to make the Apple II).

In retrospect, this strategy for the Lisa-Macintosh was more wishful thinking than a well-thought-out plan. Although based on highly innovative design concepts, Lisa's sales never reached expectations, and the design of the Macintosh required a number of iterations before it could meet the needs of its evolving market. Such critical issues as customer segments, distribution channels, product support, and follow-on products had not been carefully examined. In addition, little thought was given (even in the later stages of product development) to how new and existing manufacturing facilities would be coordinated.

The absence of strategic planning within the various functional groups created two problems: additional time was spent and resources were wasted on more than one dead end. Introduction of the Macintosh was originally scheduled for March of 1983, but was rescheduled for May, then July, and then late fall (before Christmas, it was hoped). Volume shipment did not actually begin until early 1984. Even with the delay, manufacturing suffered from serious problems.

The original goal was to have a highly automated factory for the Macintosh up and running at the time of its market introduction. Although there was extensive automation of material handling and testing, within eight months of the facility's opening, $7 million worth of automation equipment (one-third of the total spent on the factory) was removed because it had not proven effective.

The delay of the Macintosh's market introduction by several quarters drove Apple's earnings down dramatically and caused the stock market's valuation of the company to fall to less than half its early 1983 value. In the restructuring that followed, Apple closed the Dallas plant, laid off several hundred people (over 20 percent of the entire work force), and took a substantial writeoff. By late 1985, Apple had gone through great agony and emerged a vastly different company. Much of this had its roots in the shortcomings of the Lisa-Macintosh development effort. Although errors were certainly made during the actual execution of the project, the seeds of most of Apple's major difficulties were sown beforehand.

Using Maps: The Apple Case Revisited

Our discussion of Apple's development of the Lisa and Macintosh illustrates the problems that can occur when product and process development projects are launched without clear strategic direction. We have suggested that mapping can provide such direction. But would the existence of such maps have made any difference to Apple? Did information exist from which it could have gained valuable insight through a mapping process? We believe it did. In fact, the Apple case provides a good example of the power of functional mapping. Each of Apple's three main functions—marketing, design engineering, and manufacturing— confronted issues in the development of the Lisa-Macintosh product line that maps could have helped clarify.

Marketing. The Lisa and Macintosh were viewed primarily as engineering projects, and thus marketing issues—though they had a profound influence on both product design and ultimate sales—received secondary attention. Marketing thought of the Lisa as a high-end office product; the Macintosh was slated to serve the lower end of that market, with some application to education and home use—the phrase "appliance for the knowledge worker" summarized its basic concept. Yet information

Exнівіт 3–16

Personal Computer Market Segments and Product Development Factors, 1982*

Buyer/ Development Factors	Market Segments						Development Emphasis	
	Home	Education (K-12)	University	Home Office	Small Business (and professional)	Corporate Office	Lisa	Macintosh
Performance	⊚	⊚	●	◉	◉	◉	●	◉
Price	●	●	◉	●	●	◉	○	●
Features	⊚	⊚	◉	⊚	⊚	⊚	◉	⊚
Reliability	◉	⊚	◉	◉	◉	◉	○	◉
User friendly	◉	◉	⊚	◉	⊚	○	●	●
Connectivity	○	○	○	○	○	●	○	○
Field support	○	○	○	○	○	●	○	○
Application software	◉	◉	⊚	⊚	◉	●	⊚	◉

● Highly significant factor   ⊚ Of some importance
◉ Important factor   ○ Little role in decision; secondary factor

* In 1982, Apple identified six primary market segments, with the Lisa targeted at the corporate office and the Macintosh targeted at business and education. This chart suggests that the Lisa was a poor match with its primary target, the Macintosh, however, was a reasonably good fit with education but was not well positioned in the business market.

---

available in 1982 indicated that this concept ignored several important issues.

Exhibit 3–16 describes the major personal computer market segments in 1982, along with the emphasis placed on different criteria by each segment. A comparison of the importance placed on different criteria in Apple's development program (the right side of Exhibit 3–16) and the needs of different market segments suggests that the Lisa was a machine without a market. Additionally, though Apple intended the Macintosh for large corporations, it appeared better suited to the needs of small businesses and universities. The map thus highlights a mismatch between development objectives and market requirements that should have been apparent in 1982.

Design Engineering. The Lisa was to be both a high-end machine for offices and a technology platform for subsequent products like the Macintosh. But apparently little thought was given to the way that the Lisa itself would evolve. Nor does it appear that the Lisa-Macintosh devel-

Exhibit 3–17

Product Generations at Apple*

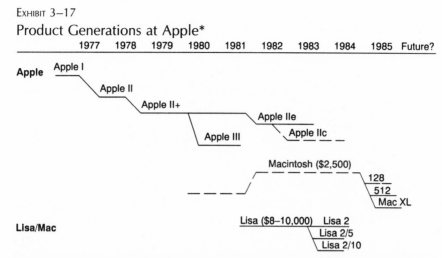

* For its first several years of existence, Apple had only one product family and simply brought out a sequence of product generations, each replacing its predecessor. While the Lisa and Macintosh were conceived as a related but entirely separate family from the Apple line, over time the Macintosh was expanded to include multiple concurrent offerings. Due to poor market fit, Lisa was dropped after only a few years.

opment team understood the implications of evolving component technology. Exhibit 3–17 is a product generation map that shows the evolution of the Apple and Lisa-Macintosh product families through 1985.

The Lisa was based on the Motorola 68000 microprocessor and employed new concepts in software (windows, icons) and user–machine interaction (the mouse). Higher-performance models were unveiled after initial introduction, but they simply incorporated additional memory. The original design of the Lisa, despite its innovativeness, did not lend itself to future evolution and development. Not only was it very expensive to manufacture, but its use of many unusual parts and design concepts made it difficult to modify. The Macintosh also was based on the 68000 microprocessor, however, and the price of memory was dropping rapidly. As a result, the Macintosh soon was able to provide most of the capabilities of the original Lisa at a fraction of the price. A product generation plan, together with a forecast of the likely evolution of component technology, would have suggested in 1982 that the Lisa was likely to be a dead end product.

Manufacturing. Apple's production experience as of 1981 had been limited largely to labor-intensive assembly in a batch processing environ-

Exhibit 3–18
Product / Process Matrix Assembly Plants*

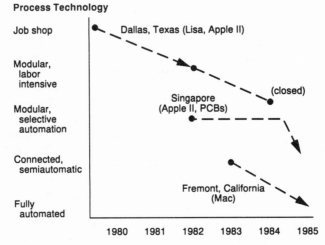

* As Apple's oldest, least automated plant, Dallas found it increasingly difficult to compete against the higher volume Singapore plant and the focused, automated Fremont plant. Eventually, with the discontinuance of the Lisa line and the relentless drive for higher volume products, Apple's senior management chose to close Dallas rather than make the imvestment required to automate it.

ment. Although the Singapore facility had some experience with automation, it was a relatively recent addition to the manufacturing organization. The Lisa required only manual assembly and fit well with Apple's capabilities, but the Macintosh was a different story. It was decided that it should be the vehicle for developing Apple's capabilities in both line-flow (as opposed to batch) processes and automated manufacturing.

Exhibit 3–18 depicts the evolution of Apple's manufacturing, from simple manual to fully integrated, automated processing. The figure highlights the major leap that the new plant—designed to use automated materials handling, automated component insertion, and (eventually) robotic assembly—represented in manufacturing technology and systems. The plan was to make the transition from unskilled workers with solder guns to automated lines in a single step. However, the various parts of the organization apparently did not have a shared understanding of what this implied, the kind of organizational capabilities that would have to be developed, or the alternatives. Thus, even where subparts of a plan existed, they were often incomplete and contradictory.

84

The concerns raised in this brief discussion of the Lisa-Macintosh development process do not reflect simply good hindsight; this information was widely available at the time and no tricks were involved in processing it. Had a set of functional maps been developed before the project began, these issues would have surfaced at Apple before it made commitments to specific target markets, product designs, and manufacturing equipment. Some decisions might have been altered as a result, but even had they remained the same, Apple would have been in a better position to manage their risks and develop the necessary supporting capabilities.

Fortunately, the lessons of this experience did not go unheeded at Apple. By 1986 it focused significant attention on its pre-project development procedures as well as on its project management capabilities. Each of its manufacturing facilities defined its process improvement path over time. The product development and advanced technology groups established clear targets for forthcoming product generations and the technologies they would enjoy. Moreover, marketing realigned its coverage of distribution channels and customer segments to better capitalize on the anticipated wave of new products. As a result, the introduction of several new products took place, well configured for their target markets and largely on schedule.

CHAPTER 4

The Aggregate Project Plan

In a vast majority of organizations, the management of development efforts focuses primarily on managing individual projects. Yet in reality, all but start-up firms almost always engage in multiple concurrent projects. Thus, they engage in a set of development efforts (both product and process) that changes as products get to the market and as new projects come up for approval. For management, this involves deciding on the set of projects to be added to the "active list," how those projects are to be scoped and defined (and their objectives), when those projects are to be started and completed, what resources will be allocated to them in what time periods, and how they will accomplish, collectively, the firm's strategy. As discussed in Chapter 2, management and direction of these activities constitutes the aggregate project plan—an important building block in the development strategy.

All firms have a set of projects that are on an "active" list—projects that have been started and not yet killed or completed. Relatively few firms arrive at such a list through a systematic process of review and decision about what the *set* ought to be. The aggregate project plan has several functions and offers firms that develop and use it several advantages. As a starting point, the plan specifies the types and mix of projects that the firm plans to undertake over the planning horizon. Laying the plan out explicitly makes it possible to balance the demands of individual projects for critical development resources with existing capacity. In technology-intensive environments, for example, it is crucial to make sure that the demands for scarce engineering talent balance appropriately with the number of engineers available.

Those demands need to be balanced over time. The aggregate project plan lays out the sequence of projects the firm plans to undertake, as well as which will be actively supported at any one time.[1] The planned project sequence establishes a framework for future decisions about adding new projects, and thus the demands on the organization resources. But it also makes explicit the kinds of capabilities the firm will be building over time. Development projects serve as a primary vehicle for building people and organizational skills. The aggregate project plan helps senior executives ensure that, collectively, individual and group project assignments make sense over time, enhancing and expanding the organization's critical capabilities.

In this chapter we examine the issues managers must confront in developing an aggregate project plan, and suggest a process for dealing with those issues in a systematic way. The first section of the chapter compares the promise of the aggregate project plan with the often problematic reality we have found in many of the firms we have studied. Simply put, most firms have too many projects. As a result, resources are overcommitted and the organization scrambles to satisfy competing development demands. Solving that problem must begin with defining the types of projects the firm is to undertake and choosing the appropriate mix of projects over time. This is the issue we examine in the second section of the chapter. We use a number of examples to explore in detail the major types of projects, paying particular attention to what next-generation or major platform projects the firm might undertake. In the third section we look at the mix and sequencing of projects over time. Two critical issues addressed in this section are the relationship of advanced development projects to platforms, and the strategy for products derived from the platform. In the last section of the chapter we lay out a process for developing an effective aggregate project plan and illustrate the implementation of the approach in an organization that had never planned its aggregate project "plan." As that company's experience suggests, the promise of the procedure we outline in the last section is to replace a weak, undermanaged aggregate project planning approach with one that is robust and effectively managed.

Aggregate Project Plans: Promise and Reality

An aggregate project plan lays out the specific development projects a firm will undertake over the relevant planning horizon. The plan establishes the types of projects the firm will complete and the relative resources the firm plans to commit to them. Thus, the plan not only lays out the sequence of projects, but also identifies the desired dates of market introduction and the associated resources required to bring each project to the market. The plan therefore establishes absolute resource requirements and explicitly allocates them to different types of projects over time.

By making explicit the set of projects a firm plans to undertake and by laying out their sequence over time, the aggregate project plan creates a framework in which the firm may address such questions as the balance between available capacity and expected requirements, and the fit between the business strategy and the specific projects a firm plans to undertake. The projects that make up the aggregate plan include new products as well as new processes and advanced development efforts. As a framework, the aggregate project plan thus helps to focus both resources and attention on the balance of effective capacity and development requirements, and on the effectiveness of the proposed set of projects in implementing the business strategy.

Part of the power of an aggregate project plan lies in the focus and direction it gives to individual development projects. Indeed, a list of the benefits and the promise of the aggregate project plan—e.g., adequate resources for project completion, a clear mission and purpose for individual projects—may sound like "nirvana" to experienced project leaders who have tried to carry out projects without an aggregate project plan. To understand this apparent inconsistency, consider the experience of a precision equipment company that we will call PreQuip, Inc.

The Overcommitment of Development Capacity

In mid 1989, the management of PreQuip became concerned about the performance of their product development process. Worried by what seemed to be a rash of late projects and a development budget that was increasing while the number of projects completed seemed to be declining, senior executives undertook a review of their active project list. Much to their surprise, they discovered that PreQuip had thirty active development projects—far more than they anticipated, and, they suspected, far more than the organization could support. For each project they obtained estimates of the remaining labor months of effort required

Exhibit 4–1

Engineering Requirements for Active Projects Compared to Available Engineering Resources at PreQuip, June 1989– December 1991*

Active Projects (formal development projects by number)	Engineering Months Required for Completion	Months to Completion (desired)	Implied Engineering Resource Allocation (engineering months)		
			1989	1990	1991
1	54	8	40	14	0
2	123	24	38	62	23
3	86	12	50	36	0
4	286	20	92	172	22
5	24	4	24	0	0
.					
.					
.					
26	352	36	48	150	120
27	75	9	62	13	0
28	215	30	40	80	95
29	153	18	60	93	0
30	29	3	29	0	0
All Other Engineering Activity (customer support, troubleshooting)	—	—	430	430	430
Total Engineering Requirements	—	—	2783	2956	2178
Available Engineering Months	—	—	960	960	960
Rate of Utilization (percent)	—	—	289.9	307.9	226.9

* This list of commitments at PreQuip indicates that for the thirty active development projects to meet their target completion dates *and* other ongoing, "sustaining" engineering activities to be carried out, almost three times as many engineering resources are needed than are currently available.

for completion and identified the expected and desired project completion dates. They compared these requirements to available development capacity, including particularly the critical resources—such as design engineering—available to support development projects.

The data developed by PreQuip's senior management are presented in Exhibit 4–1. By its own estimate, PreQuip had committed to and launched two to three times as much development activity as it was capable of completing over the 1989–1991 time period. In such an environment, it is inevitable that projects will be much later than top management expects, and much later than participants have planned in their product proposals. Furthermore, if any one project runs into unexpected trouble, there is no slack available, and it will be necessary to take resources from other projects. This causes subsequent trouble on other projects and the effects cascade. As costs of development increase and deadlines pass, there is pressure to cut corners and the firm may suffer quality problems.

This tendency to substantially overcommit development resources has been characterized by John Bennion and his colleagues at Bain and Company as the "canary cage approach" to aggregate project planning. If one thinks of a firm's existing development resources as dimensioning a canary cage, and the individual development projects as canaries, there is an optimal number and mix of sizes of canaries that can thrive in the given cage. However, what most firms do is to continually add canaries to the cage without considering how many are already in it. As each new canary enters, it becomes more crowded and the fight for survival between canaries becomes more consuming. Eventually, weaker canaries find themselves pushed to the bottom of the cage, dumped on by their fellow canaries, and they become sick, and die. Even the remaining canaries find it difficult to grow and develop in a normal way because of overcrowding in the cage.

Overcommitment of available development resources also tends to mean that a handful of key individuals show up repeatedly and concurrently on different projects. Such individuals may be key functional engineers, development specialists important to each of several projects, and even support personnel (such as an analytical test person) needed on a variety of concurrent projects. When aggregate capacity is overcommitted by 100 percent or more, these individual contributors find themselves spread across several projects at a time. The justification offered for such concurrent assignments is that, because such individuals are a scarce resource, it is important that they not have any idle time. The logic is that it is better for a project to wait for such a key resource than to have the resource waiting for the next project. While that sounds appealing, it seldom works that way in practice.

The problem is that as the number of projects increases above one, productivity rises and then falls. Extensive proprietary studies by a major computer firm and our own observations of several medical electronics firms indicate a pattern like that shown in Exhibit 4–2. When an engineer focused on a single project is given a second one, utilization often rises slightly because the engineer no longer has to wait for the activities of others involved in that single project. Instead, the engineer can move back and forth between the two projects. However, if a third, fourth, or even fifth project is added, the percentage of time spent on value-adding tasks drops rapidly, as an increasing fraction of valuable time is spent on non-value-added tasks—coordinating, remembering, or tracking down information, for example.[2] In addition, the engineer becomes the bottleneck on all of the projects to which he or she is assigned.

ExHIBIT 4–2

Productivity of Development Engineering Time*

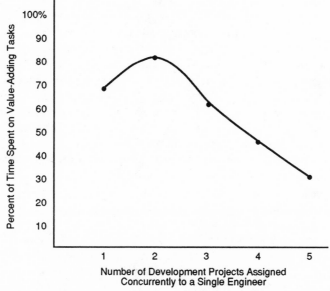

Number of Development Projects Assigned
Concurrently to a Single Engineer

* In the studies underlying this graph, the activities engaged in by development engineers were grouped into two categories—those that added value to a development project, and those that did not. This graph shows the percent of an engineer's activities in value-adding tasks.

A Reactive Mix of Development Projects

For the senior managers at PreQuip, the news that their development organization was two to three times overcommitted was bad enough. They also discovered, however, that their development resources were not focused on the critical issues for the business. After reviewing how engineers were actually spending their time, senior management discovered that the bulk of their critical resources were not focused on the major projects required to implement their business strategy. Rather, the development organization was focused on reacting to near-term pressures. This is a common problem. Short-term pressures occur daily and come from existing customers, products, competitors, and distribution channels—often with information about existing products' problems and shortcomings. This gives rise to projects that extend existing product market offerings or solve very specific customer problems. Their focus is to "sustain" the business and keep the organization's product market position viable with existing customer segments, distribution channels, and product categories.

In the PreQuip case there was no formal system to track types of projects, but a rough estimate by the vice president of engineering suggested that 60 to 70 percent of the company's development resources were devoted to "sustaining" projects or activities (much of the work was never formalized into projects). When those activities were compared to the strategic potential of developing new technology (e.g., advanced control systems) and the need to break into new markets (e.g., a smaller, lighter machine for the Asian market), and taking into account the age of the company's bread and butter product line, it was clear to PreQuip's senior management that the corporation's critical development skills and capabilities were woefully misallocated. By piling on project after project, failing to identify critical projects, and succumbing to short-term pressures, they had systematically underinvested in the most important projects for the company.

The problems at PreQuip are not unique. Most organizations fail to realize the strategic potential in new technology or markets and next-generation projects because there are too many projects, and because they pay too little attention to the strategic mission of the development effort and too much attention to short-term pressures. But it is also true that planning, shaping, and initiating longer-term, more strategic projects requires a very different kind of managerial activity. Managing next-generation (or advanced development) projects, or breaking into new markets, is much more comprehensive, ambiguous, and uncertain than reacting to short-term problems. An essential element in dealing effectively with these challenges is a well crafted aggregate project plan. The first step in developing such a plan is to define clearly the types and mix of projects the firm needs. It is to that task that we now turn.

Types of Development Projects

While a number of different dimensions could be used to classify development projects into different categories or types, perhaps the most useful relies simply on the degree of change represented by the project. As illustrated in Exhibit 4–3, the degree of product change and the degree of manufacturing process change can be combined to define several types of development projects. Distinguishing types of projects is important not only because it clarifies management's thinking about planning, staffing, and guiding of individual projects, but also because it aids in developing an aggregate project plan since each of the project types requires a different level of resource commitment. These same types also can be used in creating product and process maps, as discussed in Chapter 3.

EXHIBIT 4–3

Defining Primary "Types" of Development Projects*

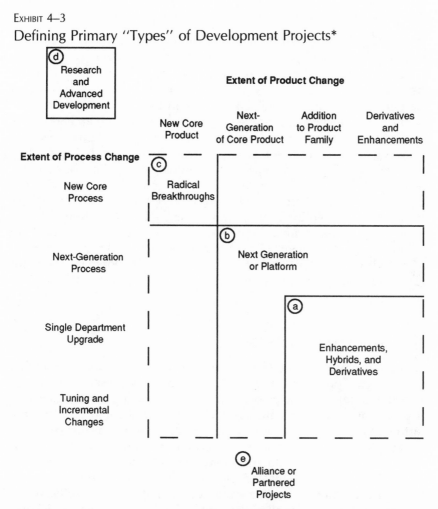

* The four primary types of projects, a through d, differ in the degree of change they require in product and process technology. The fifth type—alliance or partnered—involves joint work with another organization. While any of the four types could be partnered, it occurs most often with those involving substantial change, not with incremental or enhancement projects.

R&D/Advanced Development Projects

The boundaries of the diagram in Exhibit 4–3 define the range of commerical development projects carried out inside the firm. Two types of projects lie outside those boundaries: research and advanced development projects, and alliance or partnered projects. While projects within the primary diagram in Exhibit 4–3 focus on the introduction of viable, profitable products and processes, the focus of research and advanced development projects is the creation of knowledge—know-how and know-why—as a precursor to commerical development. Explored in more detail in Chapter 5, separating technological explorations and investigations from the application of known technologies in specific marketable products is a broadly accepted principle of technology management. Typically firms conduct advanced development in a separate group, staffed with a different set of people and equipment, than commerical development. However, over time people may move from advanced development projects to commerical development. Thus for aggregate planning purposes it is useful to include advanced development in the overall plan.

Alliance or Partnered Projects

Alliance or partnered projects also need to be considered in preparing the aggregate project plan. This type of project represents a different mode for conducting the project rather than involving a different extent of product or process change. In fact, any project could be done in a partnered mode. That is, an organization could form an alliance or create a partnership with another organization to conduct research or advanced development, to pursue a new product concept, or to develop a simple line extension. Instead of using the organization's resources alone, the partner firm often provides unique and/or significant resources (and sometimes all of the resources) and may manage the execution of the project. In recent years, firms increasingly have used partnered projects to fill in when their own resources were not delivering the development results required or when strategic opportunities were initially identified by other (often smaller) firms and acquiring a new product or process appeared less expensive or faster than duplicating the work in-house. Including partnered projects in the aggregate project plan is important because they invariably require some of a firm's own development resources, even if the partner firm does the bulk of the work. Even when the project is executed by the partner's organization, transferring the results of that project into the acquiring firm's product line, sales force, and often factories requires some of the same resources that otherwise would be available for in-house development efforts.

Incremental or Derivative Projects

In the lower right-hand corner of Exhibit 4–3 are projects that create products and processes that are derivatives, hybrids, or enhancements—what we have called sustaining projects. These range from cost-reduced versions of an existing product to add-ons or enhancements to an existing production process. As suggested by the positioning of that class of development effort, such projects include incremental product changes with little or no process change, incremental manufacturing process changes with little or no product change, and products involving incremental changes on both dimensions. Such projects usually require substantially fewer resources than projects that break new ground, because they leverage existing products or processes by extending their applicability.

Breakthrough or Radical Projects

At the other end of the spectrum are projects that involve significant change in the product and process. These "breakthrough" projects, when fully successful, establish a new core product and a new core process. They may create a whole new product category for the business or spearhead the entry of the firm into a new business. Much of the focus in such projects is on the product, because it often represents a new application or function and depends for its success on attracting and satisfying new customers. But breakthrough projects also involve significant process development; indeed, the process is likely to be critical to the success of the product. Senior management may give teams assigned to breakthrough projects some latitude in choosing the manufacturing process rather than constrain the team to use the existing plant or existing equipment and operating techniques.

Platform or Next-Generation Projects

In the middle of the spectrum between derivatives and breakthroughs lie what we call next-generation or platform projects. These projects, representing new "system" solutions for customers, involve significant change on either the manufacturing process dimension, the product dimension, or perhaps both. They provide a base for a product and process family that can be leveraged over several years, and they require significantly more resources than derivative or incremental developments. When carefully planned and executed, platform projects provide a significant base of volume and a fundamental improvement in cost, quality, and performance over the preceding generation. Thus they often are referred to as "next generation" efforts.

Platform projects deserve special emphasis in developing the aggregate project plan. Not only do they offer great competitive leverage and untapped potential in established markets, but senior managers—like those at PreQuip—often find that their organizations systematically underinvest in creating them. Understanding why, recognizing the consequences for performance, and developing guidelines for integrating platforms into the aggregate project plan thus present a significant opportunity.

Next-generation platform projects do more than create a single product and its manufacturing process. To function as a platform, a next-generation project must establish a product and a process with three essential characteristics:

1. *Core performance capabilities that match primary needs.* The solution the project develops needs to be a targeted, system solution to the needs of the core group of customers.
2. *Support of an entire product/process generation.* Platform projects create products and processes that subsequent development efforts can expand and enhance through the addition or removal of incremental features, thus creating a product and process family. While the platform must address the needs of the core customer group, it must also be adaptable and expandable.
3. *A link to previous and subsequent generations.* Platforms provide a migration path for customers, facilitating movement from one generation to the next. This ensures stability for customers as well as distribution channels, and enables the firm to leverage more fully its position and resources. Platforms do not disrupt the customer's world.

In effect, a platform project creates products (and processes) that embed an architecture for the system solution to be provided to customers. In fact, it is the architecture of the system that enables other features to be added or existing features to be removed in tailoring derivative products to special market niches. Making explicit the platform architecture helps designers, marketers, manufacturers, and general managers identify the role the platform should play in the aggregate project plan. For example, a critical choice in the aggregate project plan is whether the initial platform offering should be a fully featured version that later can be stripped down and focused as derivative products are created, or whether it ought to be a stripped-down version to which features can be added to create subsequent enhanced products. Both strategies have been pursued in similar markets. Polaroid's instant photography strategy has long been to start with a highly featured platform project, introduce it at a premium price, and then gradually remove features and create more cost-competitive versions as subsequent derivative offerings. In contrast, Kodak's single-use camera strategy in the late 1980s was to introduce a stripped down, bare bones platform—the FunSaver—to which other options and features (a panoramic lens, waterproof container, and flash) could be added to form enhanced products that were higher priced and higher performance than the original platform offering.

Using Project Types: The Benefits

The categories defined in Exhibit 4–3 are general; more specific and tailored categories may be useful in specific businesses. Explicit recognition that projects differ in ways that matter to the individual firm, and are not precise universal categories, is important. Each type of project has a different role and provides a different competitive contribution. Each requires different levels and mixes of resources, and typically generates very different results. Furthermore, because of the differences in the scope of projects and the issues associated with each of the types, requirements for success also differ.

Take, for example, the differences between platforms and derivatives. The most important of these is the front-end planning activity. While derivative projects often can represent specific, targeted responses to the requirements of small groups of customers, platform projects represent the bundling and packaging of a set of improvements into a new system solution for a much broader range of core customer needs. A successful platform project must embody sufficient improvement across a range of performance dimensions that customers will see it as a significantly better solution than either the prior platform or its targeted derivatives. Second, the new platform must combine a range of improvements in a way that no single customer may yet have thought of. Thus much more creativity, insight, and initiative are required at the front end of a platform project than a derivative project.

In addition to the challenges of front-end planning, two other differences distinguish the development of platform versus derivative projects. One is that getting convergence to a final set of specs is significantly more challenging on a platform than a derivative effort: there are many more specs that need to be defined and far fewer that are already constrained. In a derivative project, most of the issues already have been closed or severely bounded by the earlier platform effort.

The other difference characteristically highlighted is that platform projects require much more cross-functional problem solving and integration because so many issues must be defined. On a platform project, setting the specs in detail at the front end is often impractical. Instead, the project must converge over a series of months as cross-functional problem solving and conflict resolution take place. On a derivative project, setting the specs at the outset is commonplace. The focus of the project is delivering those specs by having individual functional contributors address the issues that they influence.

Getting capacity requirements clearly identified and linking projects to business strategy are first-order effects of using project categories as a framework for planning. But there are critical second-order effects that bring the organization significant advantage, particularly in making clear the interactions across projects. For example, these categories provide a useful way to link product and process development activities and plan for them jointly. Making the categories explicit highlights the similarities in needs, scope, and approaches for process and product development projects. Our experience is that most organizations spend far more time worrying about the degree of product change than about the degree of process change. In a large number of industries, achieving a better balance in the concerns and attention given to both dimensions can provide substantial competitive leverage.

There are other subtle, but substantial, effects of thinking about future projects in these terms. Project categories, for example, provide a framework for thinking not only about products and processes, but also about building development capability. Combined with a long-term planning horizon, laying out the future portfolio of projects facilitates the training and development of individuals involved in development. The primary goal of development projects is a defined product and/or process, but projects also create capabilities—particularly in human resources. A natural training path for engineers as well as marketing and manufacturing people is to begin their involvement in development by working on derivative projects, then to move to next-generation platform projects, and perhaps, for a much smaller number, to become centrally involved in breakthrough projects as experience and skills accumulate. Furthermore, key resources can be moved between research and commerical development types of activities to facilitate technology transfer and to ensure that advanced development is focused on those aspects of technology that will have the highest payoff in the market place. All of this grows out of establishing project categories as the first step in the aggregate project plan.

Choosing the Mix and Sequence of Projects

Establishing the appropriate types of projects for a particular business is the starting point for the aggregate project plan. But to put the categories to work and link them to business strategy, the firm must choose the appropriate mix of projects over the planning horizon. The mix is indicated by the percentage of a firm's development resources that are allocated to the various types of projects. Most established firms spend the majority of their development resources on incremental or derivative (sustaining) projects, whereas start-up firms spend the bulk of their development activity on radical or breakthrough projects. Additionally, some start-up firms dominated by scientists and engineers often find it difficult to make the transition from primarily research and advanced development efforts to commerical development projects. For all these types of firms, however, the issue of mix in the aggregate project portfolio needs to be readdressed periodically.

There are a number of factors that determine the most appropriate allocation of a firm's development activities across the primary types of projects. Some forces come from the firm's environment. Particularly important are industry maturity and the rate of technological innovation in the industry. As an industry matures, the opportunities for advanced development and breakthrough projects decline relative to opportunities (and customer demands) for derivative and platform projects. In fact, it is the evolution of the existing customer base, distribution channel, and competition that leads many mature firms to spend the bulk of their efforts on enhancement and derivative projects. But mix also depends on the firm's capabilities and its strategy. Given its engineering skills and manufacturing processes, for example, the returns available from enhancements and derivative projects may be quite attractive. If its strategy is to use that capability and its distribution strength to exploit market segments and niches pioneered by others, the aggregate project plan will have a higher mix of derivative projects than if the firm relied heavily on breakthrough projects. In the final analysis, the mix of project types is a strategic choice senior management makes in light of the firm's opportunities, capabilities, and strategies. The following examples illustrate how these factors combine in different firms and industries.

Changing Technology and a Focus on Platforms. In the early stages of an industry's development, firms typically compete and gain market position through products with dramatically superior performance on one or two dimensions of interest to the customer. As an industry matures and the opportunity to hit distinctive home runs on one or two technical dimensions decreases (often because technology becomes mature and shared more broadly), competitive success increasingly depends on giving customers an integrated, high-quality, system solution rather than a solution that is outstanding on only one or two dimensions of performance. In this context, platform projects become critical. Competitive success for a next-generation platform project tends to be determined by the system's collective capabilities and the excellence of the total solution on a number of different dimensions, not simply being superior on one or two dimensions.

One of the considerations in deciding when it is appropriate to go to a next-generation platform project is when there have been sufficient advances made in technology, features, and knowledge of customer needs on a range of dimensions so that they can be bundled together into a significantly better next-generation platform project. The difference between two platform generations in a given product family is not a home run on one or two dimensions, but rather greater or lesser degrees of incremental improvement on several dimensions simultaneously, integrated into a significantly better system solution. This gives the new-generation system an overall performance that is significantly superior to that achieved by the prior generation.

In the hospital bed industry, firms involved in designing, manufacturing, selling, and servicing electric hospital beds historically have faced a mature market under substantial pressure to contain capital expenditures and operating costs. In addition, technologies long had been considered mature and the payoff from new innovations largely incremental. In such a setting, it is not surprising that product generations (new platforms) have lasted from eight to twelve years. Derivatives and enhancements, however, have followed two quite different patterns. In the 1970s, as a number of hospitals in the United States were renovated and new hospitals were built, the prospect of an order for several hundred beds led firms to respond by customizing designs (doing derivative development) on almost every bed proposal. The result was extensive product line proliferation with most of the development resources being spent on derivative, incremental efforts.[3]

In the 1980s, with increased pressure for cost containment and much less new construction and renovation, Hill-Rom, the leading electric bed manufacturer, dramatically changed its resource allocation. Hill-Rom focused on developing three platform products—which shared many common parts and production processes—and providing add-on options to those basic platform designs. As a result, the mix of development projects at Hill-Rom shifted dramatically between the 1970s and 1980s from largely reactive, sustaining projects to proactive, next-generation platform efforts. In the early 1990s, with a variety of new technologies available and hospitals demanding beds that dramatically improved patient recovery and nurse productivity, Hill-Rom anticipated that generation life cycles would shorten and even more of its resources would be focused on platform projects.

Managing the Platform to Achieve Hyper-Variety. As markets mature and customers become more knowledgeable and sophisticated, the attractiveness of a standard product declines; customers seek tailored solutions. This tendency may be exacerbated if the product has a high fashion content and is sold through multiple distribution channels. In such environments, effectively managing product variety is crucial to competitive success. The market for portable cassette tape players and radios—"Walkmans"—pioneered by Sony illustrates the nature of these development challenges.

In the late 1980s Sony continued to dominate this market with over 200 models of Walkman available in 1990 alone. Yet these models were built off of three platforms, each of which had gone through periodic generational redesigns. The great bulk of Sony's development efforts were directed at a wide array of derivatives, enhancements, hybrids, and line extensions that offered something tailored to every niche, distribution channel, and competitor's product.[4]

These satisfied the full range of distribution requirements and end customer desires. Sony credited its continued dominance of the industry on this broad range of models and offerings. By basing 200-plus models on only three platform products/manufacturing processes, however, they were able to leverage their manufacturing investments dramatically and support continued improvements in cost and price in concert with continued improvements in performance. Clearly their project portfolio planning was an integral and essential part of their development and business strategies.

Choosing the mix of projects establishes how the firm will allocate resources at any point in time. But the aggregate project plan sets out how the portfolio of projects will evolve over time. Thus, choosing the sequence of projects is a critical element of the planning process. All of the project types are part of the sequence strategy, but of central interest are major platform projects for a given product family and the timing of derivative projects that will enhance and leverage that platform. When a new platform product is introduced, it usually replaces an older platform and its derivative offerings. If the new platform represents a significant improvement in system performance, several customers previously served by niche derivatives on the old platform will return to the core customer group because they will find the new system's capabilities superior to the derivative niche solution off the old platform. Thus a solid next-generation product will consolidate demand and build core volume soon after its introduction, providing leverage and scale for the primary operating assets of the firm. One reason for not usually introducing derivative products simultaneously with the next-generation platform is to take advantage of that consolidation and the competitive strength of the new platform. In addition, this allows development resources to be better leveraged: rather than working on the platform and derivatives concurrently, work can be done sequentially, without incurring any penalty in the marketplace. Experience in the world auto industry illustrates the issues involved in sequencing major platform projects.

In an extensive study of the world auto industry in the late 1980s, Clark and Fujimoto found that, on average, European platform generation designs changed every twelve years, U.S. generations changed every eight years, and Japanese generations changed every four years.[5] In exploring the sources of those differences, they discovered that European firms typically looked for larger performance improvement steps in the system solution provided by next-generation products, which took longer and were more costly to develop. When combined with lower volumes per model, this required higher prices (consistent with the higher performance characteristics) and longer design lives to earn a good return on development investments. Firms in the United States, which historically had not sought as much "perfection" in their next-generation platforms and had higher volumes per model, had found that a pattern of eight-year platform design lives was attractive. Finally, Japanese firms, faced with a more turbulent domestic market and with significant (i.e., two to one) advantages in development productivity, capitalized on performance improvements with shorter time spans between platform generations. They used development approaches that required fewer resources yet captured the latest improvements possible, enabling them to shorten the design life of platform generations to four years.

While all of the auto firms engaged in derivative enhancements in the interim years, those with longer design life patterns found it increasingly difficult to compete with the short, efficient, and system solution-oriented efforts of the Japanese firms. This competitive interaction scenario was analogous to that of the consumer electronics industry described in Chapter 1.

The timing of major platform efforts establishes the window of opportunity for derivatives and enhancements, but firms confront a number of strategic choices within the window. While many strategies for sequencing derivative projects are possible, the two depicted in Exhibit 4-4 illustrate the range of choices. Panel A of the exhibit presents the "steady stream" strategy. This scenario is often followed by business units offering a single product family derived from a single platform. Typically all of the unit's development resources will be focused on the platform during its development. Following its introduction, the team will go to work on a set of derivative projects, but their introduction will be spaced in a fairly steady stream until the development resources again focus on creation of the next generation platform and its introduction.

A very different pattern is the "secondary wave" of derivative projects, illustrated in Panel B. Business units with multiple product

Exhibit 4–4

Timing Platform and Derivative Project Sequences*

Market Introduction Year

		1	2	3	4	5	6	7	8
A. Steady Stream Strategy									
Current Platform:		Intro							
Derivative Projects:	1			Intro					
	2				Intro				
	3					Intro			
	4						Intro		
Follow-On Platform:									Intro
B. Secondary Wave Strategy									
Current Platform:		Intro							
Derivative Projects:	1					Intro			
	2						Intro		
	3						Intro		
	4						Intro		
Follow-On Platform:									Intro

* The steady stream strategy focuses first on a new platform, follows it with a steady stream of derivative projects, and eventually moves to the next generation platform. The secondary wave strategy does no enhancements immediately after the platform introduction, but instead uses derivatives later to extend the platform life and hold market share until the new platform is introduced.

lines, each having their own base platform, often pursue this strategy. The scenario works as follows: a critical mass of development resources is focused on a next-generation platform; once introduced, the key people go off to work on a platform for another product family. The recently introduced platform is left in the market for a couple of years with little or no derivative effort. As it begins to age and is challenged by competitors' newer platforms, development resources are refocused on derivatives in order to strengthen and extend the viability of the product line's existing platform in the marketplace. The wave of derivative projects provides training and feedback to those working in development and serves to prepare them for conducting the next-generation platform project. They receive market feedback on the prior platform, information on competitors' platform offerings (many of which may have been introduced recently), and information on market needs, some of which are to be addressed by the derivatives under development. Key people then bring that information together to shape the front-end definition of the next-generation platform project. Hill-Rom's electric bed approach, described earlier, is representative of this strategy.

An important variant of the "secondary wave" involves shortening the time between market introduction of major generations or platform offerings in a product family. Rather than sending the development team off to work on another product family immediately following the introduction of a new platform, they go to work immediately on a set of derivative models. This of course requires more real-time assessment of market response to the platform they have just introduced and much shorter feedback loops regarding competitors' products. Once the flurry of derivative products have been developed and introduced, the team then goes to work on the next-generation platform project for that same product family.

An excellent illustration of this secondary wave strategy is the single-use camera operations at Kodak, referred to earlier.[6] Prior to 1987, Kodak conducted a series of advanced development projects to explore alternatives for a single-use (disposable) 35 mm camera—a roll of film packaged in an inexpensive camera; once used, the film is processed and the camera discarded or recycled. A commerical version of a camera that used 110-size film was developed in the mid 1980s but without substantial market success. During 1987, a focused group of Kodak development people went to work on a first-generation platform project, largely in response to Fuji Film's demonstration of a 35 mm single-use camera. The Kodak project resulted in market introduction and volume production of the Fling 35 mm camera in January 1988 (later renamed the FunSaver). As that platform project was being completed, the front-end development resources were reassigned to two derivative projects: the Stretch (a panoramic, double-wide image version) and the Weekender (a waterproof version). By the end of 1988, both derivative projects were introduced and shipping in volume. As true derivative projects, the Stretch and Weekender took significantly less development time and fewer resources than the platform project, and required much less new tooling since they leveraged the existing automation and manufacturing process.

Thus within a year, Kodak had introduced a platform single-use camera and two derivative products. At that time it contemplated using those same resources on a third derivative product, a single-use camera with a built-in, single-use flash. However, after a couple of months of exploration, it was decided that rather than doing the flash version as a derivative project, competitively, it would be better to do it as the next-generation platform product for Kodak's 35 mm single-use family of cameras. Two things led to this conclusion. First, because of the electronic controls and connectors necessary for the flash version, substantially more development was required than for either the Stretch or Weekender derivative products. If Kodak had attempted to do the flash version as a derivative, it would have been somewhere halfway between a derivative and a platform product. The other consideration was that while the first generation was designed as disposable (and even referred to as such in some of the early advertising literature), market response suggested that Kodak would be better off positioning its cameras as single-use and recyclable. This would require a number of changes so that once the film processor removed the film, the remaining camera, lenses, and other parts of the single-use system could be recycled and reused.

The combination of both factors led Kodak to conclude that the flash version should be the first offering of the next-generation product. The product would incorporate a number of improvements to provide a better system solution, be recyclable (satisfying market desires and lowering costs), and, because the flash version would be the first to be introduced on that new platform, it would represent substantial performance improvement. In late 1990, Kodak introduced the FunSaver flash 35 mm camera and announced that, within a year, its three existing single-use offerings (FunSaver, Stretch, and Weekender) also would be recyclable. These three products were to be derivatives developed off the second generation platform—the FunSaver flash unit.

Developing an Aggregate Project Plan

Our discussion of different project types, the choice of an appropriate project mix, and the sequencing of platforms and derivatives underscores the power and importance of the aggregate project plan. Senior management at PreQuip grasped the importance of the concept as they learned about it and began to implement it. A procedure we have defined (and the one PreQuip's management followed) consists of eight sequential steps. Like any aggregate planning activity, the process does need to be repeated on a periodic basis, such as every six or twelve months.

PreQuip's management went through the first four steps of this procedure to identify the desired mix, estimate available capacity requirements, and take stock of the situation.

Step 1: Define the types or classes of development projects that are to be covered by the aggregate project plan. Most firms find it useful to start with the five categories or types outlined in Exhibit 4–3, and then refine them by specifying the characteristics to be used in deciding when individual projects encountered are of each type. This results in a set of criteria that can be used to classify any project as one of the five types.

Step 2: Define for a representative project of each type the critical resources and cycle time required for its complete development. Most often firms decide that the critical resource is the human resource, and seek to determine the full-time equivalent (FTE) development engineers, product marketing people, and manufacturing people required to go from project conception through market introduction. The cycle time is the calender time required for these activities. Firms also find it useful to specify the expected dollar cost of a representative project of each type, since that helps the organization shape its expectations and further distinguish the types of projects.

Step 3: Identify the existing resources available for development efforts (particularly the critical human resources for which the full-time equivalents were defined in Step 2) and currently active projects, with their requirements for completion. This results in explicitly identifying the available capacity and existing set of projects that will make demands on that capacity.

Step 4: Compute the capacity utilization implied by the results of Step 3. This can be done using a chart like Exhibit 4–1 that shows for appropriate time periods the amount of resources required for each of the currently "active" projects. The result is the capacity utilization of development resources over each of the next several time periods if projects are to be completed on schedule.

At the conclusion of Step 4, PreQuip's senior managers developed the summary data presented in Exhibit 4–1. The numbers were surprising. They found that total requirements over the next two quarters to complete the active projects were almost three times the available capacity. But the project mix itself was also out of balance. By breaking projects into categories based on the degree of change, they found that over 60 percent of their resources were devoted to derivative projects.

The next step for PreQuip (and for our planning procedure) was to forge a much closer link between its project mix and its strategy. Steps 5 through 7 create an aggregate project plan with this characteristic.

Step 5: Establish the desired future mix of projects by type. This entails balancing strategic choices against practical realities, in determining what percent of the critical resources should be committed to each of the five

EXHIBIT 4–5

Presenting the Aggregate Project Plan at PreQuip, 1990–1991*

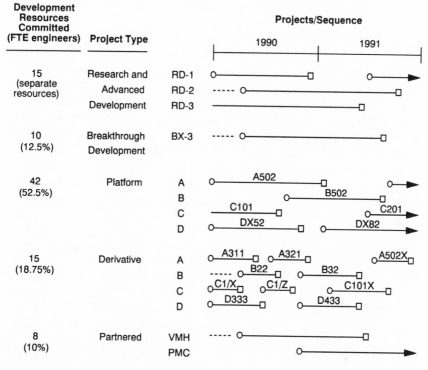

Development Resources Committed (FTE engineers)	Project Type		Projects/Sequence
			1990 / 1991
15 (separate resources)	Research and Advanced Development	RD-1 RD-2 RD-3	
10 (12.5%)	Breakthrough Development	BX-3	
42 (52.5%)	Platform	A B C D	A502 B502 C101 C201 DX52 DX82
15 (18.75%)	Derivative	A B C D	A311 A321 A502X B22 B32 C1/X C1/Z C101X D333 D433
8 (10%)	Partnered	VMH PMC	

Total development FTEs assigned: 75
Total development FTEs available: 80

O Project start   ------- Pre-project planning and analysis
□ Project completion   ——— Actual project

* In 1990–1991, PreQuip developed an aggregate project plan that matched its strategic requirements. It included advanced development (fifteen dedicated engineers working on up to three projects), breakthrough (ten engineers on one project), platform (forty-two engineers on up to four projects), derivative (fifteen engineers on up to four projects), and partnered (eight engineers on up to two projects).

types of projects. (See the left-hand column of Exhibit 4–5.) In established firms, it is common for management to conclude that half or more of the development effort should be focused on next-generation platform projects, with 10 to 20 percent focused on derivative developments and 10 to 20 percent focused on each of the other three types—research and advanced development, breakthrough development, and partnered development. It is important that the mix specified be achievable in the time horizon for which the aggregate project plan is being created and that it be appropriate given the firm's strategy, innovation opportunities, and existing product-market requirements.

Step 6: Estimate the number of projects of each type that can be undertaken concurrently with existing resources. For instance, if the critical resource is development engineers and a firm has 100 full-time equivalents in development engineering, it can use the desired mix of projects (identified in Step 5), combined with the number of full-time equivalents required for a representative project (from step 2), to determine how many projects can be undertaken concurrently. For example, if the firm wants 50 percent of its effort spent on platform projects, and it has 100 development engineers, then on average, 50 development engineers will be committed to platform projects. If representative platform projects take eight quarters to perform, and, on average, require 15–20 full-time equivalents per quarter, then the firm can undertake three platform projects concurrently given its existing resources, its estimated requirements for a typical platform project, and its desired mix of efforts.

Step 7: Decide which projects to undertake. This includes reassessing the existing projects to make sure that they should be continued, as well as determining how many new projects of each type should be started and in what time periods. This is more than just "picking projects" from the existing list. The firm may need to repackage and reformulate projects in order to define the set that offers the greatest opportunity given the firm's strategy and resources. In the example just cited, if four platform projects are already underway and it is going to be another nine months before the first two are completed, the firm should not add another platform project for nine months. If it adds one sooner, it will be pursuing the canary cage approach described earlier. A firm that is unhappy with its mix of existing projects and its overcommitment of development resources may decide to drop projects currently on the active list, add new resources, or subcontract some of its yet-to-be-started projects in order to transition faster to its desired mix and level of capacity utilization.

In PreQuip's case, senior management believed that platform projects were critical to its competitive success and required much more attention and focus. After reshaping and redefining its platform projects, PreQuip developed the aggregate project plan presented in Exhibit 4–5, which lays out a sequence of platform projects for the four product families in PreQuip's line. The painful part of the planning process is evident in the resources devoted to derivative projects. The plan calls for a substantial reduction in resources devoted to "sustaining" projects, and this required PreQuip to kill or postpone several projects. Senior management believed, however (and their belief was confirmed in subsequent events), that a more focused effort would improve development productivity. This would permit the organization to get more actual work done over the three-year planning horizon, even though there would be fewer projects in process at any one time.

Taking into account the platform and derivative resources and the engineers allocated to breakthrough projects and partnerships, the plan called for commitments of only 75 of the 80 full-time equivalent engineers in the development organization. PreQuip, thus, provided for a small "capacity cushion" in the plan. Where aggregate planning is a well-known and practiced discipline (e.g., operations management), firms have discovered that the higher the level of uncertainty about individual project requirements, the greater the need there is for a capacity cushion (slack in capacity commitments) so that those uncertainties can be accommodated without delaying all future projects. The analog in product and process development is recognizing the need to leave some percentage of the total aggregate development capacity (in PreQuip's case, 5 FTEs) uncommitted to specific projects so that as uncertainties occur throughout the year those resources can be used to cope with them.

The plan laid out in Exhibit 4–5 addresses the sequence of products and associated processes PreQuip will bring to the market over the three-year planning horizon. But if it stops there, it is incomplete. The plan must also address how these projects and other related activities will improve the performance of development. Thus, the final step of the aggregate planning process:

Step 8: Determine and integrate into the project plan changes required to improve development performance (speed, productivity, and quality) over time. Projects not only create new products, but also have the potential to build new development capability. A project may be the vehicle for introducing a new computer-aided design (CAD) system or a new approach to project organization. In addition, new systems and procedures—such as a new engineering change process—need to be planned and coordinated with ongoing development projects. Thus, the aggregate project plan needs to identify where the firm intends to make significant changes and how the changes will be connected to product and process development. In PreQuip's case, for example, the major changes were a restructuring of the engineering organization (e.g., far fewer projects per engineer) and the introduction of a new CAD system. Management planned to phase in the restructuring during the first year of the plan, while the RD-3 advanced development effort would be the pilot project for the CAD system.

As senior management at PreQuip discovered, developing an aggregate project plan involves a relatively simple and straightforward procedure. But actually carrying it out—moving from the largely ad hoc "active" project list to a robust, effective set of projects that matches and reinforces the business strategy—involves hard choices and discipline. In PreQuip's case (and in the case of every other company we have studied), the difficulty and significance of those choices have made strong leadership from senior management imperative. Without that leadership, organizations that have habitually overcommitted themselves will have great difficulty killing and postponing projects, or resisting the short-term pressures that drive the organization to spend the bulk of its resources "fighting fires."

Getting to an aggregate project plan is not easy, but working through the procedure is a crucial part of creating a development strategy. Indeed, it is crucial to understand that the specific plan itself is not as important as the planning process. The plan will change as events unfold and managers make adjustments. But choosing the mix, defining the sequence, and creating the projects to support raise crucial questions about how product and process development ought to be linked to the firm's competitive opportunities and challenges. Laying the results out in a specific plan over time gives clarity and direction to the overall development effort and helps to lay the foundation for outstanding performance in specific projects.

CHAPTER *5*

_____

Structuring the Development Funnel

The aim of any product or process development project is to take an idea from concept to reality by converging to a specific product that can meet a market need in an economical, manufacturable form. As suggested in the development strategy framework outlined in Chapter 2, the overall development process starts with a broad range of inputs and gradually refines and selects from among them, creating a handful of formal development projects that can be pushed to rapid completion and introduction. This notion of a converging funnel is illustrated in Exhibit 5–1. In its simplest form, the development funnel provides a graphic structure for thinking about the generation and screening of alternative development options, and combining a subset of these into a product concept.[1] A variety of different product and process ideas enter the funnel for investigation, but only a fraction become part of a full-fledged development project. Those that do are examined carefully before entering the narrow neck of the funnel, where significant resources are expended in transforming them into a commercial product and/or process.

The nature of the funnel is defined by the way the organization identifies, screens, reviews, and converges on the content of a development project as it moves from idea to reality.[2] The funnel establishes the

111

EXHIBIT 5–1

The Development Funnel*

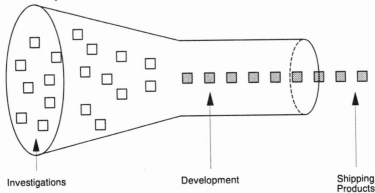

Investigations   Development   Shipping Products

* The funnel illustrates the process firms ideally go through to identify many ideas, select the few most promising for development, and focus resources to get them into the market. The small blank squares indicate ideas for investigation; darkened squares indicate ideas that are developed and applied.

overall framework for development: the generation and review of alternatives, the sequence of critical decisions, and the nature of decision making (including who is involved and the criteria used). It defines the forum for integration across and the structure within which senior managers influence the development process. In effect, the development funnel creates the architecture for the set of development activities that must occur as part of a successful development project.

In this chapter we first lay out the issues firms confront in structuring the funnel, present examples of funnels in action, and then use those examples to illustrate the power of the concept in diagnosing critical problems in the overall framework for development. In the subsequent section we turn to the question of designing the funnel for a specific business. We compare and contrast two traditional models of the development funnel, and then offer a third alternative that our work suggests is more powerful and effective. The chapter concludes with a discussion of critical challenges in using the funnel to manage development.

Basic Concepts and Their Application

Managing the development funnel involves three very different tasks or challenges. The first is to widen its mouth. To be effective, the organization must expand its knowledge base and access to information in order to increase the number of new product and new process ideas. A variety of ways of doing this—ranging from mining research labs and university relationships for more technical ideas to soliciting creative inputs from manufacturing, marketing, customers, and suppliers—will be explored later in this chapter.

The second challenge is to narrow the funnel's neck. After generating a variety of alternative concepts and ideas, management must screen them and focus resources on the most attractive opportunities. The hard part is to narrow the neck of the funnel while ensuring that a constant stream of good projects flows down it. The narrowing process must be based on a set of screening criteria that fit the company's technological opportunities while making effective use of its development resources in meeting strategic and financial needs.

Striking an effective balance between creatively widening the funnel's mouth and tough-mindedly narrowing its neck is not easy. The companies that do it best tend to combine various idea-generating mechanisms with a sequential review process. Later in this chapter we will outline alternative approaches, including front-end funding mechanisms for ensuring that ideas are ready to be screened (i.e., they receive an objective and appropriate hearing) while a systematic but fair process of screening is rigorously applied. Like capital budgeting, this task can be viewed as a resource allocation problem with all of the traditional issues of determining what data are relevant, how they should be weighted, and what they tell us about their eventual success. The goal is not just to apply limited resources to selected projects with the highest expected payoff, but to create a portfolio of projects that will meet the business objectives of the firm while enhancing the firm's strategic ability to carry out future projects.

Even with access to a number of good ideas and a process to focus on only a few, the funnel is not complete. The third challenge is to ensure that the selected projects deliver on the objectives anticipated when the project was approved. Ensuring that the project delivers as anticipated is the topic of Chapters 6 through 10. Especially relevant to this third task is Chapter 6, which considers how and when product or process specifications should be developed, when they should be modified, and how the process can be managed to convergence as opposed to being managed to a moving target.

Funnels in Practice

While the concept of the development funnel is straightforward, and the model depicted in Exhibit 5-1 apparently smooth and simple, the reality of funnels is often quite different. Even in situations where managers

EXHIBIT 5–2A
Actual Development Funnel—Medical Electronics Firm*

A. Team 1

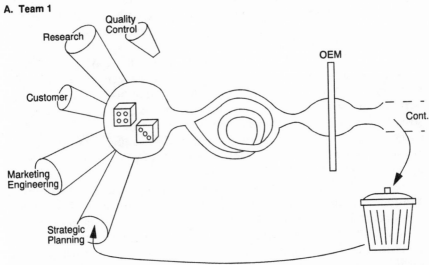

* This funnel, drawn by a group of executives, illustrates the often confused reality of actual development funnels. In this diagram, there are many funnels; choice is a random throw of the dice, and the course of development is convoluted.

---

have created a screening and review process, the actual funnel is not anything like the theory. To motivate a closer look at the funnel and to shed some light on the practical problems firms face in creating one, we have found it useful to have managers draw the funnel that actually exists in practice in their organization. Exhibits 5–2A and 5–2B present two examples from a medical electronics firm drawn by two teams of executives.

A few characteristics stand out in the first drawing. There is not just one funnel, but several, each with its own ideas and inputs into the development process. Some of these small funnels are important and well connected, while others (like QC) seem to be off in a world of their own. These ideas make up a large set of possibilities (notice how the funnel gets very wide at the beginning), but there is no clearly defined process for choosing among them. Indeed, Team 1 said, in effect, "We don't really know how projects get selected. It looks like we line them up and roll the dice." Those selected follow convoluted paths in development, with multiple loops and a lot of recycling until a few things find their way out into the market. Original equipment manufacturer (OEM) or subcontracted projects come in late, with little advanced warning or

ExHIBIT 5–2B

Actual Development Funnel—Medical Electronics Firm*

B. Team 2

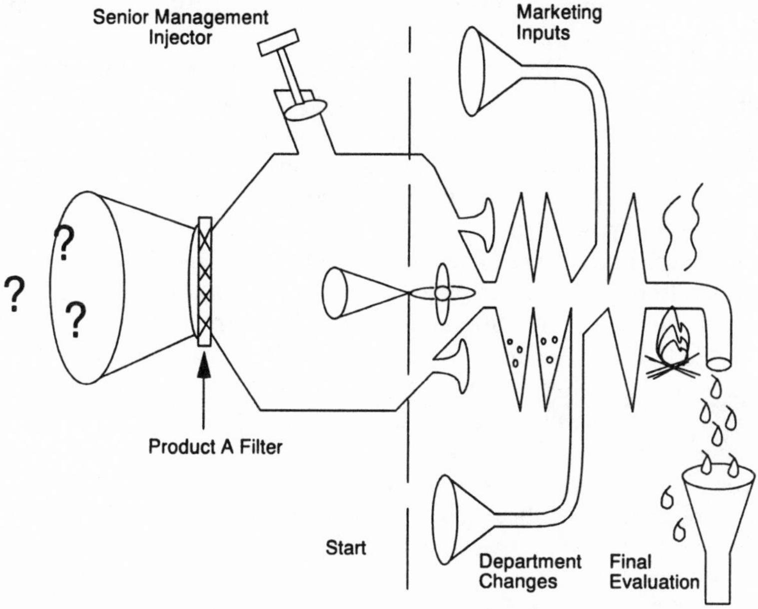

Senior Management Injector

Marketing Inputs

? ? ?

Product A Filter

Start

Department Changes

Final Evaluation

* This funnel, drawn by a group of executives, illustrates the problems firms experience with real development funnels. In this drawing, the source of ideas is uncertain, products for development get jammed up and seem to recirculate, there is a lot of heat at the end, and a few products "drip out" into the market.

analysis. Since products are often incomplete at introduction there is an ongoing development activity that lingers on. Finally, projects that fail get discarded only to be recycled through strategic planning as "new ideas."

The second funnel has similar themes. Where projects come from is uncertain, but it is clear that if the project is not a part of the Product A family (the original product line in the company) it will have a hard time getting funded. Once a project gets into the funnel, it joins many other projects that are part of the "active" list but seem to recirculate (notice the small fan in the middle of the diagram) with little progress. The team also noted that some projects enter the funnel through a special "senior management injector." These are pet projects of senior executives that seem to arrive in the development process with a big "whoosh!" behind them. Once out of the recirculation chamber, a project encounters numerous blind alleys and dead ends and also receives marketing input and departmental changes very late in its development. Finally, when something gets far enough along, senior management applies a lot of heat at the end (note the fire) and a few things drip out.

These drawings captured a sobering reality: the processes the firm used to identify, screen, select, and focus resources were fuzzy, disjointed, haphazard, and ineffective. Our experience suggests that the medical electronics company is not alone. Indeed, we have found very few companies where drawing the funnel reveals a smooth, crisp, clear, effective process. Most companies, therefore, confront a major opportunity for improving the overall development process, because getting the overall architecture of development right has great power. In the first place, getting rid of the starts and stops, the dead ends, and the convolutions eliminates a major source of confusion for the people working on the project. Additionally, an effective funnel creates a framework in which people can focus and integrate their energies and capabilities.

Creating an effective funnel, however, takes more than identifying problems and weaknesses. In addition, managers need a frame of reference to guide their choices so that the funnel they create matches the needs and opportunities they face. The first step in building that frame is to identify the critical dimensions of the funnel and how they work together to create an overall framework.

Creating the Development Funnel: Alternative Models

Exhibit 5–3 lays out three sets of dimensions that define the choices firms make about the development funnel:

- Its process for creating development projects—encouraging certain sources of new ideas and selecting which of those to support in development projects
- Its means of achieving convergence to a focused product concept and detailed design—through a set of decision-making, review, and control procedures during project execution
- Its final commitment to the market through final testing, screening, and market introduction plans

Although the large number of dimensions of choice means that in theory we could see a wide variety of funnels, in practice, many of these dimensions are closely connected. The result is that while some of the details differ, there are a few broad patterns to the choices firms make. We have presented two patterns—called Model I and Model II—in col-

EXHIBIT 5–3

Two Common Models of Development Funnels and Their Dimensions of Choice

Dimensions of Choice that Determine Funnel Characteristics	Model I (R&D Push/ Survival of the Fittest)	Model II (Single Project/ Big Bet)
Creating Development Projects		
Sources of Ideas		
Entry points	Primarily single function – R&D	Multiple functions
Direction	Bottom up/grass roots	Top down/senior management
Breadth	Wide within R&D/narrow for entire organization	Broad overall
Selection Process		
Purpose	Review/ready for next step	Go/no-go
Criteria	Internal/technical	External customer requirements/finance
Structure	Formal authorization	Informal/gut feel
People	Peer review	Senior management decision
Convergence to Concept/Detailed Design		
Process/Screens		
Timing	Technical milestones	Frequent/calendar
Purpose	Identify promising concepts	Go for one/adjustments
Criteria	Technical interest/performance	Customer requirements/finance
Formality	Signatures required	Informal
People	Peers/senior management approval	Senior management
Decision making	Consensus	Top management decision
Pattern of Convergence		
Number of options	Multiple/competing options	Single option
Width/length of neck of funnel	Wide/long	Narrow/short
Commitment to Market		
Criteria for introduction	Meets tests for performance	Meets financial targets
Decision making	Peers/top management	Top management

117

umns two and three of Exhibit 5–3. These models define approaches to the funnel that are quite common, but sufficiently different to make clear the nature of the choices firms face.

Model I

The first model is common in larger, technology-intensive firms.[3] Firms adhering to this model rely primarily on their R&D group to generate ideas for technologies and for new products and processes. They anticipate and encourage engineers and scientists to generate and explore many more ideas than will be applied in products or processes. The charge is to be creative and innovative, providing an abundance of opportunities for the larger organization to choose from.

With so many ideas, Model I then uses a series of screens—often involving peer reviews—to generate a winnowed down and manageable set of products and processes for market introduction. Early screens tend to be primarily technical in nature, focusing on technical feasibility and proof of concept. Later screens then shift to emphasize manufacturing feasibility and fundamental economics. Finally, as commercial introduction draws near, screens include added consideration of specific customer preferences, distribution channel concerns, and financial return expectations.

As a development project passes through a Model I funnel, it competes with other projects for resources. When successful, it often picks up ideas from competing projects that have lost momentum or been screened out. Many times, however, even a project that passes through the funnel successfully and is introduced to the marketplace finds itself competing with other products offered by the firm. Thus, to be successful over the long term, the resulting product must continue to compete successfully for sales, service, and customer attention, not just against products from competitors, but against products from within the firm.

The essence of the Model I funnel is a technology-driven survival of the fittest. Exhibit 5–4 graphs its characteristic funnel. The basic logic behind Model I is that of a hundred good ideas, only relatively few ever become successful products. This is due first to the fact that carrying an idea all the way from research through to market introduction is an extremely expensive proposition, and also to the notion that research can generate many more ideas than could ever be supported by the firm and absorbed by the marketplace. At each screen or hurdle, the active ideas are reviewed systematically, based on current knowledge and understanding. Only the best of those are approved for the next phase, where additional resources will be invested to prepare them for the next screen or hurdle, and to move them closer to the final form needed for eventual market introduction. But the screens are not tight enough to

Exhibit 5–4

Two Dominant Models of the Development Funnel*

A. Model I: R&D Driven, Survival of the Fittest

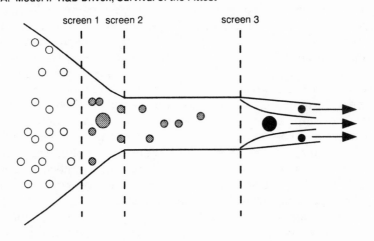

B. Model II: A Few Big Bets

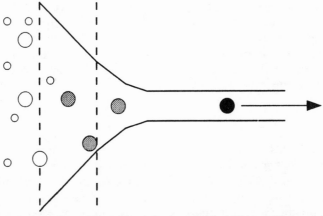

* This exhibit identifies two models of the funnel. Model I is a grass roots, bubble up model in which development is driven by R&D. Model II is a top down model common in small, entrepreneurial start-ups, in which the firm bets on a single project. The circles represent new products; shading indicates the extent of development, and size the scale of the project.

narrow the funnel substantially until market introduction is imminent.

Model I has strengths in certain kinds of markets, but a number of factors raise questions about the appropriateness of this model in a variety of industries. For many firms, a broad-ranging, exploratory research group—the vast majority of whose efforts never result in marketable products—is a luxury that few can afford. Doing such research is expensive and the forecast of which research activities would ever lead to marketable products is often too unreliable to justify such risks. Second, successful advanced development groups often become committed to turning their pet projects into marketable products, making it difficult or impractical to "kill" them. Thus, with a Model I funnel, increasing numbers of advanced development projects may find their way into commercial development. But such firms often lack the discipline and mechanisms to significantly reduce the numbers of development projects in process, and yet have insufficient resources to carry out all of them in a timely and successful manner.

A third factor that calls Model I into question is the complexity of development. As projects become increasingly complex, difficult, and expensive, it is impractical to screen out "competing projects" at the eleventh hour. While some firms respond by introducing more products to the marketplace—letting the market decide which version it prefers—this is often unsatisfactory as well.[4] Many markets simply do not grow fast enough to provide adequate rates of return by following this procedure, and too many products in the marketplace can confuse the distribution channel and final customers, and add complexity and cost in manufacturing.

Model II

Model I is a large firm model. Small firms, even those that are technically driven, have never had the luxury of following Model I. For them, the ideal model has always involved taking an idea (usually in the advanced development stage) and backing it all the way to successful product introduction. In fact, in industries such as computer peripherals, successful start-ups get that way by taking a single idea, turning it into a home run, and eventually building a product line around it. Many more start-ups have tried to imitate this approach, but failed for a myriad of reasons and disappeared in the process. When a smaller firm establishes itself using this "all-the-eggs-in-one-basket" model, they subsequently encounter a variety of challenges as they seek to repeat that success by applying the same approach on subsequent generations of products. Even mature firms, which dominate slowly evolving product market areas, often adopt this model but take more time than their smaller counterparts to execute it.

Firms that rely on the Model II development funnel generally consider a fairly wide range of ideas from a variety of sources at the outset. However, they very quickly collapse, screen, and combine them into a single project aimed at meeting a set of market needs. Most often, top management makes the call as to project boundaries, objectives, and commitment at the outset. While often influenced heavily by the backgrounds and experiences of senior management, the primary criteria for project selection, even at the outset, are market potential and financial expectations.

Throughout the execution portion of the Model II funnel, senior management requests regular reviews and updates, seeking to avoid late surprises and disappointments. With so much riding on an individual project, midcourse corrections and adjustments are common and considered appropriate. Only when serious problems arise would such a project have its market introduction postponed at the eleventh hour. Much more common is introduction as soon as feasible—even if not quite finished—with subsequent revisions and upgrades being made in the field. This flow through the funnel is illustrated in Exhibit 5–4B and can be described as a few big bets, or "all-the-eggs-in-one-basket."

While smaller firms following Model II typically have only one or two projects in process (i.e., in the narrow neck of the funnel) at any point in time, larger firms may have several projects in process under this model. However, for larger firms this most often still reflects only one or two projects per funnel for a given business unit or division. Thus in reality, even such large firms are pinning most of their new product hopes on a few bets for any given market, with many of those new products simply aimed at enhancements they hope will support and sustain an existing market position.

The success of small firms using Model II grows out of the clarity and focus that comes by necessity from betting the company on a single project. But as firms grow, using Model II may bring with it a number of problems. Model II is particularly problematic if used in large firms with multiple market segments and product families. The reality of Model II in large firms is numerous midcourse corrections, modest or even marginal market success upon introduction, and a reputation among their customers as "conservative and no longer innovative."

Exhibit 5–5 illustrates the experience of a Model II firm involved in industrial control devices in the development of a major next-generation electromechanical product. The intention of senior management in this division was to carefully serve a customer need, to apply existing technical knowledge, to identify the right product concept and features for the development effort, and then to drive that effort from advanced development through to commercial introduction in a focused project that would result in a robust, superior design, selling in volume in the

EXHIBIT 5–5

Analysis of a Specific Project's Development Funnel: Electromechanical Industrial Control Device*

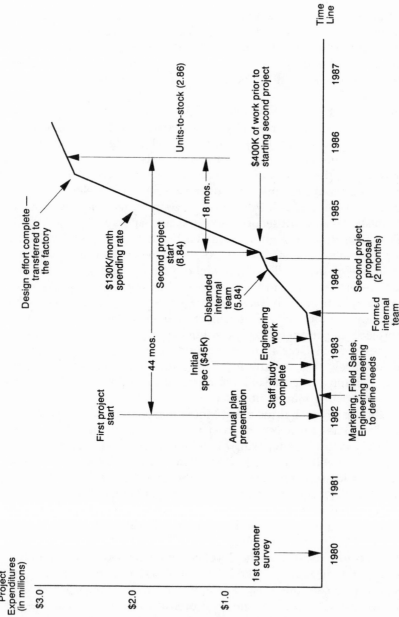

* Starting with the original customer survey and going to production units in inventory, this time line shows the major events that preceded as well as those that were part of the formal development project. It also shows the cumulative investment spent on the entire set of activities. While the "official project" was eighteen months, it was preceded by years of investigation at an identified cost of $400,000.

122

marketplace. As illustrated in Exhibit 5–5, initial customer surveys were done in 1980. By 1982, management felt the technical options and market requirements were known sufficiently to propose a major development effort as part of their annual plan. Over the next eighteen months, engineering spent close to $100,000 refining the product concept and ensuring that appropriate specs could be set and met. In early 1984 an internal development team was established, and over the next twelve months, worked vigorously—spending another $300,000—to bring the effort toward a marketable product. By mid 1984, however, management determined that while a new product was still needed for that major product family, it was not going to come out of the current development effort. The project was abandoned and the engineers went back to the drawing boards.

In late 1984, a revised proposal was made which included the use of corporate technical resources as well as resources from the division. A charter, including detailed specifications, a time line, and a $2.2 million budget, was established and approved by management at that point. The new team was indeed successful, and the product was launched on time and met the specifications. Unfortunately, however, the market had changed. Although the product was successful, a number of subsequent engineering changes were needed to refine and better target it. The firm concluded, however, that the second project had indeed been a successful execution of their "ideal Model II" funnel and that the problem with the first effort was a lack of focus, inadequate technical expertise, and a myriad of distractions that the second team avoided.

This experience underscores the problems in making Model II work in a changing, complex environment. First is that a high level of technical knowledge and completed scientific invention must be accessible to the development team if the project is to have a high probability of success and on-time completion. Similarly, the funnel structure requires that the firm have deep knowledge about the market, the competitors, and specific customer needs in advance. Second, disbanding established projects may sometimes be necessary, but it is particularly difficult, traumatic, and expensive. Third, by focusing narrowly at the outset, the funnel structure may reinforce a deliberate pace in exploring options and defining potential projects. But where time is of the essence, a leisurely pace is ineffective. The two years required in Exhibit 5–5 between the first customer survey and the initial project proposal, followed by another full year before the development team was staffed, is not viable in today's typical environment. Likewise, making extensive engineering change orders after introduction is disruptive in the marketplace and expensive and confusing to the firm. Thus both Models I and II of the funnel leave major gaps in what is "ideal" with respect to the development funnel. This becomes even more apparent once an orga-

Eхнівіт 5–6

Model III Development Funnel: Innovative and Focused*

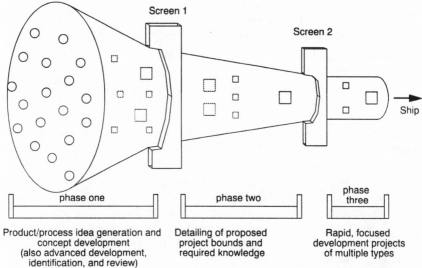

phase one	phase two	phase three
Product/process idea generation and concept development (also advanced development, identification, and review)	Detailing of proposed project bounds and required knowledge	Rapid, focused development projects of multiple types

* In Model III of the development funnel, the front end (phase one) is expanded to encourage more and better idea generation. Following an initial screening, the best of those ideas are then detailed and analyzed (phase two), ready for a go/no-go decision. At Screen 2, the approved projects are staffed and moved toward rapid introduction through a focused effort (phase three).

nization begins to sharpen its pre-project planning skills using some of the tools and concepts outlined in Chapters 2 and 3.

Model III

A much more appropriate ideal for a development funnel—Model III—combines and integrates the best features of Models I and II. In fact, it operationalizes an approach that is very close to the simple concept shape illustrated in Exhibit 5–1. We call this model "innovative and focused," and illustrate its primary characteristics in Exhibit 5–6.

The initial part of the Model III development funnel represents the concept development and idea generation for potential product/process efforts. The intent in this stage is to dramatically expand the mouth of the funnel, even beyond that envisioned in Model I. This can be done in a number of ways, gathering ideas from a variety of sources rather than just R&D.[5] One means for enlarging the mouth of the funnel is to institute procedures and incentives that encourage innovation and input from all parts of the organization as well as from customers, competitors, and suppliers. Each subfunction and group in the company needs to view itself as having significant responsibility for generating new ideas and concepts, and identifying ways in which they might be incorporated into products, services, and manufacturing processes. Providing special funding and released time for individuals to pursue and refine ideas is one type of incentive that may be needed to encourage such behavior. Recognizing individual and group contributions through competitions and awards may also be appropriate. Another way in which the need for new ideas can be addressed is through the functional maps described in Chapter 3. As each group creates those maps and plans for the activities they represent, the opportunity and need for additional development projects can be identified and responsibility for their exploration assigned.

As shown in Exhibit 5–6, a narrowing of the funnel occurs at Screen 1, which comes at the end of the product/process concept development stage. However, it is *not* a go/no-go evaluation point. Rather, it is a review by a mid-level group of managers (peers) drawn from the individual functional units to determine what additional information is needed before a go/no-go decision (Screen 2) can be made. If the organization uses a team structure to organize development, Screen 1 could be conducted by the cross-functional team. Screen 1 can be thought of as a "completeness" or "readiness" review rather than as a decision review. The intent is to periodically (at least quarterly, or perhaps monthly) review the status of those ideas in the concept development stage of the funnel. While not all ideas need to be reviewed every time, it is important that a time line be associated with individual ideas critical to carrying out the aggregate project plan. As part of this initial screen, ideas should be checked for their fit with technology and product market strategies, their potential role in executing the aggregate plan, and their appropriateness as an application of the firm's development resources. In addition, key areas of knowledge critical to the success of potential projects need to be identified and the way in which they will be accessed needs to be established.

When an idea is reviewed at the first screen, one of two outcomes is possible. If the idea is found to be complete, it can be moved into the mid-phase where project bounds are detailed and required knowledge is specified. If the idea is still incomplete and not ready to move on, then the specific tasks needed to complete it so it meets the requirements of Screen 1 can be agreed upon, assignments made for completing them, and the time at which it will next be reviewed (hopefully with all the steps completed) at a Screen 1 meeting established. In this way the product/process concept development stage can be completed effectively and efficiently, and the standards for moving to the next stage applied consistently.

An important aspect of the concept development phase that deserves highlighting is the role of advanced development. Typically, advanced development projects seek to push a technical idea or concept to the point where it is ready for inclusion in a commercial product or process development effort. The output of such advanced development projects—"proof of technical feasibility"—usually becomes a key kernel of knowledge or core concept for a specific product or process development project or provides a foundation for multiple projects. Thus advanced development projects occurring in the funnel prior to Screen 1 ensure that invention is clearly separated from commercialization.

Initiation of advanced development projects can result from different triggers: (a) a *function* may decide that an advanced development effort around a specific topic is important to their ongoing development efforts and success; (b) those involved at *Screen 1*, reviewing the development of a specific concept or idea, may recommend an advanced development effort as a way to answer specific questions (both technical and market-based) that need to precede a go/no-go decision; and (c) *senior executives* dealing with technology and/or product market strategy may identify the need for specific advanced development efforts in anticipation of subsequent development projects.

In order to coordinate resource requirements for such advanced development efforts and to ensure that the sequence of steps followed is appropriate to achieve the results desired, many organizations put the relevant resources and their management into the individual functions (engineering, marketing, and manufacturing). The logic is that most advanced development efforts are fairly narrowly focused (or can be subdivided and focused) and thus do not require cross-functional teams. The drawback in doing this is that since each of the functions has a number of operating responsibilities, they may put such advanced development projects on the "back burner," resulting in low priority. We have seen some firms counter this by separating out the key resources (primarily engineering) that will focus on advanced development, and having them handle only such requirements. Often firms transfer a few people from an advanced development effort to the follow-on commercial product or process development effort to facilitate effective "technology transfer" and ensure that those in the advanced development group do not get too far removed from the marketplace. Whatever the particular form of advanced development organization, the firm may need to create a screen prior to Screen 1 to identify promising advanced development ideas. This advanced development screen links choices about individual technologies to the aggregate project plan.

Besides reviewing ideas for completeness, Screen 1 carries out a second, important function. It begins to identify competing concepts, ideas that might be integrated into platform development projects, and those that might be most effectively embedded in enhancement or derivative projects. This sets the stage for the activity that is to take place between Screens 1 and 2—defining and creating the appropriate sequence and set of platform and derivative development projects. Thus, rather than making go/no-go decisions about potential projects as they naturally arise as individual ideas, the development group reshapes and recasts them to provide an appropriate set of platform and derivative projects to support and strengthen the product family and its coverage of the targeted markets. This also operationalizes the stated business and functional strategies. This mid-funnel phase links the development projects under consideration directly to the stated strategies and objectives of the business.

At Screen 2, senior management reviews product and process development options and selects those that will become development projects. Thus Screen 2 is a go/no-go decision point, and any project passing it will be funded and staffed with every expectation that it will be carried through to market introduction. That is, while subsequent project reviews and updates will be held with management once the project is underway in the narrow neck of the funnel, at Screen 2, management commits itself to fund the entire development effort or stops the potential project from going into formal development.

While the second phase of detailing the project bounds and required knowledge usually takes only one to two months, it has a very specific purpose: to take the data and information developed during Phase 1 (concept development) and put it in a form that will enable senior management to evaluate proposed projects against competing and complementary projects under consideration, the functional strategy maps, the aggregate project plan, and the available development resources. If approved, this statement of a project's bounds and the knowledge required for its completion become the starting point for Phase 3 project execution by the development team.

As Exhibit 5–6 indicates, under the Model III development funnel, for any product family, multiple projects typically would be in the execution phase simultaneously. However, those would generally consist of one, or at most two, platform projects and a handful of smaller derivative and enhancement projects. As a set, these projects would match the development resources available and appropriate for this product family and its associated markets, and have a high probability of delivering on the strategies and objectives specified for that business. Thus the real power of the Model III development funnel is derived from three sources: avoiding the problems inherent in Models I and II, folding a creative set of innovative ideas into a logical set of development projects, and ensuring those projects tie directly to the business strategies.

127

Diagnosing and Correcting Critical Issues in the Development Funnel

Shaping and managing the development funnel gives managers a tool to address a number of important issues that set the stage for success on individual development projects. The first phase in shaping the funnel involves diagnosing the characteristics, form, and underlying logic of the existing funnel.

We have found a straightforward four-step process extremely effective in guiding this analysis. The process is an audit of the organization's existing funnel that characterizes the pattern of choices the firm has made. The audit sets the stage for a diagnosis of the strengths and weaknesses as well as opportunities for improvement.

The *first step* in applying the funnel concept as a diagnostic tool is to lay out the basic dimensions of choice and the role the funnel plays in development with a diverse group of middle managers and functional contributors in the firm. These people should have direct knowledge of the firm's development practice. The *second step* is to divide the managers into a half dozen randomly composed teams who are asked to do three things:

- Identify the salient characteristics of their organization's actual development procedure
- Draw the organization's development funnel
- Present the drawing (through an overhead transparency) with the other five groups

In the teams, participants are encouraged to consider such characteristics as the sources of ideas for the firm's development projects, the way in which narrowing occurs, the possibility of inputs that arrive later on, and the likelihood of extra iterations during development. Participants should understand that their charge is to be creative and make it fun, but to capture graphically the essential characteristics of their organization's development funnel. The funnels presented in Exhibits 5–2A and 5–2B at the beginning of the chapter came out of precisely this process. The teams were made up of about seven people drawn from a variety of different parts of the medical electronics company.

After approximately 45 minutes of work, the *third step* is for the entire group to reconvene and for each team to present its "picture" and explain its essential elements. The funnels drawn by Teams 1 and 2 (see Exhibits 5–2A and B) are typical of the creativity that often comes out of this process. (One team we worked with drew a large pinball machine, labeling the blocking "bumpers" as different executives or departments;

the projects—as pinballs—get bounced around between bumpers, often repeatedly.)

The *fourth step* in using the funnel concept as a diagnostic tool is to have a discussion of the common themes that appear across characterizations of the development funnels made by the different teams. In the case of the medical electronics firm, the ideas from Teams 1 and 2 were reinforced in the five other teams that made presentations. Indeed, the breadth and depth of insight this simple exercise developed was remarkable. The drawings and the discussions revealed seven critical themes:

1. Ideas for new product and new process developments came from many sources, but tended not to be managed or guided.
2. The "start point" for development projects was ill defined; the tendency was to approve anything that looked reasonably good, put it on the "official list," and then see what happened.
3. During the development process, there were a number of bulges and subsequent constrictions—the funnel did not converge consistently or according to any set pattern. Some of the causes of these bulges included late redefinitions of products (the moving target), fuzzy definitions at the start point, mixing research (invention) with development (application), changing midstream the key participants assigned to individual projects, and making some decisions early that did not seem to stick later on.
4. A number of inputs that could occur early in the development process actually occurred quite late, requiring additional recycling and extra iterations.
5. Toward the end of a project, management added considerable heat to push for market introduction—often creating difficulties for other projects in process, and in many cases resulting in the introduction of products before they were fully ready.
6. A lot more went into the development funnel as "approved projects" than ever came out. Many projects simply seemed to die over time as a result of inattention and lack of progress. Of the products that did get out, it was much more likely that they would be part of Product Family A than B, even though the firm's stated strategy was to build rapidly its revenues and profits from Family B.
7. Subcontracted or "OEM" projects (referred to in Chapter 2 as "alliance projects") tended to come in very late in the process—thereby requiring considerable iterating to fit with other ongoing efforts in the firm, or getting introduced without such iterating and never quite fitting into the product line.

These themes had been discussed individually at one time or another in the medical electronics firm, but the funnel provided a framework in which their implications became clear. Moreover, the diagnosis identified opportunities for substantial improvement.

The four-step diagnostic exercise can, in a relatively short time, result in a fairly accurate description of a firm's development funnel and suggest where efforts for improvement might be focused. While some changes may be made fairly quickly and still have significant impact, others may require additional resources, involve basic changes in behavior, and take much longer. This suggests the need for a more systematic funnel improvement plan to be followed over a longer time horizon. Often such a plan can be built around three critical issues common across all development funnels—the roles of management, competition among projects, and the mix of projects pursued.

Managerial Roles. The first issue is the advisory and decision-making roles of senior and middle management. Having observed a variety of splits in these responsibilities, we think the only viable long-term solution is for middle management to do more of the day-to-day planning and decision making. Senior management does not have the time, patience, or inclination to run individual projects or to micromanage the development process. This they must delegate. However, senior management should set the agenda, determine the organization's focus, and provide many of the incentives and supports that enable middle management to do what is needed. People at the midlevels of the organization must create the rich set of options, ensure that they have been sufficiently explored, elaborated, and prepared for decision making, and be directly involved in executing the resulting development projects. Senior management trains, develops, and creates systems that encourage and make them capable of doing that. In organizations that have moved considerable distance in this direction, often the approval of all but the platform projects is delegated to those down in the organization.

The opportunity and need exists for senior management to use the development funnel as a vehicle in building the organization, the people, and their collective capabilities, not just to select development projects for top management approval and funding. The challenge is for top management to spend sufficient time initially, to start the organization down a path of improvement, and yet to be able to withdraw as appropriate and transfer greater responsibility for these activities and their continued improvement to those down in the organization. The placement of screens in the funnel is one way to formalize middle and senior management's key responsibilities.

Competing Projects. A second critical issue is when, where, and how competing concepts and projects should (or should not) be encouraged or even allowed. One of the places where we think such competition is good is in the initial phase of concept development, often through advanced development projects. There is frequently insufficient information early on to know which ideas will eventually gain market acceptance and dominance, and which will prove too limited or narrow for extensive application. Thus, many of the concepts under investigation in the front end of the funnel represent competing approaches for addressing similar issues or competing projects for meeting market requirements. (These need not be just competing technical solutions, but also might be competing marketing, field service, or distribution solutions as well.) Such competition should be allowed to continue until the second screen, the go/no-go decision point. Beyond that point head-to-head competition generally is inappropriate.

Once a development project is underway, it makes most sense to put all the resources on the best possible platform project and an associated set of derivative projects rather than divide them between an ad hoc set of projects. Only where extreme time pressures exist have we seen it make sense to have competing development projects in the execution phase. Where viable options do exist, an organization is best served by exploring them thoroughly prior to the development project phase, or tailoring alternative development projects toward markets that will sufficiently support those multiple efforts. That is, rather than have them be direct competitors for the same customers, it may make sense to target them at different subsegments and then, based on market results, decide which options and approach to push hardest in subsequent generations.

Project Mix. A third issue is providing a mix of development projects that builds both market position and desired development capabilities in areas where they have not existed previously. For example, this is particularly important in hardware companies which find their challenges shifting more toward software and manufacturing processes. If the vast majority of ideas and options that are in the funnel at a given point in time continue to be primarily hardware, the firm will increasingly find itself at a disadvantage as competitors increase their proportion of software and manufacturing process technology development projects. The need to increase the proportion of these types of projects is accentuated because collective knowledge about managing software and manufacturing process developments is much less than collective knowledge regarding hardware efforts. Similarly, if distribution channels are changing, a firm wants to be certain that its mix of development projects matches future distribution opportunities and needs, not just past channels. Managers can address the issue of project mix through the criteria they use to screen projects, and the process they use to make decisions.

For the thoughtful organization, diagnosing the reality of its existing development funnel, outlining the idealized model that best fits its environment, and implementing changes that will move it toward that improved funnel is an opportunity as well as a challenge. By creating and adopting procedures that build its capabilities through selection of a mix of ideas and practices that improve all three phases of the funnel, a firm is much more likely to have the capabilities and knowledge required for effective development projects than if it works only on improving individual projects and their outcomes.

CHAPTER 6

A Framework for Development

New products and processes come to the market through a process that first transforms ideas and concepts into working prototypes through detailed design and engineering, then tests and refines them, and finally prepares the product design and factories for commercial operation. The development funnel of Chapter 5 defines the way in which an organization proposes and selects concepts, and how these concepts converge to a specific product definition and design. At the other end of the spectrum of activity, day-to-day problem solving at the working level drives choices about the details of the design. Somewhere between the broad architecture of the funnel, and the details of specific tasks and problems, however, lies a whole set of choices the firm must make about the overall development process—how tasks and activities should be sequenced, how work should be organized, how the effort should be led and managed, what milestones should be established, how senior management will interact with the project, and the way problems should be framed and solved. In short, the development process as we define it in this chapter lays out the pattern or framework for development.

In trying to understand the nature and role of the development process, we have found the factory to be a useful analogy.[1] The funnel is like the layout of the factory and the basic structure of the flows of material and information within it. Like a layout diagram, the funnel does not define the detail. Instead, it establishes a higher level description of the physical structure and defines where and under what conditions material will come in and go out, what information will be collected centrally versus locally, and where and how people will be involved. It defines the architecture. The development process is more detailed and specific. From the factory perspective it is like the design of the production system, including the definition of the sequence of steps in the process and their location, the detailed information required to execute and control the process, the structure of the organization, and the definition of specific tasks the people will carry out. Within that framework, day-to-day work is done, problems are solved, products are produced, and projects are executed.

Like an outstanding factory, an outstanding development organization requires a coherent architecture and process that is well understood, highly capable, and in control. Too often our studies have uncovered businesses that regularly do development without an effective process. In some companies the process is so poorly understood that almost everything is implicit and subject to change within a project; there is, in effect, no process. In other companies there are so many detailed procedures and rules (many of which were devised to fix a long-forgotten problem) that no one understands or can keep track of them all. The process that exists on paper is so bureaucratic that those who follow it proceed slowly, if at all. Others regularly ignore the system, leading to confusion, rework, and delay.

Much like the infrastructure of a factory or a manufacturing organization, the detailed framework of development can have a powerful impact on performance. Creating that kind of capability, however, is not merely a functional detail. It requires senior management's focused effort and attention. The purpose of this chapter is to provide senior managers with a framework for thinking about and meeting that challenge. In the next section we outline critical dimensions of the development process and suggest the range of choices firms face. We then work through a detailed example that illustrates problems that arise when the process is not capable and in control. In the following section we examine four different "models" of the development process in practice at four companies. These models help to define the choices senior managers confront and the way in which those choices create development capability and influence performance on individual projects. The chapter concludes with brief observations on the basic principles that seem to govern effective development processes.

EXHIBIT 6–1

Basic Elements of a Project Management Framework*

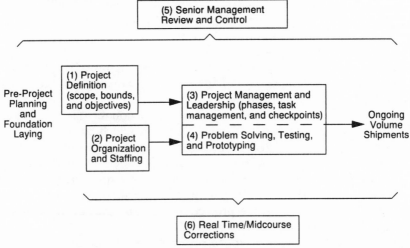

* Either implicitly or explicitly, every organization must make choices regarding these six elements in carrying out product development activities. Generally, elements (1) through (5) are considered part of the project management procedures of the organization, while element (6) is addressed on an as-needed basis.

Basic Elements of the Framework

The development process is a complex set of activities that extends over a considerable time period. As a starting point for understanding that complexity and identifying the critical choices for senior management, the six-element framework presented in Exhibit 6–1 is quite useful. Although the six elements interact to create a detailed pattern of development, they involve somewhat different issues and, at least initially, need to be understood on their own terms. Thus, before we explore how they interact, we consider the dimensions individually.

1. *Project definition.* This first element determines how the firm sets the scope of the development project, establishes the bounds for what is and is not included in it, and defines the business purposes and objectives of the project. Activities such as initial concept development, defining and scoping the project effort, obtaining both internal and external preliminary inputs, and selling the project to senior management and the entire organization are part of this element. The best indication of its completion is generally the official authorization

135

of the project and its associated goals, objectives, and resource commitments.

2. *Project organization and staffing.* This element defines who will work on the project and how they will organize to accomplish the work. Issues such as physical location, reporting relationships, the nature of individual responsibilities, specialized training and hiring, and the relationship to and use of support groups are items to be resolved as part of this basic element. Chapter 8, on organizing project teams, addresses this element in depth.

3. *Project management and leadership.* This dimension includes the nature and role of project leaders and the way in which project tasks are sequenced and managed. Choosing the type of individual given responsibility for program coordination and leadership, defining continuity in that assignment, and establishing expectations for how project roles and responsibilities will be executed are crucial to the mode of leadership on the project. The second part of this element includes the way in which tasks are divided and grouped into phases, how the work in each of those phases is monitored and managed, and the checkpoints or milestones used to signal completion of each phase.

4. *Problem solving, testing, and prototyping.* As indicated in Exhibit 6–1, this element is closely intertwined with the preceding one. However the focus here is on individual work steps, the way in which they are conducted, and the means by which the knowledge required to solve problems is developed. Central to this element is the nature of problem solving (involving both technical and managerial considerations) and the way in which testing and prototyping are used to validate progress to date, confirm the appropriateness of choices already made, and focus the project effort on the remaining tasks. This element, in combination with the preceding one of project management and leadership, largely determines the rate at which the project converges to a final, manufacturable solution ready for market introduction. We explore these issues in more detail in Chapters 7 and 10.

5. *Senior management review and control.* While senior managers do not directly perform specific tasks, their role in a project and the nature of their interaction with the project team (and project leader) is an important element of the overall framework. The way in which senior management reviews, evaluates, and modifies the project and its goals over time signals to those working on the project the degree to which responsibility has been delegated to them, and creates powerful incentives and motivation—some positive and some negative—during the course of the project. Seemingly routine patterns, such as the timing, frequency, and format of reviews, can have a significant impact on the overall effectiveness of the project.

6. *Real-time/midcourse corrections.* The ambiguity and uncertainty associated with any product or process development effort often makes feedback and revisions during the course of the project a necessity. This element deals with issues such as ongoing measurement and evaluation of project status, rescheduling, resequencing, and redefining the remaining tasks, resolving differences between problem solving in the lab and on the customer site, and determining when the organization is ready for production scale-up. Perhaps more subtle but also an important part of this element is the balance between early conflict resolution and subsequent adaptability, the relationship between unexpected early challenges and subsequent potential delays, and choices between deferring rescheduling to maintain motivation versus rescheduling early to maintain project credibility.

These six elements are like the components of a product. To work well, a product or development process needs components that function effectively. From the standpoint of development, this implies that the organization must have an effective way of defining products, must understand and appropriately deploy the mechanisms and tools for problem solving, and must understand and effectively deal with the issues involved in senior management review and control. All of this requires a depth of understanding of the individual elements. But like good components on a product, a good understanding of the elements is only part of the story. The elements must also fit well together in order to create a coherent system, and the system must be well matched to the development challenges it faces.

The experience of Medical Electronics Inc. (a manufacturer of medical instruments used in hospitals) in the development of the MEI 2010 illustrates the way the elements of the framework interact, and highlights the critical choices firms face in creating an effective development system. We have found the MEI case to be representative of the problems many firms confront in responding to the competitive imperatives for speed, productivity, and higher quality products. While there are always unique aspects in any case, the MEI experience provides a useful and relatively general context for our discussion of the principles that underlie effective development processes.[2]

The Framework for Development at Medical Electronics Incorporated

In January 1991, MEI introduced to the marketplace its portable, premature infant heart monitoring machine, the MEI 2010. While senior management was generally satisfied with the 2010 product, they were disappointed in the project management approach, particularly its inability to deliver the product on time and within budget. (The original date for market introduction had been the fall of 1989, fifteen months earlier than the actual introduction date. The overrun of the original budget had been $750,000.) This project provided an opportunity for management to use the basic elements of the development process framework to assess its approach and the connections between that approach and project results.

Background on the 2010 Portable Heart Monitoring Development Project

The development of the 2010, a unit with special capabilities for premature infant monitoring, brought together, in late 1984, several ideas that had been discussed in the organization over the preceding eighteen-to-twenty-month period. As one of the 2010 team members recalled, "This project had much more natural momentum than projects in diagnostics that MEI pursued during the same period. The organization knew how to deal with heart monitoring efforts—the main line of the business—much better than it knew how to deal with diagnostic products." While MEI's stated strategy at that time was to become a significant participant in diagnostics, a monitoring project like the 2010 seemed to go through the approval process with relative ease; in fact, if anything, the approval of the 2010 may have been too informal and too easy.

While the 2010 did not involve any radical new technologies, it was clear that it pushed the application software and graphics presentation toward more sophistication and complexity. It also involved the application of new sensor technology in the way in which sensors would be attached to the patient. Finally, both the electrical and mechanical requirements represented natural extensions of existing capabilities as the designers attempted to make this product more compact, portable, and usable in the hospital environment than existing MEI monitoring products.

A review of the stages of development used on the 2010 revealed five phases (see Exhibit 6–2 for a time line):

  I. Concept development
 II. Engineering prototyping
III. Production prototyping
 IV. Market acceptance testing
  V. Market introduction

EXHIBIT 6–2

MEI 2010 Project Time Line (Actual and Original Plan)*

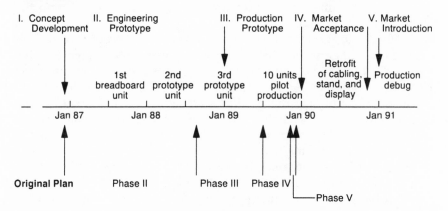

Actual Results

I. Concept Development | II. Engineering Prototype | III. Production Prototype | IV. Market Acceptance | V. Market Introduction

1st breadboard unit | 2nd prototype unit | 3rd prototype unit | 10 units pilot production | Retrofit of cabling, stand, and display | Production debug

Jan 87 | Jan 88 | Jan 89 | Jan 90 | Jan 91

Original Plan | Phase II | Phase III | Phase IV | Phase V

NOTE: Arrows indicate transition points between phases.

* This project time line outlines the planned and actual phases of the MEI 2010 project and the major prototype cycles. It makes clear that the project took longer than planned in each individual phase, making its market introduction over a year late.

These phases provide a convenient way of summarizing the history of the project. Interviews with the key functional heads, project participants, and senior management identified the salient developments.

Phase I—Concept Development. In the fall of 1984, there was no shortage of ideas regarding new product development opportunities and possible new features for existing MEI products. The issue was deciding which ideas and features to pursue, and through which projects. In the case of the 2010, the basic concept, focused on the premature infant segment, could be traced to a series of discussions between an electrical design engineer and a marketing specialist. However, several of the features (sensors, software, and data presentation graphics) came from other ideas that had been in the organization for many months, and in some cases even years. People recalled that there was a somewhat informal convergence process, during which time the ideas eventually coalesced to become the basic concept for the 2010 product. On this project the electrical design engineer involved in the original discussions became the champion within the design engineering group, convincing others that this project was a better and more challenging opportunity for the company to pursue than many of the other concepts on the drawing boards.

139

While there was ongoing discussion within marketing regarding the 2010 concept, the primary initial focus and emphasis came from the engineering disciplines. Once a marketing specialist grabbed the idea, however, it became much easier for the engineers to get it onto the "active list" of projects.

On the 2010, the transition from an idea or a concept to a specific project was rather fuzzy. The vice president of engineering recalled that at one of the executive staff meetings, he put the idea for such a product clearly on the table. As he explained the idea, the executive group warmed to it and saw the product's advantages and market growth opportunity. Within a relatively few weeks, the executive staff became solid backers of the 2010 portable heart monitoring machine targeted at the premature infant market.

A review of corporate records indicated that the project received formal budget approval (a head-count allocation for project management, a capital budget, an accounting reference number, and a target market introduction date of Fall 1989) in late 1986. While no formal written proposal could be located in early 1991, the project did appear in the 1987 business plan, prepared during the fall of 1986. By the spring of 1987, the project began to show up fairly regularly on the agenda of the monthly project reviews. (These sessions were held on the first Monday afternoon of each month and were attended by all executive staff members in town on that day—generally 80 percent of the senior management were in attendance.) Each of the "active projects" was reviewed by its project leader, in most cases a manager out of the function currently in charge of the project. (Generally project leadership passed from marketing during the formal concept approval phase to engineering during the second phase, to production during the third phase, and then back to marketing in the fourth and fifth phases.)

Phase II—Engineering Prototype. As recalled by the design engineering manager given responsibility for the 2010 project in this phase:

> We had already been doing some concept investigation and problem solving when the project received formal approval. However, within a couple of weeks of when the budget was put in place, I was appointed the engineering team leader and given three or four additional engineers who, during this phase, spent the bulk of their time on this project. I had responsibility for three other projects at the same time, but spent about 40 percent of my effort on the 2010.

In addition to responsibility for the engineering phase of four different projects, the engineering manager assigned to the 2010 also had his normal functional duties as head of the electrical engineering subgroup. Since all but one of the engineers largely dedicated to the project at this phase were electrical engineers, it was easy for him to manage them as part of his normal duties. One of the engineers, however, was a mechanical engineer, and the electrical engineering manager found working and communicating with that person somewhat more troublesome, since that mechanical engineer got his individual task assignments from the manager of the mechanical engineering subfunction.

Others in engineering recalled that the team working on the project (beyond the three or four largely dedicated engineers) was only loosely specified. This was partly a result of the basic structure of engineering at MEI, which grouped people by subfunction specialty (mechanical, electrical, software, sensors, and test), and partly because there were so many projects going on at the same time. When the 2010 moved into the engineering prototype phase, there were already fifteen to twenty projects being worked on by an engineering staff of approximately thirty-eight people spread across the five subfunctions.

By late 1987 the design engineering group had produced the first MEI prototype, albeit in a rough "breadboard" form. At that point the project became much more "real" because marketing could then "touch and feel" the concept. However, it was not until the spring of 1988—when the second engineering prototype was developed—that marketing had something solid enough to show to customers. Marketing then organized a customer focus group to help refine the desired features and the way in which they should be presented. As the product line manager for heart monitoring products recalled, "We would pass on comments and reactions to the engineers in an informal way, but since they still had numerous issues to work out before the completion of the engineering phase, we didn't really get all that involved."

Because of the strong functional and subfunctional organization at MEI, the first step in getting the work done in the engineering (or any other) phase was to decompose it into the tasks that could be done by a single function. Each of the subfunctions was then assumed to "know" how to do its assigned tasks, and project management did not seek to alter or influence those normal patterns of problem solving and task execution in any significant way.

In a very real sense, the 2010 project ebbed and flowed during this phase depending on the complexity of the issues that arose, what else the engineers were working on (competing projects), and the degree to which the monthly executive staff reviews shifted priorities on this and other projects. Fortunately the 2010 was considered relatively important throughout its duration, and did not face the major problems of rotating resources (other than the normal promotions for traditional career pathing) that many other projects did. However, 1987 and early 1988 were periods of growth for the company and a number of new people were being hired. When assigned to do engineering subtasks on the 2010, these new people often suggested new possibilities and ideas for exploration. As one senior engineer recalled, "On several occasions those new people went down paths that some of us could have told them would be futile. Unfortunately such explorations often lasted several months until the new person discovered the futility themselves, or until it happened to come to the attention of one of the more senior engineers on the project."

By late 1988, the 2010 had completed its third (or possibly fourth—it was difficult to tell) prototype cycle and was at a point where engineering felt they had validated the engineering design. At that point the project was "transferred" to production for their detailed definition of any production process changes that might be required in the factory.

Phase III—Production Prototype. In late 1988, manufacturing was brought into the process of development on the MEI 2010 in a serious way. While they had attended an occasional review session prior to that time, their policy was to wait for the validated engineering design before they began outlining production tasks, developing a detailed materials list, creating a vendor plan, and working jointly with engineering on factory test procedures. In early 1989, following a detailed review of the third engineering prototype, manufacturing outlined a work plan for this phase, the stated goal of which was "Produce a pilot batch of ten units and turn them over to quality assurance for market acceptance testing by 15 July 1989." Although the vice president of manufacturing took general responsibility for this third phase, there was one manufacturing engineer (an industrial engineer by training) who spent much of her time on the 2010 during this period. It was her effort that kept the project moving along.

Unfortunately, a number of changes in the vendor base, resulting from an ongoing vendor consolidation and improvement effort, as well as a number of requirements for tighter tolerances and improved process capabilities (much more demanding than those originally anticipated on the part of manufacturing) delayed pilot production until October 1989. The ten units produced in the pilot run consisted of only 75 percent "production vendor" supplied parts, because the remaining vendors were not able to produce the parts as quickly as needed. Thus a quarter of the parts in the ten pilot units were custom-built by local job shops and MEI's own production operations in order to get the pilot units done more quickly. The pilot units finally were turned over to quality assurance for the next phase in November 1989.

Phase IV—Market Acceptance. On the MEI 2010, as with any new MEI product, the market acceptance phase sought to validate the product and the ability of the user to achieve the desired performance in a consistent manner. This required a wide range of testing and approval processes, with the marketing manager overseeing those involving the customer, and the quality assurance (QA) manager overseeing those involving technical issues such as getting approval from the underwriter's lab (on electrical standards), the FCC (on electrical fields generated by the product), and often the FDA (on health efficacy issues). The quality assurance group also handled all clinical evaluation of the products. On the 2010, QA developed a market acceptance test plan during December of 1989. The ten units from the pilot production run were used to carry out this test plan, including life testing, government approval testing, and testing early prototypes with customers (i.e., beta site testing).

Because the project was already running late, the normal six to nine months allowed for execution of the market test plan was cut to four months. All market testing was to be completed by 1 May 1990. While there were no major delays in government approval over the next few months, the beta tests with customer sites revealed the need for some redesign of the stand on which the portable unit was mounted, the cabling used to connect some subelements of the product, and the data display device incorporated into the basic 2010 system. The first two changes were fairly minor, and by early April the parts had been redesigned, the material needed for the ten pilot units had been procured, and a retrofit had been made to each of the units.

The issue with the data display device was much more troublesome. Basically, customers found the display difficult to read and considered it of distinctly lower quality than the rest of the 2010 system. After considerable debate between marketing and engineering (because the higher quality alternative display device would raise material cost by $120 per unit and thus final system list price close to $500), it was decided in May 1989 that the higher priced display should be incorporated. This required procuring ten units of that display, adjusting the cabling, software, and other items required for it to interface smoothly with the rest of the system, and then getting customer reactions to the newly upgraded system. Work was rushed through but still not completed until October 1990.

By the fall of 1990, senior management was extremely anxious about market introduction of the 2010. While the original target introduction date had been fall 1989, in May 1990, when the handful of required changes had been identified by marketing and QA, management had set a firm target of September 1990 for introduction. Unfortunately, the delays with the display device made that unattainable. As a result the company did less testing of the 2010 on the customers' premises than originally planned. Quality assurance agreed reluctantly that they had originally set extremely high standards for product release with regard

143

to government-mandated and functional performance requirements, and that the necessary standards had been met. However, no standards had been explored and developed thoroughly with regard to customer preferences for ease of use or the field service department's requirements for serviceability. In fact, the areas of testing that were cut back generally related to ease of use and serviceability issues.

Phase V—Market Introduction. By maintaining pressure during the redesigns of Phase IV (a time when senior management also made a few changes of its own to the design), the 2010 project received top priority. However, while the market introduction phase was normally planned to take a couple of months, for the 2010, it took from 1 November to 15 January, and even that was a real stretch. Manufacturing found that it had to go back and debug some of the materials coming from the 25 percent of the vendor base who had not participated on the pilot units. A stream of engineering change orders were still in-process in mid January 1991, but marketing and manufacturing, under pressure from senior management (who wanted to show shipped units of the product in the fiscal year ending 31 January 1991), approved shipment of the first five units on 15 January. These units went to some of the firm's best customers, who themselves were anxious to receive the product they had heard so much about.

Within a few weeks, however, MEI discovered that these "best customers" also turned out to be "heavy users" of the 2010, in part because its features were so superior to other infant heart monitoring products available in their hospitals. Though these early customers were extremely pleased with the features on the machine and its ability to meet their demanding functional requirements, they soon discovered that its ease of use was not nearly as great as they had anticipated. One problem not caught earlier was the stress put on the wheels of the unit's stand. It was discovered (through field failures) that when the units were pushed into an elevator misaligned with the hallway floor, the wheels tended to crack and break off. One reason this was not caught earlier was that, because the performance at the beta test sites was so outstanding, those customers had left the units in their prenatal intensive care wings and not moved them between floors. Within the first month after market introduction, the initial handful of units required almost a quarter of their wheels to be replaced. A "crash" redesign of the wheels was then instituted, but it took another few months before the problem was resolved and the new wheels installed. This put additional stress on field service, which, combined with its normal workload, fell far behind.

A number of other small problems (most of which could have been alleviated by more thorough testing) also emerged during the first quarter of 1991. These included: small bugs in the software, occasional failures of a connector (due to a vendor problem), and difficulty on the part of sales due to a lack of training on how to figure out exactly which options a specific customer would find most useful. Thus there were a number of additional demands placed on service, including the swapping of some options once a unit was in place in the field. In April 1991 senior management hoped that all of these problems were solidly behind them, but lamented the fact that their major competitor had recently introduced a premature infant monitoring device. Though MEI's engineers considered the competitor's features not nearly as good as those on the 2010, the competitor's product seemed much easier to use in practice than their own unit.

The Development Framework at MEI

Although some of the problems in the development of the MEI 2010 were peculiar to that product, many were rooted in the company's basic framework for new product development. Exhibit 6–3 summarizes the characteristics of MEI's development framework along the six dimensions developed earlier in the chapter. The exhibit also highlights the issues those characteristics raise for designing an effective development process.

The above summary of MEI's development framework underscores the difficulty this organization has in developing a product such as the 2010 where time is of the essence, engineers need to work new features and new technology into a coherent, integrated system, and where the product functions in a complex customer environment. All of this argues for a development framework that brings a broad, system perspective to the process and facilitates cross-functional integration. As the exhibit makes clear, however, MEI's process was narrow, functionally oriented, sequential, ad hoc, and largely undisciplined. Consider how these themes play out in each of the dimensions of the framework:

Project Definition. The tone for development at MEI is set at the very outset of the process. Project definition is not managed; it follows its "natural course." Actions to define a project are a response (reaction) to a mounting groundswell and set of pressures brought to bear by the external marketplace and competitors, and finally recognized by a sufficient number of MEI marketers, designers, and managers. The result is that project definition is slow, unsystematic and haphazard. It is ad hoc and responds to individual personalities and their preferences rather than strategic business purposes. Even at the point of formal project approval, the scope of the 2010 was still quite fuzzy. Although project performance objectives regarding market introduction date and approximate resource requirements had been set, no specific quality or perfor-

Exhibit 6–3

The Development Framework at Medical Electronics Inc.

Element of the Framework	MEI Characteristics	Issues
Pre-Project/Project Definition	Reactive process; ad hoc sequence of actions; stops and starts	Achieving focus, direction, and definition without missing opportunities or styling creativity
Project Organization	Engineering focus; part-time – job shop; frequent movement of people	Creating ownership and commitment on team; achieving continuity in the face of promotion and staffing needs; business as opposed to functional team
Project Leadership/ Management	Leadership shifts by phase; sequence of phases only loosely coordinated; baton passing	Building strong leadership across the phases; establishing tight communication linkages, clear interaction between phases
Prototype/Testing	Narrow focus on functional problems; sequential problem solving	Achieving integrated problem solving; using prototyping cycles to surface broader issues that cut across disciplines
Senior Management Review and Control	Monthly meeting; reactive fire fighting; late involvement; resource reallocation	Bringing senior management direction to bear early; developing the appropriate role during the project
Real-Time Adjustments	Narrow focus on immediate problems; informal, incomplete communication; problems handled through ad hoc changes to normal process	Creating discipline; capability for early resolution of conflicts; low-level, rapid problem solving

mance objectives for the resulting product were established at that point. Even the preliminary market introduction date was set based on senior management's sense of what the market "needed," without considering any detailed work plan of what could be delivered and when.

Project Organization and Staffing. In many respects, the 2010 project was initially an engineering effort, not a comprehensive business effort. In fact, it was not until late 1988—almost a year and a half after formal project approval—that other functions began to be involved actively on an ongoing basis. During the engineering and prototyping phase, a small group of electrical engineers worked on the design of the 2010 and its various subsystems. While the core group of engineers was largely full-time, many of the other subfunction specialties (mechanical engineering, software design, sensors, and test) shared their time on the 2010 with assignments on four or five other projects. They would work periodically on the 2010, pass their work on to others, and turn their attention to another project.

146

There was also a lack of continuity in project assignments. For example, a software engineer who might work on one piece of the 2010 development would not necessarily be the same software engineer who, a few months later, worked on another piece of the project. Stability and focus in project organization and staffing thus was secondary to the firm's traditional functional and subfunctional organization structure and to the career paths and promotion policies of the functional organization. While the project appeared to be a "team" on paper, people on those assignments were neither dedicated, co-located, nor equally focused on their efforts throughout the project's duration. In essence, the project's center of gravity moved from one function to another as it proceeded through the various phases.

As with project definition, the pattern of choices found at MEI in project organization and staffing are similar to those observed in many firms—projects are an exception to the normal functional organization, and are expected and forced to adapt and accommodate to the ongoing functional structure in many subtle but important ways. It is no surprise that while personal pride may lead individual contributors to exhibit a fair level of ownership and commitment in their activities on the project, there tends to be little "team commitment." Individual contributors consider themselves to have been very effective and successful if they perform their individual tasks well. They do not, to any significant extent, judge their success and contribution in terms of overall project success.

Project Management and Leadership. Leadership in the 2010 project (and in most MEI projects) followed the same pattern as the functional center of gravity. As the projects move forward, managers in engineering, manufacturing, and marketing "pass the baton" of responsibility for project supervision. Furthermore, managers have a normal set of functional duties (such as the head of the electrical engineering group responsible during Phase II on the 2010) and often supervise three or four projects at a time. Thus any project has to compete for the time and attention of the project manager on a day-to-day basis.

This pattern is a particular problem in marketing. The product marketing person, who has a leadership responsiblity in Phases I, IV, and V (definition, acceptance, and introduction), typically is not the same person throughout. The pattern of marketing career paths at MEI has been such that product managers are people on a "fast track" that involves going back and forth between sales and sales management, and marketing and product management, with at most twelve to eighteen months in each position. Since most projects—like the 2010—spend eighteen moths or more in Phases II and III combined, it is seldom the case that the same product market manager works on Phase I (product definition) and Phases IV and V (market acceptance and market introduction). With project definition as fuzzy as it is, this means that many of the refinements and redesign iterations in Phase IV can be driven largely by the product market manager's personal preferences and experiences, rather than fundamental strategic choices that were made in the product definition phase.

The shifting pattern of leadership is connected to the way MEI breaks the project into phases and how phase completion is recognized. Each phase has a functional orientation, and the criteria for deciding whether a phase is complete are relatively narrow. In the case of the 2010, senior management marks the completion of concept definition by creating a project account number, allocating resources in the annual plan, and adding the project to the "active list." The engineering and production prototype phases end when physical units meet certain minimum requirements. The completion of market acceptance comes with a sign-off on the design by quality assurance and product marketing. While these phases and their transition points are logical and appropriate at a macro level, they provide little guidance for the ongoing, day-to-day work being done on the project. Thus it is as though the project work goes on in the middle of a forest, and only occasionally (every six to eighteen months) does the project rise above that forest—at the time of one of those transitions—and become visible to other parts of the organization.

The concept of exercising consistent management and leadership across all of the activities required for project success is foreign to MEI's development process. Rather, there are a sequence of major phases, each of which is loosely coordinated and directed within itself, but never connected to other phases. Seldom are the issues, problems, and choices in one phase directly communicated, linked, and correlated to those in another; instead, the information transfer between phases tends to be a one-shot, batch exchange from those just completing the preceding phase to those who will take responsiblity for the next.

Problem Solving, Testing, and Prototyping. With each phase focused on a narrow objective and led by a different function, it is not surprising that testing, prototyping, and verification within each phase of the 2010 was focused largely on resolving that function's issues, not working to solve cross-functional issues. Thus the nature of problem solving during the project was to solve technical problems in the engineering phase; to solve manufacturing problems in the production phase; and to solve performance and use problems in the market acceptance phase. The early prototypes did not represent total solutions (cutting across functions) for the 2010 development effort, but rather represented functional solutions. Conceptually, the sequential nature of the phases assumed that the "downstream" functions would be able to solve their problems and issues within the set of constraints and choices specified by the "upstream" functions. This was not always possible on the 2010. Many of the engineering redesigns required in the production prototype phase, and even more so in the market acceptance phase, required taking the project back through the original sequence of functions. However, with the time pressures that existed at that point, the tendency was to be very narrow and focused in those late cycles, rather than broad and integrative.

This functional decomposition approach to problem solving, testing, and prototyping is the one most commonly observed in engineering-driven firms. Unfortunately, it suffers in two major respects. First is that functional problem solving invariably proves to be suboptimal, requiring additional cycles late in the project when changes are costly and when expediency is likely to dictate compromises on performance and product quality that would not have been made had those same issues been raised and addressed much earlier. Thus the degree of integrity and integration in the final product or process suffers as a consequence.

The second problem is lost opportunity. Prototyping cycles offer a wonderful opportunity to bring together the various functions, determine the degree of progress made to date, and consider how alternative solutions might play together, at an intermediate stage. In essence, prototyping can be an important vehicle for cross-functional discussion, problem solving, and integration. However, all too often in the MEI case, the very structure of the phases and responsibility for them made it almost impossible for prototyping to be a major vehicle in achieving integration.

Senior Management Review and Control. At MEI, senior management's primary means of reviewing and controlling development projects was the monthly meeting where the executive staff would review all of the "active projects." With as many as fifteen to twenty projects on the active list, these monthly meetings tended to focus on the handful of projects that were already late in moving from one phase to another or had become bogged down in solving specific problems. In essence, management's role was after-the-fact tracking early in a project and then fire fighting, pressuring and shifting priorities later on. Such reactive demands consumed senior management's available "development attention" and prevented it from guiding and shaping proactively early on in individual projects when the leverage from such involvement would have been greatest (see Figure 2–3, Chapter 2), and when some of the the later problems could have been avoided.

The upshot of using a monthly meeting as the primary review mechanism is that senior management focuses on the wrong problems. But even the problems they do address suffer as a result. First, monthly reviews are only rarely associated with major events in the project itself.

Thus it is extremely difficult for senior management to assess just what progress had been made since the prior month, and whether or not the project is truly on track, unless it is in serious trouble. Senior management tries to manage against the calendar rather than against key events in the project itself. Furthermore, senior management does not (and cannot) take sufficient time in the monthly meetings to delve into the details of each project and connect what is happening currently with the issues likely to arise two, three, or even six months in the future as a consequence of current activities. Finally, as a result of these characteristics, the primary lever that senior management has for affecting ongoing project performance and progress is resource allocation. But that creates a vicious cycle: senior management responds to problems by reprioritizing projects and moving key resources to the current crisis. Inevitably, this "robbing Peter to pay Paul" ensures that other projects subsequently will suffer the same fate because their key resources have been removed prematurely.

Real-Time/Midcourse Corrections. With a fuzzy project definition and limited cross-functional communication, unexpected problems occurred repeatedly and real-time adjustments in design and market plans became a significant proportion of the total development effort. The pattern for addressing such unanticipated issues on the 2010 reflected the approach to problem solving in general: postpone the cross-functional aspects until a subsequent phase and deal with the immediate issues from the perspective of the function in charge of the current phase. Subsequently, functions could claim: "I did my job. This problem is not my fault. While I'm willing to help out, it's not my responsibility." In essence, conflicts and difficult issues that arose within the function were addressed narrowly and those that involved downstream functions were postponed and left for later resolution. Late in the project, when conflicts and issues arose requiring input from upstream functions, little would happen until there was sufficient management awareness of the problem that upstream resources would be reprioritized and focused on the issue.

The structure of such real-time conflict resolution at MEI was further compounded by the tendency to communicate informally and often incompletely. Because the finished prototype or pilot unit was the primary means for information transfer between functions, the downstream group generally did not fully understand and appreciate the explorations, deliberations, and choices made by upstream groups. The converse was also true. Thus, even though marketing organized focus groups during the concept definition phase, many of the recommendations coming out of them fell on deaf ears during the engineering prototype and production pilot phases, only to resurface in the market acceptance phase.

Problems with real-time adjustments were compounded by time pressures. Projects at MEI tended to go longer than originally anticipated—and well beyond the date set originally by senior management—so that engineers and marketers found themselves under severe time deadlines in the final phases. This created pressure to cut corners and skip steps in order to avoid further delays. On the 2010, engineers hoped to make up lost time by using nonproduction vendor parts for a quarter of the items going into the pilot units. The reality, however, was that cutting this corner resulted in more expensive changes later on and a deterioration in the product's design and manufacturing quality and its market impact. As with much of the development process at MEI, real-time adjustments were characterized by an absence of discipline, an absence of early conflict resolution, and an absence of low level cross-functional problem solving.

Applying the Development Framework: Comparing Four Approaches

The MEI experience suggests several issues that firms confront in designing and implementing an effective development process. We present these issues in the third column of Exhibit 6–3. Like much of what we see in product and process development, some of the issues reflect conflicting requirements: the need for focus and direction and yet creativity; the need for strong functional expertise and yet tight integration across functions. Some issues, such as strong leadership across the phases, cut against the grain of the career paths, staffing patterns, and promotion practices of the "regular" organization. MEI tried to deal with these issues through the mechanisms in its development process, but had difficulty breaking out of its narrow, functional approach. Taken individually, the general mechanisms MEI used—the "active list," budgets, approvals, phases, a project team, prototyping, and monthly reviews—could be part of an effective process. The way MEI combined them to form an overall pattern and framework, however, was ineffective in meeting the need for speed, productivity, and quality.

But there are many firms that have confronted this problem and developed far more effective processes than the one we saw at MEI. In this part of the chapter we examine four approaches to effective development and compare them in terms of our six-dimension framework. The four development frameworks come from Kodak, GE, Motorola, and Lockheed and are briefly summarized in Exhibit 6–4, which is divided into two parts. We first provide an overview of the framework in each company, including a characterization of the dominant orientation of the framework, the primary mechanisms used, and an example of the

Exhibit 6—4

Representative Approaches to Project Management

A. Overview	Kodak	General Electric	Motorola	Lockheed Skunkworks
Company's Characterization of the Process	Phases & Gates (Manufacturability Assurance Process — MAP)	Tollgate Process (see Figure 5–4)	Contract-Driven Cross-Functional Teams	Tiger Team
Dominant Characteristics	Strong functional orientation with discipline and focus in the process	Functional orientation, but cross-functional phases and a project team to achieve integration	Team focus with functional support and clear links to senior management	Fully dedicated team with control over resources and process
Key Mechanisms	Phases, gates; customer mission statement; gatekeepers	Tollgates; project manager; senior management review at milestones; cross-functional phases	Dedicated core team; general manager as project leader; the contract; senior management sponsor	Dedicated support resources; co-location; full budget authority; leader as CEO; small, hand-picked team
Major Phases in a Development Project	*6 phases* I. Customer mission/vision II. Technical demonstration III. Technical/operational feasibility IV. Capability demonstration V. Product/process design VI. Acceptance and production	*10 phases* (defined by reviews) I. Customer needs II. Concept III. Feasibility IV. Preliminary design V. Final design VI. Critical producibility VII. Market/field test VIII. Manufacturing feasibility IX. Market readiness X. Market introduction follow-up	*4+ phases* I. Product definition II. Contract development III. Development through manufacturing start-up (team defines subphases) IV. Program wrap-up (learning)	*Nonstandard* (team specifies major milestones and review procedures for those)
Dominant Type of Project	Manufacturing process; projects where technical advancement is paramount	Evolutions, enhancements, and incremental improvements; technical solutions important but balance across functions crucial; some emphasis on speed	Platform/next-generation; system solution crucial; environment turbulent; speed critical	Breakthrough projects; high risk; experimental efforts
Typical Project Duration	24–40 months	24–48 months	18–30 months	24–60 months

152

	Kodak	General Electric	Motorola	Lockheed Skunkworks
Primary Performance Drivers	a. Resource utilization b. Technical advancement	a. Risk management b. Resource utilization	a. System solution b. Speed	a. Technical performance b. Speed
B. Basic Framework Elements				
1. Project Definition	Ideas initiated from many sources; Initial funding can come from any function; "Definition" reflects funding source.	Initial phase is market need definition; Ideas initiated from many sources; Marketing must approve need/opportunity.	Phase I — "Blitz" product definition (7-day limit); Cross-functional; Colocated during definition.	Concept champion emerges (usually a technically trained general manager); Senior management agrees in principle on strategic opportunity; Team details the concept definition.
2. Project Organization and Staffing	Functions control their phase(s) of project; Functions assign people as needed; Work is done by a functional subgroup; Some overlap of R&D/engineering in Phase IV.	Representatives from each function assigned to the team at outset; Team members serve as functional liaisons; Detailed work done in the functions by staff assigned by the functional manager.	Job postings for cross-functional, dedicated/co-located core team; Part-time support groups; Core team responsible for development procedures (within broad corporate guidelines).	Project champion hand picks the team; Team relatively small, people have broad assignments; Most important support people also dedicated and co-located; Other support work subcontracted; Team develops own procedures without constraints.
3. Project Management and Leadership	Shifts from marketing (Phase I) to R&D (Phases II–IV) to engineering (Phases IV–V) to quality assurance and marketing (Phase VI); At phase transitions, a gatekeeper (upstream) releases project, and a stakeholder (downstream) accepts the project.	Program manager maintains schedule, follows up between reviews, facilitates transitions between functions; Functional managers direct the project work done by their people.	Full-time, general manager project head; Core team reports to project head; Project head is concept champion and allocates resources within the project.	Project leader is in charge — CEO of the effort; Does own hiring, training, and evaluation; Manages all aspects; Often creates an entire business unit.

153

B. Basic Framework Elements (continued)	Kodak	General Electric	Motorola	Lockheed Skunkworks
4. Problem Solving, Testing, and Prototyping	Problem solving and prototyping done largely within the functions; Many specialized test and prototype groups used as subcontractors; Quality assurance does primary testing in Phases V–VI.	Problem solving done largely within single functions; Cross-functional issues raised in reviews and later prototypes; Testing and prototyping done by specialized support groups.	Cross-functional is dominant; Prototypes are project tests, not functional tests; Substantial testing to verify 10X progress.	Cross-functional, but early phases dominated by technical concerns; Emphasis on technical performance on critical dimensions; Engineers work directly with key customer(s) and do own prototypes.
5. Senior Management Review and Control	Senior functional manager does most reviews (their resources and funds); Senior, cross-functional advisory groups used on special issues (e.g., environmental) or to achieve special coordination (e.g., international).	Occurs at key reviews; Strict criteria defined to move to next phase; Emphasis on identifying and managing risks; Management "signs" approval at each tollgate.	Senior management as sponsor and coach; Reviews tied to key project events; Manage to team "contract"; Sponsor is focal point for others on executive staff.	Periodic one-on-one between project leader and corporate top manager; Limited formal reviews, but may hold "communication" exchanges; Senior management sets aggregate resource limits; Team is largely on its own.
6. Real Time/ Midcourse Corrections	Done primarily within single functions; Send projects back to an earlier phase if major problem identified later; Major transition from R&D to engineering (technical feasibility to commercialization).	Senior management involvement in conflict resolution; In concept, vary resources and time line in response to problems; Can halt project at any review if a serious problem.	Low-level problem solving by competent, core team members; Continual, extensive communication; Revise detailed plans periodically; Team changes tasks, their sequences, and groupings.	Do what is required for success; Creative, always trying new ways; Extensive discussions of options and next steps within the team.

market and technical environment where the framework is likely to be particularly effective. The second part of the exhibit summarizes the details of the framework along the six dimensions of the development process.

It should be noted that these processes are not all equally effective; we do not present them as models for all circumstances. Our purpose here is to illustrate the existing range of approaches and mechanisms for tackling the development process, both to show how choices made in the six dimensions combine to create a pattern of development, and to suggest some of the principles managers can apply in building an effective process.

Kodak: Functional Structure and Discipline

At Eastman Kodak Company the dominant approach for managing development projects, put into place in the late 1980s and early 1990s, is referred to as the Manufacturability Assurance Process (MAP).[3] The shorthand reference used internally is "phases and gates." Kodak's evolution to this approach has been driven in part by the firm's strong technical depth and by its expertise in chemically based manufacturing processes related to film production. However, the MAP approach, with its six distinctive phases, is also being used in such diverse product categories as microfilm equipment, copiers, cameras, and medical instruments.

The six phases (named in Exhibit 6–4) take a project through an initial customer mission/vision phase, into a sequence of technical demonstration and feasibility phases managed within the R&D group, and then into a set of commercialization phases that pass from engineering through production to quality assurance and market acceptance. Kodak's motivation for this approach was to shorten development times, improve the efficiency of development efforts, and ensure a smooth transition between various functional groups during the project. Basic performance drivers for Kodak development projects typically are resource utilization and technology advancement.

The development framework at Kodak resembles the system used at MEI: both have a strong functional orientation in project leadership and use a system of phases that is largely functional in focus and operation. But Kodak has introduced a set of mechanisms that give its process a different character. The key mechanisms include the customer mission statement, the use of gatekeepers and stakeholders, well-defined procedures, and senior cross-functional advisory groups. A customer mission statement, for example, lays out the critical unmet needs the customer faces, and how the new product (or process) will meet them. In developing a new coating for its film products, for example, Kodak

155

engineers focused on the customer's need for a much tougher coating (to eliminate scratches), yet one that would offer excellent clarity. This focus led to a clear mission statement: develop a new composition that will give the customer (the film division) a coating with exceptional toughness and clarity, leading to bright, sharp photographs with no scratches.

The process clearly emphasizes the need for technical depth in the projects, but the new mechanisms attempt to achieve integration through a customer focus, common procedures, shared concepts, and the testing process. While the Kodak process thus relies on strong functional groups for direction and focus, it also establishes a common philosophy and set of procedures that provide discipline and clarity. Consider the following differences in Kodak's approach (compared to MEI):

- The front end of the process is not fuzzy; there is a clear customer focus and clear project direction.
- The transition from one phase to another—and particularly the criteria for such a transition—is much clearer.
- The quality assurance group plays a strong integrative role in the last phases of the project and brings a market-based discipline to bear.
- Senior management reviews (done by functional managers) are substantive, rather than calendar-driven.

Compared to the haphazard, confused process at MEI, Kodak's process should operate much faster (because of fewer mistakes and less rework) and use fewer resources. In many ways, therefore, we can see MAP at Kodak as an evolutionary improvement on the basic functional structure in place at MEI. Indeed, it is likely that Kodak had projects similar to the 2010 before they instituted MAP. MAP has cleaned up the process and Kodak's experience has shown substantial improvement in performance.

While the Kodak framework is inherently better than the MEI framework, largely as a result of its discipline and structure, it also fits with Kodak's business and strategy. A process such as MAP, with its strong functional orientation, appears appropriate when the strategy emphasizes technical depth and excellent technical solutions are paramount.

GE: Coordinating and Linking the Functional Process

The dominant approach to product and process development at General Electric is called the "tollgate" process.[4] With an incredibly diverse set of businesses, manufacturing processes, technologies, and markets ad-

EXHIBIT 6–5

General Electric Tollgate Process

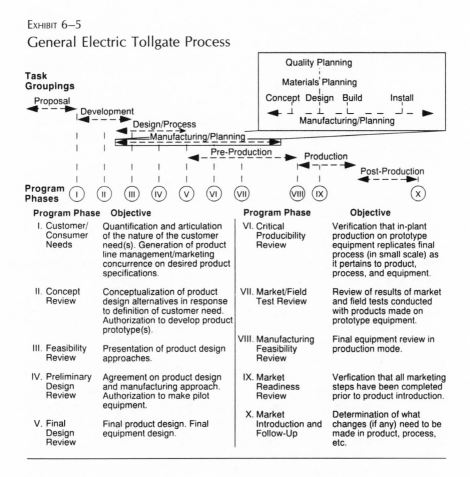

Program Phase	Objective	Program Phase	Objective
I. Customer/ Consumer Needs	Quantification and articulation of the nature of the customer need(s). Generation of product line management/marketing concurrence on desired product specifications.	VI. Critical Producibility Review	Verification that in-plant production on prototype equipment replicates final process (in small scale) as it pertains to product, process, and equipment.
II. Concept Review	Conceptualization of product design alternatives in response to definition of customer need. Authorization to develop product prototype(s).	VII. Market/Field Test Review	Review of results of market and field tests conducted with products made on prototype equipment.
III. Feasibility Review	Presentation of product design approaches.	VIII. Manufacturing Feasibility Review	Final equipment review in production mode.
IV. Preliminary Design Review	Agreement on product design and manufacturing approach. Authorization to make pilot equipment.	IX. Market Readiness Review	Verfication that all marketing steps have been completed prior to product introduction.
V. Final Design Review	Final product design. Final equipment design.	X. Market Introduction and Follow-Up	Determination of what changes (if any) need to be made in product, process, etc.

dressed by GE's divisions, the evolution to this particular approach in the mid to late 1980s was driven in part by senior management's need to control a wide range of development projects. While the bulk of the projects in most GE business units represent product line evolutions and incremental improvements, GE also wanted an approach that could be adapted to both breakthrough and platform projects.

A unique aspect of the GE tollgate approach is that its ten phases are the management review points during the development project. This is illustrated in Exhibit 6–5 where the sets of tasks are grouped together around seven themes, but the ten program phases are listed in terms of their management review purposes. The intent at GE was to create a review process with sufficiently small chunks so that the project would be unlikely to get very far off track between senior management reviews.

Additionally, as the word "tollgate" suggests, GE wanted an approach that would enable senior management to reevaluate projects and halt or redirect them as needed.

Projects to which the tollgate process is applied typically take from twenty-four to forty-eight months, depending on their scale and the type of project (incremental, platform, or breakthrough). In every case, however, the primary performance driver is the management of risk, followed by the secondary driver of maximizing resource utilization against major market opportunities.

The development process at GE shares a strong functional orientation with Kodak, but adds several elements. The phases at GE are more cross-functional in character, so that passing "tollgates" requires the involvement of several functions and applies broader criteria. Furthermore, the structure of the phases is such that there is some overlap in time, creating a need and forum for greater cross-functional interaction. Within the framework established by the tollgate system, work on the project gets done in the functions. But to achieve better interaction across functions GE has added integrative mechanisms in the way development is organized. A team of representatives from each function works under the direction of a program manager to enhance communication and coordination across functions. While the program manager's role is largely administrative, it does bring a cross-functional perspective into the process. In addition, the senior management review at each "tollgate" serves an integrative function. The reviews are closely linked to the natural progress of the project and thus are substantive in nature. Moreover, senior management involvement ensures that business (and therefore cross-functional) criteria are used in making decisions.

Like Kodak, Managing GE's diverse development efforts requires a common framework and language. Also like Kodak, much of the focus of GE's work relies on strong functional groups with depth of expertise. But GE has added more integrative mechanisms (a liaison team, program manager, cross-functional phases) and a more centralized, top management directed review process. These differences may reflect differences in environment and strategy. Historically GE often has undertaken very large projects (e.g., jet engines, plastics, turbine generators) with high technical and financial risks. A review process with close senior management involvement brings to bear an assessment of those risks, frequently, throughout the program. Compared to a process like MAP, GE's more coordinated and linked approach may be appropriate in markets, technologies, and strategies where technical solutions are crucial, but not paramount, and where other issues such as time-to-market or the fit between a technical solution and marketing strategy are more important. In such an environment the mechanisms GE employs may reduce the time required to solve problems and lead to solutions with more balance across functions.

Motorola: Cross-Functional Teams

Motorola's development framework is quite different from that followed at GE and Kodak. It is based on "contract-driven, cross-functional teams."[5] Essentially, a core cross-functional team is selected, dedicated, co-located, and put under the direction of a general manager who serves as a full-time project leader for the duration of the effort. Very early on, that core team develops a "contract" or detailed work plan, including resource requirements and anticipated performance results. Once agreed to by senior management, that contract is literally signed by both the core team members and senior management.

In the Motorola approach, there are four primary phases, but those phases cover a much broader set of activities and extended time line than do the project management phases in many other organizations. The first phase, product definition, is conducted with a cross-functional, highly focused effort. The second phase, contract development, is followed by the third and longest phase, development. This third phase covers product (or process) development from contract through manufacturing start-up. Within this phase there are several subphases, but their definitions are driven by the specifics of the individual project and are defined by the team as part of their work plan in the contract phase. The fourth phase, program wrap-up, focuses on what was learned during the project and the transfer of that learning to other parts of the Motorola organization. The dominant type of project handled at Motorola by this approach is the platform or next-generation project. Typically, goals that emerge from the first two phases represent a 10X performance improvement over the existing product or manufacturing process.

At Motorola, the typical duration of a development project is eighteen to thirty months. The impetus for this particular approach came largely from two factors. The first was a need for a "system solution" in platform or next-generation development efforts that effectively integrates across functions on a number of dimensions. Second, but close to it, was the need to speed the development process and, simultaneously, improve resource utilization.

The development framework at Motorola represents a fundamental shift in the traditional center of gravity—the functions—to a cross-functional team. Where Kodak and GE relied on the functions for basic development work, Motorola puts primary decision making and much (but not all) of the crucial detailed work in the team. In this setup, the team is where the action is, and the functions provide support to the team.

159

Consistent with the primary role of the team, leadership at the team level is much stronger and more direct than at GE, and there is much less central (corporate) direction on a day-to-day basis. The team defines its phases, working within corporate guidelines, and the team leader has broad responsibility for the effort. There are connections with senior management, but their role is much different than in the GE approach. Motorola has developed mechanisms—the contract and the senior management sponsor, for example—that give the team strategic direction, ongoing advice and coaching, and a forum for dealing with new issues. But the team leader functions as a general manager, and manages to the contract.

Motorola's framework places a premium on integration and is effective in situations where the "system solution" is what matters. In that sense, the team approach is likely to be used on platform projects where the creation of a new product or process architecture is central. In addition, the approach is likely to be more effective when markets are turbulent and fast action is essential. In those circumstances a focused team with a flexible process avoids the delays associated with coordinating across large functional groups. This is not to say that the functions are not important. Indeed, without the support of the functions and the depth of expertise the functions bring, the team would fail. But where the system is more important than specific technical solutions, and where the environment is dynamic, a more integrated development framework has advantages.

Lockheed's Skunkworks: The Autonomous Team

During World War II, Lockheed developed the "skunkworks" approach to aircraft development.[6] This approach focuses on radical or breakthrough projects, where the resultant product or manufacturing process is likely to create a whole new business or market opportunity. The essence of this approach is that a dedicated "tiger team" is formed and removed from the ongoing part of the business. That team is given complete responsibility, with no strings attached, for developing the new product or process.

Consistent with the Lockheed skunkworks approach is the notion that the major phases in the development effort should be specified by the team rather than some bureaucracy or standard set of procedures. Thus the team determines all the major milestones, and manages itself against those. Since projects undertaken as "breakthroughs" tend to involve substantial technical advancement, their duration can be fairly lengthy. At Lockheed, such skunkworks-managed projects take from twenty-four to sixty months. The primary performance driver typically is technical excellence on one or two factors of critical importance to the customer, with speed of development a close secondary driver of the effort.

Motorola's process has a strong team orientation, but the team is closely linked to the functions for support activities and part of the basic development work. At Lockheed, the team has direct control over most of the resources and decisions involved in the project, and the other dimensions of the development framework support the concept of an autonomous team. The team works within a set of guidelines on procedures (e.g, standards for testing) and has budget limits it must meet. But there are limited senior management reviews outside the team, and the team and its leadership have broad discretion on phases, practices, methods, and approaches.

Lockheed has implemented the autonomous team framework with mechanisms that reinforce team identification and the creation of a highly focused effort. The team contains the key resources required for the project, including support activities such as a model shop, and team members are handpicked by the team leader. The people involved in the project have broad skills and assignments, so that compared to other development approaches at Lockheed, the number of people involved is relatively small. All the people are co-located to ensure a high level of interaction and effective communication.

With its own budget and resources and with control over its procedures and process, the team can chart its own course and do what needs to be done to accomplish its mission. It does not have to be bound by precedent in other products or in existing systems, and is thus ideal for breakthrough projects where the intent is precisely to break new ground. It may also be effective in experimental situations or in advanced development where the objective is to explore new technical or commercial territory. But it is unlikely to be effective for platform projects that must connect to other products and processes or as the basic system of development for ongoing improvements and enhancements. Indeed, the skunkworks approach needs a larger organization and system to provide skills and resources.

Creating an Effective Development Process: Common Themes and Basic Principles

The four development frameworks presented in Exhibit 6–4 span a continuum that ranges from Kodak, with its strong functional leadership and phases on the left, to Lockheed's skunkworks, with its almost complete autonomy on the right. Along the spectrum, choices in the six dimensions of the development process differ significantly and the mechanisms used to implement those choices are likewise quite different. They appear to be appropriate for quite different circumstances and have different implications for development performance. Yet a close look at these approaches suggests common themes and some basic principles that apply to all effective development processes. As a summary to the chapter and to set the stage for a more in-depth examination of certain aspects of the development process in subsequent chapters, we look briefly at five: customer focus, discipline, coherence, fit, and sharing the pattern.[7]

Customer Focus. A central challenge in any development process is to achieve integration across functions and yet obtain excellent solutions to functional problems. The frameworks in Exhibit 6–4 use several mechanisms to achieve integration, but the one that seems both common and most powerful is customer focus. A focus on the customer's requirements and *unmet* needs can be a powerful, unifying force. But bringing the customer into focus is a challenge. It requires an effort to understand and articulate what the *future* customer's requirements and unmet needs are (and will be). And it requires the capability to translate those needs into terms that everyone can understand and use in detailed actions and decisions.

Discipline. Most development processes—and those in place at Kodak, GE, Motorola, and Lockheed are no exception—are complex. They involve hundreds (even thousands) of decisions, many different people, competing interests, and multiple objectives. There are many approaches to coping with complexity, but the effective processes have discipline in common. The use of phases, clear criteria for moving forward, testing procedures, and prototyping are an effort to bring order and clarity to the process. Excessive rules, bureaucratic procedures and guidelines can, of course, stifle creativity, drain excitement, and bog down the project in a morass of red tape. Procedures, phases, and rules must be streamlined, appropriate, and adaptable. But discipline is crucial in achieving the rigor, thoroughness, and consistency that excellent development requires.

Coherence in Detail. No matter what its basic structure or focus, an effective development process must achieve a high level of coherence among its different elements. To be effective, for example, the approach to leadership must be consistent with and reinforce the way the project is staffed and organized. The mechanisms used to connect senior management to the project must reinforce the phases of development and the criteria for moving from one to another. This coherence across dimensions must pertain at the detail level; coherence in the large or at the level of principle is not enough. What matters is that small details, such as the timing and criteria for testing within a function for a particular component, match the overall phase of development and its milestone criteria. To take another example, the details of who gets selected for a project and the skills they have must match and respond to the approach to organization as well as problem solving in the framework.

Fit with the Mission. Each of the processes outlined in Exhibit 6–4 is better tuned to some environments than others. Establishing a fit between the process and the competitive, market, and technical imperatives that confront the project is essential to effectiveness. But establishing fit is not like plugging in a formula. Environments are complex and variable and firms continually need to monitor and adapt in those dimensions that are crucial to particular objectives. Take, for example, technical depth. If, as at Kodak, technical depth is crucial, the firm needs to understand what parts of its process drive technical excellence (e.g., testing procedures, particular skills and tools), and the implications that changes in the environment (e.g., new technology, new market requirements) may have for them. In addition, firms may face several environments and need more than one approach to development.

Sharing the Pattern. If the development framework is coherent, all of the dimensions work together to create a *pattern* of development—a model of how ideas are transformed into commercial products and processes. If articulated within the organization, the pattern becomes a shared language and framework for development. This is a crucial part of an effective development process. A common framework, especially if there is understanding about the way the elements work together to achieve results, offers direction and guidance in making the myriad of decisions that create products and processes. Things work faster and more efficiently because the framework helps people understand what must be done, when, and how. It also greatly facilitates the intensive communication at the heart of effective development.

Principles as Guidelines

We have argued that creating an effective development process is like building a great factory. Much of what goes into it is very specific to the particular product and process, markets and customers, and strategy. Our discussion suggests that dimensions common to the process provide senior managers a framework for making choices in the design of the process, and for improving the process over time (see Chapter 11 for additional discussion of this topic). Beyond the common dimensions, however, there are also basic principles that underlie effective performance no matter what kind of development process the firm uses.

These basic principles may serve as guideposts for senior managers as they move their organizations along the path toward truly outstanding development. Creating and nurturing a great development process involves many crucial details, but from time to time it is quite useful to ask: "Do we have a strong customer focus in our process?" "Do we have discipline and thoroughness in what we do?" "Do we have coherence in the details?" "Is there a good fit with the mission?" "Have we articulated and shared the pattern?" These questions are not easy to answer, but failing to ask them robs the development process of strong direction and leadership. To ask them well requires a grasp of development at the working level. In the next four chapters we examine in greater depth issues that are critical to making the detailed development process work effectively: integration across functions, leadership and organization, tools and methods for problem solving, and the prototyping process.

CHAPTER 7

Cross-Functional Integration

Product and process development create advantage in competition by delivering to the marketplace great products that attract customers and deliver exceptional quality and value. Great products and processes are much more than a clever design, novel technical solution, distinctive package, catchy promotion, or advanced equipment. Outstanding development requires effective action from all of the major functions in the business. From engineering one needs good designs, well-executed tests, and high-quality prototypes; from marketing, thoughtful product positioning, solid customer analysis, and well-thought-out product plans; from manufacturing, capable processes, precise cost estimates, and skillfull pilot production and ramp-up. But there is more than this. Great products and processes are achieved when all of these functional activities fit well together. They not only match in consistency, but they reinforce one another. In short, outstanding development requires integration across the functions. Furthermore, if new products and processes are to be developed rapidly and efficiently, the firm must develop the capability to achieve integration across the functions in a timely and effective way.

This chapter examines the principles that underlie effective cross-functional integration.[1] We begin with a look at the role of the functions in the development of the MEI 2010 described in Chapter 6. The MEI experience highlights the traditional functional activities in the traditional process, and makes clear where integrative activities were missing. We then illustrate what cross-functional integration means by looking at a framework for the interaction between engineering, manufacturing, and marketing during the development process. The final section of the chapter examines what it takes to achieve integration. We focus in particular on integration at the working level and the role of senior management in creating a context where effective integration will flourish.

The MEI Experience

The development of the 2010 portable premature infant heart monitor at MEI was dominated by the engineering function, but important and essential work was accomplished in marketing, manufacturing, quality assurance, and field service. These activities typically fell within the natural charter of the functional areas. Exhibit 7–1 lays out the major activities accomplished in the functional areas during the development of the 2010 product, arrayed according to the development process phases at MEI. Although a problem in the 2010 development project was the absence of clear phases, we have used the stated phases apparent in the sequence of development activities at MEI.

The 2010 began as a concept and was defined during concept development through interactions between design engineering and marketing. In order for the corporation to approve investment in the project, marketing and engineering combined to give definition to the concept, apply estimates of costs and investment, and develop projections of likely volumes, revenues, and profits. Approval by senior management triggered the design, construction, and testing of prototypes, as well as interaction with customers, as the organization moved to put ideas and concepts into practice. Once an engineering prototype was completed and verified, manufacturing moved in through the production prototype phase to define the process and develop the manufacturing system to be used in commercial production. This required identification of the process steps and their sequence, development of a bill of materials, selection of vendors, and ordering of tooling.

The production prototype phase culminated in the production of a small batch of the 2010 product. With pilot units in hand, quality assurance took the proposed product into customer tests while engineering handled redesign work that followed testing and customers' reactions to the product. As testing moved forward, manufacturing prepared to ramp up for volume production while marketing trained the sales force and developed promotional programs. Once the product was launched

Exhibit 7-1

Functional Activities in the MEI 2010 Development Process

Functions	Standard Phases of Development					
	Concept Development	Product Planning	Engineering Prototype	Production Prototype	Market Acceptance	Market Introduction
Engineering	Early discussions with marketing; take lead in developing and pushing product ideas; investigate ideas	Prepare budget and timetable	Build and test breadboard models; build complete prototype; validate design	Develop test procedures for in-process testing	Redesign product based on customer feedback	
Marketing	Provide input on customer needs and potential concepts; investigate concepts	Provide input to engineering on prices, volumes	Talk to customers; product focus groups to refine features			Develop literature on product; train sales force
Quality Assurance					Develop test plan; conduct customer tests	
Manufacturing		Make rough cost estimates		Develop materials list; define process; select vendors; develop tooling; produce pilot batch		Establish distribution; ramp up production to commercial volumes
Field Service						Train customer service representatives; support customers

into the market, field service supported customers in the use of the product.

Looking across the phases of development within each function in Exhibit 7–1, we find a set of activities that seems natural. Engineering puts ideas into hardware and software and conducts tests, marketing establishes linkages to the customer, and manufacturing makes the product. Each of these activities not only is essential to the development of the product and the process, but falls within the traditional definition of the function's role and mission in the organization. In spite of the fact that each function seems to have carried out its basic mission in this project, however, the project itself was problematic. Before arriving at a commercially viable product that met customer needs and operated effectively within the customer's system, the product had to undergo significant redesign. Moreover, it took the organization a long time to move from product concept to market introduction of a viable commercial product. Although the product itself delivered new features and performance that customers found attractive, the project failed to create the potential advantage that appeared so attractive at the outset of the project.

The outcome of the 2010 project suggests the need for a closer look at the activities accomplished in the development project as well as the timing and sequence of functional involvement. It is apparent, in retrospect, that some of what the functions did could have been done earlier and in a way that connected more closely to the work in other functions. Moreover, some activities that cut across functions simply did not get done. We examine what this means with two examples from the MEI project. The first deals with the relationship between engineering and manufacturing,[2] while the second focuses on the connection between marketing and engineering design.[3]

Engineering-Manufacturing Integration in the 2010 Project

When the MEI engineering organization set out to develop an infant heart monitor, the challenge was to take existing core concepts and technology and develop and package them in a new, smaller, light-weight, portable design. The product, as it emerged, was a design with a much smaller package and lower weight, but with many more features requiring new components, tighter tolerances, and more capable manufacturing processes. Though the design was built on the core technology and was eventually manufactured in an existing plant, manufacturing had to do a significant amount of process development in order to create the required design capabilities. The problem in all of this was that engineering did the design of the product at a time when manufacturing was neither focused on nor involved in the project. Likewise, manufacturing focused on the design and development of the process, including the flows of material, the sequence of processing steps, and the development of tools, *after* the engineers had established the product's basic architecture and implemented that architecture in hardware and software.

Because the design of the product and process were accomplished somewhat in isolation, the overall development of a completed design and manufacturing process was slow and required a great deal of rework, which ate up significant resources. Consider, for example, the selection of vendors. Choosing the vendors to work on the project began in late 1986, many months after product design had been launched. Assumptions made by designers about components and parts availability turned out to be inaccurate. Consolidation in the vendor base had occurred, eliminating some production facilities and components from the supply base. In addition, the design required and had assumed a certain level of process capability that vendors did not possess. All of these problems created a mismatch between the requirements of the design and the capabilities and availability of suppliers.

Achieving an integrated product and process design requires a very different approach. The focus of such an approach is to bring design choices into contact with process capabilities, and process capabilities into contact with design requirements early enough in the process that the two can influence and shape one another in a timely and effective way. In an integrated process, the solution to the vendor selection problem is apparent. The question of which vendors to use could have been examined early in the process as design needs and requirements emerged. Moreover, vendor qualification could have addressed at that early stage, much more directly and substantively, required process capabilities. Finally, the suppliers themselves could have been brought into the discussion at an early stage of the design process in order to obtain firsthand information and insight about potential problems and opportunities inherent in the choices the designers were making.

Solving the vendor selection problem involves doing things earlier, and doing things that cut across the traditional functions. Making that happen necessitates, in effect, what we call "cross-functional integration." Cross-functional integration requires in the first instance that the timing and substance of the activities in the various functions be coordinated. Integration, however, is more than mere coordination. Arriving at integrated solutions means that the actions taken in the functions support and reinforce one another. In the case of product design and process engineering, for example, integration across these two functions means that the design of the product comprehends and exploits the potential and capability inherent in the production process. It also means that the production process delivers the capability and performance required by the design. Achieving an integrated design clearly means doing old things earlier, but it also means doing a new set of things. For example, engineers in the MEI 2010 project had very little interaction or contact with manufacturing engineers on joint issues. In an integrated setup, designers communicate with manufacturing engineers on a variety of joint issues. This requires establishing a forum and context in which joint communication is effective: engineers must comprehend issues of manufacturability, foster skills in developing designs that are robust and exploit manufacturing capability, and be prepared to share designs. Likewise, manufacturing engineers must become oriented to customer satisfaction: they must comprehend issues of product performance and cost, and be prepared to deliver and develop manufacturing capability that will allow the design to achieve its objectives in the marketplace.

In order to make integrated design effective, therefore, the manufacturing organization must undertake process development and process planning up front in the project. In the case of the 2010, for example, had the manufacturing organization understood the implications of the design they could have developed the capability to hold tighter tolerances much earlier in the program. This requires that the manufacturing organization come to the table with a fairly deep understanding of its process capabilities and of the potential developments that lie ahead in its own planning.

Engineering-Marketing Integration at MEI

The interaction between engineering and marketing poses similar problems of timing, communication, and joint activity. In the 2010 project, marketing developed a good product concept in interaction with design engineering as far as the basic idea (a portable unit) and some of the features were concerned. Engineering did the design of the hardware and software, and marketing talked with customers and conducted clinics. The actual design that emerged from this process, however, did not fit well into the customer's system and did not deliver on all of the important features. While the basic concept was sound and the organization delivered many features that customers found attractive, the problems with the wheels, cart, and difficult-to-read display caused delay and rework and some damage to the perception of the product in the market.

Achieving an integrated solution implies that the design makes use of deep understanding and insight about the customer and the customer's potential use of the product. In this context, a particularly crucial problem is selecting which customer or customers to work with early in development. Some firms choose to work with "lead customers" who adopt new ideas early and help to push the state-of-the-art. Others choose a target customer whose requirements are judged to be representative of the broader market. Still others choose to work with customers to gain a broader perspective. The choice is important because the customer will influence the direction of the project. But the choice may also be critical because of what it means for the longer term relationship with the customer. If things work out well, the relationship may be strengthened. But the relationship may be hurt if, for example, the project leader decides that satisfying the customer's requests would take the project in the wrong direction. The customer may have idiosyncratic needs or may request something extreme that the team feels it cannot deliver within the project framework. Picking the right customer is thus critical.

With the right customer, getting deep insight is a matter of understanding the customer's system. In the case of the 2010, for example, this included knowing not only the needs of the customer's system, but also how the monitor functioned, how the hospital personnel interacted with it, and how they might have used it when it was portable. That insight came partly from marketers who knew the customer intimately, and partly from bringing the emerging product design into direct contact with potential customers.

Knowledge about the customer can help to guide engineering design, but it is also important that the design make use of and exploit the capabilities of the marketing organization in its relationships with customers. That includes its skills and resources in market research, promotion, distribution, customer sales, and support. But integration also means that marketing must develop the capabilities that the design requires.

While many of these activities occurred ultimately in the course of the 2010 project, they did not occur early enough to avoid difficult, expensive, and time-consuming rework and redesign. Thus, integration requires shifting the timing of a whole set of activities to earlier in the process. But, there is also a new set of activities required to support an integrated solution.

Marketers, for example, need to work with customers to develop insight that goes beyond product specifications.[4] They need to establish an understanding of the future customer's desired experience with the product. There may be much more here than simply identifying the right mix of technical specifications. Customers, for example, may care about aspects of the product that are not clearly identified or that may be difficult to articulate. Moreover, since the "customers" that will buy the product are in the future, marketing needs to identify underlying trends in customer requirements. All of this suggests that effective involvement of marketing in the early stages of product development requires marketing imagination.

Taking a broader view of the customer and the product is important, because it allows marketers and engineers to anticipate problems and opportunities early in development. But that will only occur if the concept development process focuses on system characteristics of the product. In the MEI 2010 case, for example, an integrated approach would have looked not just at the monitor, but at the customer interfaces, the cart it would travel on, and the procedures for using it. Engineers would be involved in that process to establish an architecture for the product as a system.

Engineers are also important in making it possible to confront the product architecture and the product concept with customer experience early in the process. The key is the construction of early system prototypes. In the heart monitor case, for example, such prototypes might capture some, but not all, of the functionality of the monitor, but could portray physically the package, the cart, the user interface, and the way the product will be used. Such prototypes could be the basis for early tests with customers, conducted jointly by marketing and engineering.

A Framework for Cross-Functional Integration

Achieving cross-functional integration changes what the functions do, when they do it, and how they get the work done. In order to illustrate the impact that integration has on the role of the functions in product development, we have laid out an example of development phases and functional activities in Exhibit 7–2. The table examines three of the major functions involved in development—engineering (with a focus on product design), marketing (including marketing research and sales), and manufacturing (including process development, manufacturing engineering, and plant operations). Within each function, we have identified the major activities in each of the phases of development.

The phases in Exhibit 7–2 are defined by critical milestones along the development path from initial concept to full commercial operation. The sequence begins with concept development and proceeds through product planning, detailed design and development, commercial preparation, and market introduction. We have divided the detailed design and development phase into two parts. The first focuses on verification of the product design and related process development, including design of tooling and equipment. The second phase focuses on verification of process design, with refinement of the product. This particular config-

EXHIBIT 7–2

Functional Activities Under Cross-Functional Integration

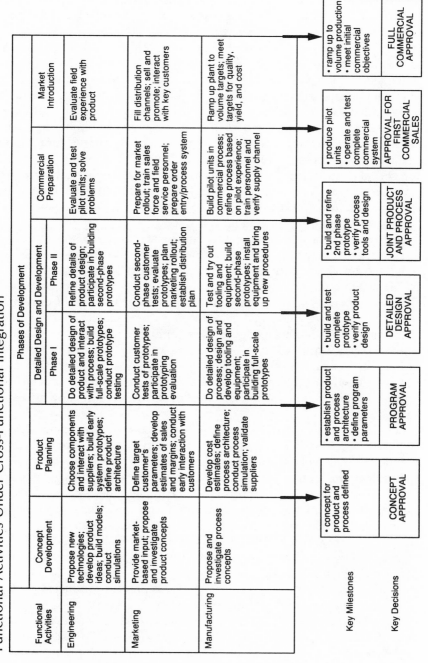

Functional Activities	Concept Development	Product Planning	Detailed Design and Development — Phase I	Detailed Design and Development — Phase II	Commercial Preparation	Market Introduction
Engineering	Propose new technologies; develop product ideas; build models; conduct simulations	Choose components and interact with suppliers; build early system prototypes; define product architecture	Do detailed design of product and interact with process; build full-scale prototypes; conduct prototype testing	Refine details of product design; participate in building second-phase prototypes	Evaluate and test pilot units; solve problems	Evaluate field experience with product
Marketing	Provide market-based input; propose and investigate product concepts	Define target customer's parameters; develop estimates of sales and margins; conduct early interaction with customers	Conduct customer tests of prototypes; participate in prototyping evaluation	Conduct second-phase customer tests; evaluate prototypes; plan marketing rollout; establish distribution plan	Prepare for market rollout; train sales force and field service personnel; prepare order entry/process system	Fill distribution channels; sell and promote; interact with key customers
Manufacturing	Propose and investigate process concepts	Develop cost estimates; define process architecture; conduct process simulation; validate suppliers	Do detailed design of process; design and develop tooling and equipment; participate in building full-scale prototypes	Test and try out tooling and equipment; build second-phase prototypes; install equipment and bring up new procedures	Build pilot units in commercial process; refine process based on pilot experience; train personnel and verify supply channel	Ramp up plant to volume targets; meet targets for quality, yield, and cost
Key Milestones	• concept for product and process defined	• establish product and process architecture • define program parameters	• build and test complete prototype • verify product design	• build and refine 2nd phase prototype • verify process tools and design	• produce pilot units • operate and test complete commercial system	• ramp up to volume production • meet initial commercial objectives
Key Decisions	CONCEPT APPROVAL	PROGRAM APPROVAL	DETAILED DESIGN APPROVAL	JOINT PRODUCT AND PROCESS APPROVAL	APPROVAL FOR FIRST COMMERCIAL SALES	FULL COMMERCIAL APPROVAL

uration assumes that tooling and equipment development for the process requires somewhat longer lead time than the detailed design of the product. The product and the process are jointly designed, but the pattern of verification and testing (product first, process second) reflects the different lead times involved. The end result of the detailed design and development phase is joint product and process approval.

As laid out in Exhibit 7–2, development does not end with the first shipment from the commercial production process. Rather, we have added a market introduction phase, during which the manufacturing organization ramps up the production process to meet volume targets as well as targets for initial quality, yield, and cost. At the same time, marketing is involved in filling the distribution channels and establishing critical relationships with key customers. As we envision it here, the development process concludes when the organization has brought the design of the product, its marketing and distribution, and its manufacturing to the point of full commercial viability.

Compared to the highly segmented and sequential process used in the development of the MEI 2010, the much more integrated process in Exhibit 7–2 involves each of the functions in each of the phases. Thus, manufacturing not only plays its traditional role in preparing the product and the process for commercial production at the end of development, but is actively engaged in proposing concepts and investigating them at the very earliest stage of development. Similarly, marketing does not wait until full-scale engineering prototypes are complete to interact with customers and bring customer insight and information into the process. The net effect of these changes in the timing of activities is to pull forward in time the activity and involvement of the downstream functions.

But that is not all. It is evident that the greater integration across functions requires the addition of specific activities that support cross-functional work. For example, engineering builds very early system prototypes in order to support marketing's desire to develop richer customer insight early in the process. To complete the circle, engineers participate with marketing in interacting with customers in order to strengthen and deepen their understanding of the experience the product will create for future customers. Manufacturing establishes process concepts in the concept development phase and does process development and planning in collaboration with design engineers. Moreover, prototype testing and evaluation is a business process conducted jointly by all the functions involved in development.

The involvement of the functions in different phases of development is reinforced by the structure of decision making and the sequence of milestones envisioned in the development process. People from each function not only participate in the decision making at each milestone, but the milestones themselves focus attention on how the activity in each of the functions fits together with activity in the other functions. Thus, for example, the milestone at the conclusion of Phase I of detailed design and development is not an "engineering" milestone. Although attention focuses on the question of whether or not the product design captures the product concept, that question is framed in terms of marketing's activities in concept development and customer testing, manufacturing's activities in designing and developing the process, as well as the technical details of the design of the product itself. It is in effect an integrated milestone that looks at the progress of development from the standpoint of the emerging system, including engineering design, marketing, and manufacturing development.

Achieving Cross-Functional Integration

Not all development projects need deep, cross-functional integration. Where product designs are stable (or change only in a minor way), customer requirements are well defined, the interfaces between functions are clear and well established, and lifecycles and lead times are long, functional groups may develop new products effectively with a modest amount of coordination through procedures and the occasional meeting. But where markets and technologies are more dynamic and time is a more critical element of competition, deeper, more intensive cross-functional integration is crucial to effective development.

A starting point for achieving effective integration is the framework laid out in Exhibit 7–2. But simply devising and even implementing a framework of this kind does not ensure that the designs, tools, or market plans will be truly integrated. Cross-functional integration that really matters occurs when individual design engineers work together with individual marketers or process engineers to solve joint problems in development. Thus, to be truly effective, cross-functional integration must be much more than a scheme for linking in time the activities of the functions, and even more than adding new kinds of activities that support cross-functional interaction. True cross-functional integration occurs at the working level. It rests on a foundation of tight linkages in time and in communication between individuals and groups working on closely related problems.[5]

The extent to which problem solving is integrated in product development shows up most forcibly in relationships between individuals or engineering groups where the output of one is the input for the other—we will use here as an example the relationship between a design group responsible for the design of a plastic part and a process engineering group responsible for designing the mold that will be used in producing the part. The upstream group—in this case, the part designers—establishes the physical dimensions of the part, how it will interface with other parts within the system, the surface characteristics of the part, and the particular material to be used in its construction. All of these decisions—dimensions, tolerances, interfaces, surface characteristics, and materials—become inputs into production of the part. The mold designer's problem is to create a mold (or set of molds, particularly if the part is to be produced in volume) that will give the part its shape and surface characteristics, but will also be sufficiently durable, cost effective, and operational that the part can be manufactured in volume (can withstand repeated use, without breaking or sticking) reliably at low cost. How these two engineering groups work together determines the extent and effectiveness of integration in the design and development of the part and its associated mold.

Patterns of Communication

A critical element of the interaction between the upstream and the downstream group is the pattern of communication.[6] Four dimensions of the communication pattern—richness, frequency, direction, and timing—jointly determine its quality and effectiveness. Exhibit 7-3 presents the dimensions and their associated range of choice. The ends of the spectra in Exhibit 7-3 represent polar opposites in integration. On the left we have a pattern that is sparse, infrequent, one-way, and late. In this pattern, upstream engineers transmit information in formal documents that appear at the conclusion of a design process in finished form with little backup information about alternatives and no scope for feedback. In contrast, the pattern on the right is rich, frequent, reciprocal, and early. Here upstream engineers meet face to face with their downstream counterparts early in the design process and share preliminary ideas with sketches, models, and notes. Feedback is a natural part of this pattern. Whereas the first pattern is little and late, the second is early and often.

The choices firms make about communication between upstream and downstream groups play an important role in shaping the nature of cross-functional integration. But there are also choices about how to link the actual work in the two groups in time. The key issue is the extent to which work is done in parallel. Exhibit 7-4 puts the communication patterns together with different approaches to parallel activity to create four modes of upstream-downstream interaction.

The first panel depicts what we call the *serial mode* of interaction. This is a classic relationship in which the downstream group waits to begin its work until the upstream group has completely finished its design. The completed design is transmitted to the downstream group in a

Exhibit 7–3
Dimensions of Communication Between Upstream and
Downstream Groups*

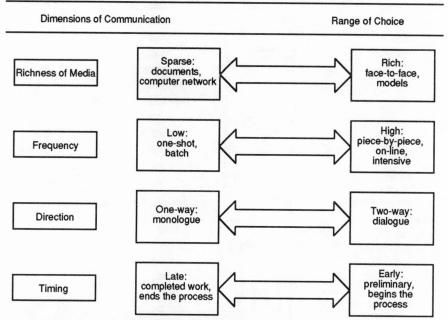

* This exhibit illustrates the range of choice firms have in determining the pattern of communication between upstream (for example, design) and downstream (for example, process) engineering groups. The boxes represent endpoints of a spectrum for each dimension of communication, while the arrows indicate the range of choice (for example, sparse to rich).

one-shot transmission of information. This one way "batch" style of communication may not convey all of the important nuances and background to the final design, nor does it necessarily comprehend the strengths and opportunities afforded by the downstream group. In that sense, the problem solving that lies behind the design of the product and that will produce the design of the mold is not integrated.

The second mode—what we call *"early start in the dark"*—links the upstream and downstream groups in time, but continues to employ a batch style of communication. This mode of interaction often occurs where the downstream group faces a deadline that it feels cannot be met without an early start on the project. But the upstream group communicates only at the end of its work, so the downstream group may be surprised by the design and may experience a period of confusion as it tries to adjust its work to the upstream design. While the net result may

EXHIBIT 7—4
Four Modes of Upstream-Downstream Interaction*

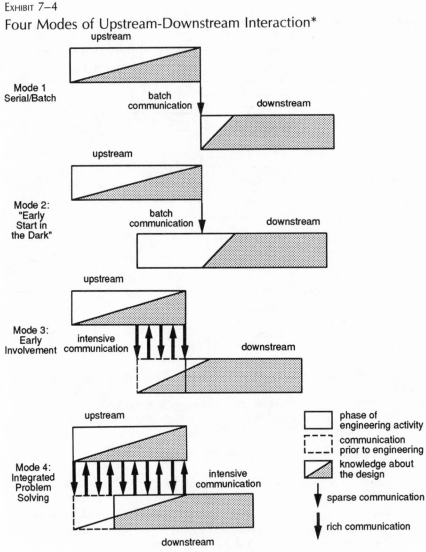

* Using the dimensions of communication in Exhibit 7–3, we define four modes of interaction between upstream and downstream groups. In Mode 1, communication is sparse, infrequent, one-way, and late; the information is serial and lengthy. Mode 2 maintains the pattern of communication, but moves up the starting point. Modes 3 and 4 make communication richer and more frequent (Mode 3) and starting much earlier (Mode 4).

be some reduction in overall lead time, the extent of the surprise and confusion can often be sufficient to make the actual process longer than the process in mode one. Although the downstream group works in parallel with the upstream group, and in this sense they are "concurrent," in actuality they operate without information and the problem solving cycles in the two organizations are not linked.

The third mode—what we call the *early involvement mode*—begins to move toward real integration. In this mode, the upstream and downstream players engage in an interactive pattern of communication. The upstream group, however, is still involved in the design of the part well before the downstream group begins its work. Thus, while the downstream group develops insight about the emerging design, and participates through feedback and interaction in the design process, it waits until the design is complete before undertaking problem solving in its own domain. The pattern of communication we envision here not only occurs earlier than it does in modes one and two, but involves two-way communication of preliminary, fragmentary information. For example, instead of waiting until the design is complete, engineers in the upstream group share preliminary analysis, alternative designs, and tentative proposals with their downstream colleagues. Similarly, the downstream group shares its views about capabilities of the downstream process, the constraints they face in designing the molds, and the relative merits of alternative concepts under discussion. Although they wait to begin work on the mold design until the part design is complete, the downstream group benefits from early involvement in two ways. First, the part design reflects a much better understanding of the issues confronting the process engineers than was true in either modes one or two. Second, the mold designers themselves have a much better sense of the issues and objectives embodied in the design. The net effect is that they are able to complete their work with fewer delays and downstream changes. In this sense, problem solving in the downstream and upstream groups is much more integrated.

The last mode in Exhibit 7–4—what we call *integrated problem solving*—links the upstream and downstream groups in time and in the pattern of communication. In this mode, downstream engineers not only participate in a preliminary and ongoing dialogue with their upstream counterparts, but use that information and insight to get a flying start on their own work. This changes the content of the downstream work in the early phases of upstream design, and is also likely to change fundamentally the content of communication between the two groups. Whereas in mode three the content of feedback from downstream engineers must rely on past practice, theoretical knowledge, and engineering judgment, under integrated problem solving that feedback will also reflect actual practice in attempting to implement the upstream design.

Communication that is rich, bilateral, and intense is an important, even essential, element of integrated problem solving. Where problem solving between upstream and downstream groups is intimately connected, the practice of "throwing the design (blueprints) over the wall"—inherent in mode one—will not support timely mutual adaptation of product and process design. What is needed to capture the nuance and detail important for joint problem solving is face-to-face discussion, direct observation, interaction with physical prototypes, and computer-based representations. Moreover, that intimate, rich pattern of communication must occur in a timely way so that action may be taken to avoid costly mistakes downstream. This does not mean the absence of conflict but rather the honest, open consideration of alternatives, and resolution based on data, analyses, and joint, creative problem solving. The essence of mutual adjustment is real time coordination between upstream and downstream groups. In this way design engineers take into account the preliminary results of process engineering problem solving in order to make products easier and less expensive to manufacture. Likewise, process engineers shape their problem-solving efforts in order to deliver the capabilities required by the upstream design. But this kind of mutual adjustment begins only after downstream problem solving has begun.

Capabilities and Relationships

Integrated problem solving relies on early action by the downstream group, dense, rich dialogue between upstream and downstream participants, and a style of problem solving that is broader and more comprehensive than one experiences in the more narrow functional focus inherent in mode one. Indeed, effective integration places heavy demands on the organization. The engineering process must link problem solving cycles in time; communication must be rich, precise, and intense; and the relationship between upstream and downstream groups must support and reinforce early and frequent exchange of constraints, ideas, and objectives. Moreover, because the problem solving across traditional functional boundaries occurs in real time, the capacity for quick and effective action is critical. Thus, effective integration relies on a specific set of capabilities, attitudes, and relationships.

Upstream Capabilities. From the perspective of the upstream engineering group, the challenge is to meet performance objectives in a way that complements downstream work and makes use of what the downstream can do. Making this happen requires skills and capabilities that go beyond the narrow technical ability to accomplish the upstream task. Three capabilities seem particularly important.

Downstream-friendly solutions. The first challenge is to create what we call "downstream-friendly" solutions. Upstream engineers must be knowledgeable about downstream constraints and capabilities. They must learn to use techniques for promoting early and continued communication with the downstream group, and to acquire relevant knowledge and experience from previous projects. A variety of methods have been developed in recent years, including design for manufacturability, value engineering, failure mode and effects analysis, and Taguchi Methods®, each of which is designed to enhance the upstream group's ability to predict the consequences of its actions and to devise solutions to its own problems that are downstream-friendly.

The objective here is not simply to make life easy for the downstream engineers. It is true that ignorance of downstream constraints hampers integrated problem solving, and may create very expensive and time-consuming engineering changes. It is also true, however, that excessive attention to downstream problems may hamper the commercial appeal of the design. Overemphasis on manufacturability or overreliance on simple parts may reduce downstream problems but render the product less attractive. Thus, downstream constraints must be carefully balanced with issues of design quality in order to maximize the total customer experience inherent in joint upstream-downstream solutions.

Error-free design. With an emphasis on creating downstream-friendly solutions, upstream engineers can have a substantial impact on the number of engineering changes and the time required to complete downstream work. But many such changes and much expensive time wasted are not due to lack of knowledge of downstream constraints or capabilities, but simply to outright mistakes. We have in mind things such as errors in copying documents, typing a "6" instead of a "9," sending a document to the wrong location, and so forth. Such minor details often have insidious consequences. In the first place, if not caught early, such errors require downstream engineering changes that are costly and time consuming, but add no value to the overall quality of the product. Second, such errors are often very difficult to track down once they have been propagated in the system. Third, they erode the mutual respect needed for groups to work as peers.

For all these reasons, error-free design is critical in achieving integrated problem solving. Designing it right the first time is a matter in the first instance of attention to detail, and discipline in the activities of individual engineers. But effective design reviews, testing, and engineering discipline can dramatically reduce or eliminate mistakes and errors.

Quick problem solving. Even where solutions are relatively friendly and careless mistakes have been eliminated, disagreements and conflict between upstream and downstream groups are inevitable in situations where the product is complex and customers are demanding. When differences arise, dealing with them effectively is enhanced by quick problem-solving capabilities in the upstream group. Faster design-build-test cycles in the upstream facilitate short feedback loops and quick mutual adjustment. When a problem arises downstream that requires upstream adjustment, the speed with which the upstream group can effect a new solution is critical in achieving responsive, fast action. Time is of the essence in this context. Since problem solving is mutual, getting to new alternatives quickly allows the downstream group to maintain its focus and complete its work in an integrated fashion. In organizations that have achieved integrated problem solving, there is a major difference between having a preliminary design done in two weeks rather than in four. In a slow organization those two weeks are not very important. In this case quick action supports integration.

Downstream Capabilities. Among downstream engineers, the challenge is to get a flying start on development before getting complete information. Moreover, that flying start must not create so many constraints on the design that it loses its appeal in the market. Moving fast, but moving effectively in the downstream depends on three capabilities.

Forecasting from upstream clues. In order to get a flying start, downstream engineers must start working on solving problems that have not been well defined. In that context, it is essential that downstream engineers develop the ability to forecast what the upstream group is likely to do. This requires that the downstream group develop skill in finding and using clues about upstream work. In combination with insight and understanding about previous patterns of upstream behavior, these clues become the basis for downstream action. For example, mold designers may know that the part designers are particularly worried about the strength of the part. They may also have learned from conversations with the part engineers that the alternative solutions include changes in the internal structure of the part. And given the way that the part designers have approached these issues in the past, the concern about strength means the part is likely to have internal ribs. These clues can therefore be the basis for initial mold design and planning.

Regular and close communication between downstream and upstream engineers is essential to finding clues and to using them effectively. But the downstream engineers need not be passive in this process. Once they discern a particular issue and a particular design direction, they may offer suggestions or counterproposals. If those suggestions are focused on helping the upstream engineers in solving their part design problems effectively—"if you want to go with small ribs, we can give you very tight tolerances that will cut down flash"—and are not simply expedients to make life in the downstream simple—"small ribs won't work; go with large ribs, they are easier to make"—the ideas from the downstream are much more likely to improve overall design and enhance the achievement of an integrated solution. Furthermore, active downstream involvement is likely to increase the quality of the clues and thus the forecasts they generate.

Managing risk. Getting off to a flying start based on a forecast of likely upstream action is a course fraught with risk. Downstream engineers must know how to make tradeoffs between the risk of a given change and the benefit of an early start. Moreover, they need to be skilled in managing the tradeoff so that the early start is made in a way that reduces risk. Take, for example, the case of process engineers trying to develop molds. Based on early clues from the part designers, and intensive discussion, mold engineers may identify sections of the part that are unlikely to undergo significant adjustment and change. Other sections of the part, however, may be less firm. This gives them the ability to begin mold design and construction by establishing the basic configuration and then using cutting margins (excess material that can be pared back once the final dimensions have been established) to allow a flying start. There is a significant amount of know-how involved in making such knife-edge tradeoffs. This implies that integration of problem solving requires significant skill in applying deliberate and detailed analysis and calculation in support of fast action.

Coping with unexpected changes. Even the best forecasters and the most clever downstream engineers will encounter unexpected changes in design. Given this fact of life, the downstream group needs to be flexible and skilled at quick diagnosis and quick remedy. Just as fast action in the upstream group facilitates mutual adaptation and integration, quick adjustment to unexpected changes on the part of the downstream group is essential to avoiding long delays and idle resources in development.

The ability to move quickly in reacting to unexpected changes relies on skill in problem diagnosis, and organizational capability in mobilizing resources and in focusing attention and effort on the important problems. But there is also the matter of raw engineering talent. It is one thing to get an organization to run tests quickly, build tools rapidly, and have decisions made promptly. But it is quite another to be able to size up a situation, identify a solution, and designate the appropriate test. Simply stated, downstream organizations that are fast and effective have many excellent engineers. Downstream (and upstream) groups that are slow have a few very good engineers and many others that only follow routine procedure and look up specifications in handbooks. While these groups may arrive at solutions given enough time, the name of the game in integrated problem solving is speed. In this case, there is no substitute for competence.

Attitudes Toward Integration

The effective deployment of upstream and downstream skills and capabilities in achieving integrated problem solving depends on fundamental attitudes that affect the relationship between upstream and downstream groups. People in the upstream group, for example, must be willing to share early preliminary information with their downstream colleagues. A perfectionist mentality, an attitude of "I won't give you anything now, because I know I'll have to change it later and I know that I will take the blame for it," is anathema to integrated problem solving. Likewise, people in the downstream must be willing to take risks based on their best forecast of the future. They must be comfortable in a very ambiguous environment. A "wait and see" attitude, an attitude of "don't talk to me until you are absolutely sure the design is done," may appear to minimize the risks of change, but is in fact a cultural obstacle to effective integration.

A sense of mutual trust and joint responsibility is essential to integrated problem solving. Once product engineers have worked hard to reduce unnecessary changes, they must trust the manufacturing process group's willingness and ability to cope with the changes that might emerge in the course of development. If process engineers trust product engineers to help them overcome manufacturing difficulties, they will be more willing and more capable to get a flying start.

Mutual trust hinges on mutual commitment to one another's success. Without such commitment engineers are less likely to expose themselves to the personal risks inherent in integrated problem solving. And there are risks. Integration requires that engineers in the upstream and downstream let their colleagues see what actually goes on in their respective departments. It exposes weaknesses and mistakes and makes clear the limits of their ability much more than does the sequential batch mode of operation.

Effective integration is also built on shared responsiblity for the results of upstream-downstream collaboration. Where integrated problem solving prevails, the objective of the upstream group can not simply be a completed design, nor can the downstream group focus its attention solely on a well-conceived set of tools or processes. Both groups must recognize that the objective is a high-quality, low-cost part that fits well with other parts under development, that comes off the production line at commercial volume levels with the styling, surface finish, cost, and structural integrity to satisfy customer expectations, and that is available for the targeted market introduction. This is a very complex objective that neither the upstream nor the downstream group completely controls. In order to achieve the objective, therefore, there must be joint responsibility for joint output.

The Role of Senior Management

Our discussion thus far has focused on integrated problem solving at the level of individual work groups and engineers, and the role of the functional groups in the overall development process. We have argued that effective problem solving and cross-functional integration relies on individual skill, attitudes, and relationships across functional boundaries that facilitate intensive communication. Although the analysis has direct impact on the activities of functional managers and members of individual work groups, achieving integration across functions at each of these levels requires the support of, and focused action from, senior management.

Senior management establishes the context in which functional interaction and individual problem solving occur. In the first place, senior management may substantially shape the development process that establishes the sequence of functional activity, and the pattern and timing of functional involvement in development. By directly affecting what functional managers and functional specialists actually do in their daily work and in interaction with one another, senior management not only establishes a framework for integration, but can also lay out and communicate what the ideal pattern of involvement, interaction, and collaboration ought to be. Furthermore, senior management can put that pattern into effect in the day-to-day activities in which they participate directly. For example, how senior functional managers such as the vice presidents of manufacturing and engineering work together, the way they communicate with each other, and the degree of respect and trust that develops in their relationship have an important shaping influence on the members of their organizations and thus on the overall pattern of integration in the development process.

But senior management's role in building effective integration extends beyond establishing frameworks and patterns. Senior management also can have an important influence on the skills in the organization, the barriers to respect and trust that may exist between functions and work groups, and the tools, methods, and languages that are essential to effective cross-functional problem solving.

It is evident from our earlier discussion that effective integration requires a different set of skills than one finds in the traditional, sequential, functionally oriented development process. In an integrated set up, for example, an effective process engineer must not only be knowledgeable about equipment design, process layout, or tool design, but must also have an appreciation of product design and be oriented toward customer satisfaction. Moreover, that engineer must be skilled in quick problem diagnosis and problem solving. Senior management can play an important role in assuring the depth and quality of the skills and capabilities of its engineers by investing in education, training, and experience. All three are essential.

Education in the basic principles that underlie effective joint product-process design, for example, endows an engineer with knowledge and understanding that can be applied in a variety of different circumstances. *Training* in specific methods and procedures gives an engineer tools to use in solving specific kinds of problems. Finally, providing an engineer experience outside a specific discipline or function gives a much better feel for the nature of the problems that confront people in other functions, and also gives a better perspective on the way different functions interact.

Varied *experience* can also be an important element in senior management's attack on the barriers to respect, trust, and effective integration. One of the most important barriers to respect and trust is a simple lack of understanding of the nature of the work, processes, and constraints under which functional counterparts operate. Experience can help to build this imperative understanding.

Promotion and Compensation

Lack of understanding is only part of the problem. Organizations often create distance between functional groups through their policies on promotion and compensation, distance that is far greater than might arise naturally because of specialized expertise and focus. In a large industrial products company that we studied, for example, the sales organization had become the only route into general management. People with technical backgrounds and skills quickly learned to suppress those interests and move into sales if they wanted to move up in the organization. The effect was to create an implicit "second class" status for the engineering organization. Subsequent efforts to integrate marketing and engineering in order to improve development ran into serious problems.

Similar issues pertain to questions of compensation. In a semiconductor company that we studied we found wide differences in compensation practices between engineering and manufacturing. For example, a job in manufacturing engineering with the same level of responsibility (same number of direct reports, same budget authority, same degree of impact on competitive position) would often be rated two or three job grades below a comparable position in design engineering. Although due partly to extrinsic factors and widespread in other electronics firms, the message was clear: manufacturing engineering was not as important, nor populated by people as talented, as design engineering. It is not surprising that the company's initial efforts to encourage more effective interaction between design engineering and manufacturing were not successful. In fact, changing the compensation structure was a critical first step in achieving true cross-functional integration.

In addition to educating people and giving them cross-functional experience, and beyond breaking down barriers to trust and respect, senior management can influence the quality and effectiveness of cross-functional integration by investing in tools and methods that create a language in which different functional specialists can communicate and interact. We will have more to say about tools and methods in Chapter 9, but it is evident that investment in computer-based design and manufacturing systems, and in techniques and methods for design for manufacturability, or robust design, can not only facilitate more effective action within the function, but can provide a basis for more effective communication and functional integration. Electronic media, for example, have come to play an increasingly important role in the connection between product design and process development. Computer-aided design and computer-aided manufacturing (CAD-CAM) data representing a complex part, for example, enable much more accurate transmission of design information to mold engineers than traditional line drawings and models. This is partly because digital information (CAD-CAM), unlike analog information (drawings and models), is less subject to error accumulation through duplication, and partly because CAD-CAM can eliminate some of the steps required by the traditional approach and thereby reduce the length of the communication chain. Where such systems exist, and where both product designers and process engineers have been trained to use the system effectively, it can stimulate and enhance cross-functional interaction.

CHAPTER 8

Organizing and Leading Project Teams

Effective product and process development requires both that all of the organizational groups involved develop and bring to bear the appropriate specialized capabilities, and that the efforts of all of these groups be appropriately integrated. For most young, small organizations, particularly those still in the start-up phase, the organization structure and the role of the project manager are not burning issues, although certainly product and process development are of critical importance. The entire organization finds itself focused on a single major development project, and the CEO or some other senior executive exercises strong project leadership. Furthermore, the various functional managers naturally take broad responsibility not only for their parts of the project but for the successful outcome of the entire effort. Thus while a number of issues—involving cross-functional problem solving, refining product and process specifications, and integrating product performance with customer needs—challenge the organization, only modest amounts of their energy gets spent on how best to organize the project and direct its execution.

In large, mature firms that over time have established strong functional groups (especially in engineering, but also in marketing and manufacturing) with extensive specialization, have large numbers of people, and have a number of ongoing operating concerns as well as development project concerns, the challenge of organizing and leading product and process development efforts is increased dramatically. In such firms, development projects become the exception for the ongoing operating organization rather than representing their primary focus of attention. Even for those on the project, years of experience and the establishment of a broad range of systems—covering everything from career paths to performance evaluation, and from reporting relationships to breadth of job definitions—create both physical and organizational distance between individual contributors and among organizational subfunctions. Often this is complicated further by organization structures in marketing that are based on product families and market segments, organization structures in engineering based on functional disciplines and technical focus, and organization structures in manufacturing operations that are a mix between functional and product market. The result is that in large, mature organizations, team organization and the leadership of development efforts is a major challenge. This is accentuated as organizations find their traditionally stable markets and competitive environments challenged by new entrants, new technologies, and rapidly changing customer demands.

It is no surprise in such an environment that, by 1990, the concept of "teams"—especially cross-functional teams—had become almost a fad in the management literature.[1] However, as organizations experimented with such teams, they discovered that success with a cross-functional team required much more than simply "naming" the team and setting up a regular schedule of team meetings. In fact, many firms who had adopted the team solution found their managers increasingly stretched, with less time for substantive work, and projects taking just as long—if not longer—for completion. This was in sharp contrast to a handful of firms in different industries who apparently had discovered the "keys to success" in making such teams work effectively.

Some of the most dramatic stories in the popular press relating to fast-cycle turnaround and time-based competitive advantage have attributed success to effective team organizations and project leadership. Particularly compelling has been the work of Clark and Fujimoto[2] in the world auto industry. In a nutshell, their findings suggest that the best firms in the auto industry have cut traditional new car development cycle times significantly; in the process, they have delivered better products and, in many cases, more than doubled the productivity of critical development engineering resources. These leading firms in the auto industry seem to have developed a much more effective way to organize and lead development projects than their slower, less efficient rivals.

The focus of this chapter is on the range of organizational options for directing development projects and their associated options for project leadership. We begin by outlining four types of project organization structures and their primary differences. This includes consideration of the differences in the roles and responsibilities of the project leader as well as those of individual team members, and their relationship with the traditional functional groups and with senior executives. The section also explores the evolution of organizations over time, an understanding of which helps explain the pervasive yet subtle nature of the patterns that influence team structures and their effectiveness.

The subsequent section focuses on a type of organization structure and leadership—heavyweight project teams—that seems particularly promising in today's environment, yet is strikingly absent in many mature organizations. The nature of such heavyweight teams and the dimensions along which they differ from their much more prevalent counterparts, "lightweight" teams, is also explored. The intent in this section is to illustrate how such heavyweight project teams and their project leaders function, and thus some of the things that an organization must do to create and utilize such a capability. While such teams are powerful in certain settings, they are not without their own unique issues and challenges, and those are the focus of the final portion of this section.

Next, we turn attention to the need for firms to match their required types of projects (a topic discussed in Chapter 4) with the appropriate project organization structure and leadership mode. Using a number of examples, this segment develops the idea that organizations, while needing a "dominant mode" for product and process development, also need alternate modes for other less frequent, yet essential, types of projects.

We conclude the chapter by exploring some of the approaches that firms have found effective in building a range of team capabilities. These vary from how to improve existing approaches to creating credible new approaches, to making sure that multiple approaches to development can coexist and be strengthened in the organization over the longer term. We hope that by the end of the chapter the reader will conclude—as we have—that this is indeed a high-leverage aspect of project execution, and that while it has no simple answers, there are several principles that can be pursued to significant advantage.

Project Organization and Leadership

Our work has identified four dominant structures around which project activities can be organized. Each has an associated project leadership role. The result is a range of options for managing development projects, each with its own unique strengths and weaknesses. The four basic types of development team structures are illustrated in Exhibit 8–1.[3]

Exhibit 8–1

Types of Development Teams*

1. Functional Team Structure

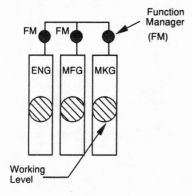

2. Lightweight Team Structure

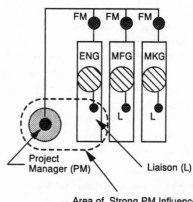

Area of Strong PM Influence

3. Heavyweight Team Structure

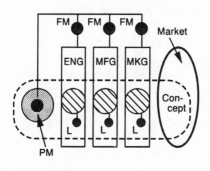

4. Autonomous Team Structure

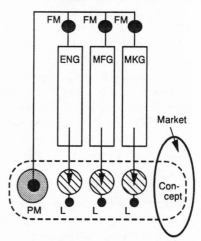

* This exhibit depicts four levels of teams: functional, where the work is completed in the function and coordinated by functional managers; lightweight, where a coordinator works through liaison representatives but has little influence over the work; heavyweight, where a strong leader exerts direct, integrating influence across all functions; and autonomous, where a heavyweight team is removed from the function, dedicated to a single project, and co-located.

Functional Team Structure. The upper left-hand corner depicts the traditional functional organization found in larger, more mature firms. People are grouped together principally by discipline, each working under the direction of a specialized subfunction manager and a senior functional manager. Within each engineering discipline, for example, specific engineers specialize in various aspects of the product or process under development. Representative groupings would include industrial, maintenance, and manufacturing process engineering under the subcategory of manufacturing engineering, and electrical, mechanical, software, and test engineering under the subcategory of R&D or design engineering.

The work of the different subfunctions and functions is to coordinate ideas through a set of detailed specifications agreed to by all parties at the start of the project, and by occasional meetings where issues that cut across groups are discussed. Over time, primary responsibility for the project passes sequentially—although often not smoothly—from one function to the next. This might be thought of as shifting the center of gravity in the project as time passes. The transfer of project responsibility from one function to the next is sometimes referred to as "the hand-off," or, less euphemistically, but probably more accurately, as "throwing it over the wall."

This organization structure has a number of major strengths as well as weaknesses. One strength is that those managers who control the resources also control performance of the project tasks that need to occur in their area. Thus the traditional wisdom of aligning responsibility and authority tends to be followed here. The rub is that to make it work, the set of tasks must be subdivided at the outset of the project, requiring a decomposition of the entire development activity into a set of separable, somewhat independent tasks. Unfortunately, on most development efforts, not all required activities are known at the outset, nor can they all be easily and realistically subdivided into separable pieces. The primary weakness of this approach thus shows up in limited coordination and integration.

Another major strength of this approach is that most career paths are functional in nature until one reaches a general management level in the firm. This mode of project organization ensures that the work done on a project is judged, evaluated, and rewarded by the same subfunction and functional managers who make the decisions about career paths. The associated disadvantage is that individual contributions to a development project tend to be judged largely independently of overall project success. The traditional tenet cited is that individuals cannot be evaluated fairly on outcomes over which they have little or no control. But as a practical matter, that often means that no one directly involved in the details of the project is responsible for the project results finally achieved.

A third primary strength of the functional project organization is that it ensures that specialized expertise is brought to bear on the key technical issues. With such an organization in a company such as an auto manufacturer, the same person or small group of people literally can be responsible for the design of every windshield wiper or door lock over a wide range of development efforts. Thus the functions and subfunctions capture the benefits of prior experience and become the keepers of the organization's depth of knowledge while ensuring that it is systematically applied over time and across projects. The disadvantage is that every development project will differ somewhat in its objectives and performance requirements, and it is unlikely that specialists developing a single component—such as a windshield wiper or door lock—will do so very differently on one project than on another. Their tendency will be to design what the consider the "best" component or subsystem, where best is defined by technical parameters in the areas of their expertise rather than by overall system characteristics or specific customer requirements dictated by the market for which this development effort is aimed.

Lightweight Team Structure. The second approach, outlined in Exhibit 8–1 in the upper right-hand quadrant, is called the lightweight project team approach. Like the functional structure, those assigned to the team reside physically in their functional areas, but each functional organization designates a liaison person to "represent" it on a project coordinating committee. These liaison representatives work with a "lightweight project manager," usually a design engineer or product marketing manager, who has responsibility for coordinating the activities of the different functions. In most cases, the lightweight project team represents a fairly minor modification to the traditional functional team. In fact, it usually occurs as an add-on to a traditional functional organization, with the liaison person having that functional liaison role added to his or her other duties. The position of lightweight project manager, however, does tend to be a type of overall coordination assignment not present in the traditional functional team structure.

The project manager in this approach is a "lightweight" in two important respects. First, he or she is generally a middle- or junior-level person who, although having considerable expertise, usually has little status or influence in the organization. Often these people have spent a handful of years in one of the functions, and this assignment is seen as a "broadening experience," a chance for them to move out of that function. Second, although they are responsible for informing and coordinating the activities of the functional organizations, the key resources (including engineers on the project) remain under the control of their respective functional managers. Lightweight project managers do not have power to reassign people or reallocate resources. Much of their time is spent confirming schedules, updating time lines, and expediting across groups. Typically such project leaders spend no more than 25 percent of their time on a single project.

The primary strengths and weaknesses of the lightweight project team are those stated previously for the functional project structure. In addition, however, there is now at least one person who, over the course of the project, looks across functions and seeks to make certain that individual tasks—especially those on the critical path—get done in a timely fashion, and that everyone is kept aware of potential cross-functional issues and what is going on elsewhere on this particular project. Thus improved communication and coordination are the added strengths expected by an organization that moves from a functional to a lightweight team structure.

The weakness is the fact that the project manager is "lightweight." The power still resides with the subfunction and functional managers; as a consequence, expectations for improved efficiency, speed, and project quality from moving to the lightweight team structure are seldom met. Lightweight project leaders find themselves tolerated at best, and often ignored and even preempted. This can easily become a "no-win" situation for the individual thus assigned.

Heavyweight Team Structure. The third approach, outlined in the lower left of Exhibit 8–1, is the heavyweight project team. In contrast to the lightweight setup, the heavyweight project manager has direct access to and responsibility for the work of all those involved in the project. Such project leaders are "heavyweights" in two respects. First, they are senior managers within the organization. In some organizations they are at the same level or even outrank the functional managers. As a result, not only do they have expertise and experience, they also wield significant organizational clout. Second, heavyweight project leaders have primary influence over the people working on the development effort and supervise their work directly through key functional people on the core teams. Often, the core group of people are dedicated and physically co-located with that heavyweight project leader. However, the longer-term career development of individual contributors continues to rest with their functional managers rather than the project leader because they are not assigned to a project team on a permanent basis.

There are a number of dimensions—in addition to stature within the organization and resource control—along which lightweight project managers differ. Several of these are summarized in Exhibit 8–2. Each is shown along a continuum, suggesting that the difference between light-

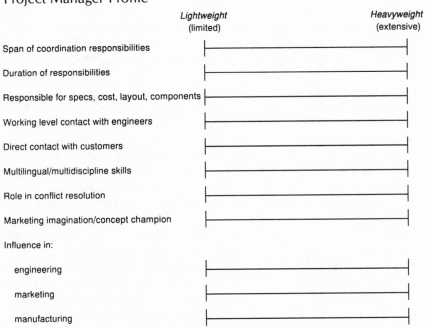

EXHIBIT 8–2

Project Manager Profile*

	Lightweight (limited)	Heavyweight (extensive)
Span of coordination responsibilities		
Duration of responsibilities		
Responsible for specs, cost, layout, components		
Working level contact with engineers		
Direct contact with customers		
Multilingual/multidiscipline skills		
Role in conflict resolution		
Marketing imagination/concept champion		
Influence in:		
engineering		
marketing		
manufacturing		

* Project managers take on a variety of roles and responsibilities, eleven of which are depicted here. How much of a heavyweight (versus lightweight) project manager role occurs on a specific project is determined by how extensive a role the project manager takes in each of these areas.

weight and heavyweight team structures is more one of degree than an all-or-none issue. By presenting these dimensions of difference on a continuum, it also is easy to have teams and their project managers assess their own position relative to "degree" of lightweight versus heavyweight characteristics.

The heavyweight team structure has a number of advantages and strengths, but also an associated set of weaknesses. Because this team structure is observed much less frequently in practice and yet seems to have tremendous potential for a wide range of organizations, it will be discussed in detail in the next section. We will leave our discussion of strengths and weaknesses to the conclusion of that in-depth exploration.

Autonomous Team Structure. The fourth form of project structure, outlined in the lower right-hand portion of Exhibit 8–1, is the autonomous team structure, often referred to as the "tiger team." Under this structure, individuals from the different fuctional areas are formally assigned, dedicated, and co-located to the project team. The project leader is a heavyweight in the organization and is given full control over the resources contributed by the different functional groups. Furthermore, that project leader becomes the sole evaluator of the contribution made by individual team members.

In essence, the autonomous team is given a "clean sheet of paper" with regards to the development project and all of its aspects and details. Typically, such tiger teams are not required to follow existing organizational practices and procedures, but are allowed to create their own. This includes establishing incentives and rewards as well as norms for behavior. However, they understand that as a team they will be held fully accountable for the final results of the project. If the project does not succeed as planned, the responsibility will be theirs and no one else's.

The fundamental strength of the autonomous team structure is focus. Everything that the individual team members and the team leader do is concentrated on making the project successful. Because of their focus, tiger teams tend to do well at rapid, efficient new product and new process development. They handle cross-functional integration in a particularly effective manner. This often may be due in part to their being able to attract and select team participants much more freely than the other project structures.

The countering disadvantage is that they take little or nothing as "given"; thus, they are likely to expand the bounds of their project definition and tackle redesign of the entire product and its components and subassemblies rather than looking for opportunities to utilize existing materials, designs, and organizational relationships. Their solutions tend to be unique, making it more difficult to fold the resulting product and process—and, in many cases, the team members themselves—back into the traditional organization upon project completion. As a consequence, such tiger teams often become the birthplace of new business units or they experience unusually high turnover following project completion.

Senior managers often become nervous at the prospects of a tiger team because they are asked to delegate much more responsibility and control to the team and its project leader than under any of the other organization structures. Unless clear guidelines have been established in advance, it is extremely difficult during the project for senior managers to make mid-course corrections or exercise substantial influence without destroying the team. More than one team has "gotten away" from senior management and created major problems.

The Evolution of Development Organization

Because of the wide range of situations in which firms find themselves, it is not surprising that different organizations tend to gravitate toward one particular team structure as their dominant mode for doing development projects. While that dominant mode may evolve over time, at any point in time the procedures and systems in place in the organization encourage all projects to follow that same mode with only minor variations. Sometimes exceptions will be allowed when a project clearly requires something different than the dominant mode, but those will be viewed as exceptions.

It is interesting in this regard to refer back to the framework and six basic elements of project management discussed in Chapter 5. In that chapter, the project management approaches of four different firms—Kodak, General Electric, Motorola, and Lockheed Skunkworks—were described. Each of those is an example of one of the four types of development structures summarized in Exhibit 8–1. The Kodak MAP process is an effective form of the functional structure. The GE system of tollgates, with a heavy dose of senior management review and control, is a fairly effective form of the lightweight, or perhaps middleweight, team. The Motorola cross-functional contract approach is a particularly effective implementation of the heavyweight team. Finally, the skunkworks set-up at Lockheed is a clear illustration of the tiger or autonomous team. The history of each of these firms, their competitive environment, and their particular strategies have resulted in each choosing a different dominant mode for conducting its development activities. These patterns of choice and evolution can be generalized, and help to explain practices currently observed in a variety of firms and industries.

As discussed at the outset of this chapter, start-up firms typically focus their entire organization on a single development project. The characteristics of that environment and the mode in which they carry out development efforts are reflective of those described above for the autonomous or tiger team structure. In essence, the entire organization is on the team, and because of their small size, they are physically co-located and dedicated to this activity. Furthermore, because these organizations are new, those doing the work are given extensive leeway to define performance evaluation and reward systems and to create procedures and approaches that they think will be most effective in that development environment. They fully understand that if the primary project does not succeed, they will pay the consequences and will have no one to blame but themselves.

As a start-up firm grows and completes its initial handful of projects, it invariably faces the issue of how to balance operating needs (selling, producing, distributing, and servicing previously designed products using previously designed processes) with the need for ongoing product and process development efforts. The initial solution often is one that closely resembles a move toward a heavyweight team structure. Because the next development project (often a next-generation platform project) is so important, a strong functional or general manager is put in charge of it and the firm adjusts its fledgling functional organization to balance that heavyweight team. While the transition is not always smooth as different managers learn to share power and coexist, the organization is usually small enough that senior people quickly recognize when the balance needs to shift one way or the other, and take appropriate action. The result often is a successful sequence of major development efforts over a period of half a dozen or more years.

Depending on the maximum volume that a single platform product (and its related derivatives) can support, at some point the organization faces increasing pressure to develop multiple projects that will be done concurrently and in support of multiple product lines. For many firms this is a traumatic period, and in today's world it is often avoided by the single-product, five-to-ten-year-old organization selling out (being acquired) by a much larger, multiple-product line firm.

Whether or not the firm remains independent as it moves to multiple product lines, invariably a functional organization begins to dominate. After all, the functions have responsibility for sustaining the existing activities of the firm (which account for an increasingly large portion of the resources and influence on performance results), and it seems natural to divide up development responsibility among those functions. The result is an organization whose primary approach to development is the functional team structure. Over time, that structure and its associated project manager approach handles an increasing number of projects, a large portion of which are sustaining or derivative in nature. In fact, when major (platform) or breakthrough projects are called for, they are likely to be viewed as "development engineering projects" as opposed to true business projects. If the firm has continued to follow a competitive strategy of technical distinctiveness and superior features in its product performance, it seems natural that the functional team structure be applied in development.

For projects that are incremental and sustaining in nature, the functional structure is a comfortable approach, because the stable environment and the limited amount of change involved in such projects makes it relatively easy to subdivide tasks and to pass the project successfully from one function to another. Thus firms that have come to dominate their market—and often its associated technologies—may, for years and even decades, find the functional team structure very satisfactory for handling development efforts. However, if the rates of change in technology, competitive positions, and customer requirements accelerate, that functional team structure may be found wanting.

Mature organizations whose environments have shifted in recent years increasingly sense that their traditional functional structure is too slow, too costly, and not sufficiently customer-focused to compete with smaller, nimbler organizations who use tiger and heavyweight team structures to develop whole new product offerings and platforms. Not wanting to upset all of their existing procedures or discard what have been major strengths in their traditional functional team structure, they choose naturally to add lightweight project managers and liaisons in hopes of becoming faster, less costly, and more on target in their efforts. If they do find themselves imminently threatened on a substantial product line, they may complement this lightweight team structure with an occasional tiger team. However, for the majority of their development projects, they are anxious to make the lightweight team structure work, thereby overcoming some of the weaknesses of their traditional approach while maintaining its major strengths.

Depending on the evolution and duration of these higher rates of change, such mature organizations may find that creating a heavyweight team structure capability is the only way to effectively compete against their most focused, effective competitors. Furthermore, because the lightweight-heavyweight difference represents a continuum, they are able to move in that direction at whatever pace they find most appropriate. From our experience, this natural evolution helps explain the trends that can be observed in a wide range of industries with regard to approaches to project management.

The challenge for any single firm is to make sure that its dominant mode matches its environment and its strategic imperatives, and that the firm develops capabilities that allow it to apply alternative modes when those are deemed most appropriate for particular projects. To make the organization and leadership characteristics of their dominant approach fully effective also requires two other things. First is making sure that the types and mix or projects undertaken (a major topic discussed in Chapter 4) are indeed appropriate for their environment, and that the mix matches what they have selected as their dominant team structure. This was what happened at Motorola when they developed their cross-functional, contract team approach in the late 1980s. Prior to that time their approach had been largely functional, adding some lightweight project managers to help speed development efforts. During the mid 1980s, they discovered that next-generation platform projects were the key to their longer-term success, and that such projects required that a heavyweight team structure be developed and applied throughout the corporation.

The second thing an organization must do is make sure that its human resource selection, training, and development policies, as well as its organizational systems, provide the mix of skills in the quantities needed by the overall development strategy. As stated repeatedly in earlier chapters, development projects represent not only the application of those skills and abilities and the capturing of their value in the market-place, but also the further enhancement and expansion of those development capabilities so that they will be available for future projects.

The Heavyweight Team Structure

In many popular and academic discussions of reducing time-to-market, or making major changes in design quality or development productivity, cross-functional, heavyweight teams often are an important part of the proposed solution. Teams offer improved communication, stronger identification with and commitment to the project, and a focus for cross-functional problem solving. The evidence suggests that when managed effectively, heavyweight teams can indeed bring significant advantage in improved development. Consider the experience of Motorola in developing its Bandit line of pagers.

The Bandit Pager: An Example of a Heavyweight Team

An excellent example of an effective heavyweight team structure was that used by the Motorola Communications Sector on the development of its "Bandit" pager.[4] The project charter was to develop an automated, onshore, profitable production operation for its high-volume Bravo pager line. (This is the belt-worn pager that Motorola sold from the mid 1980s into the early 1990s.) The core team on the Motorola Bandit project consisted of a heavyweight project leader and eight other individuals. These individuals, who were dedicated and co-located, represented industrial engineering, robotics, process engineering, procurement, and product design/Computer Integrated Manufacturing (CIM). The need for these functions was dictated by the nature of the Bandit platform automation project and its focus on manufacturing technology with a minimal change in product technology. In addition, a human resource person and an accounting/finance person were also part of the core team. The human resource person was particularly active early on as subteam positions were defined and jobs posted throughout Motorola's Communications Sector. Additionally, the human resource person played an important role as training and development of operating support people were needed later on. The accounting/finance person was invaluable in "costing out" different options and performing detailed analysis of options and choices identified during the course of the project.

An eighth member of the core team was a Hewlett Packard employee. Hewlett Packard was chosen as the vendor for the "software backplane," providing an HP 3000 computer and the integrated software communication network that linked individual automated workstations together, downloaded controls and instructions during production operations, and captured quality and other operating performance data. Because of the importance of HP support to the success of the overall project, it was felt essential that they be represented on the core team.

Not only was this core team co-located, it was housed in a corner of the existing engineering/manufacturing facility used by Motorola Telecommunications in Boynton Beach, Florida. The team chose to enclose in glass the area where the automated production line was to be set up so that others in the factory would be able to track the progress on this project and, hopefully, be more willing to offer suggestions and adopt the lessons learned from it in their own production and engineering environments. The team chose to call their project "Bandit" to indicate their willingness to take ideas from literally anywhere.

The heavyweight project leader, Scott Shamlin, was described by team members as "a crusader," "a renegade," and "a workaholic." Shamlin became the champion for the Bandit effort. He was a hands-on manager with several years of experience in operations, and played a major role in stimulating and facilitating communication across functions. Moreover, he helped to articulate a vision of the Bandit line, and to infuse it into the detailed work of the project team. His goal was to make sure the new manufacturing process worked for the pager line, but would also provide real insight for many other production lines in Motorola's Communications Sector.

On the Motorola Bandit project, a contract book was created and signed early on by the core team members and senior management. The contract book provided the blueprint and work plan for the team's efforts. Initially, the team's executive sponsor—although not formally identified as such—was George Fisher, the Sector Executive. He made the original investment proposal to the board of directors and was an early champion and supporter, as well as direct supervisor in selecting the project leader and helping get the team underway. Subsequently, the vice president and general manager of the Paging Products division filled the role of executive sponsor.

Throughout the project, the heavyweight team took responsibility for the substance of its work, the means by which that work was accomplished, and the results that it provided. The overall results of the project were extremely satisfying to the team and to Motorola. The project was completed in eighteen months as per the contract book, and that represented about half the time of a normal project of such magnitude. In addition, the automated production operation was up and running with process tolerances of five sigma (referring to the degree of precision achieved by the manufacturing processes) at the completion of that eighteen-month period. Ongoing production verified that the cost objectives (substantially reduced direct costs and improved profit margins) had indeed been met, and product reliability was even higher than the standards already achieved on the offshore versions of the Bravo product. Finally, a variety of lessons were successfully transferred to other parts of the sector's operations, and additional heavyweight teams have proven the viability and robustness of the approach in Motorola's business and further refined its effectiveness as the dominant mode throughout the corporation.

The Challenge of Heavyweight Teams

Motorola's experience with the Bandit underscores the potential power available in the use of heavyweight teams. But the experience also makes clear that there is more to creating an effective heavyweight team capability than selecting a leader and forming a team. By their very nature—product (or process) focused, strong, independent leadership, broad skills and cross-functional perspective, clear mission—heavyweight teams create potential conflict with the functional organization and raise questions about the nature of senior management's influence and control. And even the advantages of the team approach bring with them potential disadvantages that may hurt development performance if not recognized and addressed.

Take, for example, the advantages of ownership and commitment. One of the most striking advantages of the heavyweight team is the ownership and commitment that arise among core team members, enabling tough issues to be addressed and major challenges to be overcome in a timely and effective fashion. Identifying with the product and creating a sense of esprit de corps motivates team members to extend themselves and do what needs to be done to help the team succeed. But such teams sometimes expand the definition of their role and the scope of the project, and get carried away with themselves and their abilities. We have seen heavyweight teams become autonomous tiger teams and go off on a tangent because senior executives gave insufficient direction and the bounds of the team were only vaguely specified at the outset. Even if the team stays focused, the rest of the organization may see themselves as "second class." Although the core team may not make that distinction explicit, it happens because the team has responsibilities and authority beyond those commonly given to functional team members. Thus, such projects can inadvertently become the "haves" and other, smaller projects the "have-nots" with regard to key resources and management attention.

Support activities are particularly vulnerable to an excess of ownership and commitment. Often the heavyweight team will want to have the same control over secondary support activities as it does over the primary tasks performed by dedicated team members. When the heavyweight team has to wait for prototypes to be constructed, analytical tests to be performed, or quality assurance procedures to be conducted, their natural response is to "demand" top priority with the support organization or to be allowed to go outside and subcontract to independent groups. While these may sometimes be the appropriate choices, establishing make-buy guidelines and clear priorities that can be applied to all projects—perhaps changing service levels provided by support groups (rather than maintaining the traditional emphasis on resource utilization)—or having support groups provide capacity and advisory technical services but letting team members do more of the actual task work in those support areas may be other needed changes. Whatever the particular actions the organization takes, the challenge is to achieve a balance between the needs of the individual project and the needs of the broader organization.

Much the same is true of the advantage the heavyweight team brings in the integration and integrity it provides through a system solution to a set of customer needs. Getting all of the components and subsystems to complement one another and to address effectively the fundamental requirements of the core customer segment can result in a winning platform product and/or process. The team achieves an effective system design by using generalist skills applied by broadly trained team members, with fewer specialists and, on occasion, less depth in individual component solutions and technical problem solving.

But the lack of depth may disclose a disadvantage. Some of the individual components or subassemblies may not attain the same level of technical excellence they would under a more traditional functional team structure. For instance, in the case of an automobile, generalists often can develop a windshield wiper system that is extremely complementary and integrated with the total car system and its core concept. But they also may embed in their windshield wiper design some potential weaknesses or flaws that might have been caught by a functional team of specialists who had designed a long series of windshield wipers. To counter this potential disadvantage, many organizations have found that more testing of completed units is required to discover such possible flaws, and that review of components and subassemblies by expert specialists may be very worthwhile. In some cases, the quality assurance function has expanded its role to make sure sufficient technical specialists review designs at appropriate points so that such weaknesses can be minimized.

Managing the Challenges of Heavyweight Teams

Problems with depth in technical solutions and allocations of support resources suggest the tension that exists between heavyweight teams and the functional groups where much of the work gets done. The problem with the teams exceeding their bounds reflects in part how teams manage themselves, in part how boundaries are set, and in part the ongoing relationship between the team and senior management. Dealing with these issues requires the development of mechanisms and practices that reinforce the basic thrust of the team—ownership, focus, system architecture, integrity—and yet improve the team's ability to take advantage of the strengths of the supporting functional organization—technical depth, consistency across projects, senior management direction. We have grouped the mechanisms and problems into six categories of management action: the project charter, the contract, staffing, leadership, team responsibility, and the executive sponsor.

The Project Charter. A heavyweight project team needs a clear mission. One way to capture that mission in a concise way is in an explicit, measurable project charter. Such a charter sets broad performance objectives and usually is articulated even before the core team is selected; thus, joining the core team includes accepting the charter established by senior management. A typical charter for a heavyweight project would be the following;

> "The resulting product will be selected and ramped by Company XYZ during Quarter 4 of calendar year 1991, at a minimum of a 20% gross margin."

This charter is representative of an industrial products firm whose product goes into a system sold by its customers. Company XYZ is the leading customer for a certain family of products, and this project is focused on developing the next-generation platform offering in that family.

The argument for this team charter is that if the heavyweight program results in that platform product being chosen by the leading customer in the segment by a certain date and at a certain gross margin, it will have demonstrated that the next-generation platform is not only viable, but likely to be very successful over the next three to five years. Projects and settings for which such a charter might be appropriate would include a microprocessor being developed for a new computer system, a diesel engine being developed for the heavy equipment industry, or a certain type of slitting and folding piece of equipment being developed for the newspaper printing press industry. Even in a medical diagnostics business with hundreds of customers, a charter that sets a goal of "capturing 30 percent of market purchases in the second twelve months during which the product is offered" sets a clear charter for the team. The objective is to have a clear project charter that will set appropriate expectations as to the nature of success for that effort.

The Contract Book. A charter lays out the mission in broad terms. The contract book defines, in detail, the basic plan to achieve the stated goal. Creating a contract book occurs at the outset, as soon as the core team and heavyweight project leader have been designated and given the project charter by senior management. While it can take a variety of forms, the concept is that the team develops its own detailed work plan by which it will conduct the project, it estimates the resources that will be required, and it outlines the results that will be achieved. The contract book thus elaborates on how the team plans to achieve the chartered performance, and what resources it will require. The table of contents of a typical heavyweight team contract book is shown in Exhibit 8–3. Such documents range from twenty-five to a hundred pages, depending on the complexity of the project and level of detail desired by the team and senior management before proceeding. A common practice following negotiation and acceptance of this contract between the team and senior management is for the individuals from both groups to sign the contract book as an indication of their commitment to honor the plan and achieve those results.

The core team may take anywhere from a long week to a few months to create and complete the contract book. The duration depends on the experience of the team, the expectations of senior management, and the level of detail being pursued. As indicated in Chapter 6, Motorola, after several years of experience, decided that a maximum of seven days should be allowed for this activity. Having watched other heavyweight teams—particularly in organizations with no prior experience in using such a structure—take up to several months, we can appreciate why Motorola has nicknamed this the "blitz phase" and decided that the time allowed should be kept to a minimum.

Staffing. As suggested in Exhibit 8–1, a heavyweight team includes a group of core cross-functional team members who are dedicated (and usually physically co-located) for the duration of the development effort. Typically there is one core team member from each primary function of the organization; for instance, in several electronics firms we have observed core teams consisting of six functional participants—design engineering, marketing, quality assurance, manufacturing, finance, and

205

EXHIBIT 8–3

Heavyweight Team Contract Book—Major Sections*

- Executive Summary

- Business Plan and Purposes

- Development Plan

  - Schedule
  - Materials
  - Resources

- Product Design Plan

- Quality Plan

- Manufacturing Plan

- Project Deliverables

- Performance Measurement and Incentives

* The contract book for a heavyweight team contains detailed plans and objectives for the project, including the time table, resource requirements, and product performance specifications. Often this twenty-five- to one-hundred-page document is signed by the six to eight core team members and senior management.

human resources. Individually, core team members represent their functions and provide leadership for their function's inputs to the project. Collectively, they constitute a management team that works under the direction of the heavyweight project manager and takes responsibility for managing the overall development effort.

While frequently there are other participants—especially from design engineering early on and manufacturing later on—who may be dedicated to such a heavyweight team for several months, those participants usually are not made part of the core team that provides guidance and overall direction for the effort. However, they may well be co-located and, over time, develop the same level of ownership and commitment to the project as those on the core team. The primary difference is that the core team members help manage the total project and the coordination and integration of individual functional efforts, whereas other dedicated team members work primarily within a single function or subfunction.

The question is often raised as to whether these dedicated team members—who may be working full-time on the project for several months—are actually part of the core team. Different firms choose to handle this issue in different ways, but those with considerable experience tend to distinguish between core and other dedicated (and often co-located) team members. The difference between the two groups is one of management responsibility for the core group that is not shared equally by the others. Also, it is primarily the half a dozen members of the core group who will be dedicated throughout the duration of the project, with other subfunctional contributors having a portion of their time reassigned to other projects before this heavyweight project is fully completed.

Additionally, whether physical co-location is essential is often questioned in such teams. We have seen it work both ways. Given the complexity of development projects, and especially the uncertainty and ambiguity often associated with major projects like those assigned to heavyweight teams, physical co-location has several advantages over even the best of on-line communication approaches. With physical co-location, real-time problems that arise are much more likely to be addressed effectively with all of the functions represented and present than when they are separate and must either wait for a periodic meeting or use remote communication links to open up cross-functional discussions.

A final issue often raised is whether an individual can be a core team member on more than one heavyweight team at the same time. If the rule for a core team member is that 80 percent or more of his or her time must be spent on the heavyweight project, then the answer to this question is no. Frequently, however, a choice must be made between someone being on two core teams—for example, from the finance or human resource function—or putting a different individual on one of those teams who has neither the experience nor stature to be a full peer with the other core team members. In the majority of cases we have seen, experienced organizations opt to put the same person on two teams to ensure the peer relationship and level of contribution required, even though it means having one person on two teams and with two desks. They then work diligently to develop other people in the function so that multiple team assignments will not be necessary in the future.

Sometimes multiple assignments will also be justified on the basis that a function such as finance does not need a full-time person on a project. In most instances, however, there are a variety of potential value-adding tasks that are broader than finance's traditional contribution. A person largely dedicated to the core team will search for those opportunities and the project will be better because of it. The risk of allowing core team members to be assigned to multiple projects is that they will not be available when their inputs are most needed, nor will they be as committed to project success as their peers. They become secondary core team members, and the full potential of the heavyweight team structure fails to be realized.

Project Leadership. Heavyweight teams require a distinctive style of leadership.[5] A number of differences between lightweight and heavyweight project managers were highlighted in Exhibit 8–2. Three of those are particularly distinctive. First, heavyweight project leaders manage, lead, and evaluate other members of the core team. They are also the persons to whom the core team reports throughout the project's duration. Another distinctive aspect of heavyweight team leaders is that, rather than being neutral or a facilitator with regard to substantive issues requiring problem solving and conflict resolution, they are concept champions. That is, they see themselves as championing the basic core concept around which the platform product and/or process is being shaped. They make sure that those who work on subtasks of the project understand the core concept. Thus they play a central role in ensuring the system integrity of the final product and/or process.

Finally, the heavyweight project manager carries out his or her role in a very different fashion than the lightweight project manager. Most lightweights spend the bulk of their time working at a desk, with paper. They revise schedules, get frequent updates, and encourage people to meet previously agreed upon deadlines. The heavyweight project manager spends little time at a desk, is out talking to project contributors, and makes sure that decisions are made and implemented whenever and wherever needed. Some of the ways in which the heavyweight project manager achieves project results are highlighted by the five roles illustrated in Exhibit 8–4 for a heavyweight project manager on a platform development project in the auto industry.

The *first role* of the heavyweight project manager is to provide for the team a direct interpretation of the market and customer needs. This involves gathering market data directly from customers, dealers, and industry shows, as well as through systematic study and contact with the firm's marketing organization. A *second role* is to become a multilingual translator, not just taking marketing information to the various functions involved in the project, but being fluent in the language of each of those functions and making sure the translation and communication going on among the functions—particularly between customer needs and product specifications—are done effectively.

A *third role* is the direct engineering manager, orchestrating, directing, and coordinating the various engineering subfunctions. Because of the size of auto development programs and the number of types of engineering disciplines that must be brought to bear, it is essential in a heavyweight structure that the project manager be able to work directly with each of those engineering subfunctions on a day-to-day basis and ensure that their work will indeed integrate and support that of others and serve to execute effectively the chosen product concept.

A *fourth role* is best described as staying in motion: out of the office

Exhibit 8—4

The Heavyweight Project Manager

Role	Description
Direct Market Interpreter	Gathers firsthand information from customers, distributor visits, industry shows; has own marketing budget, market study team, direct contact and discussions with customers
Multilingual Translator	Fluency in language of customers, engineers, marketers, stylists; translator between customer experience/requirements and engineering specifications
"Direct" Engineering Manager	Orchestra conductor, evangelist of conceptual integrity and coordinator of component development; direct eye-to-eye discussions with working-level engineers; shows up in drafting room, looks over engineers' shoulders
Program Manager "in motion"	Out of the office, not too many meetings, not too much paperwork, face-to-face communication, conflict resolution manager
Concept Infuser	Concept guardian, confronts conflicts, not only reacts but implements own philosophy; ultimate decision maker, coordination of details and creation of harmony

conducting face-to-face sessions, and highlighting and resolving potential conflicts as soon as possible. A *final role* is that of concept champion. Here the heavyweight project manager becomes the guardian of the concept and not only reacts and responds to the interests of others, but also sees that the choices made are consistent and in harmony with the basic concept. This requires a careful blend of communication and teaching skills so that individual contributors and their groups understand the core concept, and then sufficient concept and conflict resolution skills to ensure that tough issues are raised and addressed in a timely fashion.

It should be apparent from this description that heavyweight project managers earn the respect and right to carry out these roles based on prior experience, carefully developed skills, and status earned over time, rather than simply being endowed through a designation on the part of senior management. A qualified leader who can play those roles as a heavyweight project manager is a prerequisite to an effective heavyweight team structure.

Team Member Responsibilities. People who serve on a heavyweight team have responsibilities that extend beyond their usual functional assign-

Exhibit 8–5

Responsibilities of Heavyweight Core Team Members*

Functional Hat Accountabilities

- Ensuring functional expertise on the project
- Representing the functional perspective on the project
- Ensuring that subobjectives are met that depend on their function
- Ensuring that functional issues impacting the team are raised proactively within the team

Team Hat Accountabilities

- Sharing responsibility for team results
- Reconstituting tasks and content
- Establishing reporting and other organizational relationships
- Participating in monitoring and improving team performance
- Sharing responsibility for ensuring effective team processes
- Examining issues from an executive point of view
  (answering the question, "Is this the appropriate business response for the company?")
- Understanding, recognizing, and responsibly challenging the boundaries of the project
  and team process

* The six to eight core team members of a heavyweight development team have two types of responsibility. One is that of representing their function and ensuring that the project tasks associated with their function are completed as planned. The other is that of helping to manage the team's activities and ensuring that the commitments made in the contract book are met.

---

ment. As illustrated in Exhibit 8–5, these are of two primary types. Functional hat responsibilities are those accepted by the individual core team member as a representative of their function. For example, the core team member from marketing is responsible for ensuring that appropriate marketing expertise is brought to bear on the project, that a marketing perspective is provided on all key issues of the project, that project subobjectives dependent on the marketing function are met in a timely fashion, and that marketing issues that impact other functions are raised proactively within the team. Each core team member wears a functional hat which makes him or her the focal point and manager responsible for a function that delivers its unique contribution to the overall project.

But each core team member also wears a team hat. In addition to representing his or her function, each core team member accepts responsibility for overall team results. In this role, the core team shares responsibility with the heavyweight project manager for the development procedures followed by the team, and for the overall results that those procedures deliver. The core team is accountable for the success of the project, and can blame no one but itself if it fails to manage the project, execute the tasks, and deliver the performance agreed upon at the outset.

What is unique in the core team members' responsibilities is not so much their accountability for tasks in their own function, but the fact that they are responsible for how those tasks are subdivided, organized, and accomplished. Unlike the traditional functional team structure, which takes as given the subdivision of tasks and the means by which those tasks will be conducted and completed, the core heavyweight team is given the power and responsibility to change the substance of those tasks when doing so will improve the performance of the project. Since this is a role that core team members do not play under a lightweight or functional team structure, it is often the most difficult for them to accept fully and learn to apply. It is essential, however, if the heavyweight team is to realize its full potential. Often core team members came to view these new skills as a major contribution to their career and its development.

The Executive Sponsor. With so much more accountability delegated to the project team, it is not surprising that establishing effective relationships with senior management requires special mechanisms. The need is for senior management to retain the ability to guide the project and its leader, while empowering the team to lead and act. The definition of such a person is an executive sponsor. This sponsor takes on the role of coach and mentor for the heavyweight project leader and core team, and seeks to maintain close, ongoing contact with the team's efforts. Typically such a sponsor might be the vice president of engineering, marketing, or manufacturing for the business unit. In addition to serving as a coach for the team, the executive sponsor serves as a liaison through which other members of the executive staff must work in interfacing with the team. If other members of senior management have concerns or inputs to voice or need current information on project status, communication takes place through the executive sponsor. This reduces the number of mixed signals received by the team and clarifies for the organization the reporting and evaluation relationship between the team and senior management. It also increases the burden on the assigned executive sponsor to set appropriate limits and bounds on the team so that organizational surprises are avoided.

Often the executive sponsor and team find it useful to identify and distinguish those areas where the team clearly has decision-making power and control and need not check with their executive sponsor before moving ahead from areas where other organizational concerns require review. In one electronics firm that has used heavyweight teams for some time, one of the early meetings between the executive sponsor and the core team focuses on generating a list of areas where the executive sponsor expects to provide oversight and be consulted because those areas are of great concern to the entire executive staff and represent areas where team actions may well raise policy issues for the larger organization. In this firm, areas over which the executive staff want to maintain some control include:

- Resource commitment—head count, fixed costs, expenses outside the approved project plan
- Pricing for major customers and major accounts
- Potential slips in major milestone dates (the executive sponsor wants early warning and recovery plans)
- Plans for the transition from development project to operating status
- Thorough reviews at major milestones or every three months, whichever occurs sooner
- Review of incentive rewards that have company-wide implications for consistency and equity
- Cross-project issues such as resource optimization, prioritization, and balance.

Identifying these areas of potential concern at the outset can help the executive sponsor and the core team better carry out their assigned responsibilities. It also helps other executives feel more comfortable working through the executive sponsor when they have concerns, since they know these "boundary issues" have been articulated and are jointly understood.

The Necessity of Fundamental Change

Compared to a traditional functional organization, creating a team that is "heavy," a team with effective leadership, strong problem-solving skills and, the ability to integrate across functions, requires basic changes in the way development works. But it also requires change in the fundamental behavior of engineers, designers, and marketers in their day-to-day work. A comparison of two development teams, each working in the computer industry, illustrates the depth of change required to realize fully the power of the heavyweight team.

The two teams, A and B, launched the development of a small computer system, each aimed at a different market at about the same time. Both teams had market introduction targets within the next twelve months. By chance, both products were to use an identical, custom-designed microprocessor chip in addition to other unique and standard chips.

The situation[6] illustrating the nature of the challenge in creating an effective heavyweight team structure where none had existed previously arose when each team sent this identical, custom-designed chip—call it "supercontroller"—to the vendor for pilot production. Initially, the vendor quoted a twenty-week turnaround to both teams. At the time of the quote, the supercontroller chip was already on the critical path for Team B, with a planned turnaround of eleven weeks. Thus, every week saved on that chip would save one week in the overall project schedule. Furthermore, Team B already was anticipating that it would be late in meeting its initial market introduction target date. When the twenty-week vendor lead time issue first came up in a Team B meeting, Jim, the core team member from engineering, reported that they were working on accelerating the delivery date, but that the vendor was a large company known for its slowness. Suggestions from other core team members on how to accelerate the delivery were politely rebuffed, including one suggestion to have a senior executive contact their counterpart at the vendor. While Team B's Company did considerable business with the chip vendor, Jim did not consider that suggestion promising.

For Team A, the original quote of a twenty-week turnaround still left a little slack, and thus initially the supercontroller chip was not on the critical path. Within a couple of weeks, however, other changes in the activities and schedule put this chip on Team A's critical path, and the issue received immediate attention. When raised at the team's weekly meeting, Fred, the core team member from manufacturing, stated that he thought the turnaround time quoted was too long and that he would try to reduce it. At the next meeting of Team A, Fred brought some good news: through discussions with the vendor, he had been able to get a commitment that pulled in the delivery of the supercontroller chip by eleven weeks! That is, rather than the original twenty-week quote, the vendor was now willing to assure a nine-week cycle. Furthermore, Fred thought that the quote might be reduced even further by a phone call from one of the company's senior manufacturing executives to a contact of his at the vendor. Jim and Fred clearly had different approaches to solving the same problem. But what makes this episode so instructive is that Teams A and B (and Jim and Fred) were in the same company. Not only were they in the same company, but the company had developed a structure for project management, including guidelines on roles and responsibilities of team members. Thus, Jim and Fred worked in the same basic system. But their approaches were very different. Consider what happened shortly after Jim obtained the new commitment from the vendor.

Two days later, Team B held one of its regular team meetings. The supercontroller chip again came up during the status review, and no change from the original schedule was identified. Since the finance person, Ann, served on both teams and had been present at Team A's meeting, she told Team B that Team A had reduced the cycle time from twenty to nine weeks. Jim responded that the core team was aware that Team A had made such efforts, but that the information concerning nine weeks was not correct, and that the original twenty-week delivery date still held. Furthermore, Jim indicated that Fred's efforts (on behalf of Team A) had caused some disruption internally, and in the future it was important that Team A not take such initiatives before coordinating with Team B. Jim stated that this was particularly true when an outside vendor was involved, and closed the topic by saying that a meeting to clear up the situation would be held that afternoon with Fred from Team A and Team B's engineering and purchasing people.

The next afternoon there was a Team A meeting which Ann attended. At that meeting Fred confirmed the accelerated delivery schedule for the supercontroller chip. Eleven weeks had indeed been clipped out of the schedule to the benefit of both Teams A and B. At a subsequent Team B meeting, Jim confirmed the new schedule for Team B. Curious about the differences in perspective, Ann decided to learn more about this situation. On the one hand, Team A had identified an obstacle and removed it from its path; Team B had identified an identical obstacle and failed to move it at all.

In a follow-up discussion with Ann, Fred pointed out that the Team B person negotiating with the vendor was the engineering manager responsible for development of the supercontroller chip. That manager knew the chip's technical requirements, but had little experience dealing with chip vendors. (He had long been a specialist in circuit design.) Without that experience, he had a hard time pushing back against the vendor's "standard line." Fred's manufacturing experience with several chip vendors enabled him to calibrate the vendor's dates against his best-case experience and extract an earlier commitment.

Fred's experience, therefore, told him that the vendor's initial commitment did not make sense. But there was more. Fred had also bought into the team's charter, and the long lead time on the supercontroller chip stood in the way of the team's success. So, Fred went after it and figured out how to get it off the critical path. In contrast, Jim—who had worked in the traditional functional organization for many years—saw vendor relations on a pilot build as his job, but did not see getting the vendor to shorten the cycle time as his responsibility, or even within the range of his authority. He was more concerned with avoiding conflict and not disturbing the water than with achieving the overarching goal of the team.

It is interesting to note that in the case of Team B, engineering raised the issue, and, while unwilling to take aggressive steps to resolve it, also blocked the resolution of the issue on the part of others. In Team A, however, while the issue came up initially through engineering, it was Fred in manufacturing who proactively went after it. In the case of Team B, getting a prototype chip returned from a vendor was still being treated as an "engineering responsibility," whereas in the case of Team A, it was treated as a "team responsibility." Since Fred was the person best qualified to attack that issue, he did so.

Both Team A and Team B had a charter, a contract, a co-located core team staffed with generalists, a project leader, articulated responsibilities, and an executive sponsor. Yet Jim's and Fred's understanding of what these things meant for them personally and for the team at the detailed, working level was quite different. While the teams had been through similar training and team start-up processes, Jim apparently saw the new approach as a different organizational framework within which work would get done as before. Fred seemed to see it as an opportunity to work in a different way—to take responsibility for reconfiguring tasks, drawing skills, and resources, where required, for getting the job done in the best way possible.

Although both teams were "heavyweight" in theory, Fred's team was much "heavier" in its operation and impact. Heaviness, then, is not just a matter of structure and mechanism, but of attitudes and behavior. Firms that try to create heavyweight teams without making the deep changes needed to realize the power in the team's structure will find the team approach problematic. Those intent on using teams for platform projects and willing to make the basic changes we have discussed here, will enjoy the advantages of focus, integration and effectiveness.

Building Capability for Multiple Approaches

Not all projects that firms undertake require the creation of a dedicated cross-functional heavyweight team. Heavyweight teams may be highly effective for platforms or next-generation development, but they approach overkill for those projects so small that only a few engineers need to work on the project. Others may require a significant technical advance, or involve the creation of a whole new business. Indeed, we can easily imagine a situation in which the firm would need capability in all four of the project organization types that we have discussed in this chapter.

But creating a portfolio of approaches is complicated by the tendency for development organizations to adopt a dominant orientation or a standard approach to leadership and organization. That dominant orientation in firms determines what is easy and likely to work, and what is hard and likely to be less effective. It thus determines the range of approaches and projects the firm can hope to apply and carry out.

In the four models of development organization we presented in this chapter, two represent a dominant orientation—the functional structure, and the heavyweight team. Firms whose basic systems, skills, practices, and mechanisms are functional, for example, will find it relatively easy to implement lightweight teams. The lightweight setup is largely functional with an overlay of light coordination. Moving to a heavyweight team, however, is much more difficult, and is unlikely to be fully successful if the functional structure remains the dominant orientation. Like Jim and Team A, a functional orientation runs deep and affects behavior in subtle ways, ways that make a heavyweight structure difficult. Without basic changes in systems, practices, attitudes, and behaviors, attempts to add a heavyweight team capability in what is essentially a functional organization may create a "middleweight" approach, but are unlikely to build a true heavyweight team.

In contrast, firms that have teams as their dominant orientation and have built their systems, training efforts, communication structures, and patterns of leadership around heavyweight teams, will find it relatively easy to implement autonomous tiger teams. And unlike the functional structure, they will find it possible to work a lightweight and functional approach as well. Because the heavyweight team has a functional organization carrying out detailed work and support activities, carrying out lightweight projects or even functional projects involves adjustments in the standard approach (e.g., teams are not dedicated or co-located, task structure is defined by function rather than team) instead of adding new activities or capabilities that conflict with the established system. Of course, the lightweight teams are likely to be somewhat "heavier" than if the dominant orientation were functional. But that may have positive consequences as well.

The experience of Chaparral Steel illustrates the challenge and the advantages of building capability for several approaches to development.[7] Located in Midlothian, Texas, thirty miles south of Dallas, by the early 1990s Chaparral was producing well over a million tons per year of steel products used in forging (high alloy) and construction (structural) products. Using an electric furnace, a continuous caster, and a rolling mill to convert steel scrap into various milled products, Chaparral had continued to improve its performance through a variety of product and process development efforts. Chaparral defined three types of projects: major advanced development, platform, and incremental. Projects of the first type might require an expenditure of $3–$5 million over a period of three to five years, but would provide a breakthrough product or process. Platform projects might require $500,000 to $1 million in development expenses and take twelve to twenty-four months to execute. Incremental projects typically incurred development expenditures of $100,000–$200,000 dollars, lasted a couple of months, and provided very quick payback. At any point in time, the organization might have forty or fifty development projects underway, of which no more than a couple would be major advanced development efforts, perhaps three to five would be platform efforts, and the remainder would be incremental efforts.

Because of the cost competitiveness of their industry and the operating demands required for profitable products and processes, Chaparral conducts all of its development efforts on its factory floor and staffs them primarily with line people. However, the team structure and project leadership used for each of the three types varies considerably. The incremental projects are almost all done by functional subgroups with a lightweight project manager. However, with so many projects going on and projects being so common, everyone understands the role of the lightweight project manager and wants to be supportive: they know, at some point, they will be one of those lightweight project managers and will desire the same kind of treatment. Thus the support and cooperation provided to lightweight project managers tends to be substantially greater than in many traditional functional organizations. The platform projects are headed up by heavyweight project managers who have probably been a department manager and, following completion of the platform effort, will go back to being a department manager. The advanced development projects are put under the direction of one of seven general foreman who report directly to the vice president of manufacturing (or one of the other vice presidents). These major projects start as advanced development efforts; once technical feasibility is proven they quickly become breakthrough projects, but with little or no change in team composition.

For Chaparral, this mix of approaches has served it well in satisfying the range of development opportunities and challenges faced in their business. Depending on the mix of technical depth, coordination and integration of known tasks, the level of system integration, and the degree of breakthrough and new thinking required, Chaparral can pick a team structure, a project manager, and an overall management approach that makes sense for the situation. Expectations have been established over more than a decade and thus procedures and approaches—as well as their governing principles—are well known throughout the organization.

It thus appears that the central choice is whether the firm wants the capability to run effective heavyweight teams in its development portfolio. If so, it must create the heavyweight team as its dominant orientation. With a functional orientation, the firm's effective capabilities will range from a functional structure to "middleweight" systems. Tiger teams could also exist as a wholly independent, separate activity. With heavyweight teams as the dominant orientation, the firm's capabilities could range from the tiger team to the functional structure, although steps then must be taken to ensure that the team orientation does not limit the depth of technical skill developed in the functional organization.

CHAPTER 9

Tools and Methods

A fundamental challenge in developing a new product or process is to combine engineering detail—specific dimensions, parts parameters, materials, and components—into a coherent whole. What attracts and delights customers in a new product, and what is compelling in a new process, is system performance. As we have argued thus far in this book, achieving superior performance in a new product or process demands getting the strategy right, laying out an effective aggregate plan, creating an overall process that effectively integrates the functions, and creating communications processes, skills, and capabilities that support effective cross-functional interaction. All of these things are crucial, but in the final analysis, when we search for an understanding of truly outstanding development, we must eventually get down to the working level where individual designers, marketers, and engineers work together to make detailed decisions and solve specific problems. The magic in an outstanding product or a superior process is in the details. Thus, detailed problem solving is at the core of outstanding development.

Effective problem solving and the methods and tools used to accomplish it are the focus of Chapters 9 and 10. Problems may arise in any phase of development and concern all the functions. Thus, we are interested in understanding how individuals, work groups, and organizations carry out problem solving in product and process engineering, marketing, field service, and manufacturing. In this context a "problem" occurs when developers encounter a gap between the current design (or plan, process, or prototype) and customer requirements. In the development of the MEI 2010, discussed in Chapter 6, engineers encountered a screen problem on the monitor's display device. Through testing and interaction with customers it became apparent that nurses experienced a glare that obscured information and made the display difficult to read. The nurses' experience signaled the existence of a problem, but did not define it precisely enough to allow immediate solution. Excessive glare could be the result of an inappropriate display angle, inappropriate materials, absence of control in the manufacturing process, or any number of underlying causes. When confronted by this gap between customer needs and product performance, the development team faces a number of ways of meeting customer expectations. Although there may be a team member responsible for the display, solving excessive glare is likely to involve issues that extend beyond that narrow functional domain. Thus, the problem cuts across disciplines and perhaps even functions.

How the development team takes action to close the gap—the way it frames and defines the problem, generates alternatives, organizes and conducts tasks, and implements solutions—detemines the speed, efficiency, and effectiveness of problem solving. Where such problems are critical to overall system performance, drive program lead time, involve significant resources, or have decisive influence on a customer's perception of the product or process as a whole, the effectiveness of problem solving at the detailed local level can have a powerful influence on the overall performance of the development process. Effective problem solving at the working level is not a sufficient condition for overall success, but in our experience, it is a critical and necessary part of an outstanding development process.

The remainder of this chapter is divided into three parts. We first lay out a framework for thinking about problem solving at the detailed level. Using what we call the "design-build-test" cycle, we identify activities that seem to be crucial in solving problems and suggest some of the problems and pitfalls that often accompany traditional methods. In the second part of the chapter we study examples of formal approaches to problem solving. These "structured methodologies"—in particular, quality function deployment (QFD) and design for manufacturability (DFM)—have been developed to deal with the challenge of solving detailed problems that cut across traditional disciplines, departments, and functions. We then turn to an examination of new computer-based systems and methods. The computer has the potential to change in fundamental ways the nature of development, including the modes of solving detailed problems. Our focus in this section of the chapter is on systems that facilitate communication, manage large-scale databases, and provide a means for capturing knowledge generated through the problem-solving process. We conclude with observations and discussion of the implications of such computer systems for management.

Although our focus is on activities that occur at a very detailed level in the development process, our perspective in this chapter remains that of the general manager. We have argued in previous chapters that the role of the general manager is to build capability and create effective processes in the organization. It is our view that carrying out that role requires an in-depth understanding of the problem solving process at the working level. General managers need to understand the process not only because changes in it often provide significant leverage for improving development, but also because such an understanding can be an important guide in making investment decisions about processes and capabilities. Furthermore, deep understanding may be useful as general managers make specific decisions about specific projects. With a framework for thinking about detailed problem solving and an understanding of modern methods and systems, general managers will be in a much better position to evaluate the potential and progress of specific products or processes under development.

A Framework: The Design-Build Test Cycle

The essence of product and process development problems may be defined as a performance gap between current practice or designs and the desired target. Whether it is a component within a system or a single part, whether it is a new process layout in the plant or a new piece of equipment, the fundamental problem is to design and develop something that will close the gap between current performance and the requirements of the new product or process. If the old system or existing design already meets requirements, then the design problem is trivial. But where a gap exists, developers must search for new concepts that will deliver the desired level of performance.

Consider, for example, the problem of developing a gear system for the automatic film rewinder in a new camera.[1] Exhibit 9–1 illustrates the placement of the gear system in a simple schematic diagram of the automatic rewinder in a new camera design. In this example, a company that we shall call New West Photo has launched a project to develop a new product to compete in the compact, easy-to-use, 35 mm camera market. The designers have determined that the new camera must have an improved automatic rewind system. The rewinder performs two functions: it advances the film one position after each shot, and it rewinds the film when the roll is finished. The rewinder is powered by a battery which drives an electric motor connected to a film roller

Exhibit 9–1

The Gear System in an Auto Rewinder for a 35 mm Camera

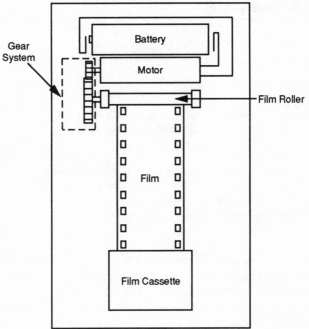

NOTE: The gear system is drawn with two gears for illustration only. The number of gears is a design parameter and designs with more than two gears are possible.

by the gear system. After preliminary testing of an initial design, it became clear that the design was too noisy, bulky, and expensive. Thus, the design problem in this example is to develop a gear system for a rewinder that takes less space and is less noisy and less expensive.

From the standpoint of the gear system, the new design involves establishing a fit between two very different aspects of the system. The first is what we will call "design parameters." These are the decisions under the control of the designers or engineers. Typical design parameters in a gear system include the diameter of the gears, the profiles of the gear teeth, gear thickness, and the manufacturing tolerances associated with each. Other design parameters include the number of gears, the materials used in the gears, and the types of lubrication.

The second aspect of the system is "customer attributes," or customer requirements. From a customer's perspective, the gear system is important because of its impact on the performance of the film rewind system. Framed in these terms, customers care about speed (wait time), sound,

221

EXHIBIT 9–2

Selected Design Parameters for Gears and Customer Attributes in a Film Rewind System

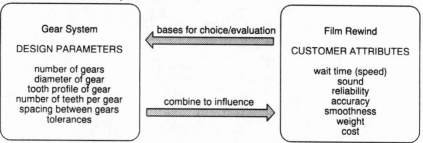

NOTE: Design parameters create a gear system that influences attributes of the film rewind system that customers care about. These attributes are, in turn, the basis for evaluation and choice of design parameters.

reliability, size, and cost. These attributes are only a part of a broad set that customers evaluate when deciding whether to buy a specific camera, and are the attributes most directly connected to the performance of the gear system. Since performance is influenced by design parameters, they are closely linked to customer attributes. But there is not a one-to-one correspondence between a specific design parameter and a specific customer attribute. Indeed, for the most part, a given customer attribute is determined or influenced by several design parameters. Furthermore, customer requirements reflect the performance of the system as a whole. As long as the gear system is sufficiently quiet, customers do not care whether it is because the gear is intrinsically quiet or because the camera case muffles the noise effectively. However, while both approaches may satisfy a customer's desire for a quiet camera, they have very different implications for cost and weight. Thus, the example of noise illustrates problems of tradeoffs in design. Design parameters often interact in ways that impose choices on designers. An important challenge of design, therefore, is to select design parameters that strike an effective balance among competing customer attributes.[2]

Exhibit 9–2 lays out the basic relationship between design parameters and customer attributes, using our gear design example. System design parameters for the gear system include the number of gears, the diameter and tooth profile for each gear (and hence the number of teeth and spacing between gears), and associated manufacturing tolerances. These design parameters influence important customer attributes of the rewind system such as wait time (the time a photographer must wait between photographs or at the end of a roll), sound (it is important to maintain a balance—some sound is necessary to indicate to the customer that the mechanism is working, but too much "noise" disturbs the photographer's subjects and may be unpleasant to the photographer), reliability, accuracy, smoothness, weight, and cost. These attributes are the basis for customer evaluation of a particular film rewind system, and therefore become the basis for choice and evaluation of alternative gear design parameters.

The Design-Build-Test Cycle

Striking an effective balance among customer attributes and closing the gap in performance is the focus of problem solving in development.[3] Solving problems is a learning process. No matter how much an engineer, a marketer, or a manufacturer may know about a given problem, there are always unique aspects of any new system that must be understood before an effective design may be developed. Except for the easiest of problems, developers are unlikely to come up with a complete, effective design in a single iteration. Instead, developers go through several iterations, learning a little more about the problem and alternative solutions each time, as they converge to a final design and complete, detailed specifications.

Each iteration or problem-solving cycle consists of three phases illustrated in Exhibit 9–3. In the *design phase*, a developer frames the problem and establishes goals for the problem-solving process. Problem framing is crucial, since the apparent gaps in performance that we observe are often caused by underlying conditions that are difficult to observe and characterize. A problem with noise, for example, may be caused by the type of material, gear width, tooth profile, gear train alignment, or a variety of other design parameters, including the precision of the manufacturing process. But the frame we put on a problem also depends on how we define the objectives. In the case of noise, for example, it may be apparent because of customer feedback that the old design had undesirable noise characteristics. A clear objective of the new system could be, therefore, to reduce noise below a given threshold level. A deeper understanding of the problem, however, may suggest that customers like to hear the rewind system working. Thus, the objective may not be simply to reduce noise below some threshold, but rather to create the right kind of sound—a sound that is distinct but soft and nonabrasive.

Once the developer has framed the problem, the next step in the design phase is to generate alternatives. Based on the developer's understanding of the relationship between design parameters and customer attributes, several alternative designs for physical models may be appropriate. The purpose of the alternative designs may be to explore the relationship between design parameters and specific customer at-

Exhibit 9–3

The Design-Build-Test Cycle in Problem Solving*
Phases of Problem Solving

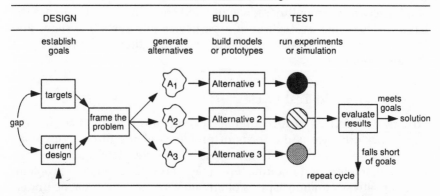

DESIGN	BUILD	TEST
establish goals	generate alternatives	build models or prototypes	run experiments or simulation

* The diagram illustates the design-build-test cycle. Goals are set, problems framed, alternatives developed, models or prototypes built, and tests conducted. If the test reveals a solution, the process stops. If no solution is found or the goals are not yet reached, the cycle is repeated. Note that repeating the cycle may involve revising the goals. Later cycles are often of shorter duration than earlier cycles.

tributes. If the particular design cycle under discussion comes at a later stage of development, the purpose of the alternative designs may be to refine an established concept.

In the second, or *build phase* of the problem-solving cycle, the developer builds working models of the design alternatives. The purpose of the second phase is to put alternative designs into a form that allows for testing. Depending upon what a developer is trying to learn, the working models may take several forms. At an early stage of gear development, for example, a developer may implement alternatives electronically in a computer-aided design (CAD) workstation, using the computer to display graphically and visually the gears' characteristics. For some purposes it may be useful to take the build phase one step further, creating alternatives using easy-to-work with materials such as plastic or soft metals. While computer simulation may provide sufficient information to arrive at effective solutions, later-stage testing and development may require the building of physical prototypes using materials and production processes that are reasonably close to those used in a commercial process.

In the third or *test phase* of the problem-solving cycle, working models, prototypes, or computer-generated images are tested. Depending upon the purposes of the particular problem-solving cycle, the tests may focus on a particular dimension or may involve full-scale system evaluation. In the case of gear noise, for example, an early testing scheme may examine the decibel level generated by alternative designs. Such a test could be run in a testing laboratory and the results used to generate an understanding of the connection between different design parameters and the overall noise level. Subsequently, given designs may be implemented with prototype parts and tested with potential customers.

Although conducting tests appears relatively straightforward, in practice getting good information out of the testing phase requires very careful forethought and skilled execution of a test plan. In a laboratory setting, test engineers worry about things such as accuracy, precision, and the ability to calibrate measurements. In addition, tests are subject to noise, or random variation caused by fluctuations in the environment that have not been accounted for or controlled. In order to cope with noise from vibration, temperature, humidity, and even stray magnetic fields, engineers often repeat tests several times to identify the amount of noise in the testing process. Even when engineers have well-designed procedures to deal with noise and have established instruments and processes to ensure accurate and precise measurement, there is still the problem of fidelity. Fidelity refers to the extent to which the test being conducted reflects the actual case of interest. With respect to gears in the film rewind system, the issue is whether a laboratory test of decibel levels reflects the way customers will perceive noise in the use of the camera. Yet even when the test moves into the field, the issue of fidelity continues to come into play. For example, developers must be concerned that the customers involved in the field tests are representative of the customers they are trying to reach, and that the conditions under which the tests are conducted effectively represent the mode in which the camera actually will be used.

A single design-build-test cycle generates insight and information about the connection between specific design parameters and customer attributes. That information becomes the basis for a new design-build-test cycle and the process continues until developers arrive at a solution—a design—that meets the requirements. Thus, the effectiveness of problem solving in development depends not only on the speed, productivity, and quality of each individual step in the cycle, but also on the number of cycles required to achieve a solution. The number of cycles depends directly on the extent to which activities at each of the problem-solving steps are linked and integrated. However, the number of cycles and their length also depends on the processes and procedures established by management and thus can be viewed as critical development decisions.

While it is important that individual activities in problem solving—the design of alternatives, building of prototypes and conducting of tests—be carried out effectively, performance in problem solving depends on establishing effective connections between these activities. If the tests conducted are not planned with a clear understanding of design objectives and the nature of the problem being solved, then the information developed may be only partially useful in the hands of the designers. If the prototypes or models built do not reflect design intent, they likewise will fail to deliver powerful information in the problem-solving process. The absence of close connections in the different steps of problem solving leads to multiple reiterations and extra cycles, and thus longer development times and lower productivity.

The issue of connectedness between problem-solving cycles also arises in the relationship between the individual part or component and the larger system in which it is embedded. In the case of the film rewinder, for example, problem solving around the gear system must be connected not only to the design of the new rewinder, but to manufacturing and vendor process development as well. Moreover, establishing targets for the design of the gear system is connected to choices about customer attributes and thus to problem solving going on in marketing. Each of these problem-solving cycles must be linked if the overall system is to be coherent. It is not enough to do a good job designing a gear system; the solutions developed must be consistent with solutions developed in manufacturing or marketing. Thus, effective problem solving at the working level is a matter of skill and capability in carrying out individual tasks in individual design-build-test cycles, as well as a matter of effectively linking and integrating problem-solving cycles in closely related areas.

Structured Methodologies for Effective Problem Solving

The challenge in effective problem solving is both to execute individual elements of the cycle (and individual cycles) rapidly and well, and to link individual cycles so that solutions are coherent. As pressure for improved performance in lead time, cost, and quality has increased, firms have adopted a variety of methods to improve problem solving. At first glance many of these methods appear to be little more than applied common sense—plan your work, think before you act, consider the consequences, and do it right the first time. While common sense is an all-too-rare commodity, there is more to structured methods than a straightforward application of what everyone already knows. The difficulty is in finding a method and logic that works where people, information, objectives, and capabilities interact in a complex system. Indeed, for people intimately familiar with detailed problem solving in traditional development processes, the ebb and flow of problem formulation and solution within and across functions and departments often has an illogical, surreal quality to it. Consider the following vignettes drawn from a project to develop a gear system for a new camera:

226

Developing the Auto Rewind System

Bob Hancock, a design engineer in the gear design department, read through Beth Lardner's report on the new camera project. Lardner, the project liaison engineer for gear design, had summarized a recent design meeting:

> The critical design issues for us are clearly cost, reliability, and speed of rewind. The targets are aggressive, but within our reach. [Hancock smiled when he read that line.] I have enclosed marketing's specifications and the project timing plan.

As he read through the specifications, Hancock noted that most of what marketing wanted conformed to the standard specifications for gears used in the gear design department. There would be some problems in meeting both the speed and cost objectives, but he had some ideas to try out. And there were some new requirements for sound. The marketing group was asking for "sound that is quiet, but effective." While that sounded pretty vague, Lardner's notes in the margin indicated that noise below 60 decibels was the target.

(*Three months later.*) Bob Hancock could not believe his eyes. Beth Lardner's latest report on the design of the rewind system called for another redesign to improve sound. This was the fifth iteration on the specifications and the project was already five weeks behind and slipping. After the first two iterations it had become clear that somebody in marketing really cared about sound. Hancock's tests had shown that meeting the noise requirement was likely to create problems in cost (his design called for more teeth per gear and higher precision in machining). But that was not all. Even after the design met the decibel target, marketing's feedback was that the sound wasn't "crisp" enough.

(*Nine months later.*) Ellen Gaither, an engineer in the gear engineering department, looked over the latest report from the test department on the new gear system for the auto rewinder. The gears had failed life testing again! Ellen walked down the hall and put the report in front of her supervisor, Randy Etheridge, stating:

> Randy, this is really weird. The redesign of the gear teeth we put into prototype last month should have worked. All of our tests indicated that we had solved the failure problem. And now this! There must be something funny going on in processing. We keep getting these process notification reports that tell us our designs are not feasible because of tolerances, but the plant should be able to handle this. There's got to be something else going on, but Jankowski (liaison engineer for gear engineering) doesn't seem to be able to get any data out of process engineering.

227

While Gaither was talking to Etheridge, another conversation was going on in process engineering between Rod McQuarrie (process engineer) and Eddie Robertson (gear machining supervisor):

> Robertson: I told you that new design wouldn't work. We just can't hold the tolerances on that drive gear without taking a hit on our costs. We must have sent through five or six process notification sheets on that design. You've got to get the engineers to change their approach.
>
> McQuarrie: Yeah, I know. But I'm not sure that the tolerances are behind this life test problem. We've got to work on the tolerances to hit our cost target, but I think something else is going on in this reliability problem.

Structured Methods

The problem-solving attempts depicted in these vignettes are characteristic of organizations that rely on highly specialized engineers working in an environment in which communication occurs through formal documents and intermediaries, with few common methods and limited language to facilitate cross-functional problem solving. Hancock goes through cycles of redesign because the relative importance of different attributes is vague, and because new requirements for sound are difficult to translate into terms with which he can work. Gaither and McQuarrie both think "something else is going on," but they have been playing engineering "Ping-pong," throwing the problem back and forth with little headway and limited resolution.

Indeed, the root cause of the life-testing problem was a change in the metal being used in the gears (a change made by the supplier and unknown to either department) and a control problem in one of the heat treating processes in the plant. The patterns of communications in use (formal documents, indirect through intermediaries) and the absence of a shared framework and language made it very difficult (and thus time consuming and expensive) for people in gear engineering and process engineering to arrive at a common formulation of the problem and thus an effective solution.[4]

Structured methodologies—formal procedures with structured tasks, and explicit representations of issues and choices—for design and development have been formulated to deal with these problems. In this section, we illustrate two commonly used methodologies. Although both of these methods have application throughout the development process, we apply them to a very specific phase of development. The first, quality function deployment, we apply to the early stages of development where targets are set and the basic product or process architecture is established. The second, design for manufacturability, we apply to the later phases of development, where detailed engineering linking product and process design is the focus of development effort. In both cases, we use our gear design problem to illustrate the methodology. Our intent here is not to provide a detailed treatment of each method. Rather, we use a very simple example to illustrate the nature of the methodology and its potential role in creating effective problem solving at the working level.

Quality Function Deployment

Quality function deployment, or QFD, is a method used to identify critical customer attributes and to create a specific link between customer attributes and design parameters.[5] The method uses matrices to organize information and to help marketers and design engineers answer three primary questions: What attributes are critical to our customers? What design parameters are important in driving those customer attributes? What should the design parameter targets be for the new design?

The organizing framework for the QFD process is a planning tool called the "house of quality." Each step in the QFD process involves building up an element of the house of quality. Exhibit 9–4 lays out a simplified house of quality for our gear system design problem. Working as a team, design engineers and marketers *first establish critical customer attributes for the product*. These attributes become the rows of the central matrix of the house of quality. Customer attributes may be expressed in terms that customers use in describing their use and perceptions of the product. Working together, the team may also group various attributes to create a broader category that simplifies the planning and analysis. In our example, we have singled out six attributes for analysis: speed, quiet operation, crisp and accurate sound, cost, size, and reliability. The team also establishes weightings that represent the relative importance of the different attributes from the customer's perspective. Using percentages (the complete set of weightings adds up to 100 percent), we have indicated that of the six attributes, our target customers (sophisticated amateur photographers) place most emphasis on speed and reliability, although taken together the two dimensions of sound are relatively important.

Once customer requirements have been identified, in the *second* step the team establishes *the critical design parameters that drive system performance*. These parameters describe the part or product in measurable terms and should be directly linked to customer attributes. The selected design parameters form the columns of the central matrix. Exhibit 9–4 presents four parameters: number of teeth, lubricant, tooth thickness, and manufacturing precision.

The *third* step in the QFD process is *to fill in the body of the central matrix*.

229

Exhibit 9–4

The "House of Quality" for a Gear Design Problem at New West Photo*

Customer Requirements	Design Parameters	Importance (%)	Number of teeth per gear	Lubricant	Tooth thickness	Manufacturing precision	Competitive Data on Customer Perceptions of Current Products
	Speed (low wait time)	25		−		0	
	Quiet	10	+	++	−	+	
	Crisp and accurate sound	9					
	Low cost	12	− −	−	+	−	
	Compact	10		0	−	+	
	Reliable	34	−	0	+	++	

Competitive Data on Customer Perceptions of Current Products

1 2 3 4 5

poor   excellent

● New West
X Competitor 1
■ Competitor 2

* The "house of quality" relates primary customer requirements to the major design parameters about which the development team will make design choices. The right-hand side shows customer perceptions of existing competitive products, while the top portion shows the interrelationship of the design parameters.

Each cell in the matrix represents a potential link between a design parameter and a customer attribute. This "relationship matrix" indicates both the direction and the strength of the relationship. Numbers or symbols may be used to establish the character of the relationship. Depending upon the extent of engineering knowledge, the team may be able to assign very specific values to the relationship. For other relationships, where less information is available, the value may be only qualitative in nature. In the gear design problem, for example, we have used simple pluses and minuses to indicate the nature and strength of the relationships. Increasing the number of teeth per gear, for example, reduces gear noise and thus has a positive impact on the customer attribute "quiet." However, increasing the number of teeth requires better tooling and more machining time. As a result, increasing the number of teeth may increase the cost and have a negative impact on the customer attribute "low cost." Such an evaluation of the relationship between design parameters and customer attributes evolves through an interactive process based on engineering experience, information from customers, and data from statistical analysis or designed experiments.

Two additional types of information complete the house of quality. The *fourth* step focuses on *customer perceptions of the company's existing product compared to its competitors.* The company's relative position on each customer attribute provides insight both as to where problems in the market may exist, and where opportunities for potential advantage may lie. New West Photo's existing designs are perceived as relatively low cost, and their automatic rewind systems are relatively slow, noisy, and bulky. In contrast, Competitor 1 has an edge in both cost and performance.

The *fifth* and last piece of analysis in the house of quality is the interrelationship or *interaction between design parameters.* In order to establish these interactions, the house of quality builds two diagonals—up and to the left, and up and to the right—growing out of each column of the matrix. The cells of this "roof matrix" indicate the strength and direction of interrelationships among design parameters. The negative sign in the cell connecting lubricants and number of teeth indicates that increasing the value of one (e.g., using lubricants to reduce noise) tends to decrease the value of the others (e.g., with a better lubricant, the design engineer can tolerate fewer teeth per gear) in engineering design. The roof matrix thus makes clear important tradeoffs that may exist in selecting design parameters, and may identify opportunities for improvements that add important second- or third-order consequences. A new lubricant, for example, may improve smoothness and reduce noise, therefore allowing for a gear design with less precise manufacturing requirements and lower cost.

When the analysis behind the house of quality is complete, the de-

231

velopment team has a summary of critical customer attributes, the design parameters most closely connected to them, the pattern of interactions among those design parameters, and potential opportunities for improving competitive position. But until the house of quality is actually used—until the team establishes targets for critical design parameters, and thus customer attributes—the house of quality is only a summary of information. The QFD process creates a framework within which the issues may be examined in a fruitful and effective way, but hard choices must still be made.

Consider, for example, the problem of sound in the gear system. The house of quality suggests that overall noise level performance is not competitive; the current auto rewind system is too noisy. Moreover, the sound that the auto rewind creates is less "crisp" and "accurate" than competitors' products. Since the sound has a relatively high importance, it is clearly a problem area and an item for focus in the early-stage design process. The most important design parameters for sound are the tooth profiles in the gears and type of lubricant used. (Though other design parameters may have some influence, these two are clearly the most critical.) As far as "crisp" and "accurate" are concerned, however, the cells in the relationship matrix are blank. The implication is that while a crisp and accurate sound is an important attribute from the customer's standpoint, there is little engineering knowledge about the design parameters that drive it.

Before proceeding to establish targets, therefore, it is necessary to investigate the underlying sources of a crisp and accurate sound through discussions with customers and perhaps through experiments involving different camera designs (especially competitive modes that come close to the desired sound). Such experimental evidence may help characterize the customer attribute (e.g., crisp and accurate may be driven by a particular pattern of high frequency sounds) and identify the parameters that influence it. We may find, for example, that the number of gears used in the system as well as the diameter and tooth profiles of each gear are the major factors behind a crisp and accurate sound, although other parameters may have some influence. We may also find however, that design parameters not on the list are important—for example, harmonics in the gear train caused by poor gear-train alignment. Important at this stage of the development process is to use relatively inexpensive experiments to identify the requirements and underlying design parameters. This is far more effective than going through a series of preliminary design iterations that provide little insight into the underlying issues.

In addition to getting a crisp and accurate sound, the noise in the gear system must be reduced. If we focus on the two most important drivers of noise—tooth profile and lubricants—we can use the house of quality to identify the important issues that must be examined in setting targets for those parameters. Improving the tooth profile, for example, is likely to affect manufacturing costs and tooth thickness (to retain strength), and therefore space. A change in the lubricant system could bear some of the burden in reducing noise, but that may also increase cost. At this (early) stage in the design process, the team may weigh costs and benefits and set targets for the lubricant and tooth profile that reduce noise, even at the expense of some additional cost. But the team may also decide that this is an area worth further investigation during the detailed design phase (e.g., looking at additional alternatives or running special experiments to increase knowledge about the sources of gear noise). This may be a tough issue, but it is much better to address it early and within a common framework than to address it late from different perspectives and on a random trial-and-error basis.

QFD has power because it provides a common language and framework within which design engineers and marketers may fruitfully interact. The house of quality makes interrelationships and inherent design choices explicit. It gives precision to the conversations and discussions that go on in identifying design objectives and critical design parameters. By clarifying a very complex and ambiguous situation, the house of quality facilitates early consideration of difficult issues and helps to identify gaps in engineering and marketing knowledge. But QFD, and the "house of quality" in particular, is a tool to be used with focus and flexibility. It needs to be adapted to fit the circumstances of particular products and processes, and it needs to be used where it will have the most value. Many users of QFD have horror stories about design teams that literally fill up wall after wall with matrices so complicated that no one understands them. The organization's time and energy is absorbed in the minutiae of nuts and bolts and no one concentrates on those design parameters that are most crucial in driving customer attributes or in doing the experiments that will provide real insight.

Once an organization has developed some experience with QFD as a process, it becomes apparent that the formal methodology—the specific matrices and the filling in of cells, columns, and rows—is less important than the underlying philosophy and framework for analysis, discussion, and experimentation. Moreover, QFD can be a way to build and store knowledge crucial to the design and development of particular products or processes. Thus, to have its most significant impact, QFD needs to be managed as a framework for communications and analysis, and as a methodology for building and summarizing knowledge about the linkages between design parameters and customer attributes.

Yet even where QFD is understood and used effectively, outstanding firms do not rely on formal procedure or mechanisms by themselves. QFD is a useful framework. But there really is no substitute for engi-

233

neers who understand customers, or for marketing specialists who understand the basic technology of the product. Thus, while formal methods like QFD have an important role to play, they are at their most powerful when used in a development organization where engineers interact directly with customers and have experience in dealing with issues of marketing, and where marketing specialists are comfortable with the technology and have experience interacting with engineers on technical problems. In this, as in so much of development, there is no substitute for competence and understanding the territory of one's functional counterpart.

Design for Manufacturability

In the early phases of development—when attention focuses on establishing overall objectives, laying out product architecture, and setting target design parameters—a methodology like QFD provides a useful framework for cross-functional integration. Much of the analysis and discussion may focus on design engineering and marketing, but manufacturing issues arise at the earliest phases of this process and may be incorporated quite easily in the QFD framework. As development proceeds through detailed engineering, manufacturing issues become acute as engineers begin to establish specific processing requirements and build prototypes. In a traditional, sequential setup (like the one at New West Photo in which Rod McQuarrie and Ellen Gaither found themselves involved), manufacturing issues arise directly only after parts engineers have established basic design parameters and built and tested prototypes for functionality. In order to bring issues of manufacturability into the design process earlier, many firms have implemented "design for manufacturability" (DFM) methods. Like QFD, DFM is a summary category that includes a wide variety of methods.[6] Here we examine two kinds of DFM methods—design rules and design for producibility—and then apply them to our gear system design problem.

Design Rules. The idea that product (or manufacturing process) design needs to comprehend the constraints and capabilities in the downstream manufacturing process has been recognized since the earliest days of mass production. Henry Ford's famous dictum, "any color as long as it's black," illustrates a rule that expresses a process constraint for product designers. Today, design rules are used in a variety of industries ranging from semiconductors to specialty chemicals, and from structural steel to consumer appliances. In essence, design rules express the boundaries within which the manufacturing process operates in terms of the issues confronting product designers. In the case of the new gear

Exhibit 9–5
Design Rules for Fabricated-Assembled Products*

Rule	Intended Impact on Performance
Minimize the number of parts in a design	Simplify assembly; reduce direct labor; reduce material handling and inventory costs
Minimize the number of part numbers (use common parts)	Reduce material handling and inventory costs; improve economies of scale (increase volume through commonality)
Eliminate adjustments	Reduce assembly errors; allow automation; increase capacity and throughput
Eliminate fasteners	Simplify assembly; reduce direct labor cost; reduce squeaks and rattles; improve durability; allow automation
Eliminate jigs and fixtures	Reduce line changeover cost; lower required investment

* Design rules provide directional guidance for designers across a variety of dimensions. Product developers often must choose among conflicting guidelines and determine how far to push in pursuing a given guideline.

system, design rules might be expressed in terms of allowable gear size, tolerances on machining dimensions, production volumes, material types, surface finish characteristics, aging and heat treating requirements, and other processing characteristics that determine critical design parameters. The basic idea behind design rules is to establish an envelope within which the manufacturing process is capable of meeting design requirements. Manufacturing engineers send a message to product designers which says, "if you design within this envelope, our manufacturing process can meet your requirements for volume, cost, quality, and product performance."

If the rules are up to date and accurate, and if product designers have a process for comparing their designs against the rules, design rules can be quite useful in highlighting potential problems early in the design process and identifying high leverage areas for process development. Indeed, one of the outcomes of a design rule process can be choices by the firm to invest in expanding the boundaries of the envelope.

Some firms have expanded the notion of design rules to include principles of design whose application will improve manufacturing performance. Exhibit 9–5 provides examples of such "rules of thumb" for a fabricated, assembled product. These rules reflect experience in which overhead costs (of material handing or inventory tracking, for example) are driven by the number of parts in the total manufacturing system. They also reflect problems with quality where a product design requires careful adjustment of components or subassemblies, or where assembly involves fasteners (e.g., screws, nuts, and bolts) that are difficult to control and are often the source of reliability problems. The rule "eliminate jigs and fixtures" is intended to lower the cost of production line changeovers and reduce the investment required for a new product. Where a product requires parts positioning for transport or assembly, process engineers often use jigs and fixtures to hold the piece in place. If there are many different models or many different products produced in the same assembly facility, an important part of the cost and time for changeover from one product to another is associated with changing jigs and fixtures. A "jigless" design, therefore, may make the assembly process much more flexible.

Experience has shown that the application of such design rules of thumb can have an extraordinary impact on manufacturing cost and productivity. NCR, for example, has shown that application of design for manufacturability concepts like those articulated in Exhibit 9–5 can result in significant reductions in assembly time, the number of parts required in its products, the number of tools and fasteners required, and the number of suppliers involved in the production system. In the NCR 2760—an electronic cash register—DFM methodology resulted in major savings over the predecessor product: a 75 percent reduction in assembly time, 85 percent fewer parts, 65 percent fewer suppliers, no tools required for assembly, no fasteners in the design, and 75 percent less direct labor time (resulting in design lifetime direct labor savings estimated at over $1 million).[7]

Design for Producibility. Rules of thumb like "minimize the number of parts" have often produced dramatic results, particularly in contexts where previous designs have been highly complex and difficult to manufacture. But experience in a number of industries suggests the need to broaden the principles of DFM to encompass a more comprehensive notion of manufacturing system performance. More modern applications of the DFM principle—such as Boothroyd's design-for-assembly concepts—typically focus on an individual part and consider ways to simplify it, combine it with others to reduce the total number of parts, or modify it for easier assembly. Most of these DFM methods are designed to reduce direct labor and manufacturing overhead costs or to improve in-plant quality. But there are other dimensions of manufacturing performance that may suffer as a result of applying traditional DFM rules of thumb.

Take, for example, lead time in product development. Application of the rule "minimize the number of parts" often results in designers combining several simple parts into one complex part. This has the effect of reducing assembly time, inventory carrying costs, and costs associated with managing specific part numbers, and in general makes the product easier to assemble at a lower cost. But it also requires a very complex mold for production. If the new part is on the critical path of the development project, the complexity of the mold may increase development lead time significantly. In a competitive market, increased lead time means that revenues will occur further in the future, and may be smaller because of the loss of early potential customers. Exhibit 9–6 summarizes examples developed by Karl Ulrich that illustrate the impact of alternative designs on overall manufacturing system performance, including the cost associated with lead time. These examples suggest that where parts are on the critical path, application of the rule of thumb that calls for minimizing the number of parts may be very expensive.

The solution to this dilemma is not to abandon DFM principles; rather, it is to embed issues of the number of parts, the choice of fasteners, and other issues associated with traditional DFM rules in a much more comprehensive analysis of manufacturing system performance. This requires methods to evaluate the implications of differences in lead time associated with alternative designs. It may also require rethinking the way that a particular process fits into the overall manufacturing system. The interaction between specific parts and products and the manufacturing system is evident in the issue of manufacturing flexibility.

Take, for example, the situation in which a firm like New West Photo manufactures many different camera models in the same plant. Given increasingly fragmented markets and the need to offer specialized products that meet the requirements and demands of increasingly diversified customers, the plant needs the capability to produce a high variety of products at low cost. Moreover, it needs to be able to respond effectively to shifts in the product mix that occur from time to time in unexpected ways. In this context, flexibility with respect to variety and responsiveness to shifts in product mix are important dimensions of manufacturing performance.

The design of the product may have an important influence on the flexibility actually achieved in manufacturing, but improving system flexibility is unlikely to occur by focusing on the design of a single part or even a single camera. What is required is an approach to design that comprehends the product family as a whole. Dan Whitney has described an approach to modularized design that he calls the "combinatorial method":

Exhibit 9–6

Impact on Manufacturing Performance (Lifetime Cost) of Alternative Designs for Fasteners in a High-Volume Camera Cover*

	Basic Parameters		Lifetime Impact on Cost if Design Shifts from Option 1 to Option 2 (000s of $)
	Option 1: Snap Fit Camera cover is assembled to camera base with snap fit plastic fasteners molded into cover	Option 2: Screws Camera cover is assembled to camera base with four screws	
Material Cost	included in molding cost	screws add 8¢/unit	+254
Labor Cost	easy to assemble	additional assembly time of 15 seconds	+204
Capital Cost	more complex molds	lower tooling costs	−41
System Cost	fewer parts; less material handling	four new parts; one new vendor	+487
Time Cost	longer lead time on molds	simpler mold design and shorter lead time	−2,598
	Total (negative implies net benefit)		−1,694

NOTE: Cost changes are based on an activity cost model developed by Karl Ulrich and his associates. They assume 4 million units produced over the life of the camera, and use prices and cost estimates from experience at Polaroid. For additional information, see K. Ulrich et al., "A Framework for Including the Value of Time in Design-for-Manufacturing Decision Making," M.I.T. Working Paper #3243-9-MSA, February 1991.

* The design matrix identifies the relationship between the manufacturing process design parameters and the product design parameters. The performance matrix shows the relationship between the process design parameters and the performance parameters of the manufacturing process.

The combinatorial method, carried out by marketing and engineering team members, divides a product into generic parts or subassemblies, and identifies the necessary variations of each. The product is then designed to permit any combination of variations of these basic parts to go together physically and functionally. (If there are six basic parts and three varieties of each, for example, the company can build 3^6 or 729 different models.)[8]

When designers and marketers use this kind of methodology to develop a new platform product, they develop not only a specific product, but an architecture for an entire family of products. In the case of our gear design problem, a firm using modular design would not design a new automatic rewind system every time it brought out a new version of a particular camera. Instead, the project to develop the platform product would include an effort to develop a new rewinder and a new gear system that designers would use in several future versions of that product. Engineers working on the platform would design the rewinder to fit a given space constraint and would establish interfaces (how the parts fit together physically, how control is achieved, how the users interact with the rewinder) to guide future development efforts. Future versions of the platform product might incorporate improvements in the rewinder and the gear system, but these improvements would occur within the framework established by the platform product. When subsequent development focuses on introduction of a new member of the family, designers work within the architecture of parts, interfaces, and subassemblies established by the basic platform product. Although adjustments may be required to meet specific requirements, these must be examined within the context of the basic architecture and with respect to their implications for overall system performance.

Implementing DFM. Thus far our discussion of DFM has moved from a relatively narrow definition of specific design rules to a much broader concept of producibility. We have broadened and deepened the scope of DFM in two ways. First, we have redefined performance to include total manufacturing system behavior, including the role of time and flexibility. Second, we have broadened the focus of design itself to include the architecture of a family of products, including the modular design of parts and components and the establishment of interfaces. In all of this analysis, the basic thrust is very similar—to create designs that comprehend the constraints and opportunities in the manufacturing system broadly defined.

Framed in these terms, implementation of a DFM methodology involves: (1) establishing the envelope for the existing process; (2) identifying important connections between design choices and manufacturing system performance; and (3) establishing key dimensions of the product architecture and its impact on the overall manufacturing system. To do this, developers require a design process that structures thinking and establishes critical relationships. Such a process may involve design checklists used by all engineers, procedures for calculating manufacturing system costs (and other dimensions of performance), or creating access to a library of established parts that are consistent with product architecture and capable of providing required functionality (e.g., the engineer does not need to specify a different electric motor for every new camera design).

One can image such a set of procedures as a static, one-way process in which design engineers take the existing manufacturing process as given and design around those constraints. For firms with unwieldy designs, such a static approach to DFM may have significant benefits. Moreover, for some products—particularly derivative products or products that extend an established design—such an approach may be highly effective. But for platform products that represent a new generation of technology or a new segment of the market, such an approach may miss crucial opportunities to change the manufacturing process in order to enhance the performance of the product and manufacturing system. To exploit its full potential, DFM has to be an interactive, integrative process in which product and process engineers create a joint product-process design. In such a setting, product design choices comprehend key process restraints, but the process itself may also change (through process development and investment) to enhance capability and provide what the emerging design requires.

Exhibit 9–7 lays out one approach to integrating detailed product and process design in what we shall call the "house of producibility" (or, perhaps more accurately, the duplex of producibility).[9] Using our gear system example we have developed two matrices: a design matrix that links product and process design parameters; and a manufacturing performance matrix that connects process design parameters to manufacturing system performance. In the design matrix, process-oriented product design parameters make up the columns of the matrix, while process design parameters create the rows. In the performance matrix, the process parameters become the columns, while the dimensions of manufacturing system performance make up the rows.

In the design matrix, the numbers in the cells indicate the direction and strength of the relationship between choices in gear design and gear processing (i.e., 1 = modest effort, 5 = strong impact). For example, an increase in the number of gears moderately increases the number of tools, makes material handling more complex, and increases the number of assembly operations. A narrowing of the tolerances on tooth profile increases required precision, and will change the metal removal sequence significantly. We have used qualitative symbols to represent these linkages in the design matrix, but engineers may be able to express these relationships more precisely. The relationships rest on knowledge about the existing process, but may also draw on theoretical knowledge in order to allow for new process ideas. For example, new methods for metal removal (e.g., laser machining) might change the way a product design parameter affects the process design. Such a new process might increase the range of metal removal capability, thus reducing the com-

EXHIBIT 9–7

The "House of Producibility" for a Gear Design Problem at New West Photo

DESIGN MATRIX — Product Design Parameters

Process Design Parameters	number of gears	tooth profile tolerances	material strength
number and complexity of tools	+2	+3	+2
complexity of metal removal sequence		+4	
material handling	+3		
number of heat treating steps	+2		+4
precision	0	+5	
number of assembly operations	+5		

PERFORMANCE MATRIX — Process Design Parameters

Manufacturing Performance Parameters	importance	complexity of tools	metal removal complexity	material handling	heat treating	precision	assembly operations
labor cost	10		+2		+2	+2	+5
system cost	15	+3	+3	+5	+2	+4	+4
reliability	35	?	-3	0		+3	-3
lead time	15	+5	0	0		+2	0
flexibility	5	-3	0	-3		+2	-2
material cost	20	+2	+3		-2	+1	+2

plexity of the metal removal sequence required for any given product design. The implication is that the new process would change the sensitivity of the process to design changes and would be incorporated into the design (and performance) matrix by changing the relationships recorded in the appropriate cells.

The performance matrix links changes in the gear manufacturing process to manufacturing system performance. Here we have adopted a broad definition of performance to include time-to-market, flexibility, and total system cost. In this context, the process design parameters are drivers of manufacturing system performance. The cells in the matrix indicate the sensitivity of different performance dimensions to changes in process design, with the same relative ratings used in the design matrix. Increasing the complexity of tooling, for example, has a substantial impact on lead time (assuming the part in question is on the critical path), reduces flexibility (because of changeover costs) and adds to overall system cost because of increased maintenance.

As it stands in Exhibit 9–7, the house of producibility helps engineers clarify the implications of their design choices for manufacturing system performance. But we need not take the empty cells (which may indicate absence of knowledge) or the relative sensitivity of performance to process design as fixed. The framework allows individuals from different functions to identify opportunities for increasing knowledge and introducing new processes.

Both the design and performance matrices embody DFM principles in the parameters used for analysis as well as in the linkages between them. The gear design parameters used in the design matrix, for example, are "process-oriented" parameters. They include not only dimensions critical to gear performance from the customer's standpoint, but also aspects of gear design that are important from the standpoint of the production process. Likewise, linkages established between parameters and manufacturing systems performance may be based on DFM rules of thumb, as well as on more systematic analysis that one typically finds in a variety of DFM methodologies. Although the cells of the performance matrix as portrayed in Exhibit 9–7 are qualitative in character, detailed calculations of cost—or of any other manufacturing performance dimension—could he used to give the linkage a quantitative basis.

As we saw in our discussion of the house of quality, the most important aspect of an effective problem-solving process is neither the matrix itself nor the other formal tools used to organize knowledge and information. Indeed, a variety of other formats may prove highly useful, including network diagrams that provide a more graphic depiction of the critical interrelationships among the parameters. Moreover, we could elaborate the design and performance matrices—add a "roof" to them, add competitive information on manufacturing performance for perspective, or summarize quantitatively the relative importance of different dimensions of performance. Other refinements, such as quantitative targets for process parameters or indications of the relative significance of different design parameters, could also be developed.

Whether in simple or complex form, the point of the matrices remains the same: to facilitate integration of product and process design and to bring issues of producibility (broadly defined) to the center of the development process. The critical issues here are exactly those we found in the earlier QFD analysis: language, framework, communication, discipline, and focus. Indeed, there is a fundamental unity in the substance and process of the various methodologies we have examined in this section of the chapter. Whether we are looking at design targets or issues of producibility, the methods focus attention on customer requirements (in the field or in the plant), linkages between design parameters and performance, and the tradeoffs among them. Moreover, the process behind the substance—the systematic listing of dimensions and parameters, establishing qualitative and quantitative estimates of critical linkages, assessing their relative importance, and structuring choices around the evidence derived from these analyses—not only provides a useful way to organize and use knowledge, but also creates a new framework for cross-functional interaction. As we have noted before, such methods are not a substitute for design engineers who are knowledgeable and oriented toward manufacturing system performance, or manufacturing engineers who are sensitive to customer needs. These tools and methods complement and make those integrative skills even more effective.

The tools and methods do change the nature of the development process. The focus in applying them, therefore, should not be just to do old things better. This is a new set of activities and interactions; a new way to frame and solve problems. Structured methods are not a panacea, but they have a role to play in making working-level problem solving more effective. They create a common framework and language and, if applied well, raise important tradeoffs and conflicts early, thus saving valuable time and resources. They make holes in the organization's knowledge about critical relationships apparent and provide a basis for capturing and using knowledge important in making choices about design.

Computer-Based Systems

In the Appendix to this chapter we examine developments in advanced computer systems that may have a profound influence on the nature of the development process. Computer-aided design and manufacturing systems are in widespread use today. Advanced systems, involving sophisticated database capability, electronic interchange of data, and intelligent support for group interaction, are under development. Such systems have the potential to greatly improve problem solving processes. The computer system itself, however, is not a panacea. Commercial hardware and software systems are unlikely to be a source of competitive advantage; instead, advantage will lie in an organization's ability to develop proprietary software and coherently integrate software, hardware, and "humanware" into an effective system. Human creativity, face-to-face contact, and interpersonal communication will continue to be an integral, essential aspect of product and process development. What will be different is the context in which face-to-face communication and human creativity have their application.

The kinds of systems we have outlined in the Appendix combine graphics, databases, and problem-solving methods, and may afford development groups rapid access to data, drawings, models, and analysis—all within a consistent framework. Today, data on customer experience, manufacturing processes, and alternative designs often are organized in incompatible formats, processed in very different computer systems, and managed by different organizations. New systems will create open access to common databases and provide a consistent framework within which designers, process engineers, and marketers may probe the underlying sources of the problems they confront. The problem-solving group will still employ face-to-face communication, but the conversations are likely to be very different. Communication will be faster and occur within a new (informed) framework, possibly using new media. These new systems in effect may provide a new "language" that will allow difficult functional groups with their own "dialects" to develop shared understanding.

Observations and Implications for Management

It is clear that advanced computer-based systems have the potential for significant impact. It is also clear that a fragmented organization with parochial philosophies and substantial barriers to communication will frustrate even the most clever and powerful computer system. In this respect, automating information and communications in the development process has much in common with the automation of manufacturing processes. Companies have learned, often by sad experience, that automation in manufacturing is most powerful and effective when applied in a manufacturing process that is well-characterized, capable, and in control. Many firms have seen automation as the means by which they would achieve a well-characterized, capable, in-control process. But these companies have learned that attempts to automate a manufacturing process that is not in control only serves to highlight and underscore much more sharply the inherent weaknesses, absence of understanding, and gaps of knowledge in the process.

An analogous outcome is likely in the application of advanced computer-based systems for design and development. Organizations that have broken down barriers to communication across functions, implemented a development process that integrates functional activities, developed a facility for and capability in structured methods for problem solving, and cultivated an organizational structure and approach to leadership that complements and reinforces cross-functional integration are likely to find advanced computer-based systems not only easier to implement but much more powerful in their effects on the speed, efficiency, and quality of problem solving. Of course, some organizations may see the implementation of such a computer-based system as the catalyst that will spur an organization to greater integration. In either case, it is important to understand that effective implementation of such systems requires significant change from the traditional, sequential, parochial development organization.

Appendix to Chapter 9

Structured methods can play an important role in moving an organization toward effective problem solving. They provide a framework for cross-functional interaction and a common language that marketers and design and manufacturing engineers can use to create a shared understanding of their joint problems in development. But even where structured methods are deeply ingrained in the organization, the speed, efficiency, and quality of problem solving will depend on how rapidly and efficiently the organization can access the right data, how quickly the information moves from one source of knowledge to another, how well the organization uses the data it has to establish critical relationships and linkages, and how effectively the organization captures what it learns from experience. In effect, the challenge of quickly and efficiently moving complex data and storing and accessing knowledge in complex systems offers significant additional opportunity for improvements in problem solving.

In short, information systems that harness the power of the computer to store, manipulate, process, and communicate information across different functional groups and projects have the potential to play a crucial role in improving the effectiveness of problem solving at the working level. The amount of information (and in manual systems, the amount of paper) required to solve even moderately complex problems effectively can be daunting. A variety of studies have shown that in electro-mechanical products, such as home appliances, computers, or consumer electronics, engineers spend as little as a half to a third of their time doing real engineering.[1] The rest of their time is spent filling out forms, attending meetings, tracking down data, and traveling to the next activity. This is true even in organizations where computer-based systems are in use. Indeed, it appears that the application of the computer to the problems of design and development has focused primarily on automating existing engineering tasks. Much less progress has been made in using computer systems to integrate problem solving.

Computers, of course, have had a major impact in some settings, particularly in applications like drafting and in industries like semiconductor design where many of the design problems can be represented in two dimensions. Furthermore, recent developments in computer-aided engineering (CAE) systems allow engineers to simulate the performance of designs electronically and thus provide the means for faster, lower-cost analysis. By building engineering equations into the software, CAE systems can aid engineers in the selection of design parameters. In designing something like a gear system, an advanced CAE system will evaluate the merits of the gear design based on theoretical equations and previous experience. Advanced systems may also embody something of an "expert system" which may suggest alternative design concepts based on input provided by the design engineer.

All of these applications of computer-based tools are useful and important. By giving engineers rapid feedback on the potential performance of their designs, these tools can improve initial design quality and substitute, at least in part, for expensive physical model building and prototype construction. For very complex systems, prototypes are likely to continue to be necessary, but their quality can be increased and the number of prototypes required can be substantially reduced with the application of the new computer-based tools. Tools that automate existing design tasks, however, fall short of the potential in the computer, and in information technology in general, to change fundamentally the way problem solving (particularly across functional groups) gets done. What is needed is a system that not only provides tools for analysis and design, but also changes the way people in different functions communicate, cope with large-scale, complex data, and capture and store knowledge. To illustrate what such systems might look like, what they might accomplish, and what the challenges in their design and implementation might be, we consider how systems might be applied to our gear design problem.

Four Generations of Computer-Based Design Systems

Exhibit A–1 lays out four generations of competitor-based systems that take us progressively from automating existing tasks to creating a fully

EXHIBIT A–1

Four Generations of Computer-Based Design and Development Systems

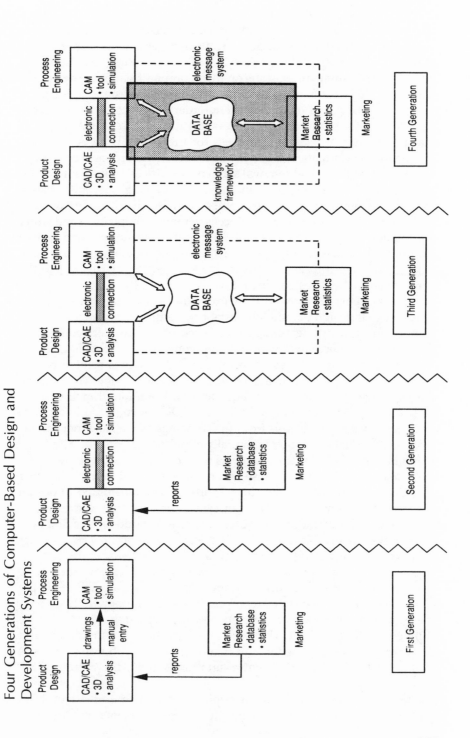

integrated system for managing the design process and the information, data, and knowledge that underlie it. In first generation systems, gear designers work with CAD software that allows them to draw alternative gear designs in three dimensions on their computer screens. The system has embedded in it analytical routines that help a design engineer examine the behavior of the gear system under design consideration. The gear designer's counterpart in process engineering uses a CAM system that programs the machining process for the gears. The CAM system also has some simulation capability that allows the process engineer to explore alternative metal removal sequences (such as heat treating steps using alternative materials). Finally, the marketing specialist uses a workstation with access to a customer database that includes data on sales by model, warranty experience, customer complaints, and other information received from customers through the field sales and service organization. The marketing specialist can also access a market research database that has information based on customer surveys, as well as the result of special studies conducted on specific products.

These systems are powerful in executing individual tasks such as selecting gear design parameters, establishing processing sequences, or identifying attractive feature sets for products. However, connecting these individual activities within a first-generation system is complex and time consuming. A design from the CAD system is printed out on a plotter and manually transferred to process engineering. (In fact, the drawings are transported manually through the internal mail system. They actually move around on little carts.) Once recognized by process engineering, the dimensions from the drawings as well as other important specifications are entered manually into the CAM system. Similarly, the marketing specialist does analysis on the workstation and then prepares reports and memos. These reports are circulated in the marketing organization and, after review and approval, are transmitted to design engineering. (They typically are not sent to process engineering.)

Compared to the traditional system without computers, this first generation system has a number of significant advantages. Design engineers consider many more alternatives quickly and efficiently, process engineers are able to execute a process plan for new designs much more quickly than before, and marketing specialists have greatly increased the amount of analysis that they accomplish for a given program. Even with these advantages, however, problem solving across departments can be cumbersome and difficult. There are lags in the flow of information, and designers, process engineers, and marketers work with different kinds of data and make very different assumptions about the nature of the problems they face.

The second-generation system depicted in Exhibit A–1 attempts to deal with some of these problems. In the second-generation system, interfaces are developed and communication links established so that gear design information may be transmitted electronically directly to the CAM system. Creating such an integrating CAD-CAM system eliminates a great deal of paperwork, avoids errors associated with translation from computer systems to paper, and reduces the amount of time required to complete a design. Design information moves across the network in digital format, allowing process and design engineers to work with the identical design. Marketing specialists, however, are still working with reports and memos, and the CAD-CAM linkage applies to the current design but captures neither previous experience nor alternatives considered on the current design.

The third-generation system focuses on the issues just cited. This system links the databases in design, engineering, and marketing, establishing a common interface among them. The combined database tracks historical experience with gear design and provides tools that allow engineers and marketers to analyze the data and establish important interrelationships, and allows engineers in different functions to keep track of design changes and maintain consistent information about development status. The third-generation system also provides a facility for sending and receiving messages, such as "post-it" notes attached to drawings and other documents. This allows the participants in development to communicate with each other about current design problems. The final element of the third-generation system is a local archive that allows a design engineer, for example, to store notes, test results, and important messages pertaining to particular issues in the design.

The fourth-generation system takes integration across product and process design and marketing an important step further. Where the third-generation system established a common database, the focus of the fourth-generation system may use a network diagram to structure the relationship between design parameters and customer attributes. Using common software and a common interface (everyone's workstation has access to the same software and the screens everyone sees are the same, even in real time), the system allows design engineers, process engineers, and marketers working together as a team to define important parameters, attributes, and connections. The system also provides access to supporting data, analysis, and information that lie behind a particular relationship.

An example of an Advanced Computer-Based Design System

In order to illustrate a fourth-generation system, we have applied a system developed by Salzberg and Watkins to the gear design problem.[3] This system uses a network structure to organize information about

Exhibit A–2

Sample Screen for Advanced Computer-Based Design System:
Databases Related to Gear Machining

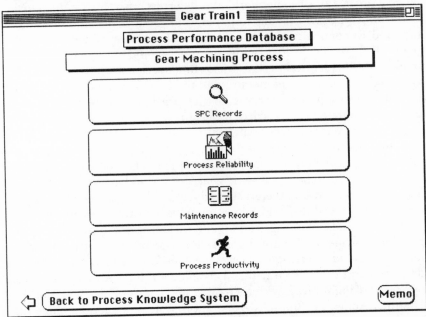

NOTE: From a system developed by Steven Salzberg and Michael Watkins. See Salzberg
and Watkins, "Managing Information for Concurrent Engineering: Challenges and
Barriers," *Research in Engineering Design*, 2 (1990), pp. 35–52.

attributes and parameters, and provides clear connections between the
choices engineers and marketers must make and underlying supporting
analyses and data. Exhibits A–2 to A–6 are examples of the screens that
engineers might use when working with the system. Exhibit A–2, for
example, shows a screen that allows an engineer to select among different databases related to the gear machining process. Some of these
databases contain statistical data while others include graphs or digi-
tized drawings. By selecting the process productivity database, an engineer can access a process flow diagram which indicates the sequence
of operations required to process a gear (see Exhibit A–3). The screen in
Exhibit A–3 provides further access to information on problem histories
associated with a given step in the process, process performance data,
and engineering drawings for this process.

Exhibit A–4 presents a network diagram connecting customer attributes to gear design parameters. The system allows engineers to cre-

EXHIBIT A–3

Sample Screen for Advanced Computer-Based Design System:
The Gear Machining Process

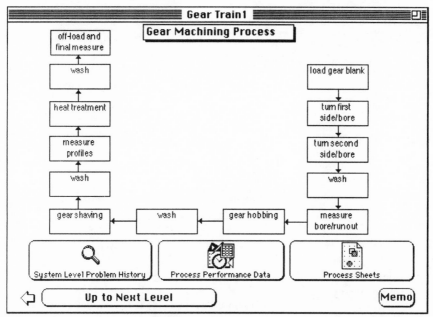

NOTE: From a system developed by Steven Salzberg and Michael Watkins. See Salzberg and Watkins, "Managing Information for Concurrent Engineering: Challenges and Barriers," *Research in Engineering Design*, 2 (1990), pp. 35–52.

ate their own diagrams and establish connections between attributes and parameters. Each parameter entered in the network diagram is connected to a variety of other databases. An engineer interested in gear spacing, for example, could easily pull up detailed drawings of that parameter in the system. Such a detailed drawing is illustrated in Exhibit A–5. The screen includes not only a schematic of alternative gear designs, but also a description of the particular parameter and access to further information related to this design aspect. Thus, an engineer working on gear design can easily access information, drawings, process reliability data, and other information relevant to the selection of a specific design parameter. The same access to underlying data and information would be available for customer attributes. Exhibit A–6 summarizes detailed information about customer attributes compared to competitor experience. This screen provides competitive information as well as data reflecting customer experience in the field.

EXHIBIT A–4

Sample Screen for Advanced Computer-Based Design System:
Network Diagram Connecting Design Parameters and
Customer Attributes

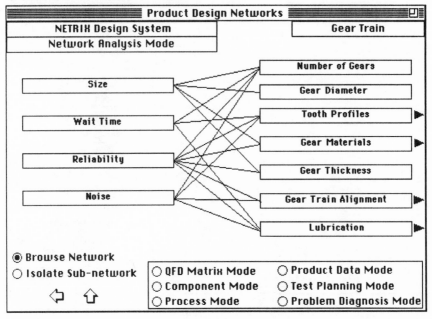

NOTE: From a system developed by Steven Salzberg and Michael Watkins. See Salzberg and Watkins, "Managing Information for Concurrent Engineering: Challenges and Barriers," *Research in Engineering Design*, 2 (1990), pp. 35–52.

The network diagrams and the connections to the databases and analytical tools become the framework within which the team jointly develops its knowledge about the design. In effect, the fourth generation system provides a more complete and electronic format for the kind of structured methodology we depicted earlier in discussing QFD and DFM. By joining the databases, analytical tools, and critical relationship diagrams in one system, the fourth-generation system shortens feedback loops drastically, makes access to data easier and more consistent, and enhances the ability of development team members to communicate and collaborate. Moreover, because the results of analysis and problem solving are captured and stored in computer memory, the fourth-generation system facilitates organizational learning. With the ease of appending notes, comments, and test results, the system becomes a framework within which the design team can communicate, manage complex data, and create and store knowledge about design and development.

Exhibit A–5

Sample Screen for Advanced Computer-Based Design System: Detailed Drawing of Tooth Profile

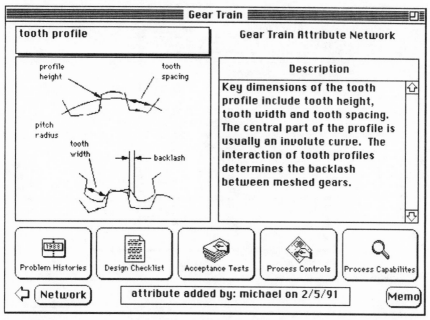

NOTE: From a system developed by Steven Salzberg and Michael Watkins. See Salzberg and Watkins, "Managing Information for Concurrent Engineering: Challenges and Barriers," *Research in Engineering Design*, 2 (1990), pp. 35–52.

One can, of course, imagine further generations of computer systems. Systems may be developed, for example, that provide intelligent support to the design team. By intelligent support, we mean the ability to discern patterns in the actions of the human design team—patterns that indicate the design teams are overlooking certain important issues or pursuing alternatives that experience has proven problematic. Such an intelligent system could track the pattern and flag inconsistencies, oversights, or impending problems. Furthermore, such systems could aid designers by suggesting design alternatives based on information about desired customer attributes or process performance. Such fifth-generation systems are not a substitute for human intelligence and creativity; rather, they use the power of the computer for computation, memory, and high-speed processing to complement and enhance the power of the human mind.

First- and second-generation computer systems are widely used, and a number of firms have begun to implement third-generation systems.

EXHIBIT A–6

Sample Screen for Advanced Computer-Based Design System: Detailed Customer Attributes and Competitor Comparisons

System Quality								
Netrix Product Design Data **Competitor Comparison**				**New West** **Competitor 1**		**Gear Train**		
Attribute	**![1]**	**Best in Class**			**TGW[2]**		**TGR[3]**	
		own	comp	diff	own	comp	own	comp
low wait time	22	3.5	5	−1.5	4	5	3	4.5
quiet	10	3	4	−1	3	5	3	4.5
crisp	11	3	4.5	−1.5	4	3	2.5	4
low cost	16	4	4.5	−.5	4.5	4.5	3.5	4.5
compact	13	2	4.5	−2.5	3	4	2.5	4
reliable	22	5	4	+1	5	3.5	4.5	3

Change Attributes

[1]Relative importance
[2]Things gone wrong
[3]Things gone right

NOTE: From a system developed by Steven Salzberg and Michael Watkins. See Salzberg and Watkins, "Managing Information for Concurrent Engineering: Challenges and Barriers," *Research in Engineering Design*, 2 (1990), pp. 35–52.

Companies such as Intergraph and Computervision have developed commercial software designed to provide third-generation capability. Fourth-generation systems, however, represent the frontier of computer-based system development for product and process design. They are an active focus of ongoing development, and some firms have developed prototypes and begun to implement custom versions of such design systems.

CHAPTER 10

Prototype Test Cycles

*T*raditionally, managers have treated prototyping as a technical tool to be used by engineers responsible for the progress of technical activities and related development efforts. The natural flow and focus of traditional prototyping has generally progressed as illustrated in Exhibit 10–1: from overall concept to detailed component engineering and finally to producible units made by the operating system. That is, an initial concept prototype tends to be a rough cut done at the system level, and the final pilot production prototype also is at the system level, albeit in a finished form. In between, the prototypes are done at the component or subsystem level and deal with the detailed technical choices being considered and evaluated at that stage of development.

The premise regarding prototyping in this chapter is considerably different. It is that prototyping—the build and test activities of each design-build test cycle—is a key management tool for guiding development projects. It is not just a technical tool. Instead of getting extensively involved only in the final state (pilot production) of prototyping—much like the pattern depicted in Exhibit 2–1 of Chapter 2—managers can and should be involved in each cycle. Even more importantly, management can use prototyping cycles to guide and pace development projects and to assess their progress, pinpoint unresolved issues, and focus resources and attention. Senior managers, functional heads, and project leaders who do not understand and fully utilize the power of

Exhibit 10–1

Traditional Path of Design-Build-Test Cycles*

Progression of Prototyping Cycles

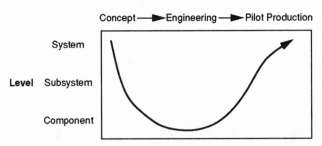

* Traditionally, the initial design-build-test cycle is done at the system level as a prototype of the concept. The next few cycles are then done primarily by engineering at the component level and eventually at the subsystem level. The final prototyping is done at the system level, usually as a pilot production design-build-test cycle.

prototyping unintentionally handicap their efforts to achieve rapid, effective, and productive development results.

Prototyping is a common activity that is of high leverage because of the central role it plays in the basic building blocks of development projects—the sequence of design-build-test cycles. Prototypes answer questions about customer reactions, industrial design, durability, fit and finish, and manufacturing cost. Furthermore, prototypes can take many forms—simulation (such as CAD modeling, finite element analysis, or heat transfer approximations), breadboards and mockups (such as styrofoam block models or parts made through stereolithography, and functional products (such as a first-unit circuit board, engineering-built engines, and pre-production washing machines). In each case, however, the basic cycle consists of taking the current thinking regarding the design, building a prototype that embodies the key aspects of that thinking, and then testing that prototype to determine where additional design refinements are and are not needed.

Prototyping in Major Appliance Development Projects

Data gathered from three firms in the major appliance industry in the mid 1980s illustrate the nature of the sequence of prototyping cycles and the management leverage inherent in them. These data, and the design-build-test cycles they reflect, are summarized in Exhibit 10–2.

Perhaps the most striking difference among the development efforts of these major appliance firms is that a major new product development

256

EXHIBIT 10–2

Prototype Cycles and Design Timetables (in Months): Major Appliances*

Event/Activity	Companies A & B Prototyping Cycles	Company A	Company B	Company C	Company C Prototyping Cycles
Pre-feasibility scoping		1-3	2-6	3	
Drawing for feasibility, sample		1-2	1-2	1	
Build sample		1-2	1	1	Cycle (1)
Test sample	Cycle (1)	2-5	2	3	
Drawings for design geometry			design	2	
Build design geometry			frozen	2	Cycle (2)
Test design geometry				3	
Complete drawings for issue		2	2	1	
Build evaluation models				2	Cycle (3)
Test evaluation models (drawing release)				3	
Tool release			2		
Tooling time	Cycle (2)	2-4	2-3	6	Cycle (4)
Inspect samples				2	
Prepare and conduct pre-pilot run				1	
Testing of product		1	1	2	
Prepare and conduct pilot run	Cycle (3)			1	Cycle (5)
Prepare for production		2-3	1	3	
Total Development Project Cycle Time		12-22 months	14-20 months	36 months	

* For these three firms, the development process involves a similar sequence of tasks. However, at Companies A and B, these are grouped into three prototyping (design-build-test) cycles, while at Company C, these are grouped into five prototyping cycles. One result is that Companies A and B develop products in twenty-two months or less, while Company C requires thirty-six months.

effort takes twelve to twenty-two months and fourteen to twenty months at Companies A and B, respectively, whereas at Company C, it takes thirty-six months. Looking at where that total time is spent reveals a very different pattern for the two faster firms than for Company C. The source of that difference is reflected in the number and duration of the design-build-test cycles needed by each firm.

At Companies A and B, a major development effort requires three primary prototyping cycles. Each consists of articulating current thinking and detail regarding the design, preparing one or more prototypes of that design, and then testing and evaluating those units, thus setting the stage for the subsequent cycle. The initial cycle for Companies A and B consists of taking the product concept, preparing sample drawings, building and testing a prototype unit based on those drawings, and completing the final drawings. While there are undoubtedly some small subcycles, the allocation of calendar time suggests they must be relatively minor if this first cycle takes from seven to fourteen months. Subsequently, these two companies do a second cycle which takes three to six months and involves preparing tooling for the factory, producing samples from that tooling, assembling units from such sample parts (as part of a pre-pilot production run), and complete testing of the resulting units. Finally, these firms engage in a third cycle of one to three months—the pilot production run—where revisions from the second cycle are incorporated into the final product and process designs, and the entire system is tested by building pilot production units. Customers evaluate those units, final revisions are made, and plans for volume production of the new product are approved. Market rollout and production ramp-up then follow.

In stark contrast, Company C engages in five separate design-build-test cycles. The first cycle, planned to take ten months, is analogous to the first cycle at Companies A and B, but ends without completion of a fully functional prototype unit. A second cycle of six months is required to refine the design geometry, tolerances, and physical relationship of the subassemblies. The results of those two cycles then are combined into a third cycle, which takes five months and builds a handful of final engineering models that can be tested and evaluated. The output of that third cycle is a set of final revisions to the engineering drawings.

Company C's fourth cycle is analogous to the second cycle at Companies A and B, but requires eleven months versus the three to six required by the other two firms. The aim at all three companies is to procure and test the tooling and to plan out a pre-pilot production run. The prototypes built during the pre-pilot run are then tested thoroughly, and final revisions are made to the design of the product and its manufacturing process. Finally, Company C engages in a fifth prototyping and test cycle—pilot production—that is analogous to the third cycle pursued at Companies A and B. However, Company C requires four months rather than the one to three months required by Companies A and B.

It is instructive to contrast the substantive differences between Companies A and B and Company C. One difference is that activity and cycle durations in the first two firms generally are anticipated to vary from project to project, whereas Company C anticipates that the planned duration of each cycle will be the same on every project. An even more striking difference is Company C's sequence of five design-build-test cycles. Companies A and B have compressed the time from concept to pre-production, while Company C has subdivided project steps to reduce complexity and "level of concurrency." Their intent has been to reduce what they perceive as the risks of costly mistakes. However, Company C, like Companies A and B, would claim that it is pushing hard to reduce its product development cycle time. So why does it use five cycles instead of three?

One response might be for Company C to drop steps and do prototypes like its faster competitors, but that is likely to be a recipe for disaster. The real explanation for the number and duration of these cycles at Company C lies in how rapidly their organization solves problems, learns, and converges to a final design. Because of poor communications, a narrow technical focus, and an excessively segmented process, Company C needs five cycles to reach a final design that can be produced in volume, while Companies A and B need only three. Furthermore, because of the way Company C handles the sequence of individual activities and the way they structure and manage the project, they also need more time to complete each cycle. If management arbitrarily were to cut that time or eliminate one or two cycles, many issues would go unresolved, leading to serious problems in production and the field.

Conceptually, any development project can be thought of (and usually is, at least implicitly) as a sequence of design-build-test cycles. Within each cycle, the prototype serves as a focal point for problem solving, testing communications, and conflict resolution. Furthermore, it forces specificity in design, provides feedback about the choices made thus far, and highlights remaining unresolved issues. By creating a physical embodiment of the design's current state, engineers are able to study critical issues of functionality, marketing can test and explore customer needs and reactions, and manufacturing can determine the feasibility and options it has for producing the product in volume.

But in spite of prototyping's substantial potential and leverage, Company C treats it as a technical and tactical concern. Even after reviewing the data in Exhibit 10–2, management at Company C did not conceive of prototyping as a management tool. They did not grasp the nature of the process and its potential role in making development work more effectively. The same seems to hold true even for industries where new product development is the basis of competition, and the speed of development and resulting product performance are the focus of the firm's stated strategy. For example, in the engineering workstation segment of the computer industry, where firms such as Sun Microsystems, Sony, Hewlett Packard, Apollo (now HP-Apollo), and IBM compete for a large, growing market, recent studies reveal differences in the number and duration of such cycles even greater than in major appliances—from as few as three cycles with durations as short as 100 days each, to as many as eleven cycles with durations as long as 200 days each.[1] Furthermore, the variety of ways in which prototyping cycles are managed and linked to the product development effort itself are as numerous as the number of firms in the industry.

Prototyping and Management Leverage

Our argument—of which we hope to convince the reader by the end of this chapter—is that prototyping and its role in design-build-test cycles is a core element of development and a major area of opportunity for managements seeking to improve the effectiveness and efficiency of their development process.[2] Increasing the rate and amount of learning that occurs in each cycle and then linking cycles in a sequence that is effective both technically and managerially permits an organization to shorter the duration and number of cycles needed to develop high-quality products and manufacturing processes and get to market significantly faster than competitors. That is exactly what Companies A and B in the major appliance industry had done by the mid 1980s, and what leading firms in the workstation industry were pursuing a few years later. By the early 1990s, firms in a range of industries increasingly viewed prototyping as an area of major opportunity in their efforts to improve product and process development capability.

The remainder of this chapter is organized into three sections. We first examine the basic elements of prototyping and its traditional role in technical problem solving. We illustrate the traditional approach in the left panel of Exhibit 10–3. In this approach there are four cycles—concept, design verification, engineering verification, and pilot production. It is important that management understand the traditional, technical role both as a reference point in planning improvements and because the use of prototyping as an important management tool is *in addition to* its technical purposes, not as a substitute for them. We conclude that section with a review of "best practice" procedures than can significantly enhance prototyping's contribution to technical problem solving.

The subsequent section focuses on the opportunity to restructure significantly the sequence, number, and duration of prototyping cycles into what we refer to as a periodic pattern of prototyping. The periodic approach is depicted in the right panel of Exhibit 10–3. In this approach, there are four main stages, but, within the second and third stage, there are shorter prototyping cycles that occur at regular intervals. This approach appears particularly promising for platform or next-generation product or manufacturing process projects carried out by a cross-

Exhibit 10–3

Contrasting Approaches to Prototyping Cycles*

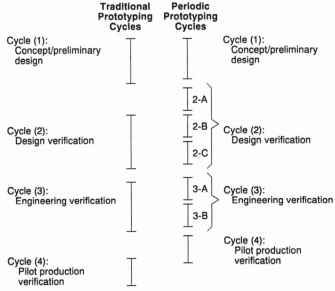

* In many engineering intensive industries, product development tasks are grouped into four phases or cycles, each with its own prototyping cycle. Adopting a pattern of periodic prototyping does not replace those four phases, but does add several shorter, more integrated prototyping cycles. This can lead to higher quality products and shorter overall development time.

functional team. The approach and its benefits are illustrated using Motorola's highly successful "Bandit" pager project.

The final section then looks at the opportunity and benefits accruing when management matches the prototyping approach used with the type of development project. We suggest that rather than using a single approach to prototyping, varying the approach to match the needs of different types of projects can enhance both its technical and managerial roles and contribute significantly to the competitive success of individual development projects.

The Traditional Approach to Prototyping.

The goal of new product and process development is to create a product and/or process that provides customers with the form and functionality they require. Superior products are distinctive and exceed customer

261

EXHIBIT 10–4

Automotive Product Development Prototyping*

A. Primary Prototyping Cycles

Cycle	Focus of Testing and Refinement
Stage 0 – Architectural	Basic layout and aesthetics
Stage 1 – Subsystem	Subsystem characteristics
Stage 2 – System	System characteristics
Stage 3 – Verification	Confirm system characteristics
Stage 4 – Pilot	Production system
Stage 5 – Production Start-Up	Volume ramp-up of production

B. Cost and Representativeness of Different Types of Prototypes

	CAD Model	Clay Model	Engineering Prototype	Pilot Production
Cost:				
Cost	Low	Low	Medium	High
Time	Low	Low	Medium	High
Representativeness:				
Form	Medium	High	High	High
Fit	Low	Medium	High	High
Function	Low	Low	High	High
Materials	Low	Low	High	High
Process	Low	Low	Low/Medium	High

* For automotive companies, there are up to six prototyping cycles in new car development, each with a different focus and purpose. There are also different types of prototypes that can be developed, each with its own advantages and disadvantages.

---

expectations in ways that are difficult for competitors to match. Meeting this goal requires outstanding design quality—a design that provides what the customer needs and wants—and superb manufacturability—a product that uses process capabilities efficiently and reliably to meet the final design specifications. The purpose of prototyping is to demonstrate to the organization that the design has outstanding quality and high levels of manufacturability. In addition, early prototyping cycles indicate how far development has progressed toward this goal and what is still required to reach it.

The auto industry provides a useful example of a traditional approach to prototyping. The various forms of primary design-build-test cycles used in the auto industry are summarized in the top portion of Exhibit 10–4.[3] The development cycles progress from architecture or product concept, through subsystem and system evaluation and verification, on to pilot production system verification, and eventually to production start-up. The evolution is from a basic product concept, its aesthetics, and shape, through the design engineering of specifications that provide product functionality. Much of the product design is verified as a total system in Stage 3, following which attention and responsibility shifts toward the production system that will build the car, and eventually to the factory floor where volume production will take place. Since different prototype cycles have different purposes, different functions traditionally have taken responsibility for each one: early cycles have been the responsibility and domain of industrial designers and body engineers; middle cycles, the responsibility of various subsystem quality assurance engineers; and final cycles, the responsibility of manufacturing process engineers and factory operations.

Not only does the locus of responsibility shift for various prototype cycles; the cost and time to create and form prototypes shifts as well. As illustrated in the bottom portion of Exhibit 10–4, initial prototypes of components and subsystems in today's environment are computeraided design (CAD) models, while the early exterior prototypes are made of clay or other formable materials like plastic. These are then followed by engineering-built subsystem and system prototypes. Eventually complete automobiles are constructed on a pilot production line, and finally, on the factory floor using operating systems. As indicated, the early physical prototype forms tend to be low cost and can be constructed fairly quickly. Later forms of auto prototypes become much more expensive and take longer to create.

If cost and time to develop were the only considerations, prototypes would be built in the cheapest and fastest way possible. There is another dimension of primary interest in new product and process development efforts, however: fidelity or representativeness—the degrees to which the prototype represents what the customer eventually will receive in the manufactured product, and what manufacturing operations eventually will produce with their production processes. The bottom of Exhibit 10–4 suggests a number of subdimensions of representativeness that apply in the development of automobile prototypes. These include form, fit, function, materials, and process. The most representative prototype is one produced on the production floor to the final design specs; the least representative is the clay or CAD model. However, each has its role and place in a development effort.

Linking Development Phases and Prototype Cycles

Prototypes play an important role in the testing of the design and thus in the progress of the project. They provide critical information about

EXHIBIT 10–5

Workstation Product Development Prototyping*

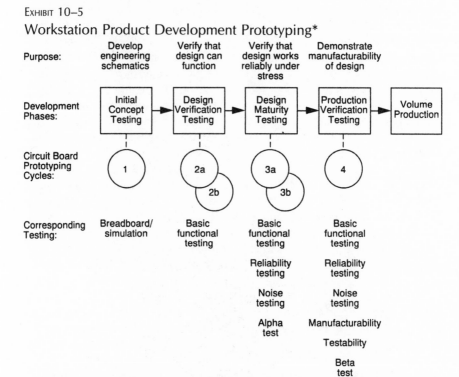

Purpose:	Develop engineering schematics	Verify that design can function	Verify that design works reliably under stress	Demonstrate manufacturability of design

Development Phases:	Initial Concept Testing	Design Verification Testing	Design Maturity Testing	Production Verification Testing	Volume Production

Circuit Board Prototyping Cycles:	1	2a 2b	3a 3b	4

Corresponding Testing:	Breadboard/ simulation	Basic functional testing	Basic functional testing	Basic functional testing
			Reliability testing	Reliability testing
			Noise testing	Noise testing
			Alpha test	Manufacturability
				Testability
			Beta test	

* In the development of a new engineering workstation, there are four primary types of prototyping cycles, each with its own purposes and set of related tests. Often, a complex development project will require two or more cycles of types 2 and 3 to ensure completion of the tasks in that phase before moving on to the next phase.

the design and its potential to meet project objectives. How firms connect prototyping to the major phases of development, therefore, is a crucial dimension of the development process. We present these connections for the engineering workstation industry in Exhibit 10–5. Like development in much of the computer and electronic equipment industry, workstation development is generally organized into four phases. Each phase is completed when certain requirements, embedded in "testing hurdles," have been met. Initial concept development ends when a breadboard model or simulated version demonstrates feasibility of the basic product and its core concepts. Design verification ends when a prototype unit demonstrates the functionality required for the product to meet the performance requirements in its intended competitive segment. Design maturity ends when the prototype from that phase works reliably under stress and conditions beginning to approach those representative of the customer's environment. Finally, product verification ends when the prototype from that phase not only demonstrates functionality in a representative customer setting, but also passes tests related to manufacturability and testability. Completion of the last phase signals that the product is ready for volume production.

Much like the sequence of prototype/test cycles used in a traditional automotive development project, workstation firms generally shift primary responsibility and involvement from engineering to manufacturing as the project progresses. It is not until design maturity testing that manufacturing plays a significant role in developing the prototypes. Engineering builds early prototypes exclusively or exercises direct control. By the production verification phase, the full responsibility for prototyping rests with production; design engineers usually are anxious to get on to another project. That prototype cycle is not of major interest or concern to them.

Issues and Choices in Prototyping: Improving the Traditional Model Through "Best Practice"

In its traditional form, prototyping is technically driven, managed by different functions in different phases, and focused primarily on design evaluation and verification. If done well, this form of prototyping has important strengths, including close ties between the type of prototype, the phase of development, and the function most knowledgeable and interested in prototyping performance. But this passing of responsibility may have the effect of limiting communications and understanding across functions. Later we shall offer a different model of prototyping that may deal with some of the problems found in the traditional approach. Even within the traditional framework, however, firms face a range of choices that influence the effectiveness of the prototyping process, and present important opportunities for improvement.

Evidence from a variety of industries suggests four "best practices" that apply to any firm and any prototyping cycle:

Low-Cost Prototypes. As illustrated in Exhibit 10–4, the progression from inexpensive, simple models and prototypes to complex, expensive ones generally is correlated inversely with the representatives that those prototypes have to the customer situation in which the product and/or process will be applied. Typically, simple industrial design models (showing form and shape), computer-aided engineering (CAE) models, and simulation models are considerably less expensive to construct than pilot production units. Making better use of these classes of models and seeking ways to improve their representatives can strengthen significantly prototyping's contribution to development efforts. Actions as simple as choosing outside providers of prototyping services who have equipment comparable to that in one's own factory can help in this regard.

Prototyping Process Quality. Studies of prototyping practice invariably reveal many simple but costly mistakes in both building and testing prototypes that never should have occurred. Whether it is misreading a drawing, reversing an overlay, or failing to check a material before using it, making sure that the prototyping process is a "quality process" can improve significantly the reliability and learning that occur in each cycle. Similarly, improving the response time in prototyping—what is often referred to as rapid prototyping—can also be extremely beneficial. Shorter, more accurate feedback cycles provide better, more usable information to those waiting for the results of prototyping.

This is especially true in early phases where the prototype represents "current thinking" and where that thinking continues to progress, even while the prototype is being constructed and tested. The faster such cycles can be completed, the more valuable and timely will be the information provided to development engineers. While this may seem obvious, speed is not always so highly valued. In one setting development engineers joked about "birth dates" for prototype units—it took more than a full year to construct and test units from a single prototyping cycle.

Timing and Sequence. Experience has taught most firms not to overlap individual prototype cycles. When cycles are overlapped, people lose track of the status of the project, which problems have been solved, and which should be given top priority in the current cycle. Ensuring that testing is completed following the production of prototypes and getting closure on each learning cycle is an important practice. Then, waiting to start the build portion of the next cycle until appropriate amounts of additional design have been completed ensures that each cycle provides the maximum progress.

Building Knowledge. Using prototypes to capture and enhance the knowledge regarding prototyping and the principles of effective design-build-test cycles provides real leverage to an organization. This practice includes continually improving the quality, speed, and efficiency of the prototyping process, and strengthening prototyping's representativeness and its ability to capture critical problems at each stage of development. Systematic study of the types of problems that can and should be solved in each cycle during the development effort can help identify better ways to plan those cycles and realize their full potential.

Dimensions of Choice in Prototyping

These four areas of practice apply to any development effort, but there are other dimensions of the traditional prototyping process where choice may depend on the type of product and the objectives of the project. Even here, however, recognizing these dimensions and making choices explicit may improve the performance of prototyping. In order to make the choices and their implications clear, Exhibit 10–6 lists several dimensions of the prototyping process and defines a particular set of choices for the standard, traditional prototyping model, a revised version of the traditional model, and an alternative model that we shall call periodic prototyping.

Our discussion of the traditional prototyping system has concentrated on the first three dimensions in Exhibit 10–6: the driving force, focus, and control over prototyping. The traditional model is technical, focused on design intent and largely controlled by engineering until the later phases. What we have called the revised version preserves the basic thrust of the traditional model, but adds a focus on customers and a drive for commerical performance. This implies that the criteria engineers use in the revised model will be broader and more customer-focused.

The last four dimensions define important issues in the way proto-typing is structured, and the two models illustrate the range of choices firms face. Who builds the prototypes, for instance, is an issue of great import in the project. For example, in rapidly changing markets where speed is crucial, it is not unusual for engineers responsible for early phases of product development to press hard for the freedom to sub-contract the construction of early prototype units. Their argument, often relevant in larger firms, is that the in-house "specialists" in prototyping tend to focus on asset utilization at the expense of fast feedback on prototypes. When construction is subcontracted, design engineering has the flexibility to decide how much it is willing to pay for fast cycles.

The "who builds" issue is particularly important in the middle phases of the traditional prototyping models. These prototype build and test cycles are controlled by engineering, but provide an important opportunity for manufacturing learning and input. In the engineering work-station industry cited earlier (see Exhibit 10–5), this usually arises in the design maturity test (DMT) phase of prototyping. There are very different choices for building prototypes in that cycle. These are shown in Exhibit 10–7. One is to leave it under the control of engineering, but outsource to a prototype supplier who will meet engineering's service requirements. Another is to have it done by a specialized group located in engineering—typically called a "model shop"—which will meet en-gineering's service requirements and yet benefit from the scale and prox-

Exhibit 10–6

Dimensions of Prototyping: Three Models*

DIMENSIONS	MODELS		
	Standard Traditional	Revised Traditional	Periodic
Driving Force	Technical performance	Technical/commercial performance	System performance/cross-functional integration
Focus	Evaluate design intent	Design intent/customer satisfaction	Superior system solution
Control of Cycles			
Early	Engineering	Engineering	Heavyweight team
Middle	Engineering	Engineering	Heavyweight team
Late	Manufacturing	Manufacturing	Heavyweight team
Responsibility for Building			
Early	Subcontracted	Engineering model shop	Engineering model shop
Middle	Engineering model shop	Model shop in manufacturing	Manufacturing/production line
Late	Plant	Plant	Commercial production line
Role/Involvement of Customers	Limited to testing in late phases	Early: evaluation of mock-ups Late: system evaluation	Early: customer test of prototypes Late: extensive customer field tests
Test Criteria	Early: functionality by component Late: system functionality	Early: functionality/fidelity Late: system functionality/fidelity	Product: system functionality Process: system functionality
Link to Management Milestones	Limited; milestone reviews based on calendar	Milestones tied to prototype phases	Prototype cycles are the management milestones

* Most firms have a dominant model for how they conduct their prototyping cycles, established by a set of choices they make regarding several important dimensions. Three quite different models observed in practice are the standard traditional, the revised traditional, and the periodic.

268

Exhibit 10–7

Prototyping Choices in the Mid-Phase of Workstation Development Projects*

DVT: Design Verification Testing
DMT: Design Maturity Testing
PVT: Production Verification Testing

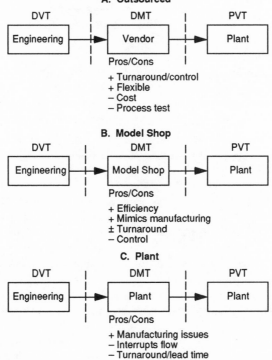

A. Outsourced

DVT | DMT | PVT

Engineering → Vendor → Plant

Pros/Cons

+ Turnaround/control
+ Flexible
– Cost
– Process test

B. Model Shop

DVT | DMT | PVT

Engineering → Model Shop → Plant

Pros/Cons

+ Efficiency
+ Mimics manufacturing
± Turnaround
– Control

C. Plant

DVT | DMT | PVT

Engineering → Plant → Plant

Pros/Cons

+ Manufacturing issues
– Interrupts flow
– Turnaround/lead time

* In the development of a new engineering workstation, the middle phase of design maturity testing may be carried out in three quite different locations, each with its own approach, mode of operation, and pros and cons: outsourced (by a specialized subcontractor), the model shop (by a specialist group in engineering or production), or the plant (by the regular production staff).

imity advantages available from doing many prototype cycles on different projects. Still another option is to have prototypes built in the factory. This ensures early involvement and consideration of manufacturing issues, but is likely to raise howls from engineering if they experience longer response times and get feedback (test results) on a set of manufacturability issues that they may not have considered the primary concern for that phase.

Under the traditional model in Exhibit 10–6, the firm has subcontracted early prototypes, done the middle phase in an engineering model shop, and the late prototypes in the plant. The revised model brings early prototypes in-house, does the middle phase in a model shop located in manufacturing, and does the prototypes in the plant. This set-up emphasizes manufacturability and capturing prototype knowledge inside the firm. As a general rule, in-house groups do not move quickly. Thus, an additional action we have seen a handful of firms take is to change the performance dimensions used to measure specialized prototyping groups to reflect "service level objectives" rather than primarily asset utilization objectives.

Since the primary focus of the traditional model is technical functionality, customers play a small role until the late phases of development. The role of customers, however, is an important choice. Often the engineers responsible for early prototype build and test cycles are so focused on technical issues that they see little need to provide units for marketing to test prototypes with customers. Often engineers view themselves as good judges of customer reactions. That may be true in some products, but where customers may have input that is relevant to choices being made in the early cycles, attractive options exists for involving them directly. These include having development engineers talk with customers, having marketing run focus groups with early prototypes, and producing additional prototype units in a subcycle (but without slowing down or hindering the main prototyping cycle) and getting customer comments that can feed back into development one cycle later.

We have added customer tests of early mock-ups under the revised model of Exhibit 10–6. Involving customers at this stage, however, requires some care and considerable skill. When the Coca Cola Company ran early tests of its New Coke with customers, the results suggested strong support for the new product.[4] But the tests only focused on taste, and the testers never asked: "How would you feel about this new product if it were to *replace* Coke?" The remarkable protests that took Coca-Cola by surprise when it replaced Old Coke with New Coke (and led to the reintroduction of "Classic" Coke) suggests the dangers of ill-conceived early customer involvement in development.

The question of appropriate tests and test criteria goes beyond customer involvement. Typically the connection between a prototype unit and its testing focuses on specific functionalities the organization feels must be resolved in that phase of development. However, it is important that testing explicitly address the *representativeness* of that prototype to the final environment in which it will be applied. Two examples help to illustrate this. In one, a piece of equipment (part of a process development project) was tested extensively in the supplier's plant as part of an early prototype cycle. Though the equipment planned for the customer's plant appeared identical, the supplier's environment sufficiently constrained the testing done that it turned out not to be representative of the commerical environment. In another case, an early prototype component was adjusted by its builder so that it would work in the system-level prototype. The adjustments could not be replicated by standard production equipment, however. Though the prototype builder thought he was doing exactly what was needed so testing could be done on the subsystem, the testing did not raise explicitly the issue of whether similar units with those tolerances could be produced on the factory floor. A major redesign subsequently was required when the initial design—which had worked in the prototype—could not be made in the factory.

Test procedure choices must not only consider what is needed in that particular phase, but also capture important issues of representativeness for the entire project. Some organizations have found that creating "test strategies" that span the duration of the development project, not just individual phases, is one way to get at this. Others have sought to have specialized groups (for example, quality assurance) do the bulk of the testing in hopes that the group's cumulative experience will ensure that representativeness issues are addressed early and appropriately. The broader criteria for testing—including fidelity—that we have added in the revised model of Exhibit 10–6 is consistent with the commercial focus of that model and its deeper involvement with customers.

The final dimension of choice shown in Exhibit 10–6 is the link between completion of prototyping cycles and management milestone reviews during the project. As indicated in Chapter 6, some firms choose to link milestone reviews almost exclusively to completion of a prototype build and test cycle while others—like our traditional model in Exhibit 10–6—schedule milestone reviews based on the calendar (for example, every three months) rather than waiting for completion of a particular prototyping cycle. Though most would agree that reviews connected to a prototyping cycle tend to be more objective and thorough with regard to work actually accomplished and what remains to be done, when a given cycle is running late (by weeks or even months, as is sometimes the case) or when it has been several months since a cycle was completed, a milestone review that is not tied to completion of a prototyping cycle is called for. Alternatively, when a project appears to be in trouble, an additional prototyping cycle might be inserted to refocus the effort and provide senior management with a reference point for a midcourse assessment and review.

Consequences of the Traditional Approach

The results of applying best practice principles and thoughtful planning to the traditional cycles can result in significant leverage and improvement in the overall development effort. The revised model in Exhibit 10–6, for example, is likely to avoid some of the late changes caused by potential mismatches between the design and the manufacturing process inherent in the traditional model. Further, the broadening of criteria for testing may uncover potential problems with customer acceptance and reliability in the field that the traditional prototyping cycles would miss. In the right environment—manufacturability is important and the product must fit in a customer's system—the revised model may be a substantial improvement. However, the very nature of the traditional approach to prototyping—with its shifting of responsibility from one function to another and its primary emphasis on its technical role—has important consequences for management at the project, functional, and senior levels of the organization.

First, it reinforces and legitimizes the separation of design engineering and manufacturing process engineering and limits the overlap between these two functions. When design engineers are responsible for a prototype build and test cycle, their focus is primarily on design feasibility (and the ability of the product to meet customer requirements, usually as stated by marketing). When manufacturing is responsible for the cycle, their focus is on resource utilization and manufacturability. Thus, under the traditional model—whether standard or revised—early prototyping cycles differ from later ones in primary emphasis and their focus of attention, as well as in who has primary responsibility for them. This shifting focus also affects learning. Because the prototypes generally are built by different people in early and later cycles, there can be substantial information and potential learning generated on early (or later) cycles that fails to get transferred and utilized later on (or on subsequent projects). While some information gets transferred from one cycle to another in the physical prototype units, it is much less than is available and much less than might be transferred under a different system.

The functional, somewhat fragmented nature of responsibility in the traditional model also affects how the product is tested. In the traditional model, it is not until late in the product development effort that a prototype build and test cycle occurs where the entire organization's contributions are brought together and tested as a system. Early prototype cycles are, by their design, tests of only subparts of the final product and/or manufacturing system. As a result, cross-functional issues tend not to get highlighted or raised until late in the development effort. Because of the cost and time required for prototyping, particularly in early phases, and because only a subpart (a single function) of the organization tests and evaluates early prototypes, relatively few units get constructed in early cycles. It is not until pilot production that most firms build a substantial number of prototype units. This means that prototype units may be a scarce resource early on and will tend to be "hoarded" by the function who manages the cycle that created them. Thus even if marketing and manufacturing could get a head start on certain system issues using early prototypes, they may not be able to get their hands on them. Furthermore, the testing that is done on early units tends to be narrow, aimed at resolving specific functional issues. It is not until late in the development effort that system-wide testing and exploration of subtle interactions with the customer's environment tend to be explored fully. At that point, most organizations are anxious to move toward market introduction, and the temptation is to underinvest in broad testing of the full product with intended customers.

Prototyping: A Managerial Perspective

Even with thoughtful adjustment and attention to speed, quality, and building knowledge, the traditional prototyping model has inherent limitations. Particularly where cross-functional integration is crucial and the system is central to customer choice and competition, the traditional model will fail to deliver all the leverage and power that prototyping can provide. Capturing that power, however, requires a basic rethinking of the model of prototyping. A starting point for that alternative approach is the recognition that prototyping can play crucial *managerial* roles in development, in addition to its more traditional, technical roles. Prototyping seems particularly well suited to four roles in development management:

Feedback and Learning. Prototypes create insight about a variety of dimensions of the product, ranging from such factors as form, style, and feel, to functionality, performance, and interactions with the customer's environment and existing support systems. As a result of that feedback individual functions as well as the broader organization can learn the degree to which choices made thus far are likely to achieve the intended results, what refinements still need to be made, and what work remains for project completion. While much of this learning is technical in nature, some is commercial and can play a significant role in helping to assess what skills are critical, defining the opportunities and need for integration, and suggesting choices that can provide superior advantage over competitors.

Communication and Information Sharing. The physical object represented by the prototype becomes the vehicle by which different contributors can focus and articulate their concerns and issues, and reach agreement on the best ways to resolve conflicts and solve problems. Because even simple prototypes can convey substantial amounts of information, they serve as a bridge between individuals and groups with very different backgrounds, experiences, and interests. Thus management can use prototypes to gauge, share, and extend organizational knowledge.

Outside Evaluation. Prototypes make possible an "in-process" look and assessment on the part of suppliers and customers. They give management the basis for assessing progress to date and making plans to integrate the firm's needs and development efforts with its suppliers and customers. A not inconsequential aspect of this role is providing credibility in the marketplace. The prototype tells customers that the development effort is, in fact, progressing and deserving of the customer's attention. Management can use prototypes to help set expectations and influence behavior on the part of anticipated customers. In addition, prototypes can be used with suppliers, the financial community, and even others within the firm. We have seen early prototypes shared with employees to generate enthusiasm and excitement well beyond those directly involved, and with senior management to get their support for key development strategies.

Establishing, Pacing, and Monitoring the Development Schedule. Since the number, duration, and frequency of prototyping cycles are closely linked to the critical path of the development project, managing those cycles is often the best way to manage the rate of convergence and the cycle time of the overall development effort. Companies A and B in the appliance example of Exhibit 10–2 had used prototyping in this role to improve dramatically their product development performance. Management systematically had recombined and grouped functional tasks into three design-build-test cycles (versus the five cycles at Company C), ensured that each cycle achieved its knowledge-building goals, and instilled the discipline needed to complete those cycles as planned.

Periodic Prototyping—An Approach for Platform Projects

The managerial roles that prototypes might play are particularly important in platform projects. By its nature, a platform lays down the architecture for a whole family of products and thus confronts the organization with a range of system issues. Moreover, the complexity and extent of performance improvement of a platform effort is likely to create important cross-functional issues. In that context, an approach to prototyping that fulfills the technical role, but exploits managerial potential more than the traditional model, could be of substantial value.

One approach that meets these criteria is called "periodic prototyping." Its basic characteristics are presented in Exhibit 10–6. We have seen it used by a handful of firms on major platform projects with a heavyweight team. In addition, periodic prototyping appears best suited for medium-to high-volume products where functional integration and system performance are likely to be key determinants of success in the marketplace and where the cost of prototypes is relatively small. Next-generation platform efforts on products ranging from computers to disk drives, and from medical devices to home appliances, would be candidates for this approach; commercial aircraft or turbine generators would not. What is different in periodic prototyping is that integration is a concern throughout all cycles, even the early ones, and prototyping is done on a calendar basis rather than a phase completion basis. The goal is to balance the technical and managerial roles of prototyping as effectively as possible. An example is perhaps the best way to illustrate the fundamental characteristics of periodic prototyping.

The Motorola Bandit pager project, referenced in Chapter 8, utilized periodic prototyping. As illustrated in Exhibit 10–8, the prototyping schedule set up by the cross-functional heavyweight team started with an initial demonstration breadboard unit built in the lab. The first design-build-test cycle was conducted by the development engineering function, as it traditionally would have been. The next five cycles, however, were done using a periodic approach. The team set a date on which each of the prototype builds would occur, and then stuck to that date whether or not each function had completed all of its tasks originally planned as prerequisites to that cycle.

Prototype build #1, scheduled for 10 January 1987, was conducted on that date with the participation of the entire cross-functional team. This early cycle, as well as every subsequent cycle, involved the integrated effort of all project participants. Obviously, at the time of each cycle, some functions were further along in their project tasks than were others. As shown at the bottom of Exhibit 10–8, for prototype build #1, the traditional pager factory provided the front end activities required for that prototyping cycle (development of the printed circuit boards), and the back end of the cycle (assembly and test) was done manually in the Bandit factory area. (The new production line was still under construction.) Though eventually the entire cycle would be conducted on the Bandit pager production line with highly automated robotics linked through computer-integrated manufacturing software, the intent was to build full units with everyone involved even in the first full prototype cycle.

The subsequent cycles (#2 through pilot) also involved all of the functions and were done in the factory. Increasingly, those cycles were done with the equipment and systems that would finally be used on an ongoing operating basis. If for some reason a function, like factory software, had not completed all of its planned steps prior to a scheduled

EXHIBIT 10–8

Periodic Prototyping—Motorola Bandit Pager*

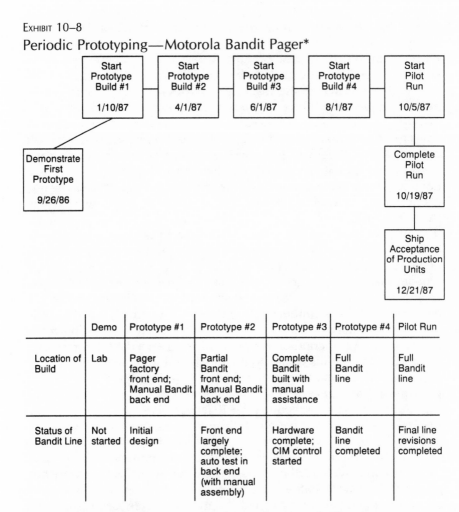

	Demo	Prototype #1	Prototype #2	Prototype #3	Prototype #4	Pilot Run
Location of Build	Lab	Pager factory front end; Manual Bandit back end	Partial Bandit front end; Manual Bandit back end	Complete Bandit built with manual assistance	Full Bandit line	Full Bandit line
Status of Bandit Line	Not started	Initial design	Front end largely complete; auto test in back end (with manual assembly)	Hardware complete; CIM control started	Bandit line completed	Final line revisions completed

* On the Motorola Bandit project, after the initial prototype build, subsequent prototyping cycles were done periodically (generally every two months.) This facilitated the regular testing of progress on all aspects of the system design and allowed the design-build-test cycles to be used as an integrating mechanism on a periodic basis throughout the project.

---

prototype build date, such as the phase 2 build scheduled for 1 April, the cycle would not be delayed. Instead, the prototyping schedule would proceed as planned, but the factory software group would have to fill in manually, as required. In addition, the software group would be expected to document what was incomplete, the corrective actions to be taken, and the expected status by the next build (#3 scheduled for 1

June). This approach places substantial pressure on all project participants to meet their commitments, but also provides objective feedback on their real status, motivates them to get back on track, and ensures them of receiving the "help" needed from others.

Characteristics of Periodic Prototyping

The Motorola Bandit project highlights several important differences between the periodic prototyping model and the traditional model. With the periodic approach, prototyping is done on a regular schedule (for example, every other month), and that schedule is adhered to whether or not all anticipated tasks have been completed. Each function goes with what it has and fills in on an ad hoc basis as required. Thus functions continue to be responsible for completion of their individual tasks and activities as part of the prototyping cycle, but know others on the project are depending on them.

Once the prototyping schedule has been specified, it is relatively easy for each of the functions to state what tasks they plan to have completed by each prototype build date. This stimulates the functional groups to think about restructuring and regrouping tasks and then resequencing and altering the timing traditionally followed. Initially, they may move as many tasks as possible into earlier prototype build cycles. Over time they may be even more creative, finding ways to further "front load" early cycles and eventually dropping late cycles that no longer are needed. Thus, periodic prototyping leads to innovative solutions to task planning issues.

Because every function is involved in every prototyping cycle (with the possible exception of the first one), each cycle provides a set of physical activities that brings together all the key players (periodically) to communicate the status of their portion of the project's tasks and to see the status of counterpart activities on the project. Each prototype build becomes an opportunity for regrouping and recalibrating. The amount of information exchanged and the detailed problem-solving focus that occurs in each cycle is substantially greater than under the traditional pattern. Cross-functional exchanges are especially strengthened.

Given their cross-functional nature, prototyping cycles become timely review points for senior management as well as the core team. The focus of those reviews is product-driven and objective, because both the status of each individual function's activities (based on what they have to do manually or on an ad hoc basis to complete the cycle) and how cross-functional issues are being raised and resolved are clear. The result of each cycle is shared understanding of what needs to happen in the next cycle to make substantial progress.

277

Shared understanding and learning for the project as a whole is also increased because of the number of units produced. In each cycle, many more units are produced than those needed for a single function; every function ends up with units it can test, evaluate, and study as a result of even the early cycles. Functions that traditionally only had units for testing late in the development project now have units much sooner, and the quality assurance function can initiate its activities—including life testing and customer evaluations—with the first cycle. The result is much more thorough testing across a broad range of variables. This is particularly valuable in next-generation platform efforts that target an improved system solution for the marketplace.

Not only does learning increase within the project, but, over time, an organization using periodic prototyping can more easily and systematically improve its development capabilities. Since project pacing and momentum are controlled and reflected in the progress that occurs over a sequence of design-build-test cycles, and since cycles are now on a regular calendar and every cycle involves all the key functions, it is much easier to track progress and identify problem areas. When done on multiple projects, the organization can examine systematically what tasks, if moved to an earlier cycle, would have the most leverage. Eventually, as sufficient learning is moved to earlier cycles, the number of cycles may be reduced.

Prerequisites for Periodic Prototyping

Periodic prototyping has significant advantages, but it requires particular organizational capability and a particular development process. It requires, for example, that all of the functions with key roles at some point during the development effort be involved throughout the project's duration. Thus heavyweight teams, with their cross-functional emphasis, are a natural for the periodic approach. The team must be given authority and responsibility to plan the organizing, sequencing, and timing of individual tasks on a project. Since this "goes with the territory" of heavyweight project teams, it is much easier in that environment than it would be in the traditional functional environment, where the functions have control of individual project tasks, their sequence, and their form of execution.

Because the firm builds many more prototype units in the periodic model, prototype units must be sufficiently inexpensive that the approach is feasible. However, prototypes do not have to be "cheap." Organizations that have adopted periodic prototyping have found that spending an additional $500,000 on prototyping units and materials (over that spent under the traditional approach) is money well spent. We've seen products that range in value from a few cents per unit to a few thousand dollars per unit developed with this periodic approach.

Support groups have a particularly crucial role to play. Groups such as the model shop and quality assurance or analytical testing must have the capacity to meet the requirements associated with the periodic proto- typing schedule. Once familiar with the approach, scheduling support resources tends to be easier under periodic prototyping than under the conventional approach. This is because the prototyping schedule is locked in early and adhered to. Thus support groups can plan their resource requirements knowing the schedule will be followed. A major problem in the traditional approach to prototyping is that support groups often discover at the last minute that a project needs their help, and they are unable to balance and coordinate demands across multiple projects.

Periodic prototyping seems best suited to platform projects where there is substantial payoff from achieving a better system solution. In a breakthrough project where the leverage is in excelling on a single, groundbreaking feature or technical component, forcing adherence to preset dates for prototype build cycles and forcing early cycles to incor- porate inputs from all the functions may complicate the project unnec- essarily and make it too complex to be managed realistically. Thus periodic prototyping is not the answer in every situation, but in many, it holds significant promise.

Matching Prototyping and Development Project Requirements

Under the right conditions, periodic prototyping is an attractive, appro- priate model for design-build-test cycles. But a different set of factors may make a well-conceived traditional approach to prototyping attrac- tive and appropriate. Even within these two broad models, however, a number of variables associated with different types of projects deter- mine what pattern of prototyping choices will be most effective. A key opportunity for management is to match the details of the design-build- test cycles with the requirements of each specific development project. Making that match requires an understanding of the characteristics of different prototyping patterns and the decisions that determine them.

Our discussion thus far has identified three critical characteristics of the project's environment that determine the appropriate dominant ori- entation of the prototyping process. While these characteristics may be present to different degrees in any project, we shall focus here on rela- tively "pure" types of projects in order to illustrate the key relation- ships. The three characteristics are:

1. The relative importance of advanced, innovative technical developments in driving superior product performance
2. The relative importance of a balanced, total system solution to customer choice
3. The relative importance of manufacturability (i.e., manufacturing cost and reliability) in competition and customer decisions

When one of these characteristics dominates a project's environment, the pattern of prototyping must adapt to that basic thrust. Consider the following three projects and their associated prototyping patterns.

Technical Breakthrough (advanced semiconductor manufacturing equipment). In this project, achieving superior technical performance is the name of the game. Prototyping thus focuses on rapid service and quick turnaround to provide engineers with timely and effective feedback. Because the product pushes the state of the art, design specifications are not frozen, but remain somewhat flexible until customers have had a chance to test early versions. Control of prototypes remains with engineering until very late in the program and issues of manufacturability receive less concern than product performance. Finally, the criteria for testing are related to technical performance, and representativeness becomes a factor only in later cycles.

Platform System (next-generation microwave oven). In this project the crucial issue is product architecture and the behavior of the product as a complete system. An effective design requires the integration of physical dimensions, ergonomics, software, sensors, aesthetics, ease of use, safety, and issues of reliability. Prototyping focuses on team learning and representativeness. Control over prototypes and prototyping rests with the heavyweight team doing the platform project, and testing criteria pertain to the performance of the system. Specifications are established relatively early in the program, but are broadly defined to allow for adaptation in later, derivative versions of the product.

Incremental Refinement (new version of desktop printer with improved reliability and lower cost). In this project cost and reliability are paramount. The new product is based on an established platform so that the basic architecture is unchanged. What matters is a major improvement in manufacturability. Prototyping focuses on early involvement and input from manufacturing. The quality of prototypes, particularly their representativeness, is the primary performance dimension used to evaluate the prototyping activity. Specifications are frozen early, since the basic product is well established and the target market is well known. While design engineers play a critical role in this project (e.g., changing the design to make it more reliable), control over prototypes passes to manufacturing relatively early in order to give issues of cost and reliability high priority.

These descriptions underscore the different patterns of prototyping appropriate for different kinds of projects. Exhibit 10–9 summarizes the patterns and indicates the problems that may arise when projects and the mode of prototyping are mismatched.

The first prototyping model—rapid response to engineering—is well suited to the technical breakthrough project run by an autonomous team. We assume that the rapid response mode uses best practice in quality, in using cost-effective processes and materials, and in tying prototypes to project milestones. But in its control, organization, focus and testing criteria, the rapid response to engineering model is dedicated to the support of technical innovation. Using a modified version of the traditional model with its emphasis on technical performance, the rapid response mode provides early feedback, flexible scheduling, quick response to the needs of design engineers, and a focus on achieving significant advances in the state of the art of technical performance.

While the rapid response mode is effective in technical breakthrough projects, it has serious limits when applied to platform projects or incremental improvements. A glance down the first column of Exhibit 10–9 indicates the central problem—lack of balance and integration. A more appropriate mode for platform projects is the integrated system model, a variation of periodic prototyping described above. Here representativeness is the crucial criterion, and the organization reflects the emphasis on balance across functions and the performance of the system as a whole. All functions participate in each stage of prototyping, and the heavyweight team controls the focus, criteria, and evaluation of prototyping. Because of the importance of the total system, the team places less emphasis on narrow technical criteria in specific components, and more on how specific component designs interact with and influence other elements of the product. In this setup the focus of prototyping is convergence to a system design and integration across functions.

Of course, one can imagine platform projects where technical excellence in a narrow sense is more important that we have indicated. In that circumstance, managers would need to adjust the mode of prototyping, particularly in the early stages, to give more weight to technical problem solving. Depending on the nature of the problems and the technology, this might involve creating a staged process in which the team adds advanced engineering prototypes to its schedule in the early stages of development. Subsequent stages might then move to a system focus.

The last mode of prototyping—replicate manufacturing early—is well suited to incremental improvement projects where issues of manufacturability are central. Given a stable architecture and an established

Exhibit 10–9

Matching Three Models of Prototyping and Three Types of Projects*

Models of Prototyping: Dominant Orientation

PROJECT TYPE	Model I	Model II (periodic prototyping)	Model III
	Rapid Response to Engineering	Integrated System Solution	Replicate Manufacturing Early
	• rapid turnaround • flexible specs • engineering control • technical focus	• team learning • specs established early • team control • system integration	• prototype quality • established specs • manufacturing control • manufacturability
Breakthrough (technical)	– creative, innovative results – fast response enhances feedback – manufacturing in late performance and features – easily overcome problems with manufacturing	– system focus causes technical compromise – complexity and uncertainty slow down technical work – constraints of system limit innovation	– slow turnaround; late introductions – engineers out of loop – performance suffers, leading to many late engineering changes
Platform (new architecture)	– technical focus skews architecture, hurts balance – system performance suffers in field leading to design revisions	– system focus achieves clear interfaces, integration – team learning leads to early design convergence – team control facilitates communication, eliminates late design changes	– manufacturing focus hurts design balance – performance inadequate, leading to late design revisions
Incremental (stable architecture)	– lack early manufacturing involvement – late revisions required for manufacturability	– team approach is overkill; complicates project – system focus leads to late revisions because of technical (processing) problems	– early involvement solves problems in design – smooth ramp-up – enhanced reliability and cost performance

* The type of development project—breakthrough, platform, or incremental—determines the most appropriate model of prototyping. However, since most firms use the same model of prototyping for all their development projects, it is useful to recognize the implications of each model for the various types of development projects.

market, design changes focus on making the product easier to make and more reliable in operation. In some respects, this mode is the manufacturing version of the traditional model—manufacturability criteria top the agenda, the prototypes are built by manufacturing, and manufacturing controls the focus, direction, and evaluation of prototypes. Representativeness, particularly the fit with the volume production process, is the principal criterion for evaluation.

Such an approach, as the third column in Exhibit 10–9 suggests, is not effective for a technical breakthrough project. Issues of manufacturability may be important even there, but a prototyping process that focuses on those issues may not yield the quick, rapid insights design engineers need to make significant advances in the state of the art. Replicating manufacturing early is also less effective in a platform project because of issues of balance. However, if the platform has a high manufacturability content, early manufacturing involvement and emphasis—even more than we would get in an integrated system approach—may be important.

Matching the mode of prototyping, particularly the focus, criteria, control, and pattern of functional involvement, can play an important role in improving development performance. No matter what the type of project, there are certain practices and characteristics (such as quality, timeliness, efficient use of materials and processes) that contribute to superior performance. But dimensions of control, involvement, and criteria represent crucial choices that drive the behavior of the prototyping system. The concepts we have developed here provide managers with a framework for systematic evaluation of existing patterns, their drivers, and their impact on development. With a close look at the set of projects, and the needs of specific projects, managers can develop new patterns of prototyping that better match project requirements. Prototyping represents a significant tool for managing development projects, and changing the prototyping process represents an important tool for improving development performance.

CHAPTER 11

Learning from Development Projects

*I*n the new industrial competition, both survival and advantage depend on upon the ability to sustain improvements in product development performance. In a world of intense international competition, where customers are sophisticated and demanding and technologies are diverse and dramatic in their effects, those who stand still in product and process development will neither prosper nor survive. The ability to sustain significant improvements in development over long periods of time rests on the capability to learn from experience. What is crucial in improving development is insight and understanding about how the organization works in practice. Studies that benchmark the best practice among competitors or that generate new concepts and frameworks may prove valuable in establishing perspective, but solving the problems that limit performance requires a detailed understanding of the root causes of those problems as they play out in the specific circumstances of the organization's development process. Thus, learning from experience is crucial.

In the context of product and process development, learning from experience means learning from development projects. But organizational learning is not a natural outcome of development projects, even in successful development efforts. There seem to be two fundamental problems. The first is that the performance that matters is often a result of complex interactions within the overall development system. Moreover, the connection between cause and effect may be separated significantly in time and place. In some instances, for example, the outcomes of interest are only evident at the conclusion of the project. Thus, while symptoms and potential causes may be observed by individuals at various points along the development path, systematic investigation requires observation of the outcomes, followed by an analysis that looks back to find the underlying causes. The second problem, however is that natural incentives in the organization favor pressing forward to the next project. Without concerted effort and focused attention on learning from the project that has just been completed, it is unlikely that engineers, marketers, or manufacturers will naturally devote time and energy to yesterday's problems. Most companies learn very little from their development experience. Those that do understand the power in improvement have developed tools and methods to help people—individually and collectively—gain insight and understanding and focus energy and attention on the problem of learning.

In this chapter, we identify the challenges that projects pose to the organizations trying to learn from them, suggest tools and methods that may be useful in meeting those challenges, and apply the ideas to specific examples. We first develop a framework for thinking about learning in a complex, ambiguous, and often confusing project environment. The framework identifies what can be learned from projects, and the general methods that seem most effective in generating insight and understanding. We then focus on the problem of capturing insight and learning and using it to change the development process. Here we examine the role of procedures, specific methods and tools, the development process itself, and specific principles that can be used to guide decisions in development. The next section of the chapter illustrates the application of the framework in what we call the project audit. The audit is a procedure for systematically developing data on the project's characteristics and performance, and conducting an analysis of the underlying sources (i.e., the causes) of the performance one observes. In addition to describing what an audit is, we present an example—taken from an actual audit—that lays out what one can learn from an audit and how the audit can be used to identify specific changes in the organization that will improve performance.

A Framework for Learning

Development projects are complex, with activity going on in many different locations, involving many different people and extended periods of time. Moreover, the outcomes we are interested in are often ambiguous—they are the result of complex interactions that may be

285

poorly characterized and not well understood. But development does have a pattern. There is a specific sequence of activities, each of which is designed to influence the character of the product or process, and each of which determines in some way development performance. There are plans that lead to designs, designs that lead to prototypes, and prototypes that are tested, piloted, and introduced. And there are critical events that seem to have a direct impact on project performance. In order to learn from development projects, therefore, we need to understand this sequence of activities and critical events. Understanding may yield leverage over the development process and create insight into what must be changed in order to seek improvement. To learn from events or sequences of activities, one needs a structure—a way to frame the problems observed. Events, activities, and their outcomes do not come neatly packaged with cause and effect well defined. Consider the following examples of critical events or activities:

- The tooling on a pump housing for a new medical instrument is delivered two months late. The tool is on the critical path of the program, and thus delays the new product significantly.
- A new piece of process equipment fails to meet quality targets during commercial ramp-up of a new production process. The process is supposed to produce perfectly round shafts for a new compressor. The shafts produced during prototype meet the specifications, but those produced during commerical ramp-up do not.
- A consumer products company discovers that its next-generation shampoo has achieved superior performance, but is far more costly than expected. Originally intended to be positioned just below premium brands in performance, but at a much lower price, the new shampoo must be either reformulated or repositioned as a "me-too" premium product.
- The doors on a new sports sedan fail water leak tests during pilot manufacturing. The sedan uses a door design similar to the design on the last three models developed by the company. Those models also failed the water leak test during pilot. The problem of water leaks with this door design was well known at the outset of the sports sedan project, but was left unresolved until pilot manufacturing.

Each of the events described above created problems for the development organization. Solving those problems required additional resources and time, and, in some cases, affected the quality of performance. Getting at the root causes of these problems could, therefore, lay the foundation for substantial improvement in development performance. But the potential for learning is not limited to things gone wrong. Consider the following examples where things went right:

- A new flexible manufacturing system experiences very rapid development (less than two years, when the average for such systems is four years) and performs at a very high level of reliability (85–90 percent) in the first few months of implementation.
- A new portable table for use in hospitals achieves dramatic market penetration in the first year of introduction. Customers report levels of satisfaction with the product that exceed competitive offerings and the prior generation by a significant amount.
- A new household appliance completes manufacturing ramp-up smoothly and in record time. The number of engineering changes introduced after completion of prototype testing is far below the normal levels achieved in previous projects.

Episodes where things go wrong (or, sometimes, right) are the raw material for learning. In Exhibit 11–1 we have presented five categories of such "critical events" and provided examples of the kinds of observations that lie behind them and issues for potential learning. What makes an event critical is its connection to an aspect of the development process that drives performance. While the event itself may be a symptom, pursuing it can lead to a deeper understanding of the forces that influence the speed, quality, and productivity of development.

Consider, for example, the first category in Exhibit 11–1—recurring problems. Here the immediate observation might involve a quality problem like the water leak that shows up in several designs. Learning, in this instance, could (and should) focus on how to solve the particular quality problem, but its recurrence suggests a basic issue with the way the organization deals with these kinds of problems. The challenge for learning, therefore, is to uncover the more fundamental source of the reoccurrence, so that once found and solved a quality problem does not reoccur. Similar observations apply to problems in the other categories in Exhibit 11–1: specific activities like carrying out a market research clinic, or conducting a product test, as well as working-level linkages, design-build-test cycles, and decision-making processes.

Individual Versus Organizational Learning

Getting at the fundamental sources of problems in the development process, however, is unlikely to occur naturally. Because the development process is so complex and involves so many different people in different groups, and because the issues cut across groups, departments, functions, and organizations, learning is likely to require careful, systematic effort.[1] Of course, some learning will occur naturally. For example, individual engineers routinely learn how to use new methods and tools—a CAD system or a testing device, for example. Engineers who

287

EXHIBIT 11-1
The Focus of Learning: Five Categories of Critical Events in Development Projects*

Category	Nature of Observations	Issues for Learning
1. Recurring problems linked to critical performance dimensions	• Persistent quality problems with design • Engineering changes at pilot for problems that could have been uncovered long before	• Does the organization capture solutions and make them permanent? • Discipline and methodology in engineering
2. Crucial individual activities/tasks and associated capabilities	• Time to complete key tasks (e.g., testing) • Quality of tasks	• Do we measure/track the right information about tasks? • Do we have the skills needed?
3. Working-level linkages (e.g., engineering – manufacturing)	• Timing of downstream (e.g., manufacturing) involvement • Degree of influence exerted by upstream and downstream on problem solving in the other group	• Do we have a process and framework for integration? • Do we have the skills, attitudes, and values that drive integration?
4. Design-build-test cycles	• Speed of the cycle/number of cycles • Quality of solutions	• Do we have the right people involved in design-build-test cycles? • Do we have the right tools, supporting resources, and skills?
5. Processes for making decisions and allocating resources	• Time required to decide/number of reiterations • Resource constraints/problems	• Are the right people involved at the right time with the right information? • Do we have too many projects? Do we have an aggregate project plan?

* Critical to improving product development capabilities is recognizing the primary areas of activity that can be altered. Through systematic observation and subsequent modification of these fundamental activities, an organization can focus its efforts and increase its rate of learning.

take on new jobs learn what is expected of them and how to do the work from their colleagues in the department. And both new and experienced people add to their repertoire of problem solutions when they encounter and solve new problems in their work.

This kind of "learning by doing" requires that engineers pay attention to the task at hand, draw inferences about cause-and-effect relationships, and develop ways of remembering what they learn. Where these conditions exist, individual learning about specific tasks may occur naturally as a by-product of doing the work. Thus, without any explicit action on the part of management, individual know-how will increase. Moreover, there may even be some transfer of that know-how within the work groups of which engineers are a part. Through the use of stories, rules of thumb, changes in procedures or methods, or other modes of communication, what one engineer learns may be shared with others working on the same or closely related tasks. Thus, for example, a gear design engineer may learn how to use a new stress analysis on a CAD system, and through this identify a way to pinpoint potential problems in design prior to prototyping. When incorporated in a story about how this tool allowed the engineer to spot a latent design problem much earlier than ever before, the know-how becomes transferable to other engineers who may use the tool to solve similar problems.

But the kinds of learning of specific interest in this chapter—about the behavior of the development system; about tasks and capabilities that cut across functional boundaries; about critical linkages at the working level between different disciplines, functions, and departments; and about complex decision and resource allocation processes—are unlikely to occur simply through "learning by doing." In this case, the "doers" tend to focus on the completion of specific tasks and activities over which they have control. But at the level of the development system, where many elements come together and interact and where the patterns of cause-and-effect relationships may be complex, there is no guarantee that the doers at the working level will observe the important interactions, let alone be able to draw complex inferences about them. Take, for example, the problem of unresolved issues showing up very late in a development program. The problem might be a leak in an automobile door seal that is observed by test engineers working on prototypes (in reality, the potential sources of the leak—and even potential solutions to the problem—are many and varied). If we look beyond the specific technical sources—which might involve the design of the rubber gasket around the door, the design of the body opening, the design of dies, or the sheet metal forming processes—we need to understand how a problem that surfaced early in the program could have remained unresolved all the way through the prototyping process. This deeper question focuses on the organizational processes and involves

289

many different departments and many different individuals. Learning about that kind of problem will require systematic effort.

The effort to learn about development system performance in a given project, and in particular about organizational processes that drive performance, must be not only systematic but also tenacious. Such learning is not easy. The problems are broad-based and often ill-defined. The data one might want to use to understand the problem and draw inferences about its sources do not come in nice neat packages. Moreover, gaining insight and improved understanding about how the development process works is only part of the solution. The organization must also determine how to change the process in order to improve its performance.

The Shaft Roundness Problem at HVAC

But systematic learning about the development process is possible. Indeed, there seem to be a small number of common denominators in successful efforts to learn from development projects. Consider the following case:

When Mark Shaw came to work on the morning of 15 October 1991, a problem with the drive shaft in the new compressor was the last thing he expected. Shaw was the project leader for a new-generation compressor at HVAC, Inc. The project was an aggressive attempt by HVAC to bring to market a new compressor design that was more compact, efficient, and quieter in operation, and that sold for half the cost of its predecessor. Shaw led a team of ten people, drawn from the different engineering disciplines within HVAC as well as from marketing, manufacturing, and finance. The team had developed a strong working relationship and the project had moved along well. The first pilot production units were scheduled for completion at the end of October. All indications were that the project was on schedule to meet its target introduction date.

When Shaw came to work that crisp autumn morning, he found a serious problem awaiting him. Kelly Fortunado, a test engineer on the team, had left the following E-mail message: "Mark: We've got a problem. The first five pilot production drive shafts we tested did not meet the specifications for roundness. This is a crucial parameter. Without it, we can not meet the performance targets in the design."

After talking to Fortunado on the phone, Shaw called a meeting of the project team. The problem was troubling because months earlier the team had thoroughly tested all of the prototype units for drive shaft roundness. Every single one had met specification. The team brainstormed on possible causes of the problem and laid out several for investigation. They checked and rechecked the tooling, machine settings, tool programming, drawings, and material specifications. They conducted experimental runs of drive shafts and subjected them to rigorous testing. This work revealed the fundamental dilemma: all of the parameters in pilot production that they could identify were identical to those employed during prototyping when the drive shafts met specification. Yet all of the drive shafts produced during the pilot production runs failed to meet the specification for roundness.

After a week of intensive effort, Shaw concluded that the problem must lie in the prototyping process. Consequently, the team went back and examined the prototype shafts. They reviewed the prototype testing data, and confirmed the earlier results—all of the prototype shafts met the specification for roundness. The team then pursued the process specification used during prototype production. In searching for answers, they discovered all the production of the prototype drive shafts had been subcontracted to an outside machine shop. Shaw, along with two other members of the team, visited the prototype machine shop and discussed the prototype work with the shop supervisor. They reviewed the processes used to machine drive shafts and interviewed all of the personnel in the machine shop involved in prototype production. Shaw and his colleagues determined that the machine shop had used the specific procedures and a machining sequence identical to the one employed in pilot production. At the same time, three other members of the team conducted interviews with the materials suppliers and with test engineers involved in prototyping. This work failed to uncover a solution; it appeared that the prototyping process had been identical to the pilot production process.

Still not satisfied with the results of their work, Shaw made another visit to the prototype machine shop. He met with the machinist who had worked most closely on the drive shaft job. After reviewing yet again the procedures used, the machine settings, and the machinist's memory of the performance of the job, Shaw was left with no explanation of the problem. Disheartened, he prepared to leave. One last time, Shaw asked the machinist: "Is there anything you can remember about this job that might help us?" The machinist shook his head; Shaw started to leave. The machinist suddenly said, "Hey, wait a minute! There was one thing. What did you guys do about that fixture problem?" In that brief question, Shaw had an answer to this problem. The machinist continued, "I took a look at the specifications on that shaft, but there was no way I could see to meet them with the kind of fixturing you had suggested. I figured out a way to modify the fixtures so I could meet the specification on the shaft. The way you had planned those fixtures, I don't think you could ever get round parts out of the process."

Shaw's investigation uncovered the fact that the machinist in the prototype shop had changed the fixtures in the machining process in order to obtain in-spec parts, but that change had never been incorporated into the process specifications. Furthermore, the machinist had never told anyone about the changes he had made. He assumed his job was to make good parts, which it was—in part. Shaw took the information from the machinist back to his manufacturing plant where the changes were introduced rapidly. The new fixturing solved the roundness problem, and the pilot production runs were carried out without further significant difficulty.

Shaw's conversation with the machinist in the prototype shop revealed several important dimensions of the roundness problem. First, the conversation revealed a solution for the immediate problem. It also revealed where the development team's assumptions had gone wrong. The team had assumed that the process specifications, in particular the design of the fixturing, used during the pilot run were identical to those used during prototype production. This turned out to be a false assumption. It was also apparent that the development systems in place failed to uncover this discrepancy. There was no mechanism for ensuring that the prototype process was completely representative of the commercial production system. Furthermore, as the team pursed the issue, they learned that the practice of subcontracting prototype part production created a potential barrier to the transfer of insight and information about the prototype parts and their associated production processes to the commercial production system. There was, indeed, nothing in the system that linked the insight of the machinist about fixturing and tooling to subsequent changes in process specifications. Finally, the machinist who worked on the prototype part did not comprehend fully the role that he played in the development process. He did understand that part of his role was to produce parts that met the design intent. But he did not know that the changes he made in fixtures and tooling should be communicated to the process engineers in order to ensure that the parts could be made round in the commerical process.

This episode could, of course, be nothing more than an idiosyncratic fluke event. But on reflection, and in comparison with other programs and processes with which they were familiar, the development team determined that the gaps they had observed in the case of the prototype drive shaft—involving linkages between prototype production and the commercial production system—were not idiosyncratic or isolated incidents. The gaps they uncovered in their search for an understanding of the roundness problem were part of a pattern of organizational practice, structure, and capability that applied to all of the parts, components, and subsystems developed at HVAC.

Themes in Systematic Organizational Learning

The HVAC case illustrates five crucial themes in successful systematic learning about the process.[2]

Learning as a Team Process. Learning goes on inside the heads of individuals. In order to create the kind of shared understanding essential to implementation of new concepts of development, however, learning must be pursued and occur within the context of the development team. Team members bring different perspectives and different capabilities, and will read evidence in different ways. This can be a powerful and important source of insight and understanding. In effect, the kind of learning that is most crucial is learning that cuts across the narrow, functionally oriented tasks in development and concentrates on the behavior of the development system. It therefore is important that the organizational processes used to learn match the learning objectives. The team process for learning is thus critical to generating insight that cuts across narrow departmental, discipline, or functional lines.

A Model of the Process. At HVAC, the search for insight about the source of the roundness problem did not occur in a random or haphazard fashion. It was guided by a model of how the development process ought to work. They understood both the technical determinants of the performance they sought (the role of process specifications, material quality, operator training, and product design) as well as the organizational processes designed to carry out the specific technical tasks. No matter what the specific issue or problem that may prompt the search for improved learning and understanding, a framework—some kind of shared model of the development process—is an important starting point for identifying potential improvement opportunities. Such models may include descriptions of the development process like those laid out in Chapter 6, some kind of funnel diagram such as that discussed in Chapter 5, or perhaps a description of the development strategy that captures current understanding of the key process dimensions and areas of leverage, including critical linkages, tasks, and important processes.

Data and Analyses. The HVAC team sought understanding of the roundness problem through data and analyses. Through experimental runs of the production plant machining process, they determined that the roundness problem was systematic. They developed and reviewed data on prototype testing of the shafts in order to pinpoint potential sources of the problem. Their conclusions were based on neither impressions nor the most recent events that they could recall, but instead were rooted in the facts of the matter. That is not to say that judgment and intuition played no part; indeed, the instincts and intuitions of the engineers and managers involved played an important role in searching out potential sources of the problem and in pursuing a range of avenues and potential leads. Such intuition and judgment are essential in learning about the development process. But where our interest centers on performance and where determinants of performance are likely to be complex, it is crucial to observe the actual activities, linkages, and decisions, and to connect them to measured criteria for evaluation.

Search for Patterns. The episodes that trigger a search for new understanding may not be representative of underlying process tendencies. They may be strongly affected by random events or idiosyncratic developments. Moreover, for any given observed outcome (like the roundness problem), there may be many different competing explanations. What is required is evidence that what appears to drive the results is in fact fundamental. We need a sense that the explanation is not only logical but also characteristic of the way the organization works. The roundness problem could have reflected nothing more than a machinist who forgot to include process specification changes in the supporting documents with the prototype parts. But as the HVAC team compared its experience with other examples of prototype part production, they recognized a pattern. This was not an isolated incident, but a recurrent theme in the relationship between prototype production and the commerical pilot operation. Indeed, the team had only to look within its own experience to identify other parts where a similar lack of knowledge and information transfer had also occurred.

Root Causes. In any problem, like the roundness of the shaft, there are numerous proximate causes that a search for understanding may uncover. Following a process that resembles peeling an onion, the team moved from recognizing that the problem had occurred to identifying the potential sources (such as failure on the part of the operators in the commerical production process to follow specifications, failure of the material supplier to deliver material according to specification, incorrect machine settings, or incorrect product design). None of these proved useful in explaining the existence of the roundness problem. They then pursued the next step, which lay in the apparent gap between the prototype testing results and the results of the pilot production run. This led them to the prototype machine shop and eventually to an understanding of the actions of the machinist in changing the tooling and fixturing. The search for understanding yielded a solution to the round-ness problem. But the team didn't stop there. They sought a deeper understanding of the root causes of the problem, which in this case involved both a machinist who did not understand the full purposes of the prototyping process and a development process that failed to create effective communication links between either prototype production and design engineering, or prototype production and the commercial pilot production line. Thus, the search for understanding involves not only establishing patterns that are characteristic, but also pursuing under-standing to its most fundamental or root level. Continually pushing this search deeper is important because it ensures that the solution devel-oped solves the immediate problem and prevents future recurrences, as well as yields insights of a broader and more lasting nature. A search for root causes will uncover opportunities for changing the development process in ways that will make for fundamental and continuous im-provement in performance.

Capturing Insight and Learning to Change the Development Process

Given a framework to guide the search for patterns and data analyses to explain the critical events we observe, the pursuit of root causes yields insight into opportunities for improvement. But it is one thing to be able to recognize, as Shaw did at HVAC, that a change in the way prototype parts get produced could improve the development process, and quite another to capture that learning and deploy it in practice. Capturing and using learning requires change in the way development gets done. In Exhibit 11–2 we have identified five areas of focus for capturing learning. Each of these areas—procedures, tools and methods, process, structure, and principles—provides a way for the organization to "remember" what it learns from development projects. These areas of focus play two im-portant roles. They are the mechanism through which managers intro-duce new capability and improve performance in development. But they are also the vehicle that managers use to capture and store what the or-ganization learns about development over time.

In addition to defining the five areas of focus, Exhibit 11–2 also pro-vides examples of changes in each that are related to one of the examples of critical events referred to earlier in the chapter. In the case of the round drive shaft problem at HVAC, for instance, what the develop-ment team learned about the prototype process could be captured through a change in the development procedures. The example we use in the table is to make production part suppliers, including the in-house

Exhibit 11-2

Capturing Learning from Development Projects*

Areas of Focus	Types of Changes to Capture Learning	Examples
Procedures	Changing the specific, detailed sequence of activities or rules that developers follow	Case: the round drive shafts Change: make production parts suppliers (including in-house factory) responsible for the quality of prototype parts
Tools/Methods	Teaching engineers and developers new skills in using specific tools and methods	Case: the shampoo that is too expensive Change: introduce QFD tools to engineering and marketing
Process	Changing the broad sequence of activities and phases that structure development	Case: the production tools delivered late Change: add a phase/activity — advanced tooling release — to the prototype and tool building process
Structure	Changing the formal organization, the locus of responsibility, and the geographic location of development activities	Case: the recurring water leaks Change: create a "door design team" composed of product and process engineers and locate members in same area
Principles	Adding to the set of ideas and values used to guide decisions in development	Case: the new FMS system developed in record time Change: a new concept — a small team of skilled generalists is far more effective at basic design and system architecture than a larger team of specialists

* In order to capture the learning available from individual development projects, attention must be focused on specific subareas and opportunities for change must be identified and pursued, as illustrated here.

manufacturing organization, responsible for the quality of prototype parts. This *change in procedure* would require the production part suppliers to establish criteria for judging the prototype parts with the development team, and would involve testing and analysis of prototype parts to ensure not only that the parts met design intent, but that the manufacturing process used to make them was representative of the commercial process.

Adding to developmental procedures, as we have done in this example, is not the only kind of change to procedures that the development organization may use to capture learning. In certain circumstances it may be important to eliminate procedures and streamline the development process in order to make it work much more effectively. In the case of the late delivery of tools, for example, it is often the case that the procedures used to approve and implement engineering changes slow down the tooling process to such an extent that long delays are commonplace. Thus, in this circumstance, one of the ways to capture that insight is to eliminate many of the levels of approval required for an engineering change. Streamlining the engineering change process thus can have substantial positive impact on the performance of the tooling design and development cycle.

The second area of focus—*tools and methods*—is important in those circumstances where the opportunity for improvement requires new capability. In the case of the shampoo that was too expensive, the search for patterns and root causes revealed that engineers and marketing personnel had little basis for communication. They did not speak each other's language. Moreover, even had they tried, there was no forum in which they could communicate effectively. One approach to capturing that insight, therefore, is to introduce the methodology and tools associated with quality function deployment (QFD) to both the engineering and marketing organizations. These tools can be customized and tailored to fit the requirements and circumstances of the particular development process in question, and can be used to capture the learning that grows out of development projects. If for example, the problem lay in the appropriate selection of the target competitor (as it did in the shampoo case—the engineers targeted the high-price, best in-class competitor), the QFD methodology can be adapted to add a competitive analysis to the main house of quality. The kind of tool and methodology, thus, becomes a vehicle to focus attention on the areas of weakness in the organization, as well as an opportunity for substantial improvement.

Introducing a methodology like QFD cannot, of course, occur in isolation. Indeed, depending upon the nature of the development process in the shampoo manufacturer, introduction of QFD methods may require a change in the sequence of activities or the phases of development. Such a change falls into the third area of focus in Exhibit 11–2—

changes in process. Whereas in previous projects, marketing may have determined the specifications for the new shampoo product and passed them to engineering for technical development, in the new QFD setup, there is an added phase and set of activities at the front end of the process. Likewise, in the case of the late tool delivery problem, one approach to improving the speed of tool development would be to enhance overlapping between product designers and tooling engineers by adding a phase or activity in the development process called advanced tooling release. This would be a decision point within the prototyping process that would precede final release of the design, but would represent a point at which the design was far enough along that authorization could be given to the tooling engineers to begin tooling design and procurement. Putting such an activity in the middle of the prototyping process requires that product designers and tooling engineers focus very early on the critical issues involved in the design and associated tools. Thus, changing the process captures insight about the importance of overlapping and, in addition, stimulates the development of required capabilities to make overlapping work.

Enhancing integration across functions is often one of the key opportunities for improving product development that surfaces as organizations learn about their development process. Changes in the development process are but one of the important determinants of the degree of integration. Another is the basic *structure* of the development organization itself. As noted in Exhibit 11–2, structure includes both the formal organization as well as the locus of responsibility and the geographic location of activities. These structural elements influence the nature of interaction across functions, the quality of decision making, and the intensity of completeness of communication. In the case of the recurring water leaks in automobile doors, for example, it became apparent through further analysis that the technical problems behind the leaks reflected important gaps in the way the manufacturing and design engineering organizations worked together. Process engineers, for example, had critical pieces of information about the performance of different design alternatives that were stored in databases inaccessible to product designers.

Moreover, individual process engineers were themselves unaware of the historical performances of alternative designs. In addition, there were critical dimensions of the design itself that were not obvious to either product designers or process engineers, because the two organizations had interacted only through formal documents and had never developed close working relationships. One way to capture these insights was to create a "door design" team, composed of both product and process engineers, that was co-located in an area of the engineering organization in which the members could interact on a daily basis. Such a change in structure would facilitate close personal interaction and enhance the quality and effectiveness of communication. It would need to be supplemented and supported by other changes in procedures, tools, and methods, allowing product and process engineers to more effectively integrate problem solving in their individual tasks. But a change in structure would provide an important organizational framework in which the new tools, methods, and procedures could be applied.

The last area of focus is the *principles* that the organization uses to guide decision-making and development activities. These principles include concepts, ideas, and values that provide more fundamental guidance in situations that may be unfamiliar. One way to capture learning in the organization is to crystallize the learning into a principle or concept that can be communicated easily and used in the future when confronting analogous decisions.

For example, in the case of the new flexible manufacturing system (FMS) developed in a very short period of time, the organization learned something about the composition of the development team. Prior FMS development projects had been accomplish by teams of specialists that were relatively large in number and were composed of individuals who brought deep but narrow expertise to the problem. In the new approach, the team was composed of a much smaller number of highly capable generalists who focused on establishing the basic design of the system, including its information architecture, basic machinery specifications, and the logic that provided system control. This high-level design team was then supplemented by a small number of specialists that were able to work within the established framework to implement the design through detailed work and decisions. The organization learned that such an approach was far more effective than its previous methodology. The learning here applied to both the procedures in the organization and the organizational structure used on FMS projects. But it also uncovered an apparent principle that the organization could apply very broadly in subsequent programs: a small team of skilled generalists is far more effective at basic design and system architecture development for a new system project than a larger team of specialists.

Taken together, the five areas of focus we have outlined in Exhibit 11–2 establish the framework for development in the organization. Capturing learning requires coming back, full circle, to this fundamental framework that guides development in the organization. The framework is where the learning process starts. Armed with that framework the organization may interpret critical events that raise questions about its current procedures, tools and methods, processes, and the structures and principles it uses to guide development. These questions and problems become devices for focusing the organization's attention on potential opportunities for learning and thus for improvement. Systematically exploring the underlying sources of both the problems and the things that went right yields insight into ways that the organization may change in order to improve itself. Those changes, however, focus on the basic framework for development. Learning does not end with recognition of cause-and-effect relationships, or with insight into the behavior of the organization. In order to be effective, it must also extend to the introduction of change into the organization—capturing the insight and incorporating it into behaviors (that is, into the way the organization does development). These changes become integral aspects of the revised framework for subsequent development projects, as the learning cycle begins again.[3]

The Project Audit: A Framework for Learning

In the previous sections of this chapter, we have identified what an organization can expect to learn from development projects and the methods that seem most fruitful in both generating and permanently capturing insight and understanding. We have argued that learning about the behavior of the development system requires a conscious, focused effort on the part of managers, engineers, designers, marketers, and manufacturers within the firm. But that effort to learn itself requires structure and organization to give it energy and coherence.

We have found the project audit—a systematic project review conducted by a cross-functional team—to be particularly useful in organizing and managing the search for understanding and insight from specific projects. In this sense, a project audit is conducted not to make sure that development has proceeded according to established rules and regulations; rather, its purpose is to help the organization learn from its experience. In effect, the audit becomes a learning project conducted by a project leader and involving individuals from the key functions represented in development. This cross-functional team reviews the project, conducts interviews with participants at all levels, and gathers data about project execution and performance. The learning logic described earlier in this chapter (developing a model for perspective, collecting data, searching for patterns, and identifying root causes) is then applied to these data and insights to identify all critical themes that seem to drive the development process and its performance. Through discussion among its members, and analysis and synthesis of insights and observations, the team develops recommendations for change that will help to capture the learning they have developed.

Exhibit 11–3 presents a set of sample questions that might structure and guide the conduct of the project audit. We have used these questions in a number of different firms and industries, and have found them useful in organizing the effort to collect the essential pieces of data and information. The questions are built around the specific categories of things to be learned from development projects, as identified in Exhibit 11–1: recurring problems linked to critical performance dimensions, individual tasks and activities, important linkages at the working level, design-build-test cycles, and processes for making decisions and allocating resources. Of course, the degree of emphasis placed in any one category, the particular questions asked, and the focus of the audit must be adapted and tailored to fit the needs and requirements of the individual situation.

The questions are a starting point for collecting data and developing insight. Once information has been collected, the team must share its observations and begin to analyze and synthesize the data. At this audit stage the team begins to search for patterns in its findings. These patterns then become the basis for a deeper search for root causes, and ultimately for recommendations for changes in fundamental aspects of the development process. The following condensed description of an actual project audit illustrates how an audit works, possible kinds of analysis and synthesis, and resulting insights.

The ABC-4 Computer Project Audit

The ABC-4, a high-performance portable computer developed by Omega Systems, was introduced into the market in October 1990. The ABC-4 grew out of advanced development work that had been done on a portable computer for the Department of Defense. The initial project proposal was formally approved in early 1988, the preliminary set of product drawings was released in December 1988, prototype units were developed and tested at beta sites during the first half of 1990, the product was announced in the summer of 1990, and initial shipments began in October.

Although portable computers represented a relatively small fraction of the total revenues of Omega Systems, the ABC-4 was regarded by the organization as a relatively important project. Market share in portable computers had fallen somewhat during the 1988–1989 time period, and Omega's position as the technical and performance leader had begun to slip. Several additional aspects of the context in which the ABC-4 was developed are important in understanding the outcomes of the project.

- During the course of the project, both the engineering function and the business unit (portable computer systems) underwent significant reorganization.

Exhibit 11–3

Framing the Project Audit: Sample Questions*

Background

- What was the motivation for the project? Why was it done at this particular time?
- What was the product strategy? Where was the greatest emphasis placed? What were the goals of the project?

Pre-Project Activities

- How many alternatives did the firm consider at the concept stage, and how, in this instance, did the particular project we are studying emerge as a development project?
- What were the sources of the ideas?
- How did the firm lay the foundation for the project in terms of establishing business and functional strategies, and how were those strategies used in the decision making/selection process?
- What does the development strategy look like?

Project Team

- Which functions within the business formally assigned people to the project on a full-time basis?
- Which functions had people assigned part-time?
- What was the basic project organization structure (e.g., purely functional, lightweight project manager, heavyweight project manager without dedicated resources, a full-scale project team with heavyweight manager, and dedicated team members from all functions)?

Project Management

- Was there a project manager – some individual who had the title of project manager or who was responsible for the project?
- If so, what was the role of the project manager? What degree of influence did she or he have over working-level decisions in marketing, engineering, and manufacturing?
- If there was no project manager, how was leadership exerted?
- What were the formal phases of development and the milestones that the project had to meet? When did they occur?
- Who was responsible for decision making and resource allocation in the project? What were the roles of functional managers, the project leader, and senior management?
- When conflicts arose in the project, how were they resolved? What kinds of conflicts were most difficult to resolve? What was the role of senior management in conflicts?

Senior Management Review and Control

- What was senior management's role in the project at different phases?
- What criteria did senior management use in reviewing the project?
- How were objectives set and defined? Using what kind of information?

EXHIBIT 11–3 (cont.)

Prototype and Test

- How was prototyping used in development?
- How many prototype cycles were there? How many prototypes were produced in each cycle?
- How was the prototype process organized (e.g., was it done by suppliers or in-house)?
- What tests were conducted? By whom?

* The project audit seeks to identify and explain—after a development effort has been completed—the connection between its management and execution and the results achieved. Six major areas for investigation and the types of questions that can be addressed in each are outlined here.

- Several concurrent development projects competed for resources during the ABC-4 project. One project, Ranger 5, was among the largest ever undertaken by the organization, and was easily an order of magnitude larger than the ABC-4 project.
- Restructuring of manufacturing at Omega Systems resulted in the closing of several plants and the shift to more outsourcing for key components. This change caught the ABC-4 project team by surprise.
- The engineering organization introduced a new engineering change notice procedure during the course of the project. The new procedure was not well understood and resulted in long turnaround cycles on changes to parts and components.

Overall, the performance of the ABC-4 project was mixed. The product itself was well received by customers but, because of its relatively late entry into the market, faced an uphill battle in a very competitive segment. The project was late according to both its own internal schedules and competitive projects. In addition, management judged the development cost to be problematic. The challenge for the project audit team was to understand the sources of problems in lead time and productivity, as well as the success of the design and development effort in producing a product judged by most customers to be outstanding. The portable computer systems division wanted to offer equally attractive products in the future, but ones that were more rapidly and efficiently developed.

A project audit team was formed, led by Marcia Karas and consisting of one member each from design engineering, process development, manufacturing operations, marketing, field service, and finance. Though the team had not been involved in developing ABC-4, members were familiar with the general performance of the effort. As the team probed the performance of the ABC-4 project, they concentrated on a set of critical events. Analysis of these key events led to an assessment of strengths and weaknesses in the six dimensions of the development process that were discussed in Chapter 6 (see Exhibit 11–4), and summarized below in an excerpt from a memo by the audit team to senior management.

> In contrast to the concerns often expressed about the ABC-4 by senior management, we found a considerable number of strengths in the way this program was organized and carried out. However, most of the strengths we uncovered were in the front end of the development process. For example, the project team was highly dedicated, was responsible for design from the very outset of the project, and was led by a very committed and talented leader who not only coordinated activity but also championed the product concept. Additionally, the product concept itself was well defined and clearly articulated so that all team members shared a common view of overall program objectives.
>
> At the same time, however, we uncovered a significant number of weaknesses in the way the program was organized and managed. Initially, because many critical events occurred late in the program, we focused our attention on activities that occurred in the later stages of development, such as prototyping and testing. As we probed the sources of problems, such as difficultly in manufacturing ramp-up, however, we uncovered problems that extended all the way back to pre-project activities. In the early stages of product planning, for example, senior management set ambitious targets for functionality and reliability, but also summarily removed three months from the normal development cycle. This strong emphasis on schedule was reinforced repeatedly during the senior management review process. As a result, the project became schedule driven to the point that the team chose to skip key tests and push ahead before critical predecessor work was complete.

The lack of team involvement in setting objectives and the challenge posed by an aggressive schedule, on top of aggressive performance goals, interacted with two other aspects of project structure to create significant problems downstream. First, senior management and the project team each seemed to regard the ABC-4 as a design engineering rather than a business project. Both groups tended to underestimate non-design tasks and developed insufficient skill and capability in downstream (e.g., manufacturing) and support (e.g., vendor selection) activities. These were precisely the areas where problems began to surface after the team had skipped tests and other critical activities. Second, the project was managed in a relatively informal way. This had important advantages in day-to-day interactions within the team, but created problems for integrating the activities of various functions. There was, in fact, no development process or structure that laid out the sequence of activities or critical milestones that needed to be accomplished. As a result, it was difficult to tell where the project was at any given time.

EXHIBIT 11–4

Strengths and Weaknesses in the Development of the ABC-4 Portable Computer*

Project Dimensions	Strengths	Weaknesses	Key Events
Pre-Project Activities	Complete concept definition; early manufacturing involvement	Top down setting of goals without team involvement; no product line strategy; management and team mismatch – team focus on performance, management on cost	Great product, but late; expensive redesign in late stages
Project Team	Dedicated core team responsible for design; strong commitment and high level of expertise	Lack of integration of new people; insufficient skill in manufacturing; inability to deliver bad news	Delays in completing prototype tasks; problems in manufacturing ramp-up
Project Management	Project leader who coordinated and championed the concept from the outset	No development process or structure; design project not a business project (underestimated non-design tasks)	Details "slipped through the cracks"; problems in manufacturing ramp-up
Senior Management Review and Control	Regular senior management reviews; willingness to support change by team	Schedule-driven development (released drawings even though design not finished); stretch targets without recognizing risks	Initial reliability problems in the field
Prototype/Test	Strong engineering/manufacturing collaboration	Skipped key tests/tested too early; no pilot production run; confusion in prototype cycles	Problems in manufacturing ramp-up; redesign late in program; in-field reliability problems
Real-Time Adjustments	Willingness to commit resources to deal with problems	Pushing ahead before tasks complete; assumed time lost early could be made up later; no measurement system to determine project status	Problems in manufacturing ramp-up; reliability problems in the field

* As the result of a systematic audit of the ABC-4 portable computer project, this exhibit shows the audit team's conclusions regarding project strengths and weaknesses in each of the six areas examined. These can then serve as a basis for making systematic changes in the development process (see Exhibit 11–5).

The upshot of these developments was that several problems remained undetected in the early stages of design and throughout the prototyping process. They became obvious only when the product had reached the customer's hands. In addition, the decision to skip pilot production (made largely because the ABC-4 was thought to be very similar to its predecessor, the ABC-3) meant that many design problems surfaced in manufacturing ramp-up: though the basic architecture of the ABC-4 was quite similar to that of the ABC-3, several new components and subsystems had been introduced and their interaction with carry-over parts was important, yet not fully tested.

The audit team's review of the strengths and weaknesses in the management and organization of the ABC-4 development project suggests several critical themes that may have more general application. Although it is relatively easy to point to specific activities that may have led to a problem, it is perhaps more useful to consider a broader pattern by focusing on a small number of critical ideas that grew out of the team's analysis. The audit team included five of these ideas in its memo to senior management.

Cutting cycle times on individual tasks. Senior management cut the time for primary task completion in the ABC-4 project (e.g., allowing six rather than eight months for prototype development). However, there was no corresponding change in support activity cycle times, nor was there a reconceptualization of the overall structure of activities that underlay the completion of those tasks. Failure to rethink the basic nature of the tasks involved and restructure the activity network meant that the only way to accomplish primary tasks in less time was postponing or skipping what were regarded as second- or third-order activities. This had a decidedly negative impact on the project. The basic concept here is that while tasks can be prioritized (e.g., design tasks as first order, testing tasks as second order, and vendor selection as third order), the full set of tasks is important to the project and its overall cycle time.

Integrating art and science. Reducing weight and cost while increasing performance made the ABC-4 (a highly engineered product) much more dependent on science than previous generations. In consequence, the assumption that many of the old parts (and production processes) could be used without change was simply invalid. Additionally, though each of the new parts was relatively straightforward, their closer interaction increased the complexity of the product exponentially. Efforts to advance the science on several elements of a product while sticking with former art on other elements (particularly where those elements are embedded and integral in the overall system) may well push the art beyond its limits.

Internal and external fit—strategy and the customer system. The strategy and position of the business called for improved performance and high reliability at market introduction (Omega needed to catch up, but had a strong market franchise). Senior management emphasized time and cost while engineering focused on speed and features. This internal gap, or mismatch, was accompanied by an external gap: the failure to consider all aspects of the customer system (especially service and reliability) in the development process. These gaps required multiple engineering changes and redesign after market introduction.

The need for a structured process. Creating a development organization and a project management system that are robust, replicable, and successful requires a structure for the development process that everyone understands and follows. This includes clearly defined stages with understood milestones that mark completion, and separable prototype cycles of design-build-test where each can be shortened and still result in maximum learning. Finally, the structure needs to provide adequate testing of three types: components, total system (finished product), and customer use. These tests should not be viewed as hurdles or gates, but as opportunities to build the experience and knowledge needed for subsequent stages.

Measuring/calibrating project status. The ability to assess and measure the status of a development project is crucial to its effective management. The ABC-4 suffered from unrealistic judgments about the amount of work remaining to be done. These judgments were, in part, driven by the absence of good measurements of project status. It is particularly crucial to measure status relative to work that remains to be done rather than only against progress to date. An accurate, detailed activity network provides the framework for determining the remaining work to be completed.

Recommendations for Action

The audit team learned much about the development process at Omega Systems, and uncovered some important opportunities for improving time to market as well as development productivity. Exhibit 11-5 presents the team's recommendations for each of the major dimensions of development, and groups them under the five kinds of changes outlined earlier in this chapter: procedures, tools/methods, the development process, organization structure, and basic development principles. The thrust of the recommendations was to make adjustments across the board, in all aspects of development, in order to change the overall pattern. Thus, recommendations that seemed systematic to the organization were highlighted. While there were many things in the ABC-4 that were special cases, Exhibit 11-5 presents those recommendations with the greatest leverage. Collectively, they had the potential to change the basic pattern of development.

A central focus of the recommendations is the role of senior management—not only in changing the senior management review process, but in introducing a new development process and in communicating fundamental principles. The audit team put forth three aspects which summarize the basic approach:

EXHIBIT 11–5
Recommendations for Change in the ABC-4 Audit*

Project Dimensions	Procedures	Tools/Methods	Process	Structure	Principles
Pre-Project Activities	Set objectives using a contract book as part of the first stage of the project	Develop maps for product generations; develop tools for customer system evaluation	Define pre-project stage (key activities)	Involve manufacturing and service people in concept development	Planning can pre-empt subsequent problems and aid in concept convergence
Project Team	New members added to team must be trained and certified	Link career expectations to project completions	Project leader must do much of the training	Use a dedicated core team with multiple functions to manage major projects	Teams need a balance of experience and youth
Project Management	Develop an activity network for each project	Introduce an activity network capability	Establish formal stages of the development process	Select project leader at outset; role includes coordination and concept leadership	Product development is a business project, not just an engineering project
Senior Management Review	Set forth competitive imperatives clearly before the project is launched	Establish a method for calibrating the status of the project (work remaining to be done)	Review thoroughly at major milestones (at least every 3 months)	Set up a senior staff mentor/coach/sponsor	Review and control against key milestones (task completion), not just schedule
Test and Prototype	All mechanical systems will be piloted before commercial release	Introduce new method for evaluating the tradeoffs between new and carryover parts	Establish clear design-build-test cycles for prototyping	Develop a test strategy that covers components, systems, and subsystems	Solve problems early
Real Time Adjustments	Regenerate activity network after major changes	Use PERT system linked to formal development stages	Establish a process for responding to new developments (maintain focus, avoid fire fighting)	Compare planned schedule against tasks remaining	Fix problems before moving forward

* Based on an audit of the ABC-4 portable computer project, a number of improvements in the development process were identified. For each of the six areas examined, changes in procedures, tools/methods, process, structure, and principles were identified and implemented, improving significantly the development efforts on subsequent projects.

Essentially, the front end of the development process and the organizational structure have been relatively solid in the past and remain quite strong. However, changes must be introduced in both areas to bring the downstream organizations (manufacturing and service) into the development process in a central way and to provide stronger, more direct links to basic business strategy.

Integration at the working level is fairly good. Engineers and manufacturing people work well together. There is a weaker relationship between engineering and marketing, and this needs attention. More importantly, however, Omega Systems must create a different context for development within which integration at the working level can take place. There really isn't a clear development process at Omega Systems. We don't need a bunch of manuals with detailed procedures. What is required is a systematic, shared process that provides an overall framework.

While the introduction of a new structure and principles is important, it is also crucial to upgrade people's skills and give them better tools with which to work. The problems are not just structure and process; there is a real need for capability in areas such as customer system analysis, activity network design, and project measurement.

In summary, the above-mentioned changes in the basic development system will allow Omega Systems to proceed more rapidly and efficiently in development, but will also preserve the organization's strengths in product design, product concept development, teamwork, and collaboration.

Conclusions and Implications

Learning from development projects is one of the most difficult things that an organization can do.[4] It requires focused effort and attention, and the willingness to make hard choices. When a firm seeks competitive advantage through its development capability, the object is to become better at designing and developing new products and processes. It is not to succeed just on a particular project, but continually to build and improve the organization's procedures, processes, leadership skills, and tools and methods in order to do things faster, more efficiently, and with higher quality.

The project audit of the ABC-4 implies that being good at learning from development projects requires many of the same skills and capabilities that being good at development itself requires. Because what we want to learn cuts across individuals, work groups, and functions to encompass the development system as a whole, and because the phenomena that we are examining are themselves complex and often ambiguous, learning needs to be organized, managed, and directed by leaders with skill, tenacity, and perspective. In this sense, a project audit (which is a primary organizing framework that we advocate for learning about development projects) is every bit as much a project—with all of the attendant requirements for leadership, collaboration across functions, clarity of process and objectives, and effective tools and methods—as the development of a new product or process.

Of course, this does not imply that individuals, small work groups, or even functions should go about their business and not pay attention to learning opportunities. Important learning must occur at each of these levels in the organization. Indeed, a development organization populated by individuals, work groups, and functions that pay attention to their experience and learn to improve their operation will be in a much better position to implement a structured learning process about the development system as a whole. Thus, from senior management's perspective, the important mission is to foster an environment in which learning takes place at each of the levels we have discussed, and to create the capability to learn about specific development projects through a process built of several elements, such as the development audit.

Although learning to learn through the development experience is not easy, making the commitment and pursuing it vigorously can have significant payoffs. Indeed, learning from projects is an important element in the organization's overall approach to improving its development capabilities. Precisely because learning and sustained improvement are inherently difficult, they provide—when done effectively—a source of competitive advantage. One need only recall the experience of Northern and Southern Electronics outlined in the first chapter of this book to recognize the power of sustained improvement in development capability. But learning from projects is only one element, albeit a crucial and vital one, in the overall problem of building development capability over a long period of time. We examine the rest of the story in the concluding chapter of this book.

CHAPTER 12

Building Development Capability

The capability to develop new products and processes rapidly and efficiently is a powerful source of competitive advantage. Our discussion of Northern and Southern Electronics in Chapter 1 underscores the importance of product and process development in every strategy and business. Of course, its relative importance depends on the particular circumstance, strategy, market, and technical environment. But a development capability that matches that environment can create a significant edge in the marketplace.

Such capability, however, is not a static characteristic of the outstanding organization. Indeed, in order to be a source of sustainable advantage, development capability must be continually expanded, upgraded, and improved. Thus, it is not enough to be good at development at a particular point in time. What is required is to be both good now and getting better all the time. That means that no matter what the position of the firm—whether the firm is an industry leader, a close second, or under significant competitive pressure because of gaps between its capabilities and those of its rivals—the ability to build development capability at a rapid rate is crucial to long-term competitive success.

One of the reasons development capability is so powerful and valuable is because building it is exceedingly difficult. The vast majority of organizations that we have studied do not improve significantly and continuously their development performance over time. Building development capability takes determination, persistence, and careful attention to those aspects of the development process that are most crucial in a given organizational situation. Those that succeed make significant investments of resources, managerial time and attention, and organizational energy. The key to effecting real change is to change the total pattern of development—the development strategy and process, the basic organizational structure and leadership, particular skills and tools, and the systems that provide the context in which development takes place.[1] Even if a whole new pattern is not required, substantial refinement and alignment of parts of that pattern may be needed.

Since firms are in many different competitive positions and face different problems and opportunities, numerous approaches to changing the pattern of development seem to work. But, behind them all are a set of common principles that appear to govern success. In this chapter, we examine four different approaches to building development capability and present specific examples of each. The examples give content to the approaches, but they also suggest the particular challenges associated with each approach. We then step back in order to identify the common themes that characterize successful building of this capability. Our intent here is to develop a set of principles that managers can use in launching and guiding efforts to improve the development of new products and processes. The chapter concludes with observations about the importance of managerial leadership in building a competitive advantage in development capability.

Four Approaches to Building Capability

The development process touches so much of what a company does that changing it often seems a daunting challenge. Indeed, efforts that start out intending to change the company's entire pattern of development in one fell swoop are likely to fail. Firms that succeed in building capability do so by finding a starting point—some aspect of the pattern of development that provides a useful vehicle through which to introduce change into the organization. In some cases, simply refining and upgrading what is fundamentally a sound approach is the appropriate starting point. In other cases, more radical change—such as establishing a whole new approach—is appropriate. In this section of the chapter, we present four different approaches to building a development capability. These represent a range of starting points and strategies for changing the pattern of development. The examples we use illustrate the interaction of approach and the firm's situation, and the challenges involved in each approach, and provide the context for identifying the common themes that characterize successful strategies for change.[2] Whatever combination of these four is pursued, sustained learning is the goal, and inevitably that requires a systematic, managed process of improvement. It simply does not happen by chance or good fortune.

Creating A Development Strategy

In organizations with complex product lines, heavy demands for improved product or process performance, and the need to effectively launch and execute multiple development projects with shorter lead times, a useful starting point for building the required capability is often the creation of a development strategy. Physio Control, a manufacturer of cardiovascular defibrillators and heart monitors used in emergency rooms, has used the creation of a development strategy as a starting point for its efforts to improve new product capability over the last few years. Based on its innovative technology, strong reputation for high quality, and strong customer service and support, Physio Control, by the mid 1950s, had established a strong market position in emergency unit defribrillators and emergency room heart monitors. That position, however, came under attack from aggressive small competitors who took advantage of regulatory and technology changes to open new product niches. Legislation in many states, for example, required a defibrillator in all emergency vehicles, thus creating a new product category— the lightweight, small, convenient defibrillator. In addition, changes in electronics technology, software, display devices, and batteries all combined to create new opportunities for products with superior power, space, weight, and communication characteristics.

The thrust of competition and of changes in the environment created a significant requirement for new products at Physio Control. The number of models in production doubled from eight to sixteen between 1985 and 1990. Over that same period, estimated product production life shrank from fourteen years to five years or less. Furthermore, because of growing customer demands and the development of new technologies, the new products under development were more complex and sophisticated than ever before.

The challenge at Physio Control, therefore, was to cope with an exploding product diversity while at the same time meeting requirements for increased responsiveness and improved productivity. Analysis of the situation by the vice president of R&D and the senior management group suggested that the proliferation of new product development projects overlaid on the existing system for development created significant bottlenecks in key support groups and a scramble for resources among competing project teams. Although there were several possible avenues for pursuing improvement and change in the development system, the senior management group saw development strategy—particularly the creation of an engineering and development capacity plan—as a critical first step in their efforts to improve performance.

The process the senior management group used to create a development strategy involved data collection and analysis completed under the direction of the relevant functional heads (the directors of R&D, manufacturing, and marketing) and discussion and synthesis among the senior management group itself. In effect, the senior management group chose to take line responsibility for the development strategy. They did not want the creation of this strategy to be perceived among themselves or in the organization as a "staff activity."

In a day-long meeting held in the spring of 1990, the senior management group focused on the question of engineering capacity. The first step was to list the projects currently under development and try to attach some priority to each one. The discussion of priorities quickly focused on the question of product strategy. It was very difficult for the members of the group to determine the relative priority of alternative projects without a clear sense of direction with respect to the overall product line. For some time marketing and engineering had been discussing the increasing rate of product proliferation and the need to achieve coherence within the product line as well as in the manufacturing organization. While these ideas had occasionally been under discussion within the senior management group, the pressure to create a development strategy brought the issues of product line strategy to the fore. After extensive discussion, a consensus emerged around the strategy for next-generation new products. That strategy called for the creation of a platform product that would serve as the basis for several follow-on products in selected market niches.

Toward the end of the day's session, as managers began to discuss the implications of the platform strategy for engineering capacity, it became clear that pursuit of that particular product strategy would require some very tough choices. The problem was that many of the projects then under development did not fit with the emerging product strategy. Since a vast expansion of the engineering organization was out of the question, it was evident that pursuit of the platform product strategy would require Physio Control to eliminate several ongoing development projects.

Over the next few months, the heads of marketing, R&D, and manufacturing reviewed the existing projects, reevaluated the platform strategy, and developed better estimates of the resource requirements for various development efforts. This review of resource requirements was particularly crucial for support groups like the model shop, testing, and quality assurance.

In a series of discussions held in the summer of 1990, senior management not only reaffirmed its product strategy, but began to lay out a more detailed sequence of projects—including the platform project scoped a few months earlier—required to realize the strategy. One of the most difficult problems Physio Control confronted in developing the aggregate project plan portion of their development strategy was defining the relationship between its current and future generations of products. Significant engineering resources at Physio Control were devoted to the support of current products. Some of that support took the form of specific projects to improve or upgrade the current products, but much of it involved specific customer requests, fixing problems, responding to crises in the field and manufacturing plant, and, in general, undertaking engineering work in order to solve specific problems. Individual marketers and engineers could always justify spending time on the current product, since doing so generated cash and earnings immediately.

In order to resolve the conflict between current and future products, senior management at Physio Control did not start with a prioritized list of projects. Rather, they asked the question: "Given our strategy, the nature of our business, and our short- and long-term objectives, what is the appropriate mix of projects we ought to pursue?" The project options they examined included major projects (to create new platforms), smaller projects (to leverage off existing platforms and thus expand the product line or open up new market segments), and ongoing support of current products. After determining the fraction of resources they wished to see devoted to each type of project, the senior management group, working with data and analysis supplied by engineering, R&D, marketing, and manufacturing, identified a prioritized list of projects within each category. The priorities established for each type of project grew out of the overall product strategy, including the business plan and aggregate project plan for the next five years. These plans identified the sequence of projects required to realize the business and product strategies. They matched this prioritized list with an estimate of development resources required to complete the project, as well as an estimate of the available capacity (given the business plan). By matching estimated requirements for high-priority projects against capacity, senior management was able to determine the set of projects within each category that their resources could support and that would deliver the desired financial results.

The net effect of the series of discussions and analyses conducted within the senior management group was a development strategy that sharply reduced the number of projects in progress at Physio Control. But the process also resulted in a much higher degree of communication and greater shared understanding of the development process and development strategy among the senior management group and key functional executives in engineering, marketing, and manufacturing.

Changing the Development Process

In companies with complex development processes and a long history of development experience, a fruitful starting point for bringing about significant change is often the overall architecture of the development process. By introducing a restructured sequence of activities and redefining both the phases of development and the milestones that characterize completion of each phase, firms may create a new framework—a new context in which engineers, marketers, and manufacturers may see new opportunities for improvement. The Ford Motor Company's efforts—identified within the firm as "concept to customer" (or "C to C")—are illustrative of such an approach and its potential benefits.[3]

In the early 1980s, Ford faced a dismal future: quality was far below competitive standards and market share was falling. In addition, the company's financial position was precarious and layoffs were ongoing. By the end of the decade, however, Ford had introduced a string of successful new products. Indeed, the Ford Explorer, introduced in the spring of 1990, may prove to be Ford's most successful product introduction ever. Despite the fact that it debuted in a down market, the four-door, four-wheel-drive sport utility vehicle sold phenomenally well.

Behind the Explorer and other successful Ford products (such as the Lincoln Continental, Probe, and Taurus) lay a decade of changes in Ford's management culture, particularly their product development process. A pivotal event in this process of change was the development of the Taurus, a family sedan with the styling, handling, and ride of a sophisticated European car. As a product, the Taurus offered a distinctive yet integrated package in which advanced aerodynamic styling was matched with a new chassis, independent rear suspension, and a front wheel drive layout.

But the Taurus was also an important "vehicle" bringing about change in the development process at Ford. It was the initial project used to improve the development process. Traditionally, Ford's development efforts had been strongly functional in character and the architecture of the development process reflected this orientation: it was schedule driven, relatively sequential in the way it organized activities, and punctuated by a series of detailed reviews that were highly proceduralized and bureaucratic. In developing the Taurus, however, Ford sought to break down barriers between functions by creating "team Taurus," the core of which included principal participants from all the functions and activities involved in the creation of the new car. The team served to coordinate and integrate the development program at the senior management level, and was the first step on a long path of organizational, attitudinal, and procedural change. The team was initially headed by Lew Veraldi, at the time the director of large car programs at Ford. As the development of the Taurus proceeded, however, it became clear that integrated development, and, in particular, development that required much less time to complete, necessitated more than a high-level core team under the direction of a single manager.

In order to cut lead time, improve quality, and bring products to market that were distinctive and attractive to customers, Ford launched the C to C process in the mid 1980s. Led by a handpicked group of engineers and product planners, the C to C project took as its mission the creation of a new architecture for product development. Its specific focus was to create a sequence of development activities and associated milestones that would result in a forty-eight-month development time (a 20–25 percent cycle time reduction) on major new development programs while improving product quality and creating products with competitively attractive features and performance.

The C to C team was led by an experienced senior engineer, and its members were drawn from most of the important engineering groups as well as product planning and marketing. Through extensive interaction with senior functional managers, the group sought in the first instance to identify the overall structure of the current development process at Ford. They determined how the process actually worked, where the milestones were, and what materials were used to make decisions. The C to C team also became the focal point for significant benchmarking activities in which Ford compared itself to its major competitors and companies outside the auto industry whose success in product development was well documented. The benchmarking activities, as well as the intensive analysis of the internal process, revealed several opportunities for significant improvement. But the group also recognized the importance of establishing fundamental principles for the creation of a new development architecture. Through a series of presentations and extensive discussion within the development organization at Ford, the group articulated and sought to create consensus around critical milestones, decision points, and criteria for decision making, as well as around patterns of responsibility and functional involvement. The following statements illustrate the principles the C to C team developed:

- Senior management review of the program should be driven by the substantive milestones rather than the calendar schedule.
- Suppliers of the production parts should be responsible for the prototypes of those parts. They may subcontract production of prototype

317

parts, but the production suppliers remain responsible for quality, performance, cost, and delivery of prototype parts.
• Parts used to manufacturer pilot vehicles should be made with production tools.

Over the course of several months, the C to C team applied these and other similar principles to define the major development milestones as well as the critical sequence of activities and patterns of responsibility. This architecture was then implemented step by step in ongoing programs and in all new efforts. Thus, once the process was defined, it was implemented in every program (and adapted to where the particular program was in its development): if a program had passed the first prototype stage, the C to C process was implemented for subsequent development activities; brand new programs were launched with the full-scale C to C process as their underlying structure.

The implementation of the C to C process was one step in a long evolutionary path in Ford's development organization. The C to C process envisioned strong cross-functional interaction and involvement throughout the development process in order to eliminate significant engineering changes and rework occasioned by poor communication and lack of shared understanding. Thus the implementation of the C to C process motivated and necessitated continual organizational change as Ford sought to formalize the team structure that grew out of the Taurus experience.

Creating Building Block Skills and Tools

In most development projects, there are a handful of critical activities that have an important influence on lead time, product quality, process reliability, and other important dimensions of project performance. For example, in some products, complex parts are manufactured using dies or molds that require a long time to design and manufacture. In situations such as these, a focused effort to substantially improve an organization's capability in executing that critical activity can often result in significant development performance improvement. Improving such critical activities often requires creating new or improved capability in basic tools and skills.

In early 1987, Eastman Kodak launched a new development project that necessitated exactly that kind of improved capability.[4]The project's intent was to develop a single-use 35 mm camera (originally called the Fling but subsequently renamed the FunSaver). The Fling project was in part a response to Fuji Film's introduction of the QuickSnap, a 35 mm single-use camera expected to be available in volume in the United States within six months. The challenge facing the Fling project was considerable: the camera needed to produce high quality images, be rugged and reliable, sell for a relatively low price, and be completed in less than forty weeks (similar Kodak projects generally took sixty-five to eighty weeks).

The Fling team determined that the only way to complete the project was to use computer-aided design (CAD) for the entire development effort. While Kodak had used CAD for individual parts, they had never done a complete camera design from start to finish with all of the parts on CAD. The challenge went further. Not only did all parts need to be designed on CAD, but CAD needed to be used in such a way as to facilitate the design and development of the long lead time tooling for the parts. Thus, the challenge for the Fling team was not only to develop the Fling, but also to create tools and a design process that would allow full utilization of CAD for all parts and would integrate parts and tooling design.

Since the traditional methods of engineering involving drawings were generally regarded by engineers as less demanding and easier to complete than a full-scale CAD-based design, the team needed to attract design engineers fully committed to the use of CAD and experienced in its intricacies. The team decided to use a Unigraphics CAD/CAM system originally developed by McDonnell Douglas for aeronautical design work. This was the third generation of CAD at Kodak, and a crucial objective of the design team was to make the CAD system user-friendly. Parts were designed by creating a series of objects such as points, lines, surfaces, and dimensions that described the part. Objects could be grouped logically in a layer, and layers could be worked on individually or overlaid to generate a single part, a subassembly, or the entire camera. The use of layers allowed engineers to see how their work and the resulting parts fit with other parts being designed by the system. It also facilitated the organization of control and change responsibility, with each layer being assigned to a single engineer who had control of change authorization. Engineers at any time could access all of the design layers in order to generate a picture of the integrated parts and subassemblies. In addition, different colors could be assigned to the layers to help differentiate them and provide perspective on how the particular part being designed fit into the overall camera.

A second major thrust of the team was to make sure that all engineers involved in the project—including design, tooling, and manufacturing— had access to the designs of all the parts. Of course, only the designer assigned control over a particular part could make final changes or additions to that design. Every night, however, all the work done by the design engineers on the project was uploaded to a central data bank. Once a design for a part was uploaded, everyone had access to it and could examine on a daily basis updated versions of the complete design.

This common database and the facility to view and examine the implications of design changes for other parts and components was an important element in achieving significant manufacturing involvement early in the design. Along with the assignment of a tool designer and manufacturing engineer to the Fling team, the ability the system provided them to examine the evolving design easily and quickly on a daily basis meant that it was easy for them to understand the preliminary versions of the design, to catch manufacturing problems early, and to add value to the design activities.

The new design system was also used for designing the molds used to fabricate the parts. The tooling designers first designed the components of the mold on the CAD system using the part design done by the product designers as a starting point. On the Fling project this step was simplified substantially by the up-front work done by the tooling designers in conjunction with the parts engineers. In addition, the user-friendly design system facilitated the tool designer's work by aligning the layers developed by the parts designer with the corresponding surface of the mold design. That system also made standard adjustments and was particularly crucial in catching design mistakes or inconsistencies.

In order to facilitate communication and ensure consistency and discipline in design, the Fling team used the CAD system to capture all design changes. When a tool designer needed a change in a part in order to simplify the tool or support recommended changes in processing, that change had to be completed by the part engineer in the CAD system. This approach was consistent with the Fling project team's view that CAD was a communications tool. Moreover, CAD made ambiguities in the design evident and simplified the process of achieving a shared perspective and understanding of the design of the part and the tools. While CAD generally involved more up-front work on the part of the designers, the team believed that there were substantial long-term benefits during this project and on future projects. In particular, the CAD system reduced substantially the time to design the molds. Tool fabrication itself was also improved because of the greater involvement of tool designers early in development through the CAD system. The Fling estimated that tool fabrication could be reduced from five weeks to one week with this system.

By developing a user-friendly CAD system, requiring that all parts be designed with it, and creating tooling design in conjunction with parts design, the Fling team effected a substantial reduction in the development cycle. In addition, the introduction of this new set of tools created significant opportunities for change in other aspects of the development process. Such changes included the creation of a strong team structure with shared responsibilities and significant up-front involvement of all critical functions.

A possible future change the team now envisions is sharply reducing the distinction between a product and tooling design engineer. It was evident to the Fling team that the CAD system made it possible for a single engineer to accomplish part design and tooling design on relatively simple parts. While there might be a need for specialization on very complex items, the great bulk of parts developed for the Fling and their respective tooling could have been combined and developed by a single engineer, assuming the engineer had received some training in both parts and tooling design. The prospect at Kodak is for significant improvements in productivity and lead time as the organization conducts additional training, gains experience in working on cross-functional teams, and further refines the CAD system and its application.

The Demonstration Project

The need to effect improvements in product development often coincides in an organization with the need for specific new products to deal with competitive threats or exploit a technical opportunity. In such circumstances organizations often find it attractive to launch what might be called a "demonstration project." Such a project is designed to teach the organization a new mode of development by employing new concepts directed at a specific product or process.

In the mid 1980s Hewlett Packard's Vancouver Division was faced with such a challenge.[5] With responsibility for HP's low-cost printing products, the division felt boxed in between low-cost impact printers developed by Japanese firms like Epson on the low end, and very expensive, high-speed printers using laser technology on the high end. With its market share and financial fortunes declining and its future in question, the division embarked on a bold strategy to deliver to the market a personal computer-based printer that would sell for less than $1,000 but would offer laser quality printing. At the same time the division desired to make a substantial improvement in the development process to achieve both reduced lead times and lower-cost manufacturing. The project, called DeskJet, was to be based on the introduction of an innovative technology—inkjet printing—in a low-cost, high-quality form for the first time.

Recognizing the ambitiousness of the program, the HP Vancouver Division created a core team at the outset and gave them a twofold mission. First, they were to design and develop a breakthrough product for the division. Second, they were to create a new development process, with significant emphasis on speed, design for manufacturability, and teamwork.

The DeskJet team was a true heavyweight team. It was one of the two major development projects in the division, and was managed by the head of R&D. In addition to having a core team including key individuals from all the major functions, at the working level critical R&D designers, mechanical and electrical engineers, software developers, and manufacturing personnel, as well as individuals from purchasing and quality control, were dedicated to the project and co-located. The combination of strong leadership, a cross-functional team at the core, and the creation of a co-located working-level group provided the organizational context in which a new development process became a reality.

In the beginning, the team focused on developing a clear and consistent product definition. They were substantially aided by well-defined targets. The strategy was to bring to market a personal printer that would sell for less than $1,000 but would offer laser quality printing. Because HP's proprietary inkjet technology had only been used in very expensive, high-end products, the DeskJet product required substantial technical development to create a print head and printing process that could be offered to the market at low cost. The product also needed to offer substantial improvements in reliability over previous HP products as well as create a platform for subsequent product generations.

The need for speed as well as the product strategy of high-quality printing at low cost, with high-volume production, called for significant integration of product and process development. In contrast to normal practice at HP, the team chose to develop the product and process designs simultaneously. Design for manufacturability (DFM) was a critical theme linking product and process designers. Working with their process colleagues, design engineers simplified the mechanical design of the product and substantially reduced the number of parts in manufacturing. In one famous example, product designers combined more than thirty parts to create a new complex part that made up the base of the printer and provided significant mechanical functions.

In addition to DFM, the team also focused on the creation of early production tools. By integrating tooling design with part design in the CAD system, the team was able to cut substantial time off mold design and mold making, thereby reducing lead time substantially. The discipline imposed within the project by the drive to get to production tools early was complemented and supported by a significant change in the prototyping process. The team scheduled prototype builds once per month during the development phases of the project in order to focus attention on objectives, provide timely feedback, and facilitate the convergence of marketing, engineering, and manufacturing activities and thinking.

Through strong leadership, teamwork, and significant technical development, the DeskJet project met with considerable success. The project was completed in a twenty-two-month cycle, compared to a thirty-six to sixty-month cycle for similar projects in the past. Given the significant technical development and manufacturing development required for the DeskJet, the twenty-two month cycle was even more remarkable. The DeskJet won the HP corporate award for the best R&D design in 1987, as well as the Datek Industry Award as Printer of the Year in 1988. Furthermore, the project achieved its basic goal of providing the market with laser quality printing on plain paper at under $1,000 and met with considerable financial success. It achieved more than double the margins of earlier products, and created sales volume substantially in excess of forecast. Finally, the DeskJet project became a model for subsequent development efforts, having "demonstrated" what was possible and how it could be achieved at HP Vancouver.

Building Capability: A Comparison of Alternatives

The four approaches or starting points for building development capability—development strategy, development process, skills and tools, and demonstration project—each bring different opportunities and risks. Moreover, while the approaches ultimately are focused on substantially improving development capabilities by creating new ways of working, they differ in their focus and sequence, and thus one may be preferred over another in different contexts. Exhibit 12–1 outlines various circumstances in which a particular approach may be selected, and suggests the opportunities and risks that accompany each approach.

In the case of creating a development strategy, for example, such an approach may be most appropriate where the product line is complex and changing and where the organization has experienced substantial increase in development requirements in the face of resource constraints. Starting the process of building new capability and development with a development strategy serves to focus existing resources and establish priorities. However, in order to succeed, it almost always requires that the organization reduce the total number of active projects. Failure to do so creates the risk that initially the organization will have a plan with no substance and no leverage for real improvement. A complementary discussion of context, opportunities, and risks applies to all three remaining approaches.

The discussion in Exhibit 12–1 suggests that the preferred context for a given approach is driven by the character of the opportunity the organization faces as well as its legacy of organizational capability and historical experience. The approach selected should both fill gaps in the organization and exploit opportunities with large payoffs. Introducing a company-wide development process, for example, is likely to be important when products are complex or the organization is large and has a

323

EXHIBIT 12-1

Comparison of Alternative Approaches to Creating Development Capability*

Approach	Context Where Approach May be Preferred	Opportunities	Risks
1. Creating a Development Strategy	• Complex, changing product line; many project opportunities • Increase in development requirements in the face of resource constraints	• Focus resources • Establish priorities (reduce projects)	• Failure to reduce number of projects hinders change • "Staff" planning exercise with no real substantive impact
2. Introducing Substantial Change to the Company-Wide Development Process	• Large organization, complex product line • Functional organization with history of sequential development	• Communicate new pattern to entire organization • Focal point for organizational energy	• Difficult to phase into ongoing projects • Adds bureaucracy to "cure" existing bureaucratic process
3. Establishing Building Block Tools and Skills	• Smaller companies or projects with history of teamwork • Fabricated parts where molds or dies are crucial	• Leverage change across many paths • Create fundamental change in way tasks are done	• Local optimization – build local skill but don't tie it to larger system • Technical (or commercial) sandbox
4. Pursuing a Demonstration Project	• Well-defined technical or market opportunity • Demand for significant development improvement for project success	• Organization sees integrated process in action • Identify challenges and problems quickly	• Project idiosyncratic – rest of organization doesn't learn • "Once and for all" mentality

* While a wide variety of approaches can be pursued in improving development capability, these four are perhaps most common. Based on the experience of dozens of firms, the opportunities and risks of each and the settings where they might be most appropriate are outlined.

history of sequential development. In that context, a new development process has significant leverage.

The risks that each of these approaches poses to an organization share common elements. In each case the challenge is to build from the starting point defined by the approach and to spread insight and understanding—as well as skill and capability—to other parts of the organization. That challenge is particularly evident in the case of building block tools and skills. If the new tools become nothing more than a set of toys for the technical or commerical personnel, the tools will not have their desired impact. Moreover, if they are introduced effectively at the local level but without attention to the complementary actions that need to be taken to make them effective within the overall development system, they likewise will have only a limited impact, and one likely to diminish with time. But this issue of spreading the effect of an approach and extending its reach applies also to an avenue for change that starts at the top. For example, introducing a new, company-wide development process can easily get bogged down in the creation of new bureaucracy and procedures rather than becoming a framework within which other supporting and complementary changes to the new process can occur. Likewise, a demonstration project can be nothing more than a single project, and may fail to teach the organization lessons that spread and extend its influence.

Creating New Development Capability: General Observations

The four approaches discussed in Exhibit 12–1 represent starting points in an organization's effort to create new development capability. Although the starting points are different, we recognize that they are the beginning of a series of changes that will, if successful, build support and momentum and pervade the development system. Management must recognize that selecting an initial approach does not mean that it will be sufficient on its own. Indeed, depending on the circumstances in the organization, it is likely that more than one of the approaches may eventually come into play as the organization proceeds on its journey to truly outstanding development capability. Although the starting points have different implications for the timing of activities and entail different implementation problems, it is useful to see them as part of a larger process of organizational change. Viewed in these terms, the four different approaches to building capability represent different starting points along a similar journey. In this section, we examine the common themes that characterize this journey.

The Path of New Capability

Whichever point an organization chooses to launch its effort in creating new capability, it must recognize that that effort is not a single step, but one of many along a path. In spite of the fact that the initial effort may involve a focused set of charges in the organization, successfully building development capability is not a matter of a single demonstration project or the introduction of new tools such as a CAD system ("We are going to improve development by introducing the XYZ CAD system"). If it is to succeed, the first effort must be followed by other changes and projects as the organization seeks to change the entire pattern of development.

This notion that building capability is a long-term process representing a path for development's evolution represents a significant change from traditional assumptions that most companies have made about the way one improves development. We compare this new concept with the traditional approach in Exhibit 12–2. In the conventional paradigm, indicated by the dashed line in the figure, managers seem to assume that development performance (here represented by cycle time on the project) can be improved by a step function process in which major changes in either procedures or systems are implemented at periodic points in time, bringing about significant improvement almost immediately. The actual pattern of change under these assumptions, however, is quite different.

As indicated by the solid line on the graph, changes in development procedures or systems are often precipitated by deterioration in performance. As lead time on development projects rises because of the addition of procedures to "catch" past mistakes, the absence of appropriate skills, or a failure to integrate across functions, senior management focuses on the need for change and improvement. But instead of making fundamental changes along a development path, the organization typically revises procedures, modifies checkpoints, or redefines subsequences of activities without addressing the real underlying problems. The result may be a modest improvement in performance which occurs almost immediately as the organization tries very hard to improve itself. As time goes on, however, the normal processes within the development system reassert themselves and the underlying problems surface once again. A repetition of this creates a sawtooth pattern of gradual deterioration followed by modest improvement and subsequent deterioration.

In organizations that substantially improve their development systems, we see a different pattern. The starting point for improvement in development performance may be any one of the four avenues that we have identified above, and may include other activities discussed in

EXHIBIT 12–2

Improvement Paths for Development Capabilities*

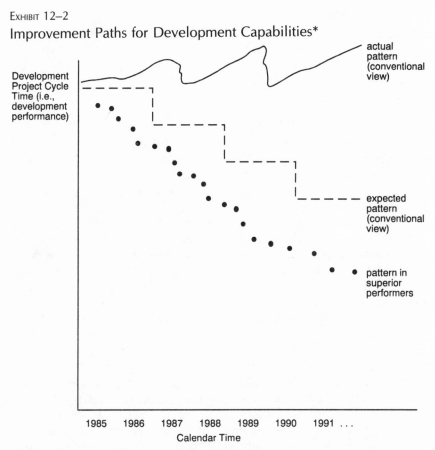

* Typically, firms envision an improvement path for product development that collects improvement ideas and periodically implements them. Unfortunately, the reality is that development processes often get encumbered over time until periodically they are simplified. Those firms that do achieve systematic improvement in development seem to do so on a continuous, incremental basis.

SOURCE: R. H. Hayes, S. C. Wheelwright, and K. B. Clark, *Dynamic Manufacturing* (New York: The Free Press, 1988), p. 337.

prior chapters. But what is striking about the high-performing organizations is the evolutionary, incremental, consistent, persistent improvement in performance in one project after another. In this approach, management focuses its attention on creating a context in which the initial starting point leads to learning and improvement, further understanding of the opportunities, and subsequent evolutionary changes in procedures that tighten, streamline, and make more effective the basic organization. Although at any one point in time the changes observed in the organization need not be radically different from previous practice, over a sustained period of time the organization not only takes on a very different character and builds a different set of capabilities, but also experiences dramatic performance improvements.

Competitive Benchmarking

Viewing the building of new development capability as a journey which is likely to extend over a significant period of time underscores the importance of fostering motivation and desire in the development organization. Managers can do several things to build this motivation and desire. Perhaps one of the most powerful levers managers can use is the process of *benchmarking* their organization against other similar organizations, thus building awareness of their competition.[6] Such efforts allow managers to channel a sense of rivalry and competition from the marketplace deep into the development organization. The effect is that individuals called on to make substantial changes in the way they work may see their efforts not in terms of some vague corporate goal, but rather in terms of very specific competitive realities. Subsequently, benchmarking against "best in class" may be especially helpful. This second type of benchmarking analysis identifies those who are best at some key aspect of development; not just from one's own industry, but from across all industries.

Benchmarking also has the effect of changing what people expect and what they see as possible. Particularly when an organization is confronted by the need to make major improvements in its process, the individuals who must bear the brunt of the change often go through a denial phase in which proposed targets for improvement (e.g., reducing development cycles or tooling lead times by 50 percent) are met with widespread skepticism and disbelief. To overcome this sense of "it can't be done," managers can use benchmarking to demonstrate that, indeed, it can be. Furthermore, benchmarking can often indicate exactly how one might go about making it happen. Establishing an external, dynamic base of reference through competitive benchmarking energizes the improvement process by giving it real-world "pull," not just the "push" of a few converted managers.

While recognizing that building capability is a path and will extend over a period of time, it is important that managers capitalize on their internal sources of insight and enthusiasm. This is likely to involve spotlighting important successes in the organization, conducting project audits in order to document improvements and learn from experience (see Chapter 11 for a discussion of project audits), and in general focusing management attention on the building process. An important element for achieving and maintaining such focus is measurement. Establishing measurements of development capability and performance that are credible may involve significant investment, but it will clarify what must be done and give an accurate idea of how the process has proceeded to date.

Building Capability Is a Development Process

Like the creation of a great product line or a significant series of outstanding manufacturing processes, building development capability occurs through a sequence of projects. Like new products and processes, building capability raises all of the questions about resource allocation, focus, capacity utilization, establishing an effective sequence of projects, priorities in development, concept leadership, and so forth. The implication is that the challenge of building capability requires a development strategy of its own. Such a development strategy for capability needs to include at least three kinds of efforts:

- *Building capability through product and process development projects.* Ongoing projects can often be a vehicle for introducing new skills or tools, and may be used as demonstration projects. Thus, as the organization creates its product or process development strategy, it needs to decide in which projects specific opportunities for improvement will be realized.
- *Independent efforts to build capability.* Outside of ongoing product and process development projects, the organization can undertake separate efforts to build new skills and tools, create new processes, and in general create new capability. For example, Ford's "concept to customer" process involved a significant effort on the part of a small team, working independently of ongoing development projects, to create a new development process. Development of CAD systems or rapid prototyping tools represents another type of separable project that builds capability. At some point, an organization must decide how to implement the capability developed in a specific product or process development project. But the creation of the capability itself may occur off-line in an independent effort.
- *Project audits.* As we emphasized in Chapter 11, project audits represent an opportunity for an organization to learn by experience. These ongoing efforts to identify opportunities for substantial change and improvement need to be coordinated with and linked to ongoing efforts in product or process development.

Taken together, a plan that lays out the organization's approach to these three kinds of efforts constitutes a kind of "development capability strategy." In addition to helping the organization focus its resources and establish priorities, the process of creating a capability strategy may help managers focus the organization's attention and communicate to the members of the organization the nature of the journey they have chosen to pursue. Thus, a capability strategy can also serve to improve identification, motivation, and desire within the organization.

Skills and Knowledge

Where it succeeds, a strategy for capability and a path for building capabilities does so because it increases the knowledge and skills of the individuals in the organization. Several kinds of knowledge and skills are crucial. In pre-project activities, for example, we have discussed in this book skills in creating strategic maps, building aggregate project plans, and creating a development strategy. To make these activities work, the people charged with their completion need to enhance their knowledge of the organization's market position, technologies, production processes, suppliers, and competitors. Moreover, they need to be educated in the fundamental principles that govern the creation of maps, development strategies, and aggregate project plans.

Within specific projects, we have identified many kinds of skills and knowledge that are essential to creating new development capability. Some are technical in nature, like those required to achieve effective product/process integration. Others are organizational, like those required to create a capability for managing heavyweight teams. Still others are commerical, like those required to develop effective product concepts and link customer requirements and unmet customer needs to the details of product planning and design.

The importance of personal knowledge and skills under any of the four approaches suggests that managers must pay close attention to the way in which individuals involved in building new capability are educated, trained, and endowed with requisite experience and perspective. First, the importance of skill and knowledge means that managers must carefully select the individuals who will lead those efforts and who will provide important guidance and input into the process. But since the building of capability is likely to occur over a period of time, it is essential that managers give attention to issues of career paths, education and training, and, in general, the development of human resources in the organization.

The issue of education and training is obvious when development improvement rests on the creation of new tools and techniques. If improvement and development involves introduction of a new CAD system, training people to use the system and educating them in the basic principles that govern its operation are straightforward. But other kinds of education are less obvious. For example, the introduction of joint product and process design requires the training of individuals in tech-

EXHIBIT 12–3

Skill and Knowledge Requirements for Improving Development Performance

Development Participants	Skill or Knowledge Requirements		
	Technical	Organizational	Commercial
Senior Corporate Managers	Understand key technical changes	Recognize importance of creating a rapid learning organization; lead and provide vision	Identify strategic business opportunities
Business Unit General Managers	Understand depth and breadth of technology	Train and select leaders; champion cross-functional teams; adapt career pathing	Target key customer segments; architect product families and generations
Team Leaders	Provide breadth of capabilities; comprehend depth requirements	Select, train, and lead development team; recognize importance of attitudes and secure functional support	Champion concept definition; competitive positioning
Team Members	Use new tools and apply technologies	Integrate cross-functional problem solving; create improved development procedures	Operationalize customer-driven concept development; refine concept based on market feedback

niques of DFM and education in the principles underlying effective integrated problem solving. These principles have to do with attitudes as well as new skills and extend beyond the narrow technical tasks confronting the product and process designers. A theme that runs throughout this book is the need for project participants to add value to the work of others, as well as do their specific job.

In a similar way, management must endow its project leaders with the intuition, skill, and judgment required to play that role in development. Education is important in that process, but there is likely to be no substitute for experience in specific functions and activities. Thus, managers must look carefully at career paths for project leaders, providing both a range of functional assignments as well as a sequence of increasingly broad and challenging project assignments. Exhibit 12–3 summarizes many of the skills and much of the knowledge required for rapid, productive, high-quality developments.

Changing Behavior and Overcoming Obstacles

The path to superior development capability is often marked by potholes and other obstacles. Building capability requires change, not just in systems or procedures, but ultimately in individual behavior. A more integrated development process, new approaches to planning, new ways of conducting prototype cycles—all of the desired changes in an organization's development process—rest on changes in the way individuals do their work on a daily basis. Thus, the challenge is to build capability while creating processes that change behavior.

It is hard enough to define new modes of behavior in a completely new situation. In most companies, however, building new development capability occurs within an existing organization. That organization must support existing products and develop new ones while simultaneously reinventing itself; senior managers do not get to call "time out" and stop, regroup, and then start over. Change and the building of new capability must go on while the organization gets real work done.

Managers thus are confronted by an ongoing organization and its need for support and success, and by the need to motivate people to change their behavior to make a future desired organization happen. This combination of new and old poses significant challenges to building capability. Indeed, there are attitudes and practices that are effective "showstoppers." In Exhibit 12–4 we provide examples of showstoppers from different organizational levels and phases of development. The list is clearly incomplete. Indeed, if we were to try to list all of the showstoppers that one encounters in building development capability, we would need many pages. The intent here is to indicate the nature of obstacles likely to confront managers who embark on a path of improved capability.

Obstacles show up throughout the organization, but are probably most difficult and prevalent at the middle ranks. Take, for example, the problem of discipline in engineering. Often, improving development capability involves instilling a new sense of discipline within the engineering organization. In the case of a new emphasis on designing it right the first time, old practices of letting changes go until later in the development process are completely dysfunctional. As Quote 3 in Exhibit 12–4 makes clear, engineers often perceive that what their supervisors really care about are the old objectives like hitting release dates, even though the release will contain mistakes that the engineers know are there and could fix now, if they took the time to do it. Implicit in the problem is an underlying willingness on the part of supervisors and managers in the system to live with the consequences of failing to catch the changes early in the process. Those consequences include late engineering changes, delays in market introduction, and quality problems in the field. Years of experience in implementing quality programs in manufacturing have taught that unless the members of the organization are convinced that management really cares about the new approach— unless they see a match between the way management talks and the

Exhibit 12–4

Showstoppers: Examples of Obstacles to Building Development Capability*

	Symptoms	Function/Level of Organization	Issues/Obstacles
1.	I've asked Jerry [head of planning] to study this for us.	Senior management	Improvement as a staff responsibility
2.	You don't need to take me through the details, just give me the bottom line.	Senior management	Lack of knowledge at the top
3.	Look, forget the new procedure. What Jack cares about is hitting the release date. Let it go and we'll ECO it in pilot.	Engineering/ middle management	Lack of discipline/willingness to live with consequences
4.	Hey, don't tell the mechanical guys about this change. Just put it through. By the time we get to prototype, it'll be too late and they'll have to accept it.	Engineering/ middle management	Failure to accept responsibility/ adversarial relationships
5.	My people can't worry about training for new tools – we've got to get these drawings released by Wednesday.	Engineering/ middle management	Short term pressures/ time horizon
6.	Wait a minute – field service is completely overworked. There's no way I can free up someone to work on this project.	Field services/ middle management	Lack of resources
7.	That's design engineering's problem. It's not my job.	Process engineering/ working level	Poor understanding/ lack of incentives
8.	I have an idea that might work, but there's no way I'm saying anything. You know the old saying around here: the nail that sticks up gets hammered.	Manufacturing/ working level	Fear/lack of trust

* Numerous patterns of behavior, many of which are subtle and deeply ingrained, can be major impediments to improving development capabilities. Examples common to different organizational levels are shown here along with their representative symptom(s) and the challenges that must be addressed to overcome them.

---

actions they take—people will not change their behavior to make the tradeoffs called for by the new approach.

Like the problem of lack of discipline, obstacles at the working level may grow out of dysfunctional attitudes or perspectives. Take, for example, the last quote in Exhibit 12–4. The individual involved is dealing with one of the most important sources of leverage in building new development capability: individual initiative and creativity. But failure to take action here reflects a lack of trust in the actions of superiors and peers. It also suggests a fear that new ideas will be rejected. Such attitudes are especially critical in building development capability, because so much of what matters in creating outstanding performance involves the total pattern of activity—process, structure, skill, and decision making.

While senior management or even a team of individuals may lay down an effective architecture from the top, successful development of capability requires the concerted involvement, effort, and, in particular, initiative and creativity of people throughout the organization. Systematic efforts to learn and improve are, of course, important, but there must also be a broad, grassroots effort to refine, streamline, and make more effective. As we emphasized in Chapter 11, people in the organization must understand that learning is not just a nice thing to have, but an essential element of successful development. It is crucial, therefore, that managers embarking on a path of improvement and capability pay close attention to the critical interfaces where distrust may be present. They also need to take action to break down those barriers of distrust by transferring people across boundaries, establishing working teams so that people can build up relationships that will support trust, and taking extraordinary measures to encourage individual creativity.

These considerations suggest that attitudes may present important obstacles to building capability. But there are also systematic problems that have to do with incentives, information, and resource allocation. The sixth quote by the field service organization is typical. Support groups that are not directly involved in detailed engineering often find themselves with substantial new responsibilities, but no new resources to carry them out. Solving this problem often requires restructuring tasks in order to give the support organizations the time and energy to participate in the crucial up-front work that will make their work more effective later on. There also may be a need for investment in expanding the capacity of support organizations in order to achieve significant improvement in development. In a project we recently studied, a new product whose lifetime revenues for the company were expected to approach $500 million had been substantially delayed because of a shortage of critical resources (e.g., two mechanical engineers). Pressure to reduce costs through across-the-board head count reductions led to a management decision that was penny wise and pound foolish.

Systemic problems are also evident in Quotes 5 and 7. Effecting change requires an understanding of the incentives faced by the individuals whose behavior must change. Once again, managers must be sensitive to those aspects of their systems that get in the way of the kinds of changes the new capabilities require. The process engineer who says "that's not my job" when required to get involved early in the design phase of a product lacks information on the purpose of such involvement and incentives to undertake it. Indeed, what the engineer means is ". . . that it is not what I get paid for, that is not how I get rewarded, there is nothing in it for me." Unless individuals understand the value awaiting them in working within the new or improved approach, it will be a long uphill battle to bring about significant change. In fact, our experience has been that once product and manufacturing engineers get involved in working together in an integrated fashion, the benefits become apparent. If the atmosphere is right—if they have been trained and their understanding is accurate—getting involved creates opportunities for them to substantially improve their performance, the quality of their work, and the performance and quality of others' work. It also influences the quality of their lives at work.

Building Capability: Management Leadership

Sustained improvement in the ability to develop new products and processes provides significant advantage in the market place. Throughout this chapter, we have tried to develop a framework that will be useful in meeting the challenge of creating sustained improvement. Although there are many different starting points and means of launching a program of continuous improvement in development capability, successful efforts share common characteristics. Managers recognize in the first instance that building capability is a journey, not a destination. The critical problem is to chart a path and sequence of efforts over time that will address the organization's opportunities and needs effectively. Because superior performance requires attention to many different elements that cut across functions, disciplines, and organizations, sustained improvement requires fundamental change in the entire pattern of product and process development. That change involves systems, procedures, and organizational structure, and also includes the skills and behavior of key individuals involved in the process.

Since product and process development touch much of what a company does, and since sustained and fundamental change must be pervasive to be effective, management leadership is a critical determinant of success. The importance of management leadership has long been recognized in academic studies of organizational change and in the popular press, but leadership may take many forms. In our study of building product and process development capability, we have seen managers approach development improvement in several ways. We organize our observations below into three modes of management leadership that represent different objectives, styles, and perspectives on the role of development in competition.

- *Mode One: Seek relief.* In the first mode—what we call "seek relief"— senior managers look to product development to solve short-term problems in their markets. Change in this mode focuses on the product itself, not the development process. Leadership in Mode One often

335

appears bold and decisive: senior managers may direct an overhaul of a product's image in the marketplace through redesign, or may develop an entirely new product line through acquisition (suitably trumpeted as a move filled with synergy and decisiveness); management may effect a repositioning of the product through the addition of new technology and features. In the short term such moves may have considerable impact, but because Mode One behavior does not focus on the underlying process of development, it does not deal with an organization's basic capability. Its focus is fundamentally short term and its impact on competitive position is unlikely to be lasting.

- *Mode Two: Close the gap.* In the second mode, managers define the problem they confront—and, therefore, the opportunity they face—in terms of a gap between their own and important competitors' performance. Comparisons with competitors, particularly those with outstanding capability, can provide managers with important information about how to focus attention and energy. Leadership in this mode often recognizes the importance of making fundamental change in development, but does so within the framework established by competitive comparisons. Any number of changes may be identified in such an analysis. Managers may focus on the introduction of a new CAD system, installing new approaches to managing teams and development, or launching an educational program to establish new directions for the organization. Compared to the "seek relief" mode, Mode Two has a number of advantages: It gets at important underlying issues and builds new capability. Leadership in this model is substantive. Managers focus on changing the organization's capacity to act in ways that will make it more effective relative to its competitors. It misses, however, some of the important long-term benefits that come when senior management understands that product and process development capability can be the basis for distinctive advantage.
- *Mode Three: Competitive advantage.* The hallmark of Mode Three is its focus on building lasting advantage in development. Managers operating in Mode Three, therefore, keep the entire horizon—both long and short term—within their purview. They recognize the importance of making immediate changes that will begin to change the organization's competitive position. They also recognize the importance of making those changes in a way that will be lasting and fundamental. They see product development as an integral part of business strategy, and recognize that building outstanding development capability can reinforce and capitalize on the things the firm does well. In doing so, development becomes a source of advantage in itself. Leadership in Mode Three is truly substantive. Managers focus not only on how work gets done, but also on helping the organization discover what new things it needs to do to be successful. While leaders operating in

Mode Two focus on adding a capability to close a gap with competitors, leaders in Mode Three rethink the organization's approach to development and create a gap that competitors may not have considered. Leaders in Mode Two may do established things better, but leaders in Mode Three concentrate on doing new things better.

While senior managers in Mode Three may do many of the things that their counterparts in Modes One and Two do (redesign products, make acquisitions, fill gaps in CAD systems, or modify organizational structure), they do so with a broad comprehensive focus. The leadership they exercise focuses on the expansive vision of what the organization ought to become in the future as well as on the substantive details of everyday work in development. In this context, effective leaders pay careful attention to both the whole and the part. The successful building of capability over a long period of time is a matter of consistency between detailed actions and the overall pattern and direction of the new development process. Creating and ensuring depth of consistency is not something even a powerful senior manager can do alone, however. Everyone involved in the development process—from the senior executive to the most recently hired bench-level engineer—must share an understanding of the overall pattern of development the organization seeks. Like a great orchestra conductor, senior managers charged with the challenge of building long-term development capability must offer the organization a powerful and compelling vision or "score" of the development future, and then direct the timing and nature of contributions of others, "bringing them in" at the appropriate time.

With a clear understanding of the development pattern that the organization seeks, senior managers can move to help the organization translate that pattern into projects designed to build specific kinds of capabilities. Moreover, their support of that effort must include actions to help solve particular problems. In this sense, effective managerial leadership is much more than encouragement. Senior managers must supply critical energy and focus for the organization's search for new capability. They not only coach and counsel with key individuals, but also help define principles and then move to educate the organization in their application.

Leadership that offers a compelling vision of the new development path—that provides energy and momentum to the organization; encourages, coaches, and supports; develops substantive principles and teaches them to the organization; and helps apply those principles in solving problems—is the kind of leadership essential to building development capability.

Notes

Chapter 1. Competing Through Development Strategy

1. For recent in-depth work on the world automobile industry, see Kim Clark and Takahiro Fujimoto, *Product Development Performance* (Boston: Harvard Business School Press, 1991); and James P. Womack, Daniel T. Jones, and Daniel Roos, *The Machine that Changed the World* (New York: Rawson Associates, 1990).
2. These data on technical diversity in automobiles come from William J. Abernathy, Kim B. Clark, and Alan M. Kantrow, *Industrial Renaissance* (New York: Basic Books, 1983).
3. For further information and analysis of developments in textiles and apparel, see Kurt Salmon Associates "Quick Response Implementation: Action Steps for Retailers, Manufacturers, and Suppliers," in Thomas Bailey, "Technology, Skills, and Education in the Apparel Industry" (Technical Paper No. 7, Conservation of Human Resources, Columbia University, November 1989).
4. Changes in the disk drive industry are examined in detail in Clayton M. Christensen, "The Development of the Magnetic Information Storage and Retrieval Industry, 1960–1987: An Analytical History," unpublished paper, Harvard Business School, December 1990.
5. The emphasis on speed is evident in the recent literature on product development. See especially George Stalk, Jr., and Thomas M. Hout, *Competing Against Time* (New York: The Free Press, 1990); and Preston G. Smith and Donald G. Reinertsen, *Developing Products in Half the Time* (New York: Van Nostrand Reinhold, 1991).

Chapter 2. The Concept of a Development Strategy

1. For more information about development experience at Plus Development, see "Plus Development Corporation (A)" (Boston: HBS Case Services, Harvard Business School), 9-687-001.

339

2. There is a large literature on technology strategy. Robert A. Burgelman and Modesto A. Maidique, *Strategic Management of Technology and Innovation* (Homewood, Illinois: Dow Jones-Irwin, 1988) provide a good overview, several cases, and references. For a European perspective see Ray Loveridge and Martyn Pitt (eds.), *The Strategic Management of Technological Innovation* (Chicester, England: John Wiley and Sons, 1990), who also provide an excellent bibliography.

3. For additional background on product/market strategy, see Glen L. Urban and John R. Hauser, *Design and Marketing of New Products* (Englewood Cliffs, New Jersey: Prentice-Hall, 1980).

4. Sony's product strategy is examined by Susan Sanderson and Vic Uzumeri, "Design-Based Incrementalism: The Walkman," Rensselaer Polytechnic Institute draft paper, 1990.

5. For an example of the implications of standards for product development in the electric motor industry, see "Reliance Electric Motor Division (A)" (Boston: HBS Case Services, Harvard Business School), 9-678-067.

6. For additional background on Honda's experience with the Today, see "Honda Today" (Boston: HBS Case Services, Harvard Business School), 9-692-044.

CHAPTER 3.   Maps and Mapping: Functional Strategies in Pre-Project Planning

1. The cable story is based on real events, but names and circumstances have been disguised.

2. Maps have been discussed in several places. See, for example, Chapter 10 of Robert H. Hayes, Steven C. Wheelwright, and Kim B. Clark, *Dynamic Manufacturing* (New York: The Free Press, 1988); and Steven C. Wheelwright and W. Earl Sasser, Jr., "The New Product Development Map," *Harvard Business Review*, May–June 1989, p. 112.

3. The Coolidge example was first developed by Sasser and Wheelwright, "The New Product Development Map," although the focus in their article was on the product generation map. Here we examine the broad range of functional maps in the business.

4. For more information on the product-process matrix and its use in developing operations strategy, see Robert H. Hayes and Steven C. Wheelwright, *Restoring Our Competitive Edge: Competing Through Manufacturing* (New York: John Wiley and Sons, 1984).

5. This example was taken from Chapter 10 of Hayes, Wheelwright, and Clark, *Dynamic Manufacturing*.

CHAPTER 4.   The Aggregate Project Plan

1. The concepts we develop in this chapter about aggregate planning for projects have analogies in other fields where aggregate planning and scheduling are important. For a review of the general problems in manufacturing, for example, see Thomas E. Vollman, William L. Berry, and D. Clay Whybark, *Manufacturing Planning and Control Systems, 2nd edition* (Homewood, Illinois: Dow Jones-Irwin, 1988). The canary cage analogy is one developed and described by John Bennion of Bain and Company.

2. Studies of time allocation among engineers have shown engineers in a typical setup where most people work on several projects and spend 25–30 percent of their time on value-adding activities (i.e., designing, testing, solving problems). The balance is taken up with travel, correcting mistakes, attending meetings, and so forth. For further analysis, see Jeffrey K. Liker and Walton M. Hancock, "Organization Systems Barriers to Engineering Effectiveness," *IEEE Transactions on Engineering Management*, EM-33(2) (1986), pp. 82–91.

3. For more background on the hospital bed market and Hill-Rom's strategy, see "BSA Industries—Belmont Division" (Boston: HBS Case Services, Harvard Business School), 9-689-049.
4. See Susan Sanderson and Vic Uzumeri, "Design-Based Incrementalism: The Walkman" (Rensselaer Polytechnic Institute draft paper, 1990), for more detail on Sony's strategy with the Walkman.
5. See Kim B. Clark and Takahiro Fujimoto, *Product Development Performance* (Boston: Harvard Business School Press, 1991), for details of this study.
6. For background on Kodak's FunSaver project, see "Kodak FunSaver" (Boston: HBS Case Services, Harvard Business School), N9-692-070.

CHAPTER 5. Structuring the Development Funnel

1. The concept of a development funnel is discussed in Robert H. Hayes, Steven C. Wheelwright, and Kim B. Clark, *Dynamic Manufacturing* (New York: The Free Press, 1988), Chapter 10.
2. There is a large literature on project selection in R&D, but our focus in this chapter is quite different. The project selection literature generally focuses on the problem of selecting among a set of projects that are relatively well defined. Here we examine the processes through which firms generate, review, and screen alternatives and determine the content of development projects as they move toward the market. For a review of this literature and a recent application see M. L. Liberatore and G. J. Titus, "The Practice of Management Science in R&D Project Management," *Management Science*, 29(8), August 1983, pp. 962–964; and Muhittin Oral, Ossama Kettani, and Pascal Lang, "A Methodology for Collective Evaluation and Selection of Industrial R&D Projects," *Management Science*, 37(7), July 1991, pp 871–885.
3. For a much more detailed discussion of project selection and resource allocation, see Albert H. Rubinstein, *Managing Technology in the Decentralized Firm* (New York: John Wiley and Sons, 1989), Chapter 7. Variants of Model I have been discussed in the literature in terms of "technology push." See Edward B. Roberts, "Managing Invention and Innovation," *Research-Technology Management*, January–February 1988, for a review of the literature.
4. Of course, if the cost of development is sufficiently low, a strategy of market determined selection—offering many possible products to the market and letting customers decide which will succeed or fail—may be effective. This seems to be the case in the Japanese consumer electronics industry.
5. For further background on the problem of generating ideas and the influence of management in the process see Norman R. Baker, Stephen G. Green, and Alden S. Bean, "How Management Can Influence the Generation of Ideas," *Research Management*, 28(6), November–December 1985, pp. 35–42; and Rubinstein, *Managing Technology*, Chapter 6.

CHAPTER 6. A Framework for Development

1. Robert H. Hayes, Steven C. Wheelwright, and Kim B. Clark, *Dynamic Manufacturing* (New York: The Free Press, 1988), use the architecture metaphor in their discussion of the system of material and information flows within a factory. See especially Chapter 7.
2. The MEI case is a composite based on actual experience at several medical technology companies. Although the case captures the basic structure of the development process, the product and other aspects of the firms have been disguised.
3. For additional background on the development process at Kodak, see the chapter on

Kodak in H. Kent Bowen, Kim Clark, Charles Holloway, and Steven Wheelwright (eds.), *Vision and Capability: High Performance Product Development in the 1990's* (New York: Oxford University Press, forthcoming). Some of the details presented here also draw on a presentation by Al Van de Moere at the Boston University School of Management Manufacturing Roundtable Seminar, "The Kodak FunSaver Story," March 20, 1991.

4. See, for example, "General Electric Lighting Business Group" (Boston: HBS Case Services, Harvard Business School), 1-689-038; and "General Electric Company: Major Appliance Business Group (A)-(C)" (Boston: HBS Case Services, Harvard Business School), 9-585-053 to 9-585-055.

5. See, for example, "Motorola, Inc.: Bandit Pager Project" (Boston: HBS Case Services, Harvard Business School), 9-690-043; Tom Inglesby (ed.), "How They Brought Home the Prize—A Visit to Motorola's Bandit Plant," *Manufacturing Systems*, April 1989, pp. 26–32; Ronald Henkoff, "What Motorola Learns from Japan," *Fortune*, April 24, 1989, pp. 157–168; and "Motorola—Boynton Beach, Florida," *Industry Week*, October 15, 1990, pp. 62–64.

6. For a recent discussion of the skunkworks at Lockheed, see Ben R. Rich, "The Skunk Works Management Style—It's No Secret," *Product and Process Innovation*, 1(2), March–April 1991, pp. 28–35.

7. Kim B. Clark and Takahiro Fujimoto, *Product Development Performance* (Boston: Harvard Business School Press, 1991), discuss the application of these principles in automobile product development. See especially Chapter 10.

CHAPTER 7.   Cross-Functional Integration

1. There is a growing literature on cross-functional integration, including recent research and writing on topics such as concurrent engineering, simultaneous engineering, cross-functional teams, overlapping problem solving, and the engineering-manufacturing interface. The classic work on integration is Paul R. Lawrence and Jay W. Lorsch, *Organization and Environment* (Homewood, Illinois: Richard D. Irwin, 1967). For a more recent discussion, see Hirotaka Takeuchi and Ikujiro Nonaka, "The New Product Development Game," *Harvard Business Review*, January–February 1986, pp. 137–146; and Kim B. Clark and Takahiro Fujimoto, *Product Development Performance* (Boston: Harvard Business School Press, 1991).

2. For further discussion of the interface between manufacturing and engineering, see Martin E. Ginn and Albert H. Rubenstein, "The R&D/Production Interface: A Case Study of New Product Commercialization," *Journal of Product Management*, 3, 1986, pp. 158–170; and James B. Quinn and James A. Mueller, "Transferring Research Results to Operations," *Harvard Business Review*, January–February 1963, pp. 49–66.

3. For additional insight into engineering-marketing integration, see Ashok K. Gupta, S. P. Raj, and David Wilemon, "The R&D-Marketing Interface in High-Technology Firms," *Journal of Product Innovation Management*, 2, 1985, pp. 12–24.

4. This challenge has achieved recent recognition in the marketing literature. See, for example, Gerald Zaltman and Vincent Barabba, *Hearing the Voice of the Market* (Boston: Harvard Business School Press, 1991).

5. Clark and Fujimoto, *Product Development Performance*, develop this perspective in their study of the world auto industry.

6. See Clark and Fujimoto, *Product Development Performance*, for further discussion of the issues and framework presented in this section. Takahiro Fujimoto, "Organizations for Effective Product Development," D.B.A. dissertatiaon, Harvard Business School, 1989, provides an in-depth review of the literature on communication in this context.

CHAPTER 8. Organizing and Leading Project Teams

1. For an example of recent literature related to leadership and organization, see Gloria Barczak and David Wilemon, "Leadership Differences in New Product Development Teams," *Journal of Product Innovation Management*, 6, 1989, pp. 259–267; Ikujiro Nonaka, "Creating Organizational Order Out of Chaos: Self-Renewal in Japanese Firms," *California Management Review*, 30(3), Spring 1988, pp. 57–73; Thomas J. Peters, *Thriving on Chaos* (New York: Alfred A. Knopf, 1988); and Robert H. Hayes, Steven C. Wheelwright, and Kim B. Clark, *Dynamic Manufacturing* (New York: The Free Press, 1987).

2. See Kim B. Clark and Takahiro Fujimoto, *Product Development Performance* (Boston: Harvard Business School Press, 1991).

3. These forms of organization were first developed in Fujimoto, "Organizations for Effective Product Development." Additional work includes Hayes, Wheelwright, and Clark, *Dynamic Manufacturing;* and Clark and Fujimoto, *Product Development Performance.* For further reading on the basis of organizing for development, see Paul R. Lawrence and Jay W. Lorsch, *Organization and Environment* (Homewood, Illinois: Richard D. Irwin, 1967); Jay R. Galbraith, *Designing Complex Organizations* (Reading, Massachusetts: Addison-Wesley, 1973); and Thomas J. Allen and Oscar Hauptman, "The Influence of Communication Technologies on Organizational Structure," *Communication Research*, 14(5), October 1987, pp. 575–578.

4. For a more extensive review of Motorola's experience with the Bandit line see "Motorola, Inc.: Bandit Pager Project" (Boston: HBS Case Services, Harvard Business School), 9-690-043.

5. For an extended discussion of this pattern of leadership and its impact in leading firms in the world auto industry, see Clark and Fujimoto, *Product Development Performance.*

6. Adapted from a description provided by Dr. Christopher Meyer, Strategic Alignment Group, Los Altos, CA.

7. For a more thorough discussion of Chaparral Steel's approach to development, see the chapter on Chaparral in H. Kent Bowen, Kim Clark, Charles Holloway, and Steven Wheelwright (eds.), *Vision and Capability: High Performance Product Development in the 1990's* (New York: Oxford University Press, forthcoming); and "Chaparral Steel: Rapid Product and Process Development" (Boston: HBS Case Services, Harvard Business School), N9-692-018.

CHAPTER 9. Tools and Methods

1. We are indebted to Geoff Gill and Michael Watkins for their help in formulating the gear design example.

2. The notion of fit between the parameters of design and the context of its use is an important theme in the literature on design. For one approach to this problem see Christopher Alexander, *Notes on the Synthesis of Form* (Cambridge: Harvard University Press, 1964).

3. The problem solving framework we use here has its roots in the work of Herbert Simon; see especially Herbert A. Simon, *The Science of the Artificial* (Cambridge: MIT Press, 1969). Design-build-test cycles and the logic of problem solving are discussed directly in Takahiro Fujimoto, "Organizations for Effective Product Development," D.B.A. dissertation, Harvard Business School, 1989; and Kim B. Clark and Takahiro Fujimoto, *Product Development Performance* (Boston: Harvard Business School Press, 1991).

4. This problem has been developed at length by Michael D. Watkins, "Managing Cross-Functional Problem-Solving in Product Development and Manufacturing: The Case of Liftgate Engineering at Ford of Europe," doctoral dissertation, Harvard Business School, 1991.

5. QFD is a methodology that originated in Mitsubishi's Kobe shipyards and was developed and extended by Toyota. There is a large literature on QFD, including works translated from Japanese. For an excellent introduction, see John R. Hauser and Don Clausing, "The House of Quality," *Harvard Business Review,* May–June 1988, pp. 63–73. In the paragraphs that follow we adapted the basic framework laid out by Hauser and Clausing and applied it to the gear design problem.

6. There is a large and growing literature on DFM. For a good introduction see Daniel E. Whitney, "Manufacturing by Design," *Harvard Business Review,* July–August 1988, pp. 83–91.

7. We have taken this example from Karl Ulrich, David Sartorius, Scott Pearson, and Mark Jakiela, "A Framework for Including the Value of Time in Design-for-Manufacturing Decision Making," M.I.T. Working Paper #3243-9-MSA, February 1991.

8. This method is described in Whitney, "Manufacturing by Design."

9. A similar concept is part of the framework developed in Hauser and Clausing, "The House of Quality."

Appendix to Chapter 9.

1. See, for example, Jeffrey K. Liker and Walton M. Hancock, "Organizational Systems Barriers to Engineering Effectiveness," *IEEE Transactions on Engineering Management,* vol. 33, No. 2 (May, 1986) pp. 82–91, who developed survey evidence that design engineers spend less than 10 pecent of their time designing new products "right the first time," and only 20 percent of their time doing actual engineering work. The rest was spent attending meetings, searching for people and information, and coordinating with other engineers.

2. This example uses the system developed by Steven Salzberg and Michael Watkins, "Managing Information for Concurrent Engineering: Challenges and Barriers," *Research in Engineering Design,* 2, 1990,pp. 35–52. We are grateful to Michael Watkins for his help with the work in this section. His work on computer-based systems provides a useful review of the literature and a detailed discussion of the computer system and its application. See Watkins, "Managing Cross-Functional Problem-Solving in Product Development and Manufacturing."

3. See Salzberg and Watkins, "Managing Information for Concurrent Engineering: Challenges and Barriers."

Chapter 10. Prototype/Test Cycles

1. For additional information on prototyping in the workstation industry, see David Ellison and Steven C. Wheelwright, "The Prototyping of PCBs in Engineering Workstation Development Projects," Harvard Business School Working Paper, 1991.

2. This point of view—that prototyping is crucial to development—has been developed in work by Phil Barkan. See, for example, Phil Barkan, Marco Iansiti, and Kim B. Clark, "Prototyping as a Core Development Process," in H. Kent Bowen, Kim Clark, Charles Holloway, and Steven Wheelwright (eds.), *Vision and Capability: High Performance Product Development in the 1990's* (New York: Oxford University Press, forthcoming).

3. For additional background on prototyping in the automobile industry, see Kim B. Clark and Takahiro Fujimoto, *Product Development Performance* (Boston: Harvard Business School Press, 1991), pp. 176–182.

4. For the story of Coca Cola's introduction of a new version of Coke, see Thomas Oliver, *The Real Coke, The Real Story* (New York: Random House, 1986).

CHAPTER 11. Learning from Development Projects

1. There is a large literature on learning in industrial settings. Much of it has to do with the "learning curve," or the observed tendency for costs (and other dimensions of peformance) to decline with increases in experience. Here we focus on directed, managed, systematic efforts to increase the firm's knowledge about development. For additional discussion of systematic learning, and learning in an organizational context, see Roger E. Bohn, "An Informal Note on Knowledge and How to Manage It" (Boston: HBS Case Services, Harvard Business School), 9-686-132; Roger E. Bohn, "Learning by Experimentation in Manufacturing," Harvard Business School Working Paper, 1987; C. M. Fiol and M. A. Lyles, "Organizational Learning," *Academy of Management Review*, 19(4), 1985, pp. 803–813; and Dorothy Leonard-Barton, "The Factory as a Learning Laboratory," Mimeograph, September 1991.
2. The themes we examine here are consistent with recent research on effective learning and organizational change. Michael Beer, Russell A. Eisenstat, and Bert Spector, *The Critical Path to Corporate Renewal* (Boston: HBS Press, 1990), for example, argue that effective learning and change needs to focus on the essential tasks and associated behavior in the organization, rather than on individual attitudes.
3. The notion that learning about new products involves a cycle of activities is a central theme in Modesto A. Maidique and B. J. Zirger, "The New Product Learning Cycle," *Research Policy*, 14, December 1985, pp. 299–313.
4. Robert H. Hayes, Steven C. Wheelwright, and Kim B. Clark, *Dynamic Manufacturing* (New York: The Free Press, 1988), discuss this issue and the general problem of creating a learning organization. See especially chapters 11 and 12 for examples that put learning about development in context.

CHAPTER 12. Building Development Capability

1. For additional reading about organizational change along these lines, see Michael Beer, Russell A. Eisenstat, and Bert Spector, *The Critical Path to Corporate Renewal* (Boston: Harvard Business School Press, 1990).
2. Chapter 12 in Robert H. Hayes, Steven C. Wheelwright, and Kim B. Clark, *Dynamic Manufacturing* (New York: The Free Press, 1988), provides additional examples from manufacturing companies of strategies for bringing about fundamental improvement in operating performance. For additional insight from experience in service businesses, see James L. Heskett, W. Earl Sasser, and Christopher W. L. Hart, *Service Breakthroughs: Changing the Rules of the Game* (New York: Free Press, 1990), especially chapters 13 and 14.
3. Ford's recent experience is documented in the chapter on Ford's development process in H. Kent Bowen, Kim Clark, Charles Holloway, and Steven Wheelwright (eds.), *Vision and Capability: High Performance Product Development in the 1990's* (New York: Oxford University Press, forthcoming).
4. For additional background and detail on Kodak's FunSaver project, see "Kodak Fun-Saver" (Boston: HBS Case Services, Harvard Business School), N9-692-070.
5. For additional background on HP's development process, see the chapter on HP in Bowen et al. (eds.), *Vision and Capability*. Chapter 12 of Hayes, Wheelwright, and Clark, *Dynamic Manufacturing*, discusses the experience of the Vancouver plant in making broad improvements in manufacturing.
6. There is a growing literature on benchmarking. For a good example of the concept and its application, see Frances Tucker, Seymour Zivan, and Robert Camp, "How to Measure Yourself Against the Best," *Harvard Business Review*, January–February 1987, p. 8.

Index

ABC-4 computer project audit,
301–9
  recommended action, 307–9
  strengths and weaknesses of,
  305, 306–7
Accord (Honda), 3, 55
Accountabilities, functional hat
  and team hat, 210–11
ACS, 24
Advanced projects. *See* R&D (advanced) projects
Advanced tooling release, 298
Advantage, competitive. *See*
  Competitive advantage
After-the-fact problem solving, 32
Aggregate project plan, 34–36,
  48–51, 86–110
  "canary cage approach" to, 90
  cycle time and, 106
  deciding on projects to undertake, 108–9
  developing, 105–10
  development performance over
  time and, 109

human resources and, 106
leadership strength and, 110
maximum concurrent projects
  and, 108
mix and sequence of projects
  and, 98–109
overcommitment of development capacity and, 88–91
promise of, 88
purposes of, 87, 88
reactive mix of development
  projects and, 91–92
resources available and capacity utilization in, 106
types of development projects
  and, 92–97, 106
Alliance (partnered) projects, 50,
  93, 94
All-the-eggs-in-one basket model
  for development funnel, 117,
  119, 120–24
Analyses, systematic organizational learning through,
  293–94

Apollo (now HP-Apollo), 259
Apple Computer, 79–85
Apple II personal computer, 80
Application, invention separated from, 38–39, 40
Applied Materials, 24
Architecture, system, 96. *See also* Development funnel
Assignments, concurrent, 90–91
Attributes
  customer, 221–22
    design parameters and, 222–23, 225
    experimental determination of, 232
    quality function deployment (QFD) and, 229
  product, 62–64
Audit, project. *See* Project audit
Auto industry, world
  efficiency imperative in, 5
  international competition in, 2–3
  sequencing major platform projects in, 102
  team organizations and project leadership in, 189
  traditional approach to prototyping in, 262–63
Automobile development process, 7
Autonomous teams. *See* Tiger (autonomous) teams

Bandit pager project (Motorola), 200–202, 261, 275
Benchmarking, competitive, 328–29
Benetton, 3
Bennion, John, 90
"Best practice" prototyping, 265–66
Breakthrough (radical) projects, 49–50

aggregate project plan and, 93, 95
skunkworks approach to, 160
start-up firms and, 99
Building block skills, 318–21, 324
Build phase of problem-solving cycle, 224
Business plan, 57
Business strategy, project categories and, 98
Business team, mapping process and, 78

CAD-CAM, 187, 249
"Canary cage approach," 90
Capabilities. *See also* Development capability
  downstream, 182
  upstream, 180
Capacity, overcommitment of, 88–91
"Capacity cushion," 109
Capacity plan, 50
Capacity requirements, project categories and, 98
Capacity utilization, aggregate project plan and, 106
Career paths, 192–93, 331
Change(s)
  organizational, 325
  unexpected, 183–84
Chaparral Steel, 216–17
Choice, prototyping and, 267–71
Coca Cola Company, 270
Combinatorial method, 237–39
Commitment in heavyweight teams, 202–3
Communication
  individual, 289
  problem solving and, 228
  prototypes and, 273–74
  upstream-downstream, 176–80

Compensation, cross-functional integration and, 186–87
Competition, 1–5. *See also* Maps, functional
in concept development, 131
critical dimensions of, 60–61
imperatives of, 4–5
industrial, 1–4
international, 2–3
performance measures and, 47
performance of, comparison with, 336
platform product generations and, 42
Competitive advantage, 336–37
of development capability, 311–12
of fast-cycle development, 20–25
technology strategy and, 36
Competitive benchmarking, 328–29
Competitor, fast-cycle, 16–25
Computer-aided design and computer-aided manufacturing (CAD-CAM), 187, 249
Computer-aided design (CAD), 247–49, 319–21
Computer-aided engineering (CAE), 246
Computer-aided manufacturing (CAM), 247–49
Computer-based tools. *See under* Problem solving
Computer industry, prototype cycle in, 259–60, 264–65
Computervision, 254
Concept development, 6, 7, 125–26, 139–40, 264
competition in, 131
in outstanding programs, 15
Concept infuser, heavyweight project manager as, 208, 209

"Concept to customer" (C to C) approach, 316–18, 329
Conflict resolution, real-time, 150–51
Contract book, 205, 206
Contract development, 159
Contract-driven, functional teams, 151–54, 159–60, 161, 197, 199
Control
of prototyping cycles, 267, 268
by senior management, 136, 146, 149–50, 305, 308
Coordination of functional teams, 192
Corrections, real-time/midcourse, 137, 146, 150–51, 305, 308
Cost(s), 23–25
of fast-cycle development, 23–25
manufacturing, 74–75
of prototyping, 262, 263, 278–79
Cost overruns, 31
Critical events, 286–87, 288
Cross-functional contract approach, 197
Cross-functional integration, 165–87
achieving, 172, 175–87
capabilities and relationships needed for, 180–84
communication patterns, 176–80
promotion and compensation in, 186–87
senior management's role in, 185–86, 187
attitudes toward, 184–85
changing development process and structure and, 298–99
defined, 169
framework for, 172–75
functional activities under, 173

Cross-functional integration (*cont.*)
in MEI 2010 development
(composite case illustration),
165–72
periodic prototyping and,
275–77
quality function deployment
(QFD) and, 234
traditional prototyping model
and, 272–73
Cross-functional interaction, 158
Cross-functional problem solving,
97–98, 228
Cross-functional teams, 151–54,
159–60, 189. *See also* Heavyweight project teams
contract-driven, 151–54, 159–60
popularity of, 189
project audit by, 285, 300–309
C to C approach, 316–18, 329
Customer(s)
development framework and,
162
heavyweight project managers
and, 208
lead, 171
perceptions of company's competitive position, 231
prototyping and role of, 268,
270, 273, 274
response to product attributes,
63–64
sophisticated and demanding,
2–3
target, 171
understanding of and insight
about, 170–72
Customer attributes, 221–22
design parameters and, 222–23,
225
experimental determination of,
232
quality function deployment
(QFD) and, 229

Customer mission statement,
155–56
Customer support, platform
product generations and, 43
Cycle time, aggregate project
plan and, 106

Data
problem solving and, 245
systematic organizational learning through, 293–94
Decision making, 174–75, 288
Delays, 31
Demonstration projects, 321–23,
324
Derivative (sustaining) projects,
50, 95
aggregate project plan and, 93,
95, 97
firm maturity and, 99
industry maturity and, 100
Model III development funnel
and, 127
number, timing, frequency,
and relationship to product/
market strategy of, 42, 43–44
patterns of, 41–42
platform projects vs., 97–98
prototyping patterns associated
with, 280–82
secondary wave strategy for,
102–5
sequencing of, 101–5
steady-stream strategy for, 102,
103
Design(s)
alternative, 223–24, 237, 238
computer-aided (CAD), 247–49,
319–21
error-free, 181
gap between performance and,
220
integrated, 169–70
tradeoffs in, 222

Design-build-test cycle, 6–7, 16, 219, 220–26. *See also* Prototyping
  in auto industry, 262–63
  as critical event, 288
  in major appliance development projects, 256–59
  traditional path of, 255, 256
Design engineering maps, 82–83
Design-for-assembly concepts, 236
Design for manufacturability (DFM), 219, 228–29, 234–43, 322
  design for producibility, 236–39
  design rules, 234–36
  implementation of, 239–43
Design matrix, 240–41, 242
Design maturity, 264–65, 269
Design maturity test (DMT) phase of prototyping, 268–69
Design parameters, 221, 222
  customer attributes and, 222–23, 225
  interaction between, 231
  quality function deployment (QFD) and, 229
Design phase of problem-solving cycle, 223, 224
Design quality, 21, 46, 262
Design verification, 264
DeskJet (Hewlett Packard), 321–23
Detail, coherence in, 162–63
Development. *See* Product development
Development, concept. *See* Concept development
Development capability, 311–37
  building, 311–37
    changing behavior and overcoming obstacles in, 331–35

by changing development process, 316–18, 324
comparison of approaches to, 323–25
competitive advantage of, 311–12
competitive benchmarking, 328–29
by creating building block skills and tools, 318–21, 324
with demonstration projects, 321–23, 324
as development process, 329–30
with development strategy, 313–16, 324
as long-term process, 326
management leadership in, 335–37
organizational change and, 325
path of new capability, 326–28
skills and knowledge necessary for, 330–37
  overcommitment of, 88–91
  project categories and, 98
Development funnel, 111–32
  challenges in managing, 112–13, 130
  creating, 116–27
    innovative-and-focused model for, 124–27
    R&D-push/survival-of-the-fittest model for, 117, 118–20
    single-project/big-bet (all-the-eggs-in-one-basket) model for, 117, 119, 120–24
  critical issues in, 130–32
    competing projects, 130–31
    managerial roles, 130
    project mix, 131–32

Development funnel (*cont.*)
  as diagnostic tool, 128–30
  factory analogy of, 133–34
  nature of, 111–12
  in practice, 113–16
  screens in, 118–20, 124, 125–27
Development goals and objec-
    tives, 34–36, 44–48
Development process
  changing to build development
    capability, 316–18, 324
  factory analogy of, 134
  learning based on shared
    model of, 293
  learning to change, 295–300
Development project(s). *See also*
    Learning from development
    projects
  advanced, 49, 93, 94, 126
  aggregate project plan and, 92–
    97, 106
  aim of, 111
  building capability through,
    329
  concurrent, 108
  conventional approach to,
    33–34
  development funnel and com-
    peting, 130–31
  financial modeling of, 45–46
  major appliance, prototyping
    in, 256–60, 274
  management and leadership of,
    136
  mix and sequences of, 98–109
    changing technology and,
      99–100
    hyper-variety and, 100–105
    reactive, 91–92
  narrow view of, 39
  organization and staffing of,
    136, 146–47
  performance measures for,
    46–47

plan, 51
resource requirements for,
    50–51
return map, 47–48
status of, 307
types of, 49–50, 99. *See also*
    specific types
Development schedule, 274
Development strategy, 28–56. *See*
    also Aggregate project plan
  for capability, 313–16, 324,
    329–30
  development goals and objec-
    tives, 44–48
  framework for, 33–36
  "great leap forward," 38
  of Honda, 53–56
  main purposes of, 34
  to meet multiple platforms,
    55
  post-project learning, 52–53
  product/market planning and
    strategy, 40–44
  project management, 51–52
  rapid inch-up, 38
  secondary wave, 102–5
  steady-stream, 102, 103
  technology planning and strat-
    egy, 36–40
Development teams. *See* Project
    team(s)
"Direct" engineering manager,
    heavyweight project manager
    as, 208, 209
Direction of communication, 176,
    177
Discipline
  development framework and,
    162
  in engineering, 332–33
Disk drives, 3
Distinctiveness, product, 30
Distribution channels, 64–65
Downstream capabilities, 182

Downstream engineers, 183–84
Downstream-friendly solutions, 181

Early-involvement mode of communication, 178, 179
Early-start-in-the-dark mode of communication, 177–79
Eastman Kodak Company
development framework at, 151–54, 155–56
disk camera, 30
FunSaver project, 97, 104–5, 318–21
Manufacturability Assurance Process (MAP), 151–54, 155, 156, 159, 197
Edsel (Ford), 30
Education, 330–31
of engineers, 186
Efficiency, imperative of, 5
Emerson Electric, 42
Employees, prototyping and assessment by, 274
Engineering. *See also* Upstream-downstream group communication
computer-aided (CAE), 246
under cross-functional integration, 172–75
cross-functional integration
with manufacturing, 168–70
with marketing, 170–72
discipline in, 332–33
heavyweight project managers and, 208
marketing and, 75–76
product/process, 6–7
rapid response to, 280, 281, 282
Engineering changes, 12–13
Engineering design, 15
Engineering maps, 62, 67–69
design, 82–83

Engineering prototype, 140–42
Engineering workstation industry, prototyping in, 259–60, 267–70
linking development phases and, 264–65
Engineers
downstream, 183–84
education and training of, 186
time allocation among, 340n2
Enhancements. *See* Derivative (sustaining) projects
Environment-organization mismatch, 29–30
Error-free design, 181
Evaluation, outside, 274
Evaluation criteria, 8
Events, critical, 286–87, 288
Executive sponsor, 211–12
Experience, cross-functional, 186
Expertise, functional project organization and, 193
Expert system, 246
Explorer (Ford), 316
External and internal fit, 306–7

Fast-cycle competitor, 16–25
Fast-cycle development, 16–25
competitive advantage of, 20–25
pricing strategy and, 23
technological gap and, 22–23
Feedback from prototypes, 273
Fidelity, 225
of prototype, 262, 263
Field service organization, obstacles in, 333, 334
Financial modeling of development projects, 45–46
Firms
mature, 192, 199
start-up, 188, 197–98
Fisher, George, 201
Fit, internal and external, 306–7

Flexible manufacturing system (FMS), 299

Focus
of autonomous teams, 196
of prototyping, 267, 268, 272

Ford Motor Company, "concept to customer" (C to C) approach of, 316–18, 329

Forecasting from upstream clues, 182

Framework for development, 133–64, 299–300. *See also* MEI 2010 development (composite case illustration)
basic elements of, 135–37
common themes and basic principles, 161–64
General Electric's tollgate process, 151–54, 156–60, 197
Kodak's Manufacturability Assurance Process (MAP), 151–54, 155, 156, 159, 197
Lockheed's skunkworks approach, 151–54, 160–61, 197
Motorola's contract-driven, functional teams, 151–54, 159–60, 161, 197, 199

Frequency of communication, 176, 177

Front-end planning, 97

Fuji Film, 104, 318

Functional decomposition approach, 148–49

Functional hat accountabilities, 210–11

Functional maps. *See* Maps, functional

Functional teams, 191, 192–93
contract-driven, 151–54, 159–60, 161, 197, 199
evolution of, 198
heavyweight teams and, 204, 216
mapping process and, 78

Functions, mismatches between, 30

Funnel, development. *See* Development funnel

FunSaver camera project (Kodak), 97, 104–5, 318–21

General Electric's tollgate process, 151–54, 156–60, 197

General manager, 220

Generational projects. *See* Platform (next-generation) development projects

Goals
development, 34–36, 44–48
technical performance, 46

"Great leap forward" strategy, 38

Greenwood Mills, 3

"Hand-off, the," 192

Hardcard® (Plus Development), 30

Hard disks, Winchester-technology, 3

Heavyweight project manager, 194–95

Heavyweight project teams, 190, 191, 194–95, 200–215
challenge of, 202–4
contract book of, 205, 206
evolution of, 198
executive sponsor of, 211–12
functional teams and, 204, 216
fundamental change necessary for, 212–15, 216
Hewlett Packard DeskJet team, 321–23
Motorola Bandit pagers development, 200–202, 261, 275
periodic prototyping and, 278
project charter of, 204–5
project leadership of, 194–95, 208–9
staffing of, 205–7

team member responsibilities
in, 209–11
Hewlett Packard, 47–48, 201, 259
"pizza bin" approach of, 39, 40
Vancouver Division DeskJet
project, 321–23
Hill-Rom, 25, 100, 104
Honda, 24, 53–56
Hospital bed industry, 100
House of producibility, 240–42
House of quality (planning tool),
229–32
HP-Apollo, 259
Human resources, 98, 106
HVAC, Inc., 290–93
Hybrid development projects, 93,
95

IBM, 38, 39, 41, 259
Impala (Chevrolet), 3
Imperatives, competitive, 4–5
Incremental projects. *See* Derivative (sustaining) projects
Individual learning, 287–90
Industrial competition, 1–4
Industry standards, 28, 42
Information sharing, prototypes
and, 273–74
Innovation, 3–4, 99
Innovative-and-focused model for
development funnel, 124–27
Insight, 285, 286. *See also* Learning from development
projects
capturing, 295–300
about customers, 170–72
team process for learning and,
293
Integrated problem solving, 178,
179–80, 184
Integration, 8–9. *See also* Cross-
functional integration
of functional teams, 192
from heavyweight team, 203

platform projects and, 97–98
problems of, 14–15
of product and process technology efforts, 38, 39, 41
in tollgate approach, 158
vertical, 71–72
Integrative maps, 73–76
Integrity from heavyweight team,
203
Interaction, cross-functional, 158
Intergraph, 254
Internal and external fit, 306–7
International competition, 2–3
Invention, application separated
from, 38–39, 40
Investment
platform product generations
and return on, 42–43
post-project learning and, 53

Jobs, Steve, 80

Karas, Marcia, 303
Kawamoto, Nobuhiko, 54
Knowledge
for building development capability, 330–37
prototyping to build, 266, 270
scientific, 2
technical, 36
Kodak. *See* Eastman Kodak Company

Lead customers, 171
Leadership, 15. *See also* Management; Project management
and leadership
aggregate project plan and, 110
Lead time, 237
Learning from development
projects, 284–310
capturing insight, 295–300
to change development process, 295–300

Learning from development (*cont.*)
framework for, 285–95
critical events in, 286–87, 288
individual vs. organizational learning, 287–90
sequence of activities, 286
systematic organizational learning, 290–95
implications of, 309–10
"learning by doing," 287–89
post-project, 52–53, 55
problems in, 284–85
project audits and, 285, 300–310
ABC–4 computer project audit, 301–9
sample questions, 301, 302–3
prototyping and, 272, 273, 278
as team process, 293
Life cycle planning, 45–46
Lightweight project teams, 191, 193–94
implementation of, 215–16
in mature organizations, 199
project managers of, 193–95, 208
Limited, The, 3, 25
Lisa personal computers (Apple), 80–85
Lockheed's skunkworks approach, 151–54, 160–61, 197
Low-cost prototypes, 265–66

Macintosh (Apple), 30, 80–85
Major appliance projects, prototyping in, 256–60, 274
Management. *See also* Project management and leadership; Senior management
after-the-fact problem solving by, 32
building development capability and, 335–37

career paths for project leaders and, 331
computer-based systems and, 244
development funnel and, 112–13, 130
mapping process and, 76–78, 79
prototyping and, 255–56, 260–61, 273–79
reviews by, 157–58, 268, 271
of risk, 183
timing and impact of attention and influence of, 32–33
Managers
general, 220
project. *See* Project managers
Manufacturability, 270. *See also* Design for manufacturability (DFM)
prototyping to demonstrate, 262
replicate-manufacturing-early prototyping model and, 281–83
Manufacturability Assurance Process (MAP), 151–54, 155, 156, 159, 197
Manufacturing
computer-aided (CAM), 247–49
cost and product complexity of, 74–75
under cross-functional integration, 172–75
cross-functional integration with engineering, 168–70
flexible manufacturing system (FMS), 299
Manufacturing maps, 62, 69–73, 83–84
Mapping, 76–79
getting most out of, 78–79
management and, 76–78, 79
objective of, 60

MAP process, 151–54, 155, 156, 159, 197
Maps, functional, 57–76
    at Apple Computer, 79–85
    case illustration, 57–60
    characteristics of, 60
    concept of, 60–62
    design engineering, 82–83
    engineering, 62, 67–69
    integrative, 73–76
    manufacturing, 62, 69–73, 83–84
    marketing, 62–67, 81–82
    need and opportunity for, 79–85
    product generation, 65–67, 83
    requirements for, 60–61
Market acceptance, 142–44
Marketing
    under cross-functional integration, 170–75
    engineering and, 75–76
Marketing maps, 62–67, 81–82
Marketing specialist, 248, 249
Market interpreter, heavyweight project manager as, 208, 209
Market introductions, 45–46, 144–45, 174
Market needs, heavyweight project managers and, 208
Market position, benefits of, 28
Markets
    fragmented and demanding, 2–3
    shifting, 29–30
Market share, 23–25
Matrix
    design, 240–41, 242
    performance, 240, 241–42
    product/process, 73–74, 84
    relationship, 229–31
    roof, 231
Matsushita, 25
Mature firms, 192, 199

Measurements of development capability and performance, 328–29
Medical devices market, 4
MEI 2010 development (composite case illustration), 138–51
    concept development, 139–40
    cross-functional integration in, 165–72
        engineering-manufacturing, 168–70
        engineering-marketing, 170–72
    market acceptance, 142–44
    market introduction, 144–45
    phases in, 166–68
    problem solving, testing, and prototyping, 146, 148–49
    project definition, 145–46
    project management and leadership, 146, 147–48
    project organization and staffing, 146–47
    prototypes, 140–42
    real time/midcourse corrections, 146, 150–51
    screen problem, 219
    senior management review and control, 146, 149–50
    time line, 139
Methods and tools. *See* Problem solving; Tools and methods
Midcourse/real-time corrections, 137, 146, 150–51, 305, 308
Middle management, development funnel and, 130
Middleweight teams, 217
Mission, fit with, 163
Mission statement, customer, 155–56
Mock-ups, 270
"Model shop," 267–69, 270
Motorola, 45–46
    Bandit pager project, 200–202, 261, 275

Motorola (*cont.*)
  contract-driven, functional
    teams, 151–54, 159–60, 161,
    197, 199
  68000 microprocessor, 83
Moving target syndrome, 29–30

National Electrical Manufacturers
  Association (NEMA), 42
NCR 2760 electronic cash regis-
  ter, 236
New Coke, 270
New product and new process
  development
  business goals related to, 45–46
  potential benefits of, 28–29
  problems in, 29–32
New West Photo, 237
Next-generation projects. *See*
  Platform (next-generation)
  development projects
Noise (random variation), 225

OEM (subcontracted) projects,
  129. *See also* Alliance (partnered) projects
Omega Systems, 301–9
Organization
  mismatches within and with-
    out, 29–30
  project, 136, 146–47
  renewal and transformation of,
    29
Organizational change, development capability and, 325
Organizational learning, 287–90
  systematic, 290–95
Organization structure. *See*
  Project team(s)
Outside evaluation, 274
Outsourcing to prototype supplier, 267, 269
Ownership in heavyweight
  teams, 202–3

Parameters
  design, 221, 222
    customer attributes and, 222–
      23, 225
    interaction between, 231
    quality function deployment
      (QFD) and, 229
  process-oriented, 242
Partnered (alliance) development
  projects, 50, 93, 94
Patterns
  of development, 41–42, 163
  systematic organizational learn-
    ing through, 294
Performance. *See also* Development capability
  aggregate project plan and, 109
  of competitor, 336
  definition of, 241
  gap between design and, 220
  measures of, 46–47
  in problem solving, 225–26
  of products, 21–22, 96
  skill and knowledge require-
    ments for improving, 330–31
  system, 218
Performance matrix, 240, 241–42
Periodic prototyping. *See under*
  Prototyping
Personal computer market segments and product development factors (1982), 82
"Phases and gates" framework,
  151–54, 155–56
Philips, 25
Physio Control, 313–15
Pilot production, 7–8, 258
"Pizza bin" approach, 39, 40
Plan. *See also* Aggregate project
  plan
  business, 57
  capacity, 50
Planning and strategy
  front-end, 97

life cycle, 45–46
product/market, 6, 7, 40–44
task, 277
technology, 36–40
Platform (next-generation) development projects, 50, 275
aggregate project plan and, 93, 95–97
derivative projects vs., 97–98
Model III development funnel and, 127
number, timing, and rate of change of, 42
patterns of, 41–42
prototyping patterns associated with, 260, 274–79, 280, 281, 282, 283
sequencing of, 101–5
technological maturity and, 99–100
Plus Development, 30
Polaroid, 96–97
Policy issues, unresolved, 31–33
Post-project learning, 52–53, 55
Pre-project activities, 34–36, 302, 305, 308
Pressures, short-term, 91–92
Pricing strategies, fast-cycle development and, 18–19, 23
Problem(s)
defined, 218–19, 220
framing of, 223
in learning, 284–85
in new product and new process development, 29–32
recurring, 287, 288
technical, 31
of unresolved issues, 289–90
Problem solving, 136, 146, 148–49, 218–54. *See also* Prototyping
after-the-fact, 32
communications and, 228

computer-based systems for, 219–20, 243–54
current applications of, 245–46
example of, 249–54
generations of, 246–49, 253–54
with intelligent support, 253
management and, 244
prototypes and, 246
cross-functional, 97–98, 228
data management and, 245
delays in, 31
design-build-test cycle of, 219, 220–26
detailed, 218
functional decomposition approach to, 148–49
integrated, 178, 179–80, 184. *See also* Cross-functional integration
integration with product development, 175–76
performance in, 225–26
quick, 181–82
structured methodologies for, 226–43, 245
design for manufacturability (DFM), 219, 228–29, 234–43, 322
quality function deployment (QFD), 219, 228, 229–34, 297–98
Process-oriented parameters, 242
Producibility
design for, 236–39
house of, 240–42
Product attributes, 62–64
Product complexity, 8, 74–75
Product definition, 159
Product development
effective, 13–16
fast-cycle, 16–25
forces driving, 2–3

Product development (*cont.*)
  phases of, 6–8
  problematic, 9–13
Product distinctiveness, 30
Product generation maps, 65–67, 83
Production prototype, 142
Production quality, 46–47
Productivity, resource, 46
Product performance, 21–22
  next-generation products, 96
Product planning, 6, 7
Product/process engineering, 6–7
Product/process generation, platform projects and, 96
Product/process matrix, 73–74, 84
Product reliability, 3
Product variety, 3–4, 100–105
Product verification phase of prototyping, 264, 265
Profits, time to market and, 21–22
Program wrap-up, 159
Project audit, 53, 285, 300–310, 329
  of ABC–4 computer, 301–9
  sample questions, 301, 302–3
Project charter, 204–5
Project definition, 135–36, 145–46
Project management and leadership, 51–52, 136, 146, 147–48
  for ABC–4 portable computer project, 305, 308
  at Honda, 55–56
  project audit questions on, 302
Project managers
  career paths of, 331
  heavyweight, 194–95, 208–9
  lightweight, 193–95, 208
Project mix, development funnel and, 131–32
Project plan. *See* Aggregate project plan
Projects, development. *See* Development project(s)

Project selection in R&D, 341*n*2
Project team(s), 188–217. *See also* Cross-functional teams
  for ABC–4 portable computer project, 305, 308
  building capability for multiple approaches, 215–17
  composition of, 299
  evolution of, 197–200
  in mature organizations, 189
  middleweight, 217
  project audit questions on, 302
  types of, 190–96. *See also specific types*
  in world auto industry, 189
Promotion, cross-functional integration and, 186–87
Prototype(s)
  computer-based tools and, 246
  engineering, 140–42
  fidelity of, 262, 263
  production, 142
Prototyping, 15, 136, 146, 148–49, 255–83
  for ABC–4 portable computer project, 305, 308
  advanced tooling release in, 298
  basic cycle of, 256
  in computer industry, 259–60, 264–65
  customer and, 268, 270, 273, 274
  forms of, 256, 263
  in major appliance projects, 256–60, 274
  management and, 255–56, 260–61, 273–79
  matching development project requirements and, 279–83
  in outstanding programs, 16
  periodic, 260–61, 274–79
    characteristics of, 277–78
    dimensions of, 268

for platform projects, 260, 274–79, 280, 281, 282
prerequisites for, 278–79
project audit questions on, 303
purpose of, 262
quality of, 266
rapid, 266
representativeness of, 262, 263, 265–66, 270–71, 292
responsibilities in, 263, 265, 267–70, 272
traditional approach to, 260, 261–73
"best practice" method of improving, 265–66
consequences of, 271–73
dimensions of choice in, 267–71
linking development phases and prototype cycles, 262–65

Quality
design, 21, 46, 262
imperative of, 5
production, 46–47
prototyping process, 266
Quality function deployment (QFD), 219, 228, 229–34, 297–98
cross-functional integration and, 234
house of quality, 229–32
implementation of, 232–33
Quantum, 25
QuickSnap (Fuji Film), 318

Radical projects. *See* Breakthrough (radical) projects
Ramp-up phase, 7, 8
Random variation (noise), 225
Rapid inch-up strategy, 38
Rapid prototyping, 266

R&D (advanced) projects, 49, 93, 94, 126
aggregate project plan and, 93, 94
project selection in, 341n2
R&D-push/survival-of-the-fittest model for development funnel, 117, 118–20
Real-time/midcourse corrections, 137, 146, 150–51, 305, 308
Recurring problems, 287, 288
Relationship matrix, 229–31
"Release," engineering, 7
Reliability, product, 3
Reliance Electric, 42
Renewal and transformation of organization, 29
Replicate-manufacturing-early prototyping model, 280, 281–83
Representativeness, 281, 283
of prototype, 262, 263, 265–66, 270–71, 292
Research projects. *See* R&D (advanced) projects
Resource allocation process as critical event, 288
Resource availability
aggregate project plan and, 106
platform product generations and, 43
Resource productivity, 46
Resource requirements for development, 50–51, 126
Resource utilization, benefits of, 28–29
Responsibilities
functional hat and team hat, 210–11
in heavyweight teams, 209–11
in problem solving, 184
in prototyping, 263, 265, 267–70, 272
Return map, development project, 47–48

Return on investment, platform
product generations and,
42–43
Reviews, management, 157–58,
268, 271
senior management, 136, 146,
149–50
of ABC–4 portable computer
project, 305, 308
during prototyping, 277
Risk(s)
in developing capability, 324,
325
managing, 183
Roof matrix, 231
Root causes, pursuing, 294–95
"Rules of thumb," 235–36

Schedule
development, 274
in periodic prototyping, 277
slippage of, 10, 11–12
Scientific knowledge, 2
Screens in development funnel,
118–20, 124, 125–27
Secondary wave strategy, 102–5
"Seek-relief" mode of leadership,
335–36
Senior management, 126
cross-functional integration
and, 185–86, 187
development framework principles as guideposts for, 164
development funnel and, 130
heavyweight team and, 211–12
modes of leadership, 335–36
perspective on learning from
development projects, 310
project audit questions on, 302
review and control by, 136,
146, 149–50
of ABC–4 portable computer
project, 305, 308
during prototyping cycles, 277

tiger teams and, 196
tollgate approach and, 158
Sequence in prototyping, "best
practice" in, 266
Serial mode of communication,
176–77, 178
Shamlin, Scott, 201
Showstoppers, 332–33
"Sign off," engineering, 7
Single-project/big-bet model for
development funnel, 117,
119, 120–24
Skills
building block, 318–21, 324
for building development capa-
bility, 330–37
Skunkworks approach, 151–54,
160–61, 197
Slippage, schedule, 10, 11–12
Solutions
downstream-friendly, 181
system, 159, 160, 203–4
Sony, 24–25, 42, 101, 259
Specifications for platform vs.
derivative projects, 97
Speed, imperative of, 4–5
Sponsor, executive, 211–12
Staffing, 136, 146–47, 205–7
Standards, industry, 28, 42
Start-up firms, 188, 197–98
Steady-stream strategy, 102, 103
Steinway & Sons, 41–42
Strategy
business, 98
development. *See* Development
strategy
project, 51
Stretch camera (Kodak), 104–5
Structured process, need for, 307
Subcontracted (OEM) projects,
129. *See also* Alliance (part-
nered) projects
Subcontracting as barrier to in-
sight and information, 292

Sun Microsystems, 259

Suppliers, 267, 269, 274

Support activities, heavyweight teams and, 203

Support groups, scheduling of, 279

Sustaining projects. *See* Derivative (sustaining) projects

System architecture, 96. *See also* Development funnel

Systematic organizational learning, 290–95

System performance, 218

System solution, 159, 160, 203–4

Target customer, 171

Task planning, 277

Tasks, cutting cycle times on, 306

Taurus (Ford), 316–17

Team hat accountabilities, 210–11

Team process, learning as, 293

Teams. *See* Project team(s)

Technical breakthroughs, prototyping patterns associated with, 280, 281, 282, 283

Technical feasibility, proof of, 126

Technical knowledge, 36

Technical performance goals, 46

Technical problems, unexpected, 31

Technological gap, fast-cycle development and, 22–23

Technological innovation, development project type and, 99

Technological maturity, platform projects and, 99–100

Technology(ies)
changing/shifting, 2, 3, 29–30, 99–100
development funnel driven by, 117, 118–20
at Honda, 54–55

integration of product and process of, 38, 39, 41

planning and strategy, 36–40

platform product generations and evolution of, 42

Testing, 136, 146, 148–49. *See also* Design-build-test cycle
in prototyping, 268, 270–71, 272–73
strategies, 271

Test phase of problem-solving cycle, 224–25

Texas Instruments, 30

Textile and apparel industry, 3–4

Tiger (autonomous) teams, 217
implementation of, 215–16
leadership of, 195–96
Lockheed's skunkworks, 151–54, 160–61, 197
structure of, 191

Time allocation among engineers, 340*n*2

Time-to-market, 15–16, 21–22, 46–47

Timing
of communication, 176, 177
in prototyping, "best practice" in, 266

Today (Honda), 54–55

Tollgate system, 151–54, 156–60, 197

Tools and methods. *See also* Problem solving
ABC-4 audit and recommended change in, 308
building block, 318–21, 324
development funnel as tool, 128–30
learning from, 295, 296, 297

Tradeoffs in design, 222

Training, 186, 330–31

Translator, heavyweight project manager as, 208, 209

Trust in problem solving, 184

Ulrich, Karl, 237
Uncertainty, 8
Upstream capabilities, 180
Upstream clues, forecasting from, 182
Upstream-downstream group communication, 176–80
dimensions of, 176, 177
early-involvement mode of, 178, 179
early-start-in-the-dark mode of, 177–79
integrated-problem-solving mode of, 178, 179–80
serial mode of, 176–77, 178

Variation, random (noise), 225
Variety, product, 3–4, 100–105

Vendors, selection of, 169
Veraldi, Lew, 317
Verification, design, 264
Vertical integration, 71–72

Walkman (Sony), 42, 101
Weekender camera (Kodak), 104–5
Whitney, Dan, 237–38
Winchester-technology hard disks, 3
Working level, obstacles at, 333–34
Working-level linkages, 288
Workstation industry, prototyping in, 259–60, 264–65, 267–70

DEVELOPMENT STRATEGY FRAMEWORK
Building Block Concepts

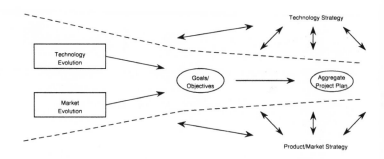

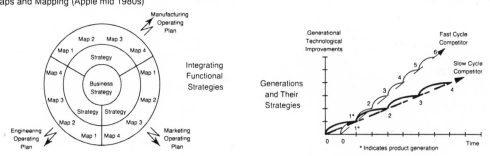

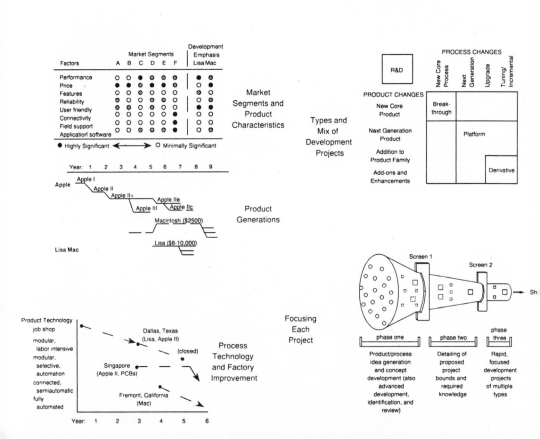